A MULTITUDE OF WOMEN

The Challenges of the Contemporary Italian Novel

A Multitude of Women looks at the ways in which both Italian literary tradition and external factors have influenced Italian women writers in rethinking the theoretical and aesthetic ties between author, text, and readership in the construction of the novel. In her analysis, Stefania Lucamante discusses the unique contributions that Italian women writers have made to the contemporary novel, addressing works by Maraini, Ferrante, Vinci, and others with reference to concepts of intertextuality and feminist theory.

This study identifies a positive deviation from literary and ideological orthodoxy in the contemporary Italian novel and considers its effect on the traditional notion of the literary canon. Lucamante argues that this development is partly due to the impact of women writers and their avoidance of conventional patterns in narrative while favouring forms that are more attuned to the ever-changing needs of society. She shows that contemporary novels by women authors reflect a major shift in thinking, and that the actual literary and aesthetic significance of the novel has been profoundly affected by female emancipation. By overturning epistemological schemas bound to a set time and place, Italian women writers are producing a more meaningful relationship with their readers while expanding the possibilities of the novel.

(Toronto Italian Studies)

STEFANIA LUCAMANTE is an associate professor of Italian in the Modern Languages and Literatures Department at The Catholic University of America.

A Multitude of Women

The Challenges of the
Contemporary Italian Novel

Stefania Lucamante

UNIVERSITY OF TORONTO PRESS
Toronto   Buffalo   London

© University of Toronto Press 2005
Toronto Buffalo London
utorontopress.com

Reprinted in paperback 2021

ISBN 978-0-8020-8725-6 (cloth)
ISBN 978-1-4875-2583-5 (paper)

Toronto Italian Studies

Library and Archives Canada Cataloguing in Publication

Title: A multitude of women : the challenges of the contemporary Italian novel / Stefania Lucamante.
Names: Lucamante, Stefania. author.
Series: Toronto Italian studies.
Description: Series statement: Toronto Italian studies | Paperback reprint. Originally published 2008. | Includes bibliographical references and index. | Includes some text in Italian.
Identifiers: Canadiana 20210120037 | ISBN 9781487526177 (softcover)
Subjects: LCSH: Italian fiction – 20th century – History and criticism. | LCSH: Italian fiction – Women authors – History and criticism. | LCSH: Women and literature – Italy – History – 20th century. | LCSH: Women in literature. | LCSH: Feminist theory.
Classification: LCC PQ4055.W6 L83 2021 | DDC 853/.914099287–dc23

Publication of this book was facilitated by a grant from The Catholic University of America.

University of Toronto Press acknowledges the financial assistance to its publishing program of the Canada Council for the Arts and the Ontario Arts Council, an agency of the Government of Ontario.

 Canada Council for the Arts   Conseil des Arts du Canada

 ONTARIO ARTS COUNCIL
CONSEIL DES ARTS DE L'ONTARIO
an Ontario government agency
un organisme du gouvernement de l'Ontario

Funded by the Government of Canada   Financé par le gouvernement du Canada

Contents

Acknowledgments vii

Abbreviations xi

Introduction: What Women Writers Do with the Knowability of the World   3

1 'Writing Is Always Playing with the Mother's Body': Mothers' Rewrites   28

2 Of Fathers and Daughters, or the Italian Family Interrupted   109

3 Italian Sexual Patho-Politics Revisited   181

Conclusions   234

Notes   243

Works Cited   297

Index   315

Acknowledgments

I have worked for some years towards the completion of this book, as many were the elements I needed to incorporate to make it what it is today. I hope the book will prove helpful to those students and scholars who share my interest in the development of the novel and persuade all its readers of the importance and merit of women's writings in Italian literature.

Since I started teaching at the Catholic University of America I have relied more and more on the understanding and generous help to pursue and complete my scholarly projects of a particular and very caring person, Dr George E. Garvey, Dean of Graduate Studies. My thanks go to him for the support he has always shown me. I am also quite grateful to the Italian Ministry of Foreign Affairs, which funded some parts of my research and writing.

I would like to thank many colleagues and friends who made *A Multitude of Women* possible through their help, advice, and patience. First of all, my heartfelt thanks to my friend and former student Kenise Lyons, whose brilliant help was essential to the initial composing of this book. My dear friend Cristina Della Coletta devoted much of her time during the summer of 2006 to the reading of my manuscript. She gave me much insight and always brilliant suggestions, showing how great friends and colleagues can be. My friends Chad Wright and Giancarlo Lombardi read my introduction, making sure that my linguistic ambiguities would no longer be there. My colleague and friend Lisa Gitelman provided me with her great wit and help in the revision of the edited manuscript. Two are the Annamarias to whom I am indebted for this book: the former Director of the Italian Cultural Institute in Washington, Annamaria Lelli, and *Leggendaria*'s founder and director, Anna Maria Crispino. They have both been instrumental in promoting discussions about some of the authors and the novels I chose for the book. While Anna Maria Crispino directed my mainly literary interest towards key issues for feminist rights in Italy and elsewhere, Annamaria Lelli introduced me to many writers whose work has become, in some cases, what readers are about to approach. My gratitude goes also to my old friend Filippo La Porta for our discussions about the destiny of Italian literature and criticism. I am also grateful to my computer wizard in Pula, Italy, Franco Puddu, for making available for me his printers, computers, and advice during very hot Sardinian summers.

Preliminary versions of some of the sections that make up the chapters of this book formed part of lectures I delivered in several institutions, among which I would like to remember the University of Wisconsin–Madison, where my dear colleague Grazia Menechella invited me along with other colleagues in 2003 to assess Italian feminisms in what turned out to be a very animated symposium (and loads of fun). Some of these lectures became articles, for whose revised and extended republication in this volume I received generous permission from the journals in which they first appeared (for which I thank Andrea Ciccarelli of *Italica* and Silvia Contarini of *Narrativa*):

'*Come prima delle madri*: Un thriller edipico dai toni *noir*,' *Narrativa* 26 (2004), 81–96.

'Il desiderio perverso e il rovesciamento del mito meduseo in *Il bacio della Medusa* di Melania Mazzucco,' *Italica* 76.2 (Summer 1999), 220–40.

'*Passaggio in ombra:* Riprese, innovazioni e soluzioni tematico-strutturali in un romanzo morantiano,' *Italian Culture* 15 (1997): 269–95.

To all my writer friends, Ippolita Avalli, Melania Mazzucco, Dacia Maraini, Francesca Mazzucato, Pia Pera, and Anna Santoro, many thanks for their creativity and inspirational words. To Maurice Dotta, my gratitude for letting me use his photo for the jacket. Finally, my gratitude to my editor, John St James, who so carefully revised the manuscript. To Ron Schoeffel and Anne Laughlin, my heartfelt thanks for their constant assistance in every detail that accompanied the journey of my book.

Special thanks to Alberto Bordignon and Laura Piccarolo of Einaudi editions, Roberto Santachiara, Marina Pescia of Edizioni e/o, Giovanna Canton and Vittoria Casarotto of Rizzoli, Vanessa Sparling of Europe Editions, and Feltrinelli publisher for kindly granting me rights for the passages of the novels reprinted here.

Permission to quote from the following is gratefully acknowledged:

Simona Vinci, *Come prima delle madri*, © 2003 and 2004 Giulio Einaudi Publisher SpA, Turin, by arrangement with Agenzia Letteraria Roberto Santachiara.

Francesca Mazzucato, *Hot Line: Storia di un'ossessione*, © 1996 Giulio Einaudi Publisher, SpA, Turin.

Melania Mazzucco, *Il bacio della medusa*, © 2007 RCS Libri SpA, Milan.

Dacia Maraini, *Un clandestino a bordo* (1996), *Il treno per Helsinki* (2000), *Lettere a Marina* (2001), © RCS Libri SpA, Milan.

I dedicate these pages to my family, to my husband and my sons, and to the memory of my father.

Abbreviations

AM	*L'amore molesto*
BM	*Il bacio della Medusa*
CPM	*Come prima delle madri*
DA	*The Days of Abandonment*
DB	*La Dea dei baci*
DL	*Diario di Lo*
DW	*The Destroyed Woman*
FR	*La femme rompue*
GA	*I giorni dell'abbandono*
HL	*Hot Line: Storia di un'ossessione*
HOL	*House of Liars*
LA	'Lettera sull'aborto'
LA?	'Letter on Abortion'
LD	*Lo's Diary*
LF	La frantumaglia
LO	*Lolita*
MS	*Menzogna e sortilegio*
PO	*Passaggio in ombra*
PPR	*Pausa per rincorsa*
TL	*Troubling Love*

A MULTITUDE OF WOMEN
The Challenges of the Contemporary Italian Novel

Introduction: What Women Writers Do with the Knowability of the World

A Multitude of Women looks at how Italian women writers have distinctively produced texts in which both Italian literary tradition and external agents of influence have assisted them in the process of rethinking the theoretical and aesthetic ties between the author, the text, and its readership in the construction of a novel. A new epistemology of the novel is the result. The scope of this book is to set forth the valuable contribution of Italian women writers to the contemporary novel and to illustrate the relevance of their female precursors' novelistic examples. Also, this study demonstrates the relevance of feminist and cultural studies in the renegotiation of the territory occupied by women's writing within the realm of the contemporary Italian novel.[1] *A Multitude of Women* further argues that the Italian novel is a territory that, far from being devoid of meaning and ideological stances, can only benefit from a positive deviation from literary and ideological orthodoxy. This deviation – the key issue of the book – is partly due to the merits of women writers and their ability to eschew obsolete patterns in narrative, while embracing expressive forms that are more attuned with the ever-changing needs of society. In fact, contemporary novels by women authors mirror a shift from previous trends in which the need for female emancipation interfered with the actual literary and aesthetic significance of the novel. By overturning epistemological schemas, chronologically bound to a set period in the history of women in Italy, female writers are producing a more profitable relationship with their readers, while expanding the possibilities of the novel, and treasuring the influence of a distinctively female novelistic tradition.

The transformation of subjectivities in the literary act of narrating today's world brings us face to face with some issues when looking at the genre of the Italian novel, the contribution to this genre by Italian women writers, and finally what feminist theory has brought to aesthetic reception and to the act of reading *tout court*. Since genres rely on an established consensus based on models of thought, it is hardly surprising to see how the novel has been recently reworked into different patterns by Italian women writers. The title of this book intentionally uses the term 'multitude'[2] to suggest the notion of a hybrid multiplicity of artistic expression of Italian female authors who eschew the formal language of scholarship and express their views on the relation of women with society in the writing of novels. In other words, to paraphrase Toni Negri and Michael Hardt's notion, multitude, 'the living alternative that grows within Empire,'[3] connotes the (possible) positive multifaceted ways deployed by women writers to refigure elements of the realist genre. This book analyses the innovative position of Italian women's thinking in their representation of a rediscussion of patriarchal and feminist tenets via literary works. If it is true that 'art is universal,' it is also true that the perspectives by which art is conceived, produced, and commented upon greatly vary. Cultural (unconscious) feminism, or better, the reconsideration of woman's position within society, is a strategic form of essentialism, as Rosi Braidotti expresses it. Cultural feminism could thus be considered the theoretical basis for my discussion on the prevailing forms in Italian women's literature. 'Women must then articulate the feminine,' Braidotti claims, invoking Gilles Deleuze; in order to do so, 'they must think it and represent it in their own terms.'[4]

This introduction defines the theoretical support for the textual analysis of the novels in the following chapters chosen to integrate theory and textual practice pragmatically according to critical parameters that might shy away from traditional philology. It illustrates the necessity to recognize new models of knowledge and to be critical of theories and approaches to literary textual practice that do not take gender difference into account. Feminist and psychoanalytic theory provide the indispensable background for a critique of the social construction of gender and its relation to other systems of privilege as seen in Italian novels. Moreover, this introduction considers the reasons why the Italian literary canon needs to be revised so that it is more flexible and can incorporate the work of women novelists. Male critical discourse and a relative lack of innovative critical tools in analysing women's literary works attest to a preoccupying absence of critical interest and knowledge that is not reflected by Italian readership at large.

Italy and the Genre of the Novel

I want to offer my point of view with respect to the more general field of the Italian novel from the mid-1990s to present. With great regularity, critics examine the lack of significant contributions/innovations/revolutions to this genre. In fact, one of the commonplaces of literary criticism has to do with the novel as a minor genre within the Italian literary tradition. In Italy this criticism is magnified by the pre-existing notion that the novel, upon touching Italian soil, undergoes extreme stress and fatigue, with only a few select Italian writers venturing into what has been traditionally considered a non-Italian genre.[5] The belief that the novel is not really part of the Italian tradition is questionable, particularly today with the abundance of archival research establishing the opposite. Denying the generic development of the novel in Italian literature does service to no one, as one falls prey, once again, to questionable models of reference of how one conceives of this specific genre. The novel captures the fragmentary, innately multicultural, even regionalistic (if one intends this term in its healthy and enriching meaning) nature of Italian reality, one that is far from – for instance – the more homogenous French tradition.[6] At the core, Italian novels portray Italian reality, Italian problems, and very Italian families. But generalizations have proved to be ineffectual for mapping such fragmentation, such a multitude of possible narratives on Italy and Italians, particularly when one considers the enduring love of Italians for foreign thinkers and foreign artists. Far from having settled into sterile fragmentation, these very characteristics have actually strengthened the genre. A constantly innovative lexicon, along with a syntactic simplification of the language in reverence to English syntax, and the capability of the novelistic genre to mediate new jargon and slang coming from other forms of communication such as television, essay writing, and media discourse at large have made it entirely possible for the novel to engage in a challenging discussion with various discourses (psychonanalysis, cultural and social studies, film, music, advertisement, etc.). The novel has become – or, better put, has indeed *remained* – one of the ideal containers for a society such as the Italian one, which has been deeply shattered by historical events such as the country's unification, fascism, world wars, the advent of communist opposition, the 'lead years' and terrorism, and, until recently, the Berlusconi era of neo-conservativism and ideological vacuum. And Italian women were always at the forefront of novelistic writings.

A Long History of Cooperation in the Making of the Novel

In a much more understated way, but no less significantly than is manifested in English and French literature, Italian women authors have always been present in the arts.[7] The second quarter of the nineteenth century witnessed the awakening of women authors in narrative discourse as well as in journalism and poetry.[8] The relative incoherence of the notion of the bourgeoisie in Italian culture often resulted in a relative lack of the energy needed by the novelistic genre to depict the very class that this genre was trying to address and depict. And yet the genre counts in its corpus many examples authored by women. Luisa Ricaldone and Anna Santoro, among other critics, have done extensive research on the literary production of women in the seventeenth, eighteenth, nineteenth, and early-twentieth centuries respectively.[9] Their work is, in this sense, irreplaceable. Only through archival research in Italian libraries for a prolonged period of time does one fully realize the importance of women's literary production. Without knowledge of this previous production by women, it would appear as if illustrious examples such as Matilde Serao, 1926 Nobel Prize–winner Grazia Deledda, Sibilla Aleramo, Ada Negri, and Neera are isolated cases that can not be inserted within a literary trajectory established before their period.

Beginning with the 1970s and the cultural activities of the feminist movement, which led to a process of understanding and fully re-evaluating women's writing, both literary and philosophical, critical works on women writers began to appear in Italy.[10] Other anthologies and critical works have followed, engaging in a productive manner the canon of Italian studies in narrative fiction and critical work on women writers, and positing the issue of difference in discourse and narrative strategies that the work of these women presented in adopting traditional subgenres, such as the thriller, the psychological novel, and the *Bildungsroman*. These anthologies' effective use of innovative techniques regarding the rereading and rewriting of a text has shown the necessity to address differently works that, if analysed with the tools of historico-philological analysis, cannot be fully understood in their importance. In analysing women's writing, Anna Santoro makes an important distinction between the writing and the actual publishing of women writers' work. Such division partly originates in an intense conflict between what the culture and the image of the period wanted women to be and look like, and their own expressive necessities.[11] In other words, what women were and what they had to appear to be in order to fit into societal models were two distinct intellectual and cultural entities. In several cases, they had to give up their intellectual ambitions, as society would not allow women to express their views freely. In her two anthologies of women's writing, Anna Santoro draws up a reading itinerary in which lesser-known authors than Aleramo and Deledda find their space[12] and includes entire generations of relatively unknown writers. Both anthologies build a 'territory of continuity' among all the novels by women that traditional literary anthologies have always neglected to acknowledge and that should, instead, be included in an Italian literary history at large. This type of critical reading is done in accordance with an interpretive key that conceives the development of a genre as a constant transformation of the society producing it, one that is not exclusively male. New novels constantly re-evaluate the properties of the genre to which they belong while offering a vivid commentary on society.

Despite the important efforts made towards the retrieval of works by Italian women writers for a possible taxonomy of their contributions – an effort of which Santoro's two anthologies are emblematic – systematizing their work seems problematic even in recent times. In his otherwise brilliant survey of Italian contemporary literature *An Introduction to Twentieth-Century Italian Literature*,[13] even my enlightened colleague Robert S. Gordon falls prey to stereotypes about women writers, hopping between Sibilla Aleramo, Anna Banti, and Natalia Ginzburg, between Anna Maria Ortese and Oriana Fallaci. He fails to provide readers with a clear sense of the situation in which these writers were active or to give a judgment of these women's aesthetic agenda. A detached tone, which raises questions about the author's familiarity with the work of these writers, permeates a subsection entitled 'gender,' with no further clarification given to the meaning of gender studies or women's studies when it comes to Italian literature. In the effort to present readers with the literary production of an entire century, Gordon's publication, an introduction to twentieth-century Italian literature, suffers from necessary limitations of space. Brevity notwithstanding, the decision to situate women writers together in an awkward chapter bearing the tile 'Other Voices' demonstrates a widespread lack of concern for women's advancement in the arts. Male Italian writers are, by contrast, placed within the subgenre of the novel in which they were most active. Each woman too should be mentioned for her use of expressive forms and approach to thematic and her contribution to the novel genre (or any other genre, for that matter). As far as history goes, one can possibly accept the concept of a fraught history, as Michel Foucault suggests, of a history composed by fractures, in which one must perforce dig into hidden realities that relate to the history of society and its perversions. In literary histories, however, one can view precisely these 'fractures' as a logical thread between the different artistic productions that until recently were considered isolated cases and to which Italian critics offered no explanations, as we will see in chapter 1 in the case of Elsa Morante and Cesare Garboli's critical notion of the 'uniqueness' of her genius.

In the evolution of the Italian women's literary paradigm, it is possible to conceive a system of women's artistic production in three phases, comparable to the historical model proposed by Elaine Showalter in *A Literature of Their Own*, her fundamental study of Anglo-Saxon women's literature.[14] Within the Italian panorama, and given the socio-historical background, Showalter's previous three-phase paradigm is subject to a temporal shift mainly due to the delay in the industrial revolution and unification of the Italian peninsula, not to mention a significantly different set of values from the Protestant and strongly individualistic one of England, or of Jansenist France. When applied to the unspoken female literary Italian canon, the categories, or periods, are, roughly: (1) an *imitative* phase, the imitation of models prevailing from the dominant tradition, the result of which is the interiorization of artistic standards and ideas in social roles; (2) a (long) phase of *protest* against such standards and values, while minority rights are embraced with a conscious need for autonomy; and (3), *self-discovery*, the search for identity, which is more complex. Finally, I would propose a fourth, and current, *hybrid* phase, to which I ascribe the writers whose work is scrutinized in this book.

Only a few generations after the (now taken for granted, though but this was certainly not always the case) mothers of the Italian twentieth-century novel, namely, Natalia Ginzburg, Elsa Morante, Anna Maria Ortese, Lalla Romano, and Alba de Céspedes, a growing number of women writers experiment with various types of novelistic writing, ranging from the historical novel to the thriller, from the erotic novel to the socially engaged one. After the denunciation of women's abuse which generated much of the literature of the 1970s, inserted into the theoretical line of the Communist Party and the feminist movement – the so-called *doppia militanza* – women writers have expressed a keen interest in the theorization of sexual difference. Aware of a notion of history that could no longer carry a strong meaning, well before Gianni Vattimo and Pier Aldo Rovatti[15] would even theorize their *weak thought*, women writers designed characters and situations in their fictional works in such a manner that, not surprisingly, distinguish them from such philosophers. Italian women writers contend that, in the establishment of new dialectics, Vattimo and Rovatti's philosophical thought does not take into account the main difference between politics per se and body politics, the reconsideration of the body as the key to a renewed understanding of the woman's position within society, an understanding that will be at the core of Italian women's writing thereafter. Also, the philosophical findings of the feminist group Diotima, philosophers who connect their studies to Plato, but also to Martin Heidegger and Hannah Arendt, retrace a new subjectivity within the search for a new order aside from the patriarchal one, finding new ways of narrating history, power, Eros and death. Postmodernism and feminism have experienced something of a parallel itinerary in the past twenty years. As the number of women writers now active in Italy is steadfastly growing, it would behoove us not merely to consider them in terms of gender, thereby avoiding too-easy categorizations, but to understand how their writings require more subtle distinctions in order to map out their contributions to modern Italian literature.

A *fausse route*? A Hybrid Theoretical Approach

On what theoretical bases does the notion of the *hybrid* phase rest? Elisabeth Badinter asks about the nature of feminism in the new millennium, in her *Fausse route*, 'How to redefine the female nature without falling back into the old patterns?'[16] A corollary to this very question could serve as the notion upon which my analysis about these *hybrid* literary texts produced by contemporary Italian female writers is built. In the shared sense of anxiety arising from our attempts to understand the role of culture in general, and literature in particular, how can we redefine female literature without 'falling back into the old patterns'? How should one analyse the innovations brought to the novel by Italian women writers without falling into essentialism, and instead enrich the literary discourse on representation of reality without relegating women's writing back into a separate chapter of literary histories? Ineffective essentialism is dangerous, as is the recurring accusation of the overestimation of works by women whose aesthetic value, according to some, holds an inconspicuous place in the history of Italian literature. They both need scrutiny and reconsideration. This book has been written to offer readings of multiple forms of contemporary Italian novelistic discourse without falling back into 'old patterns' regarding women's writing dictated by either category.

As Paola Bono states, many feminist thinkers have started to investigate their own often contradictory subject positions in the recognition of a multiple subjectivity that makes incursions into traditional feminist theory obsolete.[17] A traditional type of feminist theory does not work well with my reading of Italian women writers. In fact, in the analysis of post-1990s Italian women's literature, this book aims to bridge two different lines of feminist thought, thus constructing my own hybrid theoretical position. As an Italian active in literary studies but also sensitive to debates on this side of the Atlantic, I find Rosi Braidotti's views as well as her readings of Luce Irigaray particularly useful. The politics of situating is a relevant aspect of this appropriation of the literary world currently under way among Italian women writers. The legitimization of a multiply feminine and feminist subjectivity to which Braidotti aspires is the key to the plurality of literary voices we witness today. Her acceptance of feminism and feminist theory is a hospitable and non-hostile haven for my own genderized thinking about literature. I appreciate the writing of the American Rita Felski as well for her insightful reading about the lack of critical understanding of what feminist studies are today. A hybrid-view theoretical and textual analysis of women's novels is thus necessary for any attempt to bridge two fundamentally different perspectives on feminist theory that might cause the problem of 'reproposing some normative traits' of the signifier woman, or 'creating new norms in the name of a new feminist ethos.'[18] Though Felski and some other feminist critics in the United States are wary of Irigaray's interpretations of sexual difference, cautious as they are regarding the so-called excessive 'carnality' of European thinking, Braidotti instead embraces Irigaray's concepts because she recognizes in them the positive and joyous power that many other women thinkers have found. Both Braidotti and Felski agree on one point: the danger of letting the voices of radical feminists like Andrea Dworkin and Catharine MacKinnon take over and represent feminist studies as a homogenous field of thought[19] vastly different from the diversified views we enjoy today. To illustrate my point about the hazards of certain theories, I offer as testimony Badinter's otherwise brilliant *Fausse route* to demonstrate how in Europe several critics still represent the whole of American feminist studies by using the theories of merely two among the many contemporary American feminist thinkers. In comparison, one sees in the United States a failure to appreciate fully the work of European feminist thinkers who do not channel their work within the guidelines of an official American feminist theory, one that leaves very little space for nonconformist, non-orthodox readings of women's reality today by female literates.

Like Felski, I do not conceive of a feminist aesthetic or general theory of women and literature per se. Dogmas have seldom been useful, particularly when writing about the arts, since questioning is a basic aspect of both artistic and critical expression. Felski notes that 'feminist scholarship, like any other field, is a mixed bag, and not all of its claims are equally worthy or defensible.'[20] Indeed, resorting to the feminist theories of Dworkin and MacKinnon would be pernicious in studying contemporary Italian women writers, as their work largely depends upon and is affected by political questions and is deeply embedded in an altogether different society.[21] Felski addresses the difficulty of dealing exclusively with particular literary values and notes that 'trying to hold literature and the social world apart is a Sisyphean task: however valiantly critics try to keep art pure, external meanings keep seeping in. This is because literature is double-sided. It is not *either/or* but *both/and*.'[22] Felski also maintains that linguistic analysis, though important, cannot be a conclusive evaluation of the literary in a work; she notes that the way critics, in assessing feminist scholarship, often exaggerate by means of focusing on a few particularly radical writers is just another mistake of traditional scholarship. Feminist criticism emphasizes the 'double-sided'[23] aspect of literature and its connections to society, as it considers the novel – composed of a plot, a system of characters, a discourse, and other literary forms – from a different point of view that varies precisely because every reading is a gendered reading. Far from demonstrating its 'universality,' the novel shows instead the individuality by which each writer and his/her readership particularizes its hermeneutics.

(Italian) 'Literature after Feminism'

Felski's observations apply equally to the Italian context, where academic male critics fail to engage seriously with feminist studies, often by dismissing feminist scholarship as a mere admixture of literary and cultural studies.[24] When we examine Italian literature and culture, these problems appear to be acute. One cannot analyse Italian women writers in depth without understanding first and foremost that their world is still deeply invested in traditional values and yet besieged (in a positive way) by modern values. A serious approach to criticism of the Italian novel written by women cannot impose models of theoretical discourse that are devoid of familiarity with Italy's fragmented and kaleidoscopic society – which, if seen from extra-Italian viewpoints, might still demonstrate certain clichés, including the characterization of female Italians. It is beneficial not to isolate literature *from* its socio-political context, since in order to understand the arts, and in order to perform well the reading/analysis of what we can call 'artistic texts,' we must understand what artists draw from society. Felski's perception of the double-sidedness of literature – and of the novel as a genre in particular – is vital to the actual 'value' and permanence of the literary work. Conversely, when we study artistic texts, we acquire knowledge of the society the artists describe. By knowing the works of Italian women writers, we can appreciate a larger part of the representation of Italian society, since these texts constitute the majority of authors *and* certainly readers in the Italian literary market today. Women are at once the authors of their works and also their consumers.

Even within the parameters of the Italian readership, Italian women's literary writing is a rich locus for many artistic expressions that runs the risk of being misunderstood, chiefly because the role of women is not being consolidated within academia, the intellectual environment that still today directs critical and literary thinking in Italy. Much critical comment has been based on the belief that 'you cannot do two things at once. You can either look at literature as literature or you look at it as politics, the argument goes, but you cannot do both.'[25] Discussing John Ellis's tenets on feminist critics, Felski argues that Ellis's contention that 'feminists ... impose their obsessions on the text and hence they are not literary critics' is invalid. She also objects to Ellis's practice of literary criticism, according to which 'real critics ... respond to what a work of literature says ... without assumptions, biases or prejudices.'[26] Felski argues against the presumed 'blank slate' that a critic brings to reading a text. The personal experience, taste, and literary competence a reader brings when approaching a text makes this 'innocence' an impossible task. 'This is not to claim that literature either causes or simply reinforces the oppression of women'; as she clarifies, 'it is to argue that ideas, symbols, and myths of gender *saturate* literary works.'[27] More than the 'literary works' per se, one would contend that literary criticism in Italy as well seems to be affected by the 'troubles that gender draws.'[28] The 'multitude' of women's novelistic expressions of the last decade is witness to their varied approaches to the novelistic text. One of the most salient features in the work of contemporary women writers is a shift in the mode of investigation of reality. This shift largely consists of the use of both an understandably muted point of view and a kind of discourse that determines some of the most distinctive features in their writing vis-à-vis that of previous periods.

Felski furthers her argument by pointing to the hermeneutic circle, which allows the reader to change his/her belief about the text as the reading progresses. She asserts that, 'claiming to possess a non-ideological viewpoint is thus a deeply ideological act'[29] in itself. From what I have observed, this latter view is common in Italian women's literary studies. The novelists who claim such a 'blank-slate' view act as any minority will. As women artists, they deny any ideological viewpoint in order not to be ghettoized within the very small but active circles of Italian women intellectuals, active in philosophy, historiography, and, more generally, politics.

The *Hybrid* Phase

Contemporary women's writings mirror, as they should, the epistemic transformation undergone by the Western world since the days of the feminist movement of the 1970s. Tracing a map of women's writing of the last few years can be challenging, but it is a rewarding task, since postmodernist readings have opened up new ways of writing, and reading, the novel. In what is now generally considered the fourth generation of twentieth-century Italian women writers, situated in the years following feminism's most active period of the 1970s, the novel is once again a site for expressive research and discussion of social issues regarding youth, family, and women. When looking at the current production in the Italian women's novel, I must add a fourth phase to Elaine Showalter's model, always urging readers to make use of the 'flexibility' which Showalter recommended regarding her three-phase paradigm. The mode of *self-discovery* is sustained in this fourth phase by such a multitude of narrative forms and strategies that I believe it reasonable to call it the *hybrid* phase.

The influence of North American culture and postmodernist bricolage have greatly helped these authors in their attempt to create a truly innovative style of character narration. Consumerism, the feminization of culture, and the use of pornography as elaborated in the works of these writers clearly mirror an unprecedented and unforeseen freedom in the expression of Italian female authors. While in its generic terms discussion on consumerism probably applies more accurately to the feminist debate in the United States and to the one involving cultural studies in Great Britain, it also constructs parallels between those studies and a more specifically Italian realm of women's literary studies. The American and the British debates appear to be relevant, in fact, for identifying some factors of the cultural shift in Italian women's newest forms of literary expression. This shift is not necessarily provoked merely by changes in so-called high literature or philosophy, but is also, and particularly in the case of the female authors close to the now-defunct group of the *Cannibali* writers, originally motivated by the effects of mass culture, consumerism, and commodification of goods (i.e., the female body) *upon* 'high' literature. I have argued elsewhere for the importance of an entirely new perspective of Italian women authors' muted standpoint with respect to family, mass consumerism, pornography, and middle- and highbrow culture, as well as an emerging awareness of the female body, as a 'contested site – a battleground for competing ideologies.'[30]

I have called *hybrid* the most current phase of Italian women's writings. Their literary production forsakes the specificity of subgenres that was so often seen and theorized by studies of the 1980s. The current novels engage in a genre that is borderline diaristic-autobiographical and fictional.[31] Women writers of today conceive very different ways in which to represent the world and their female characters. They situate themselves as agents and spectators of their own existence at once, but they also perform a scrutiny and/or critique of the most obvious aspects of Italian androcentrism. Their work makes use of an almost incessant flow of sexual activity of every type (imagined and not), under whose fragile surface it is not unusual to see representations of female trauma, alienation, and desperation that these writers do not hesitate to give us in crude words that are reminiscent of, but not always limited to, masculine coprophilia and pornophilia.

This book discusses the works of authors primarily born after 1960. For them, it would have been physically impossible to participate in the happenings or demonstrations of the historical *femministe* of the 1970s. Therefore, it is hard to reproach these younger writers when we realize how deeply Italian society has changed from a vastly politicized nation into a rather 'Americanized' one, in which capitalism and economic power have taken over both the system of values inherent in the Catholic tradition as well as the secular tradition. Many of them do not belong to that generation in which radical feminism was auspicious and almost required. These younger writers, such as Melania Mazzucco, Simona Vinci, and Silvia Ballestra, were children when Ronald Reagan was in power, when *perestroika* appeared from behind the Iron Curtain. When these women were born or right afterwards, abortion was already a legalized reality in Italy, as was divorce. As a consequence, there is ample difference between past and present ways of women writers making culture and ideology available to the reader. Italian writers use notions previously explored by feminist critics and thinkers, many of which are common psychoanalytical loci of discussion, such as the mother–son theme in the conventional Italian novel, or the mother–daughter relationship commonly found in the writings of women authors.[32] Writers commit themselves to investigate these sites of research and analysis in aesthetic expressive forms. There is a willingness to believe in something, but fathers can no longer provide it for their children, regardless of gender. Mauro Covacich writes about this generation of Italians from which the women writers I analyse stem:

> I nostri padri capelloni credevano in qualcosa, poi sono arrivati i paninari degli anni Ottanta che non credevano in niente, adesso ci siamo noi che crediamo in tutto. Noi, col taglio etnico internazionale. Noi, che non sventoliamo nessuna bandiera perché sbandieriamo i diritti di tutti.[33]
> (Our hippie forefathers believed in some things, but then the eighties *paninari*,[34] who did not believe in anything, appeared on the scene. Now we believe in everything and we are ethnically international. We do not wave a particular banner because we represent the rights of all.)

If we plunged this new generation of women writers into the political and ideological situation in which intellectuals such as Dacia Maraini, Fabrizia Ramondino, Maria Rosa Cutrufelli, and Luisa Passerini lived their own aesthetic experience, many of them would probably utilize their writing as both an epistemological and also a political tool. Political and ideological engagement can take on different forms. If not in a prescriptive way, as Felski notes, writers do, nevertheless, often take a stand. Within the body of their novels that seem by necessity to be always charged, Italian women writers question sites of traditional male power in Italian society (sexual politics, the family as a problematic societal entity, the workplace) to indicate routes to a more constructive form of respectful coexistence among humans of all genders and sexual orientations. The Arendtian tenet, reiterated by Adriana Cavarero, is indeed true: 'the political sphere, exclusively human in the world, consists of the *between*, of the *in-between*, in what, while revealing their plural condition, also puts in relation and separates at once individuals.'[35]

Exemplified by the characters of Rossana Campo, particularly in *Mai sentita così bene*,[36] but also in her other novels, a new (female) rhetoric of language ('talk as you fuck') encourages readers to appreciate the often undervalued ability of women to unfold and discuss social and personal issues while chatting within their community.[37] Rossana Campo represents in many ways the quintessential post-feminist Italian writer. She uses colloquial spoken Italian as her linguistic medium to place female readership, on the same level as her characters, with everyday problems connected to love, money, and work. Reading becomes another *chiacchierata* among women, not an exercise in patience. Her characters are not lonely female protagonists. Campo sets her novels of liberated women in Paris (where she lives) and makes them experience the great disparity between their cultural and religious Catholic Italian upbringing and the choices they have made in life. They are often torn between social conformity and their genuine desires and insecurities, all supported by the author's ability to record the transgender and transcultural language they employ. Campo has created a nonchalant and plain representation of women contemporary to her while using an assorted array of sub-novelistic genres to articulate her discourse of postmodern themes from a woman's point of view. From the detective novel to the fictional autobiography, from expatriate memoirs to the father-daughter story, Campo tends to depict the most realistic image of humanity at large. This strategy is adopted in a very different way by Isabella Santacroce,[38] who uses no irony to make a situation comic or render it less dramatic, not even in the ingenious *Fluo*.[39] Instead, as early as in *Destroy*, pornographic words are brought to an intense level of poetry that enacts the dislocation of the body considered in posthuman terms, and to use this poetry to create her own vision of the world and of the female body in various stages of profound changes. More recently, Paola Presciuttini's narrating character asserts her independence from the suffocating entity of her family:

> Fuori dalla famiglia. Da un posto dove non sei nemmeno libero di mangiare quando hai fame, di andare in bagno senza che nessuno ti bussi alla porta interrompendo quell'unico momento di quiete della giornata, un posto dove le bollette sono più importanti dei sentimenti.[40]
> (Out of the family. Out of a place where you are not even free to eat when you are hungry, to go to the bathroom without someone knocking at the door interrupting the only quiet moment of the day. A place where bills are more important than feelings.)

But if it is convenient to group these post-feminist, post-nineties writers (or those generally recognized as such) in a perspective framed by post-feminist theory, it is necessary, however, to recognize that they have produced a type of narrative that differs from previous feminist models, although not disengaged from ideological issues. A literature that is neither imitative nor revolutionary mirrors aspects of women's social behaviour in the 1990s and the first decade of 2000. It has contributed to the fictionalization of a behavioural model for Italian women (and readers) that would be unthinkable without the feminist movement of the 1970s. The new model for the articulation of the Italian woman in her relationship with society and societal norms emerges from recent literary texts, whose import I have already illustrated in my work on Santacroce and Campo.

This model constructs a new type of individual with a gender that mirrors a particular social behaviour programmed and foreseen by the normative system that is, nevertheless, endowed with alternative strategies to subvert the intellectual oppression/repression of women. If a traditional approach to literary criticism fails in its understanding of women authors' representation of female desire for change that is conveyed through the stories they tell and the perspectives their narrators often take, it is, nevertheless, quite apparent that the new elements and narrative structures presented by contemporary writers are meant to redesign in concrete terms the historical relationship of the woman with the Other. The thematic elements and the narrative forms utilized by the women authors of the most militant feminist period were not in any terms segregated from the implications of postmodern consumerism. Gendered identity mirrors 'a meaning of the word woman, always open to negotiations while individuals and diverse groups fight for changes in meaning to be able to satisfy new needs'[41] that present themselves little by little. The body is extinguishing itself, or so it appears; do we really live, as they say, in a society of posthuman bodies? We should not forget that it is from the body, going back to Rosi Braidotti, that language finds it strength to say what is being lost and what we are finding today.

Women's narratives involving issues of self-discovery and the woman author's personal relationship with the term 'feminism' can rely in the *hybrid* phase on expressive forms that do not clash stylistically with the content of their works, and as a result relevant issues no longer stick out awkwardly from a literary form in which they were uneasily placed, as in some cases in the 1970s. Rather, the result of these writers' efforts is the consolidation of what I do not hesitate to call one of the most brilliant periods for novelistic writing in the Italian panorama. I argue that literature, and particularly this newly hybridized form of the novel, still contains the impetus for a vast social, political, ideological debate over the nature of human relations that it inherited from the past. In today's world, which simplifies and inhibits the complexity of ideas and the sharing across borders of ideas and ideologies, there is still plenty to explore.

Refiguring the Novel, Refiguring Criticism

To note that, even in today's Italian criticism, the existing novelistic canon still presents a problem constitutes no new scholarly observation. The reading and aesthetic evaluation of a novel can rarely count on innovative analyses of the mechanisms connecting a certain work to preceding ones, for today still originality, the criterion of 'uniqueness,' dictates a reading that cannot undermine the innovative merits of a new work, while canonical works must be kept in the rank that critics before us have decreed and must remain there. More striking, perhaps, are the ways in which the authorial intentions that women writers ascribe to their novels appear often misinterpreted or, worse, ignored.

The contribution of women to the development of the Italian novel is impressive in its duration and variety. Globalization perceived as 'the creation of new circuits of cooperation and collaboration that stretch across nations and continents and allow an unlimited number of encounters'[42] can be, by extension, a positive movement that brings Italian women writers to insert their discourse into a transnational, wider circuit of experimentation and commonalities/diversities, of recovery of the peripheral within the central, of better interaction with foreign writers facing similar issues, and finally of making their role in public action as artists better known.

Somehow Italian academics and the *critici militanti* whose reviews influence readers from the *pagine culturali* of the Italian newspapers still give their approval about the direction in which readership should go. Readers and viewers are today much more aware of the presence of women writers and artists more generally in the concurrent effort at 'represent[ing] the human kind.'[43] And yet, there is a failure to realize the shift in women writings on the part of many of our critics, particularly those operating in academia, who still find it difficult to deal with a muted point of view as expressed in contemporary literature, not to mention the work of women artists who are very much alive and well. Critics are often still anchored to stylistic criteria that appear somewhat inadequate for a comprehensive reading of what women writers of today are producing.

Emblematic of this is Massimo Onofri's recent *stroncatura* of Isabella Santacroce's novels. In a whimsical comparison with D'Annunzio's lyricism, Onofri terms her a '[s]crittrice dal basso, e del basso, la Santacroce, ma molto attratta dai processi di liricizzazione della realtà' ('writer from, and of, the bottom, Santacroce, however very interested in the process of lyricization of reality').[44] Her *inautenticità* bothers Onofri, who is perhaps more attuned to appreciate the inauthenticity of other (male) writers whose stylistic paradigm is more congenial to his textual analysis. With visible irony, Onofri wonders about Santacroce's ability to write lyrical prose, and describes hers as 'una scelta inattuale, che mescola i ritmi brevi al respiro lungo del romanzo e lo infetta col virus di flash istantanei' ('an obsolete choice that juxtaposes short rhythms to the long breath of the novel while infecting it with the virus of instant flashes').[45] Onofri's patronizing and conservative approach to Santacroce's prose is yet more evidence confirming the lack of willingness of Italian critics to find alternative practices of textual analysis in their reading of women authors' works. In its intent, Onofri's *stroncatura* mirrors quite vividly the argument made by Rita Felski about the paucity of critical tools available when it comes to a woman writer's text. When limiting the reading to the analysis of her use of metonymy, critics, and readers by default, miss the entire socio-psychoanalytical point made by a woman writer.[46] As a corollary to this, the more conventional texts by women writers suffer less from the critics' unwillingness to adopt more encompassing, more up-to-date, critical tools. These novels are often the ones, in fact, that enjoy more successful critical readings by professional reviewers, and the ones that manage to avoid hurried misunderstandings.[47]

Perhaps the reason for the frequent misreading of women's writing, and women-authored novels especially, resides in the fact that, while Italian forms of narrative are evolving at a frantic speed, the tools critics use to read them are still pretty much those utilized in the 1970s: a strong ideological commitment (now with a disillusioned bent), attention to the use of rhetorical figures, and epistemological poetics. These tools come coupled with an intransigent refusal to understand the historical shift between radical feminism and a more updated sociological one that is so prevalent in post-feminist female writing, as Felski's form of literary criticism both emblematizes and hopes for. In addition, critics are often uneasy when reading a narrative that presents themes, syntax, and stylistics that do not interest them. The case of Onofri's *stroncatura* of Santacroce's writings represents just the latest (negative) comment about young female writers in Italian literary studies. These problematic approaches to literary texts by women are often also due to a lack of interest – rather unjustified given the profile of the Italian readers' market – as well as to the actual absence of a correct knowledge of genre development, feminist studies, and theoretical debates on women's writing.

With some discomfort one notes that the reading of novels by women becomes sometimes a weapon against the whole category of women intellectuals and artists who want to construct novels fully reflective of their sexuality. A dissatisfying novel by a woman, such as Melissa P.'s first publication, brings out much misogynist criticism in Italian intellectuals that allows for sterile generalizations while directing negative comments to the entire women's literary community. Instead of noting innovations, Italian academics in particular seem to be too quick to reject works they cannot frame within a specific organizational pattern, unless it comes accompanied by an aura that makes it worthy of appreciation in an exquisite vein of conformist anticonformism. Unless, of course, it screams for scandal, as in Melissa P.'s case. Far from being a destiny, woman's body is a 'vessel' that determines how one perceives art, much like race, ethnicity, and geographic location. Whether presented in a demystifying and amused way, as in the case of Rossana Campo's characters,[48] or in the decadent atmosphere in which Isabella Santacroce's nihilistic heroines live, sex and sexuality are important spaces in twenty-first-century women's literary expression. This authorial decision to narrate sexuality in all of its implications (even through pornographic writing), proves fruitful in its representation of the female body, of the body and sexual politics, features that appear in many novels from the end of the 1990s onward. This is a narrative choice that, given the relative lack of a female erotic literary tradition, renders new Italian women writers extremely vulnerable to criticism, with the risk of yet further marginalization from the mainstream publishing tradition. After the flagrant and not-quite-representative case of Melissa P.'s first book, *Cento colpi di spazzola prima di andare a dormire* (*One Hundred Strokes of the Brush before Going to Bed*) a book that has drawn the attention of the *New York Times*'s reviewers in its American translation,[49] this kind of writing has become much more evident to a more general public – for all the wrong reasons. Instead, one could argue that the Italian novel has only been enriched by recent erotic novels by women writers, as new and fresh perspectives about the understanding of sexual practices and sexual desire bring to the fore important implications about Italian society and how women view its construction. The importance of these women writers and of their contribution to the understanding of social dynamics by sexual discourse (what Michel Foucault termed 'sex in the head')[50] are at odds with the unjustified indifference or contempt with which critics often receive and misread their work.

That a feminist reading must be a comprehensive rather than exclusionary reading of women's work is a difficult idea to disseminate. The reaction of critics like Onofri, their indifference to things they do not know, is perhaps only too human, but critiquing what one does not know, particularly with the incorrect critical tools, is not what critics are supposed to do with artistic works. In addition, the hybridized forms in which the novel as a genre has developed in a whirling process of language experimentation and narrative strategies attest to the difficulty present in expressing new perspectives on life if the criticism of authors remains based upon obsolete forms of writing. Unfixing identities is apparently the task that contemporary Italian women writers have chosen in their works. In summary, to quote Rosi Braidotti, writing is for the nomadic subject (a category to which many of us subscribe) 'a process of undoing the illusory stability of fixed identities.'[51] If Braidotti applies it particularly with respect to polyglot writers, this concept holds true particularly to some of the more challenging Italian writers.

Aesthetic Value versus Political Value, or the Logic of the Canon

Understanding and appreciating the diversity proposed by women writers in their works dealing with Italian society remains, nevertheless, quite a task, chiefly because there is a failure to analyse the way these writers position themselves within that society in their representation of the 'knowability of the world.' In fact, many scholars are still attached to traditional (stereotypical) parameters of what Italian literature should be. If we think that, according to Harold Bloom, Primo Levi's writings represent a 'prophecy' in the Italian canon, we are still far from the inclusion of women authors in what is considered the Italian canon.[52] De-canonizing Italian literature remains a challenge. Entering/revising the canon, or de-canonizing it, defining the social reality in which texts operate, redefining the novel as a 'gendered' genre, understanding the needs of readership while investigating human society: these are concerns that Italian women writers share in their however many dissimilar approaches to the novel.

Gender bias in the appreciation and reception of Italian women's writing has been debilitating, and its consequences have included the production of mis-categorizations and misconceptions. My reading of contemporary Italian women's writing aims at discussing what, in their work, has led to the ascension of a more flexible literary canon, one that is now much more expanded with respect to the reading lists that appeared in our universities many years ago. In the United States, the canon is something now looked at with difficulty and suspicion, as its very essence brings to the fore the inevitable vestiges of white male hegemony that lie dormant within it. In *Feminism Is for Everybody*, bell hooks explains the matter plainly: 'When the feminist movement exposed biases in curriculum, much of this forgotten and ignored work was "rediscovered." The formation of women's studies programs in colleges and universities provided institutional legitimation for academic focus on work on women.'[53]

Talking about the canon today generates an understandable sense of unease, because of the rather problematic calls for the insertion of texts by minority writers or, more drastically, because many vigorously claim the need for the radical elimination of 'a' canon. (This very situation can be witnessed also in the case of the visual arts.) Back in Italy, such a bastion of tradition is still highly regarded by academics, who keep confirming the need for works by Dante, Petrarch, and Manzoni in curricula and reading lists while denying the utility of reading many women authors deemed dispensable and peripheral. The canon of readings that these illustrious (male) writers unwittingly produced by virtue of their works – these were and are indeed the source of inspiration and creativity for a host of great writers – exists, and resists change. Indeed, my goal is neither to question nor a priori to expand the importance of the literary canon for a country such as Italy. I venture to say that in Italy there still exist pretty much two distinct territories in which the canonical authors keep considerable distance from the non-canonical ones. Better put, critics still like to recoil from any form of more extended 'hospitality.' Within the wide spectrum of American critical and literary theory, and after many struggles, the great divide between canonical and non-canonical has left space for a blending of the traditional need for knowledge of a canonical corpus with the accommodation of more peripheral (with respect to the canon, of course) exponents from other cultures. In the case of Italian literature, the danger resides in the exclusion from textbooks, curricula, and academic programs of the work of the so-called 'not-yet, not-now, not-canonical' writers. In other words, the danger resides in the exclusion of the work of those contemporary writers whose sense of style does not meet a set of expectations about stylistics, coupled with the nostalgia for times past, that many academics and *critici militanti* still cultivate.

American feminist critics such as Carla Kaplan can be comfortable in claiming her choice of certain texts for her book because they 'have already been established by feminist critics as a canon.'[54] This reconfirms the notion that, according to feminist theory, the transformations taking place in a multimedia society in the age of globalization can affect not only the pole of the 'others,' but also the 'centre.' This statement, this choice of texts to analyse, makes manifest shared acceptance of the multiple subjectivities that construct literary works. The same cannot be said for Italian literature. To some, even Italian women writers of the stature of Elsa Morante and Anna Maria Ortese still hardly compare to Italo Calvino and Cesare Pavese. And so, if I am still raising issues regarding the notion of canonicity years after the American debate on this topic, I do it with the full knowledge that it might sound stale.[55] However, a discussion of canon expansion is still essential when dealing with Italian women writers, for in spite of much readjustment of 'sites,' in spite of much discussion about the interaction between the 'centre' and the 'peripheral,' even today not many recognize the innovation and contribution of Italian contemporary women writers.

Contesting sites by the means of a theoretical and critical discussion (and analyses) is the duty of academics if and when it is realized that the site allocated to some authors (and their critics by default) has been unfairly assigned as a static, immobile one that deserves neither further discussion nor critical development. One can only work from within a structure to demonstrate what is not working properly. It should not be surprising that in Italian academia the canon constitutes one of the most logical points of resistance to the affirmation of women writers. The work of renovation and innovation of the novel genre by women writers in Italy today is so compelling that it demands more in-depth analyses.

The work of critics resides mainly in the comprehension, reception, and aesthetic assessment of literary works. They should be able to position works temporally and spatially, to explain why stories are narrated in a particular way and not in another, why in our own times (which will be at some point 'the past') certain subgenres are favoured over others. If we read without forcing preconceptions into a corner, we are doomed to fail in the reading of anything called 'new' or 'unknown,' not to mention in the ability to find a comfortable place for them in the aforementioned Italian canon. In Italian, '*canone*' literally means 'payment for something,' and is a term that implies the notion that the text needs to give something in return for its entrance into the literary tradition. In other words, if you belong, you need to pay a fee that can roughly parallel the sense of appeasement, of aroused interest, of challenging minds that a text should ignite in readers, particularly since its presence in the most important literary circles has been decreed. This book hopes to demonstrate the changes contemporary Italian women writers have produced in their work by way of close reading and use of theory to facilitate analysis in a direction more profitable both to the works themselves and to Italian literature in general, while banning theoretical fences and facile condemnation.

The Plan of the Book

Since one of this book's aims is to establish a thread between current Italian novels and their rich legacy, chapter 1 reconnects to the much-frequented topos of the mother–daughter relationship to elicit the discovery of a map of female intertextuality and a rereading of the female as a literary and epistemological construct. The three novels analysed – Mariateresa Di Lascia's *Passaggio in ombra*, Elena Ferrante's *I giorni dell'abbandono*, and Simona Vinci's *Come prima delle madri* – further advance this notion. By examining these three writers, chapter 1 offers ways to understand the dissemination of the legacy of some of the most important voices in women's literature and philosophy. It uncovers the rhetorical strategies these three writers utilize in retrieving narrative models created by women who were active in a different generation and indicates how they engage in a fruitful and long-lasting foray into experimental writing in the realist mode. While Di Lascia relies on a narrative pattern that approximates to Morante's in *Menzogna e sortilegio*, Ferrante and Vinci operate in radically distinct manners while also drawing on the legacy of Morante. Simona Vinci reworks the Morantian Oedipal novel in a hybrid *noir* novel divided in two parts. The first pertains to the son, the second to his mother. They are Morantian creatures, for their relationship will remain unresolved and unclear, founded on a communion of instincts rather than feelings, charged with a love that paradoxically borders on hate. Mother and son do not engage with each other. As in Morante's *Aracoeli* or *L'isola di Arturo*, mother and son love each other in a way that is bound to decompose. Vinci problematizes the Morantian notion of disillusionment, or *smagamento* as Morante would call it, for she complicates the clear transition that Morante assumes between childhood and adulthood (happiness/unhappiness). Vinci's shift from the Morantian norm in her interpretation of *smagamento* makes of her perhaps the most brilliant epigone of Morante's legacy.

Ferrante's novel *I giorni dell'abbandono* is exuberant with the Mediterranean passion and negative force that was always the underlying structure in Morante's novels (and poetry), while intertwining them with a reading of Simone de Beauvoir's *La femme rompue* and revisiting the myth of the abandoned woman, Medea. My discussion here revolves primarily around the critical and deconstructive rereading the novelist performs of *La femme rompue*, as this is a clear case of the relationship that texts entertain with each other regardless of national boundaries. In Simona Vinci's Oedipal-*noir* novel *Come prima delle madri*, it is the mother–son relationship, the boy's growing up while facing bad teachers within his own family – just like Morante's characters – that brought me to see in Morante the predecessor for Vinci and her stories of family horror. While the mother–son connection is a conventional one in the Italian novel, Morante deconstructs it in all her four novels, thus offering future writers the possibility of a different vantage point from which to constitute a relationship with Italian society, and – by default – the Italian novel. Morante's last novel, *Aracoeli*, contains some of the most evident intertextual connections with *Come prima delle madri*. The historical background of this novel, provided by the Second World War and the partisans' guerrilla actions, are suggestive of some parts of Morante's 1974 Italian epic on human suffering, *La Storia*. Despite this, the treatment of the maternal bond with the son, so acutely analysed in its destructive perversion, ties Vinci's novel to Morante's novels narrated in the first person rather than to *La Storia*. In all novels of Morante's epigones it is the first-person narrator that invariably ties the novels to Morante's.

Chapter 2 deals with an original and relatively recent development of familism. This thematic, upon which an impressive body of work in Italian literature is built, pursues a new, tangential trajectory, the narrative treatment of the father-daughter relationship. This is an important transformation from the usual mother-son theme at the core of much twentieth-century Italian literature, in which the Oedipal complex is constantly revisited, both by male authors and also by female ones, as in the case of Elsa Morante. Ippolita Avalli's *La Dea dei baci*,[56] Francesca Mazzucato's *Hot Line: Storia di un'ossessione*,[57] and Pia Pera's *Diario di Lo*,[58] a riveting reading of Vladimir Nabokov's *Lolita* are the novels examined in this chapter. In Avalli's *La Dea dei baci* the theme of the paternal relationship with power and authority (and their abuse) creates a novel written in the first person about a Northern Italian orphan at the beginning of the 1960s. The young girl's departure from the identity that a community has decreed to her must in her case necessarily coincide with the separation from her father and his law. The protagonist of Francesca Mazzucato's *Hot Line: Storia di un'ossessione* sells sex over the phone, only at night, in a town near where she lives. While at first one would think of her job as a means to an end, freeing her from old tenets of repression, the job is revealed to be inextricably connected with the trauma of her abandonment by her father – especially caused by the phone calls of his lover – when she was a little girl. Unlike Nicholson Baker's *Vox*,[59] a 1992 novel in which the two protagonists, Jim and Abby, never meet and never have sex, but sustain a long conversation making up the entire book, *Hot Line: Storia di un'ossessione* is a more intricate novel in which desire and melancholia for the father figure take over and impede the powerful suggestions arising from the protagonist's transgression and sexually provocative statements.

In the case of Pia Pera's novel, we face a different kind of paternity, an artistic one, the weight of which is felt by the author in a dialectical and positive form of 'anxiety of influence.' Known for her beautiful translation of Pushkin's *Eugene Onegin*, Pia Pera has managed to work on a parodic rewriting of a canonical text in the attempt to render justice to a mistreated character, as she considers Vladimir Nabokov's Lolita to be. Her *Diario di Lo* is a pensive parody that does not miss the ironic and even comic aspect of this literary mode. Most important, it is Dolly who now narrates her own version of 'Lolita's story,' and not her stepfather.

Chapter 3 illustrates emerging sexual politics in two diverging directions in the work of Dacia Maraini and Melania Mazzucco. Their works are scandalous and audacious, but they explore two entirely different fields of sexuality. In my analysis of Maraini's works the stress is on the theme of abortion, in Mazzucco's that of lesbianism. In Dacia Maraini's narrative works, from the outset of her career, abortion has taken a dominant role. The theme is presented and discussed in several of her novels, as well as in her subsequent reflections on abortion, which appeared for the first time in the 'Lettera sull'aborto,'[60] addressed to the late Enzo Siciliano, then general editor of *Nuovi Argomenti*. In the investigation of Melania Mazzucco's *Il bacio della Medusa*, the treatment of perverse love and its deregulating powers leads to engaging conclusions. Teresa de Lauretis's *The Practice of Love*[61] has been instrumental in my reading of perverse desire in Mazzucco's novel, as it deals with the rebuttal of the 'norm,' for it allows a discussion of normality, conformist behaviour, and construction of femininity in Italian society at the beginning of twentieth century in Mazzucco's postmodern hybrid novel.

This analysis of novels published for the most part between the 1990s and 2005 will, I hope, show what has changed in the novel thanks to the work of these women. Far from being a conclusive study, this book proposes a different type of reading of women's novels in contemporary Italy, a reading/mapping that does not seek to be influenced exclusively by feminist theory/ies, but that, instead, reflects how enriching literary and cultural studies can be when one considers the contemporary novel with a frame of mind that incorporates feminist theory. At the same time, ample space has been allotted here to several topics that are at the heart of the novel genre no matter the period, such as love, family, sex, and history, as they will always be at the core of the narratives we construct about ourselves and the society we inhabit and transform with our own bodies.

chapter 1

'Writing Is Always Playing with the Mother's Body': Mothers' Rewrites

Women writers' presence in the development of the Italian novel justifies the argument in the present chapter that these women reread, and find inspiration in, not only the texts of their male predecessors but also those by some of the most fundamental female authors. This chapter expands some of the theoretical tenets treated in the Introduction. At its core lies the analysis of the relationship between one particular literary mother, Elsa Morante, and her literary daugthers, namely, Mariateresa Di Lascia, Simona Vinci, and Elena Ferrante. My close readings illustrate how the novels of these contemporary artists[1] and their respective relationships with the inspirational figure of Elsa Morante have contributed to create for some an unofficial canon in Italian literature. A woman 'entrusts' her work with another woman who is more knowledgeable than she in a field. This practice originates in the need of the woman to establish her work in that particular field. The dissemination of a female symbolic power becomes evident in this practice, for no longer do women rely on male models for their particular interest in a topic/subject, and also because the *pratica di affidamento* organizes a profitable interaction among women, one that need not be based on sisterhood and kinship viewed merely as psychological support, but that takes actively into account the professional needs of women at work. Being a Morantian scholar, I work on the legacy that Elsa Morante and, in the case of Ferrante, the French philosopher and novelist Simone de Beauvoir have established among a newer generation of Italian women writers. Di Lascia, Ferrante, and Vinci entrust Elsa Morante with their writings because they can find in her texts not merely the thematics that are closest to their heart, but, more important, the belief that a thread connects these discussions of the world and its possible representations without their gender, their position within society, being forgotten. Interaction among texts – mediation with the mother figure – ensues precisely when a muted perspective about the locales in which their work is embedded is there to tie them together. Some readers could see this present chapter as an on-going process of canonization for Elsa Morante's works as well, as the echo of her novels has grown large in recent generations of writers. Their perception is probably accurate, as Di Lascia's, Ferrante's, and Vinci's examples are fitting practical cases in which writers look at their literary mother to have freedom of speech and postulate the advancement of their own epistemology. Only in this sense can one imagine the practice of *affidamento* as liberating. By entrusting previous literary female models with their own work, women writers facilitate the formation of a non-androcentric system of influence and reference in literature that pragmatically advances women's position in society.

Literary interaction between texts by contemporary Italian women writers should be viewed as an open forum in which to discuss the canon and its expansion beyond those texts that, until today, have been considered standard readings by, and for, women 'only.' The interaction that takes place between female writings, literary tradition, and conventional ways of reading texts needs further discussion in order to bridge these diverging paths of what one can think of today as separate female (unofficial) and male (official) canons of the Italian novel. This chapter illustrates some cases in which an enriching and liberating literary interaction – a practice of literary entrustment – between Italian female writers of different generations, far from essentializing their artistic production, is conducive to a revised notion of what can eventually be considered canonical in the near future. The long process of acculturation, emancipation, and transformation in Italian literature, one that allows today for analyses of influence and intertextuality between two Italian female writers, is something that deserves a preamble and explanation.

Trusting the Mother, Mediating the Order

What is to be treated here is, therefore, a particular dimension of the mother–daughter relationship, with the firm understanding that it is not a biological mother that is involved in this relationship, but an intellectual one. This chapter presents a critical and textual analysis of three novels in which the interaction between literary mothers and literary daughters is the most salient element of intertextuality. The notion of 'trust' implied in Luisa Muraro's *pratica dell'affidamento*[2] ('practice of entrustment') fits well with my critical approach to the discourse between contemporary Italian female writers' literary texts. In fact, traditional tenets regarding the interaction between literary texts are simply not sufficient for analysing the complex relation among these novels by women. Nevertheless, the (inter)textual analysis of these novels is mindful of, yet not limited to, Muraro's theory and subsequent interpretations and analyses.[3] Predicating, as Muraro does in her well-known theory on entrustment, that 'the arrival of the Law of the Father (of the patriarchy) that imposes itself on the positivity found in the works of the mother, separates logic from being and is the cause of our losing and re-losing of being,'[4] cannot quite be sufficient to justify the reasons why female authors refer to other women's texts. This loss needs to be connected to the notion of the sinning mothers, obliterated from society despite having procreated it.[5]

For women artists, independence can be achieved – but not solely – by reconnecting their work to a symbolic order that, reconnecting with the mother figure, presents similarities to and differences from the patriarchal one. In fact, an order that is not metaphoric but actually symbolic *and* concretely productive, where the duplicitous role of women as writers and/or readers finds the most accurate theoretical and rhetorical strategies, must take into account *also* the patriarchal voice and question it.[6] Any form of *affidamento*, of entrustment, be it articulated between members of the same gender, or otherwise, always hides a type of authority that, if acceptable – and in some case even desirable – can nevertheless be reductive, both in artistic expression and in private life. While Muraro's theory is endorsable for many valid reasons, especially for its non-conflictual and non-oppositional approach to a woman/woman mediation, there is also the awareness that authority between two women can be limiting to artistic endeavour, just as it is between two individuals of the opposite sex. 'Devouring *the* mother'[7] is what philosophers do, according to Muraro. 'Respecting' the mother – mirroring a woman's work in the literary mother's work – while engaging with the father's literary tradition can actually be very valuable when discussing the development of a woman's authorial point of view in the contemporary novel. Rather than proposing another hierarchical relationship, this time based on the mother–daughter relationship, we need to explore an appreciation of the pragmatic possibilities of the trust younger writers allocate to other women artists' texts. This is an artistic shift that makes clear how – in spite of critical and academic denial of 'authority' for women-authored novels – women writers often see other women writers' works as an indispensable frame of reference. In this symbolic order that works well for the exclusive purpose of literary analysis, there is no other hierarchy than the one the writers in question feel towards their literary models of reference. One needs to love the mothers, but not to be devoured by them either. Passion for the mother must be constructive and useful; indeed, it can make the *ordine simbolico*, when it is not separated from the desire for knowledge.[8]

In Northern American literature, as Carla Kaplan does not fail to note in her *The Erotics of Talk*, the female canon is a largely established notion that actually has defied a restrictive use of this term and allowed women's literature, like the literature of other minority groups, to enter curricula and prestigious reading lists. In Italy, however, the female canon is something yet to come, not to mention the insertion of important works by women in the traditional canon. A female literary canon does exist, but its importance is rather limited when it comes to the mainstream. Only those who work in women's studies assume such a canon exists, and know the pre-eminence of some authors vis-à-vis others. In Italian literature we are still at the stage of problematizing the (male) canon in the effort to assure more fluidity and more space to the work of women writers.

Having said all this, I want to optimistically work in the direction of a unified Italian literary canon that is flexible and culturally aware of realities other than the central, traditional ones. In other words, I want to optimistically assume that women authors indeed have a space in the canon, that they can be taught in schools without preconceptions, and that critics can analyse their work from a more expansive perspective. A liberated canon, that is, one in which, aside from the regulating tools of artistic hierarchy such as highbrow versus lowbrow categories, or universality of contents, one can analyse the work of women writers who have, by sheer originality or by creative admiration for other women writers, established an alternate route for canonicity. This route should, in turn, become another way to read the society from which such texts spring. So, mothers and daughters from a literary standpoint are the subject of this chapter, while I exclude the literal relation between mothers and daughters, one that several critics have brilliantly researched.

The mother–daughter relationship and its articulation both in philosophy and in literature has been an oft-studied topic in the last three decades of the past century. Philosophers Adrienne Rich, Hélène Cixous, Luce Irigaray, and Julia Kristeva[9] have aptly demonstrated how a feminist philosophy has to deal primarily with the mother–daughter relationship as a way to understand the formation of a female identity with respect to her mother figure. This relationship clearly is affected by the particular geographic location of both the philosophers analysing it and the writers fictionalizing this relationship that is at the very foundation of women's writing.

In *Writing Mothers and Daughters: Renegotiating the Mother in Western European Narratives by Women*, Adalgisa Giorgio maps the territory of this topic in Western Europe. In the introduction, Giorgio summarizes what three decades of studies have brought forth: the relevance of the mother–daughter relationship in the philosophical and critical orientations that each aforementioned thinker has taken while Western society was, and still is, evolving, into a new order, both economic, with the advent of the European Community, and demographic, with the new migratory phenomenon from Africa and former Communist countries.[10] Giorgio also discusses and comments upon several publications that have been very relevant in the United States discussion of the topic and that have later on spilled over into European studies in a fruitful exchange and debate. Marianne Hirsch's argument in 1989 in *The Mother-Daughter Plot: Narrative, Psychoanalysis, Feminism*[11] concerns the distance from which both fictional and theoretical feminist writing would look at the maternal. Indeed, female writers felt burdened by the psychological weight of the maternal figure in their creative process of finding new forms of expression for the identity quest and the treatment of the family in the novel. This perception was also what put Muraro to work on a philosophy of identity and subjectivity that would place the mother as the point of departure, not the father. Starting from the findings of Marianne Hirsch, Giorgio follows her theoretical line and develops her own position on the theme of the daughter's quest for the mother, adopting a cultural approach to narratives on mother–daughter relationships that takes into consideration the differences of literary renditions of the subject that might reflect the national literatures to which they belong. The topic of deterritorialization and dissolution of identity enter almost perforce in the recently redefined European context, which sees several women authors no longer expressing themselves in their native tongue, but rather adopting a foreign one, namely, the language of the country in which they have chosen to live.[12]

Giorgio aptly stresses the relation between French, North American, and Italian feminist philosophers. She steers away from facile similes, while offering a comprehensive map of feminist writings of the early

1990s, and assessing the relative lack of success, in social terms, of, for instance, Luisa Muraro's theory of the *ordine simbolico*, 'the symbolic order of the mother' which relies on the notion of *affidamento*. Within this practice, Giorgio states, 'maternal power was redefined as women's ability to enter into signifying relationships with other women, relationships, that is, which produce "thought" and mark the world with female difference.'[13] Particularly in the 1980s, women's writing in Italy kept the mother–daughter relationship as one of its key thematic elements. Emblematic (and successful) examples of this type of relationship can be found in the works of Francesca Sanvitale, Carla Cerati, and Rosetta Loy as well as of Fabrizia Ramondino (in her case the grandmother figure is a genealogical element that ensures complete linkages between women of the same family). This relationship, studied in depth in psychology by Nancy Chodorow in her 1978 *The Reproduction of Mothering*,[14] visited in philosophy by Muraro in her *L'ordine simbolico della madre*, and by other theoreticians of various fields, is destined to remain a permanent theme in women's narratives. The mother–daughter relationship is constantly revisited by way of the continual reflection of the (female) self in the image of the biological mother, as in that of another woman (a literary mother) whom the daughter has decided to entrust with her own work. In this matter mirroring effect (literary mother and daughter) competitiveness and rivalry give way to a positive and constructive complicity from which the daughter can only benefit, while the mother's work is recognized as canonical. The outcome of this interaction is unique in each mother–daughter literary example and each morphs into narrative solutions that are extremely diverse. In the case of Fabrizia Ramondino's *Althénopis*, the rejection of its protagonist of the life led by her parents, her strenuous refusal to preserve the traditions imposed by her father, who desires for her a future as a librarian, makes it possible for the girl to develop a passion for, and find more appropriate, the lifestyle of her grandmother, the *Nonna*. The *Nonna* carries a Morantian naturalness, as she has found that the distinction between nature and culture can be resolved in life in a variety of ways. Thus, there also exist narrative situations in which the maternal figure is bypassed, in an almost aprioristic discarding of a difficult relationship because it lacks that concept of sisterhood necessary to the revisiting of the relationship with the mother.

The notion of entrustment lies at the very base of my present study as a point of departure and reference, for I probably could never have been able to accommodate the problematic aspect of women writers facing the example and the legacy of other women writers without introducing entrustment into my working hypothesis. What I hope to demonstrate is that without entrustment, there is no example to take; without entrustment there would be no model to follow after internal deliberation. As chapter 2 illustrates, the relationship with the father remains a very strong and fruitful one if expressed in literary terms, but in this chapter we witness the development of what we can unproblematically call a privileged women's tradition from the twentieth century onward. Whereas in real life, Muraro's 'entrustment' can become yet another unproductive form of authority among women, in fictional writing it can become an innovative force to open the canon in Italian literature. In this practice of literary entrustment, a theoretical thread among women writers becomes possible. Working in a literary context dominated by male figures such as that which pertains in Italy, Italian women writers can instead learn a way to rely on preceding literary figures who, in turn, symbolically endorse their writing. They can establish an artistic genealogy, they can exercise a process of artistic rewriting/rereading, and syntactic-lexical reprises – just to mention a few of the elements that constitute the development and the lasting action of a body of works composing a genre, in my case the novel.

It is only by noting these existing threads that the map of Italian women's fictional narrative can be laid out. The mothers of the contemporary novel and their epigones sustain each other. The first ones will no longer be considered 'isolated cases,' while the novels of the second ones will find an ample apparatus of references in the novels of the first. Their entrustment of their literary mothers is revealed in the novels they write. Carla Kaplan and her discussion of the expression 'fantastic collaboration,' as theorized by Sandra Gilbert and Susan Gubar, should be recalled at this point. Bringing to mind how Gubar utilizes the term as an antidote to the Bloomian prevailingly male 'anxiety of influence,' Kaplan turns her attention to those 'swerves of silence' as to the palimpsests that texts by women create. While for Harold Bloom, Kaplan notes, 'misrecognition ... became an explanation of literary greatness and originality,' for feminist scholars '*women's* culture ... is one site where women's bid for recognition can succeed.'[15] According to Kaplan, as she refers to the model established by Sandra Gilbert and Susan Gubar, the female writer 'turns to other women as allies in a literary battle she wages not with them, but against her Oedipal *fathers*.'[16] If I take this tenet as valid for my work, I also want to make sure that it is taken not as a dogmatic, restrictive statement, but as one that has been determined by concrete examples, such as the ones I make in this chapter. It is useful, however, to remember this discussion about Bloomian theory as revisited by Kaplan via Gubar and Gilbert to demonstrate how, within the past century, women authors have gained a particular awareness of what accepting the text and the aesthetic sign of another woman as a model for their own entails. In a 1985 article, 'Life's Empty Pack: Notes toward a Literary Daughteronomy,' Sandra Gilbert wrote that 'the riddle of daughterhood' is a

> 'figurative empty pack,' with which ... not just every powerful literary mother but every literal mother presents her daughter. For such artists, the terror of the female precursor is not that she is an emblem of power but, rather that when she achieves her greatest strength, her power becomes self-subverting: in the moment of psychic transformation that is the moment of creativity, the literary mother, even more than the literal one, becomes the 'stern daughter of the voice of God' who paradoxically proclaims her 'allegiance to the law' she herself appears to have violated.[17]

The artistic action of women novelists no longer assumes, or is, a site for contention, even if prone to emancipation, and determined by rules connected with patriarchal voices, as Sandra Gilbert noted in her article about the authority of George Eliot as viewed by Edith Wharton. Nor is the artistic influence of previous women novelists upon the 'daughter's text' to be perceived as a gesture of kinship and sisterhood. At this point, looking at a literary mother results in the mere recognition of women writers that some expressive forms and models by women writers 'fit' better than others for their own works. It means that, if women look at the work by another woman they do so in the full recognition that they are pursuing, however innovative their way, the mode in which they can see their own artistic expression displayed at its best. At the beginning of the twenty-first century, the fear of the literary mother rarely touches the on-going desire of women to legitimate their work through that of other women precursors. The recognition of female precursors has shaped itself into more flexible traits that do not 'oblige her to speak of her own powerlessness.'[18] As Kaplan states: 'Rather than assume that identity is a fixed and stable construction to be either recognized – or misrecognized – by others, can we imagine a critical practice and a vision of literary tradition more open to the idea that identity is a fluid and inter-objective phenomenon, constructed out of a dialogic – contestatory – process, a critical practice that nuances "recognition" accordingly'?[19]

Elsa Morante and Novelistic 'Recognition'

Twenty years after Gilbert's argument about the riddle of mother's authority and daughter's powerlessness, the focus of the present chapter is to demonstrate the efficacy of Elsa Morante as a practical model in the development of the novel by contemporary Italian women artists. As Sharon Wood and I state in the introduction to *Under Arturo's Star*, Elsa Morante has now long received recognition for her innovative artistic endeavours.

> What has most attracted younger Italian writers is her unorthodox approach to literature that greatly distances her from all her contemporaries and makes her aesthetically and ideologically far more transgressive and daring. Morante uncovers their perverted underbelly, dealing with themes rarely touched on before such as homosexuality, incest, cross-dressing, the logic of madness, class struggle, drugs, and finally ecology, in other words the whole structure of the contemporary natural world which overlaps the *naturalità* of her characters, whether human or animal. In all these areas it is our contention that the anachronistic nature of Morante's work places her not behind, but ahead of her time. The almost prophetic quality of her writing is now being recognized and drawn on by younger generations.[20]

Her systematic de-masculinization of male characters, her deconstruction of male identity, coupled with the unredeemable inability of her female characters to conform to the societal constrictions placed on their gender, both already evident in her 1941 publication, the short-story collection *Il gioco segreto*, are all paradigmatic elements of her attempt to unveil the problems inherent in Italian society. These characteristics speak louder than Morante's own lack of feminist remarks to explain the import of her writing in today's Italian women's writing.

After years of strong antagonism and open opposition to Elsa Morante, the most widespread critical tendency is now that of full recognition for her work, firmly posited within the canon.[21] The Morantian legacy can be defined along several trajectories as, each writer has made a different selection and has interpreted her work in different ways. However dissimilar the choices might be for each writer, the point of departure for the analysis of Morante's work and legacy should be her notion of what a novel is. Morante was always convinced that the novel, even in its traditional meaning and form, nevertheless remained the genre best suited to analysing the modern world with respect to the individual vis-à-vis his/her relationship with an oppressive, bourgeois society. Neuroses and fears, traumas and dreams, utopia and dystopia, these topics could find a narrative medium in the novel. She, the *romanziera-raccontatrice*, assumed the role of narrator of this complex world as a dilated *racconto* on humankind. Upon learning that *Don Quixote* was her first model of reference,[22] one appreciates her notion of what a novel should be – an all-encompassing marvellous work of fiction – that is, one in which the two aspects of life, dream and reality, are enmeshed. As in Calderón de la Barca's *La vida es sueño*, so also for Morante's characters 'life is a dream.' Nevertheless, in the dream one can also find reality and an alternative to it – in Morante's words, 'Un vero romanzo, dunque, è sempre realistico, anche il più favoloso" ('A true novel, then, is always realistic, even the most imaginative one').[23] It is true, as Adalgisa Giorgio states in describing Elsa Morante's last novel, *Aracoeli*, that she did not write 'emancipatory novels,' as is clearly the case with some of Dacia Maraini's fiction, such as *Donna in guerra* or *Lettere a Marina*, or with Simone de Beauvoir's *La femme rompue*, classic feminist readings of the 1970s. Morante's works touch upon issues that are, nevertheless, linked to women in 'their relationship with the symbolic and the imaginary,'[24] while interrogating the form of the novel. Giorgio concludes that 'Morante's discourse on women in *Aracoeli* is contradictory and ambiguous, but it is certainly neither misogynist nor sexist: it reflects the complexity of current theoretical discourse on femininity and motherhood, providing a critique of certain notions and stereotypes of our culture, but at the same time exposing the traps of facile idealizations and the delusion of oversimplifications'.[25] The feminist condemnation of Morante in the 1970s and 1980s no longer gets in the way of appreciating her discussion of individuals and of the society that determines their lives. The Morantian legacy lives through deeply different trajectories as individual writers have operated a subjective selection of her legacy.

Mariateresa Di Lascia's *Passaggio in ombra*:
About the *Pessima Matrigna* Elsa

When we examine some reviews and interviews published at the time of the 1995 Strega Prize, awarded to Mariateresa Di Lascia's novel *Passaggio in ombra*, two elements that have informed these reviews emerge: many critics and artists assumed that the prize had been assigned sympathetically to the novel because of the premature death of the young writer,[26] while some argued that it had been given to Di Lascia because the novel contained evidence of craft in the exquisite making of yet another novel set in the suffocating South. In all conversations, though, the name of Morante was almost invariably set against any comment about Di Lascia's work. Morante's novels are composed of a rich material that lends itself to interpretive innovations and re-elaborations of her themes and strategies, establishing in this way a long line of ascendance that connects works provided with Charles Altieri's always current definition of what canonical works should be.[27]

Morante was Di Lascia's artistic model, at least for her only novel. The reasoning for the Morante–Di Lascia parallel varies. Writer Rosetta Loy uses it to distance (negatively) Di Lascia's novel from Morante's *Menzogna e sortilegio*, suspicious of the former's utilization of an 'old structure thirty years later.' Loy states further that she was very happy the Strega Prize had been assigned to a woman and to the Feltrinelli publisher. She was bothered though by the comparison made with Elsa Morante, a writer she much admires. Loy says to journalist Daniela Pasti, 'Ci sono delle somiglianze, ma la Di Lascia non ha quella magia. Semmai la struttura narrativa è simile; e mi chiedo che senso abbia riproporre quella struttura vecchia trent'anni dopo. Ma il libro avrà successo: è una storia molto italiana' ('There are similarities, but Di Lascia's writing does not have that magic [of Morante's writing]. Perhaps the narrative structure is similar; and I wonder what is the point in reproducing an old structure thirty years later. But the book will be successful: it is a very Italian story').[28] Of course, *Menzogna e sortilegio*, having been published in 1948, was almost fifty years older than *Passaggio in ombra*, but Loy's point is well taken.

Most critics have positively reviewed *Passaggio in ombra*, drawing it closer to the anxiety of maternity that sometimes one wants to attribute to Morante's work. One exception, created by preconception, was Cesare Garboli. Garboli has always been quite firm in denying any influence Morante might have drawn from, or given to, other texts. His was a preconception due partly to his belief that her case was quite unique, that her writing was so magisterial that no one could be quite like her. Of necessity, Garboli could not see Morante in a female literary world. He always brought the 'uniqueness' trope forth in his critical works on her novels. Garboli wrote about Di Lascia's novel in an essay on Morante, in which he drew some comparisons between *Passaggio in ombra* and *Menzogna e sortilegio*. Presenting as a fitting example a writing by Morante in which the novelist declares the negation of a difference between women's rights and those of all oppressed groups, he maintained:[29]

E nelle pagine di quel bel romanzo di cui tanto si parla, uscito qualche settimane fa, *Passaggio in ombra* di Mariateresa Di Lascia, non si sentono risuonare i passi, gli echi, le reminiscenze di *Menzogna e sortilegio*, non se ne vedono ovunque i segni e le tracce?
Ma non è la capacità di sedurre ciò che si richiede a una madre. Per quanto grande possa essere la forza di provocazione e fascinazione dei suoi romanzi, *nessuno dei messaggi della Morante ha per destinatarie le donne*, né può essere indiziato di solidarietà con la loro lotta, la loro ideologia, le loro battaglie in favore dell'emancipazione femminile ... Se a una madre si chiede di fare da educatrice, da guida, da aiuto nella difesa dei diritti della donna, se a una madre si chiede un atteggiamento solidale nei confronti del maschio, la Morante può essere considerata sì e no una pessima matrigna. Esibire le viscere materne, abbandonarsi al proprio demonio non basta. Sono donne le streghe? [30]

(And in the pages of that beautiful novel everyone is talking about, published a few weeks ago, *Passaggio in ombra* by Mariateresa Di Lascia, do we not hear the footsteps, the echoes, the reminders of *Menzogna e sortilegio*? Can we not see signs and traces of the earlier novel everywhere?
But it is not the ability to seduce that we ask of a mother. However great the power of her novels to provoke and to fascinate, none of Morante's messages are directed towards women readers, nor can they be co-opted in solidarity with their struggle, their ideology, their battles for female emancipation ... If of a mother we ask that she act as teacher, guide, help in the defense of women's rights, Morante can, at best, be considered a stepmother of the worst kind. It is not enough to exhibit maternal innards, to abandon oneself to one's own demons. Are witches to be considered women?)

While admitting the influence of Morante on other writers such as Di Lascia, Garboli purposely rejects the term *madre* in its ethical connotation, as this use could facilitate the notion of an artistic and literary legacy. He denies even the literal one, apparent, that of a spiritual guide, educator for generations of women to come, and with some cause perhaps, since Morante's reluctance to appropriate the set of values of her time and to belong to a bourgeois system while immersing herself in a world dominated by the *ragazzini* would make her role as mother impossible. Unwittingly and unbeknownst to himself, Garboli confirms Gilbert and Gubar's thesis, and omits what is more important in Morante's legacy to women artists: the competitive, agonic relationship that, both in real life and in artistic life, women entertain with each other, not 'against the male,' but about their work, about the transmission of their knowledge in the work they do.

Il saper amare è una strada diversa dal desiderio di sapere, quasi contraria, poiché questo è un indirizzare le forze passionali verso l'obiettivo della conoscenza, dichiarato per altro inattingibile, mentre il sapere amare è la messa in circolo delle forze passionali con l'attività della mente.

(Knowing how to love takes a different path than the desire for knowledge, almost opposite to it, because this means addressing the forces of passion towards the goal of knowledge, however declared to be unattainable. Knowing how to love means instead to establish synergies between the passions and mind).[31]

This agonic relationship engenders what Carla Kaplan defines as 'prescriptive ethics.'[32] Like other male critics, Garboli does not catch the relevance of the dialectics between a mother and a daughter, if intended in the artistic sense of pragmatically entrusting one's own work to another woman writer. Indeed, he wonders whether 'esistono modelli sicuri, collaudati, ai quali una donna interessata alla letteratura potrebbe rifarsi.'[33] I believe that, aside from the curious question about the sex of witches – 'sono donne le streghe?' – Garboli has excluded almost a priori the possibility that a text can function as a site of exploration and knowledge, a site for measuring and confirming the challenge that any text throws at other texts. A text is a reference for those who find within its body the source and energy to say what they want to say and, more, the not-yet-said. The categorical statements Garboli makes, that 'nessuno dei messaggi della Morante ha per destinatarie le donne,'[34] and that 'Morante non ama le donne. Le disprezza,'[35] are difficult to understand. Granted, not all writers, like Manzoni, display full awareness of their 'twenty-five readers.' However, discarding female readers a priori as possible addressees seems an unwarranted exaggeration. What were Garboli's convictions for such belligerent declarations? The cruelty with which Morante plunges the knife of her writing into female characters is neither less nor more than the force with which she attacks her male characters. All Morante's characters are oppressed; all are losing figures without nobility and with no particular talent. It is doubtful that Morante wanted to be didactic, ethical, or emancipatory. Her writing can at times assume one or more of these aspects, can satisfy all these criteria, but it is not conceived as such. Morante, precisely because she was external (or so she thought herself to be) to the bourgeois model, never proposed any model of her own. Her work, capable of meshing the subversive with the traditional in the depictions of human weakness, cowardice, and love as a site of human fragility, does not observe any gender categorization. If Garboli admits the existing connection between Morante and Di Lascia, perhaps out of too much love for the former, his argument ends up by strongly limiting the canonical attributes and power of Morante's work. Out of too much love and respect for her genius, Garboli eliminates in Morante's work the importance of the literary *exemplum* that functions as *artistic model*. He eliminates the marvellous potentialities of the Morantian sign, an eccentric and genial crossroads of foreign influences and themes typical of Italian literature.[36] In this way, Garboli severs the thread between Morante and her epigones merely to save for her work the term *originality*, used in the most conventional manner to single out the work of a female artist who does not fit any mould.

The unfounded notion that, as a non-feminist, Morante could not render, for lack of solidarity and sense of kinship, any service to the causes of women, since, according to Garboli, 'esibire le viscere materne, abbandonarsi al proprio demonio non basta' ('displaying the maternal bowels, giving yourself up to your demon is not enough')[37] needs to be refuted. Denouncing one's own demon is not a demonstration of moralism and ethical concern anyway. Why is this act 'not enough'? In another writing on *Linea d'ombra*, Elsa Morante's critic and friend Goffredo Fofi is more effective in defining the Morantian influence in Di Lascia's novel, as he utilizes analytical instruments and categories in contrast with Garboli's. More than Garboli, Fofi realizes the import of Morante as a literary mother for the prematurely deceased writer:

> La Di Lascia prende soprattutto da *Menzogna e sortilegio*, mentre viene a lei la condizione di 'creatura di confine', una di quelle creature irrisolte, che denunciano fin dall'aspetto il proprio ibrido destino' ... che la protagonista e narratrice evoca per sé nel momento in cui rievoca, che è quello della sconfitta e della decadenza ...
>
> La Di Lascia si è scelta 'madri' straordinarie, straordinariamente solitarie. Della prima, la Morante, si sente a inizio del romanzo il forte peso e si ha paura dell'imitazione, ma per vedere sciolta quest'impressione rapidissimamente, al calore di una visione e di una scrittura molto autonome.
>
> (Di Lascia draws chiefly from *Menzogna e sortilegio* while she appropriates for herself the condition of 'liminal creature.' This is one of those unresolved creatures who, beginning with their appearance, declare their own hybrid destiny ... that the protagonist and narrator suggests for herself in the moment she re-evokes, that of defeat and of decadence.

Di Lascia has chosen for herself extraordinary 'mothers.' Of the first, Morante, one feels the heavy weight in the beginning of the novel and is afraid of the imitation, but only to quickly see this fear vanish at the warmth of a very autonomous vision and writing.[38]

The act of writing does not merely signify a set of moral precepts, of savvy and prescriptive intents, these latter capable of making a female writer interesting, or even able to make proselytes among younger writers. As literature has taught, it is quite often rather the opposite. The problematic notion of being gendered writers in Italy consists almost entirely in the effort of demonstrating the 'validity' – not just the presence – of an innovative expressive and aesthetic sign, with which the strategies and techniques adopted are permeated. In order to elicit this innovative sign from the text, the practice of critical/professional reading as it is traditionally done in Italian literary criticism needs to change. To avoid relegating women's works to the confined space of isolated chapters on 'Other Voices,' a practice of reading that takes into consideration the gendered point of view of the *romanziera* is needed. Equally important in the development of literature, this practice should examine also the impact of previous male and female writers' work on the *romanziera*'s writing process and final production of the novel. Only in this way can we construct a thread between authors. Without this understanding, there can't be any understanding of seemingly 'illogical' retrievals of other women writers' work. Once this issue is clarified, we can construct a map in which the novel written by women is not confined to a chapter in Italian literary histories, but is aptly inserted and studied within, and out of, the tradition.

Pier Paolo Pasolini detected quite early the presence of a passion for the traditional novel in Elsa Morante's disposition towards the genre. In commenting on *L'isola di Arturo*, Pasolini notes the '"allusività" al grande romanzo idealmente tradizionale che si configura "a frammenti"' ('"allusivity" to the ideally traditional great novel that takes body through "fragments"'), aside from the 'assunzione dell'Italia reale, nella fattispecie meridionalistica ... a una luce di fantasia pura, che patina quei minuti dati quotidiani e vivaci, quasi "lume universale" da pala profana' ('assumption of actual Italy, specifically Southern Italy ... to a light of pure fantasy, that gives to those tiny daily and vivacious facts the patina of an almost "universal light" as in a profane wooden painting').[39] More generally, Pasolini's opinion suits all works by Morante. He, more than others, fully realized that Morante's oeuvre was 'eccentrica e irripetibile' ('excentric and unrepeatable'),[40] within the limits of any true work of art. Contrary to what even today is said of Morante, with her writing she indeed created a lasting body of expressive forms for those writers who engage in similar themes. Facing a writer whose pages seem neither to have a precise affiliation, nor to belong to a specific group whose intent was clear to many; of discerning the trait of someone who was 'senza padri ispiratori, senza sorelle o fratelli di una stessa genealogia culturale' ('with no inspiring fathers, with no sisters or brothers from the same cultural geneaology'),[41] was certainly disorienting for several critics. Perhaps because of his long frequentation and mutual collaboration with Morante, Pasolini instead saw better than others a specific role and place for Morante's narrative work – of *L'isola di Arturo* in particular – within the Italian panorama. Unlike Garboli's declaration of uniqueness, Pasolini knew where to situate Morante's writing:

> Nel quadro storico, non solo si inserisce con una serie di rapporti meccanici, ma lo modifica all'interno con la sua stessa presenza, rappresentando una nuova necessità, che i critici, anche ideologicamente impegnati, non possono ignorare, o respingere secondo schemi valevoli fino a ieri. La presenza dell'*Isola* è lì a dimostrare che una seconda fase del realismo del dopoguerra si sta iniziando, evidentemente, al di qua dello stato di emergenza in cui è nato. Ne consegue la riassunzione di forme che solo apparentemente erano superate, ma che in realtà, dentro il neorealismo stesso, si erano tramandate, quale tradizione recente (nella specie l'irregolarità sintattica e narrativa e la squisitezza): e il formarsi di nuovi tipi di 'evasività' ineluttabili in ogni situazione letteraria normale. L'opera della Morante ne indica i modi con la necessità della poesia.[42]

(Within the historical frame, not only does it find its insertion with a series of mechanical relations, but it also modifies it from within, representing therefore a necessity which critics, even those ideologically engaged, cannot ignore or reject according to criteria valid until recently. The presence of *Arturo's Island* serves to demonstrate that a second phase of postwar realism is about to begin, palpably beyond the state of emergency from which it sprang. The resulting re-employment of forms that were only seemingly obsolete, but actually were embedded already within neorealism itself, had been transmitted as recent tradition (such as syntactic and narrative irregularity and preciousness), and the forming of new types of 'elusiveness,' inevitable in any normal literary situation. Morante's work indicates the ways with the necessity of poetry.)

When one reads *Passaggio in ombra*, the only novel by Mariateresa Di Lascia, posthumously published and winner of the Strega prize in 1995, the pragmatic context for Pasolini's statements about Morante's narrative novel appears quite convincingly. The new Italian novel can, after fifty years, manage to speak of a South,[43] of a sick woman, and of her family, in a strikingly 'anxious' echo of Elisa's story. In this sense, a 1995 novel can reinscribe the parable of a character, Chiara, victim of her own disease, living within the literature of her life, which not for this reason must be identical to that of her predecessor.

Pasolini was proved right in his assertions about Morante's formulation of a post-neorealist trend and the resonance of her aesthetic findings by the novel *Passaggio in ombra*. Far from being guilty of vulgar plagiarism, Di Lascia understood and interpreted Morante's legacy. Di Lascia wanted to inscribe her work within the *Familienroman* in the same way that Morante conceived this subgenre in her *Menzogna e sortilegio*. Di Lascia retrieved from this novel the persistent Proustian motif of memory, with the backdrop of a suffocating South covered in dust, and seemingly devoid of ideological implications. Her novel appropriates the model defined by *Menzogna e sortilegio* of the dark and gloomy Southern saga, based on the repression of desires. It depicts the saga of a family whose destiny has been marked by the incurable social cancer of a single mother who gave in to her love only to find herself alone against the little town society; by a daughter affected by cyclothymia and rivalry with her beautiful mother; by a warm and tender aunt who will take the girl under her wing during childhood; of an impossible love between cousins. The 'social cancer' of being an illegitimate daughter, forces Chiara to retreat into the *stanze della memoria*, the rooms of memory. In these suffocating locales the echo of her own frustrated sense resounds like the blood flowing in her veins. But her blood, just like her senses, has become putrescent, poisoned as it is by years of such a tragic existence. Morante readers know that all these thematic elements could best describe Morante's *Menzogna e sortilegio* as well.

The complex web of terms indicating intertextuality appears quite evident to the Morante reader. Intertextual elements in Di Lascia's novel-*testament*[44] can be perceived as a nostalgic and yet necessary reprise of Morante's lyrical narrative. I will focus particularly on how intertextuality is at work in the adoption of a novel structure as Morante conceives it in *Menzogna e sortilegio*.[45] If this last text is seen as a Proustian novel with a Southern Italian background, it should come as no surprise that *Passaggio in ombra* possesses the 'largo respiro del romanzo antico' ('ample breath of the ancient novel').[46] In this, Di Lascia's novel repeats some of the strategies employed in Morante's novel, published indeed fifty years earlier. There was in Di Lascia a specific intent in producing a feeling for her novel as if it were a 'polveroso' ('dusty') novel, a novel with no ambition of 'modernity,' but quite the opposite. Readers sensed that these complicated – and yet very simple – love stories and that of Chiara's illegitimate birth could not have been published any earlier. Dust had to cover this manuscript, for she had personal reasons not to publish it earlier, but also because she aimed at narrating a love story in the old *romanzo d'appendice* fashion. The same was true for Morante's *Menzogna e sortilegio*. Cesare Garboli's reflections on Morante's treatment of love as a social pathology, love as a *sindrome socio-passionale* ('socio-passional syndrome'),[47] apply also to Di Lascia's novel, particularly if in such a treatment we value in full the relevance of the area *propre*[48] of relations, the one circumscribed by the family nucleus. In the lacerating recollection of the dramas in her family and life, Chiara, the protagonist, relives the tormented familial relations of Elisa in *Menzogna e sortilegio*. Morante's writing, more than others', even more than Anna Maria Ortese's early writings on postwar Naples, is strongly linked to the culture of the South, making her narrative constitute a necessary point of reference for any Southern saga by subsequent women writers. But in this case it so for a reason. Common to both Elisa and Chiara is the failure for detachment from lyrical tones, their shared failure to reach for a less individualistic, solipsistic dimension. This failure to react to their own situation in the present of writing, of re-composing what their past was or was imagined to be, is mirrored in a common depiction of a female narrating 'I' as virtually unable to distance itself from its own ghosts and demons, and thus never be fully resigned to accept the past for what that entailed. There is no lesson to be learned from the past, particularly when it comes to families.

The parallel treatment of the anguishing analysis of family pathologies makes it possible for the existing analogies of the two novels to be discussed on several levels. On the thematic level, it is very evident that both novels deal fundamentally with the theme of childhood reminiscence, one that coincides with the history and prehistory of the family lineage as narrated by a young woman. Its development coincides also with the painful moment of passage from childhood to adolescence of the protagonist, the one that Morante defines as *smagamento*, or 'disillusionment' with the world, until then thought to be an enchanted Eden.

This rite of passage should be perceived as Morante's and Di Lascia's characters' growing awareness of their condition of *diversity* within a reactionary and outdated society. In both narratives, Elisa's and Chiara's, events deriving from their recollection-invention take on significant proportions within the diegesis, making apparent the isolation of the protagonists from the surrounding world. There are no intermediaries between them and us. The complex analepsis of their childhood in both cases locates its space in their room-cave, as Elisa and Chiara both suffer from an illness, apparently of psychosomatic origin. In a clear dislocation of the narrator from the character, Chiara writes, '[c]osì torno al passato, e incontro la fanciulla che fui; la seguo mentre serba nel cuore la vanità immancabile di un amore eterno' (PO 210).[49] The inertia and indolence with which both narrators are afflicted, the lack of love, are annulled and exhausted by the only heroic act of their lives: writing and rewriting the story of their family, a story in which ancient wrongs they endured are unearthed, only for them to find evidence of the hereditary form of their neurosis and attitude towards lies.

There are parallels in the plot as well, which appears to be constructed not merely in terms of causality, but also on more subjective and profound elements that privilege recurring patterns, repletion, and analogy. It seems as if Elisa and Chiara go back to a particular anecdote or incident to fight the fear of having missed a sign or trace that can help to explain their current unhappiness and despair. More generally, destiny, in the person of another woman and the decision this latter has made for them, will eventually take Elisa and Chiara away from their original familial nucleus. It is the distance from their suffocating original space that will generate the mnemonic writing that finds its enduring body in the text-testament.

Mermaids *Singing in a Dusty Room*

In both novels, the reminiscence of the passage from childhood to adulthood is a process that happens after the death of another woman. In the case of Elisa, she begins to lay out the *Romanzo dei suoi* after the death of her putative mother, Rosaria, a prostitute who entertained a lasting relationship with her father, Francesco. In Chiara's case, the recording of this transition begins after the death of her aunt, Peppina Curatore, years after that of her mother, Anita. Chiara gives a brief portrait of herself in the introduction to the two parts in which the novel is divided, 'L'audacia' and 'Il silenzio.' In her current and desired isolation '[n]ella casa dove sono rimasta, dopo che tutti se ne sono andati e finalmente si è fatto silenzio' (PO 7) ('in the house where I have remained after everybody has left and over which finally silence fell'), where she can read and spend her time as she pleases, Chiara listens to the *bisbiglìo*, to the whisper of Anita and Peppina, two *mortes-vivantes* like Anna and Rosaria in *Menzogna e sortilegio*, those Quixotian *cavalieri della trista figura* who would wander in Elisa's room. Like Elisa with her mother, Anna, and the prostitute Rosaria, Chiara is a young woman still – perhaps forever – strangled between the two women who loved her most, Donna Peppina and her mother Anita. Chiara still remembers their struggles for supremacy over her love, for the love of this little girl whose leonine hair was her most characteristic trait:

> Quando donna Peppina, che mi ha amata più di ogni cosa al mondo, e per questo mi rubò a mia madre e mi mise sempre contro di lei, decise che avrei studiato, e sarei diventata una 'professorona,'[50] avevo dodici anni e stare al mondo non mi appassionava, perché l'umanità pulsa di desiderio e di passioni incontrollate e forti, che io non so provare e neanche immaginare e che, infine, mi terrorizzano.
>
> Adesso che mi viene incontro la vecchiaia e ho smesso con anticipo inspiegabile anche di avere il sangue, il mio aspetto dimesso e le rughe che tardano a venire mi difendono ancora più degli sciatti vestiti che mi coprono il corpo. Travestita così, senza età e senza sesso, finalmente me ne rido del mondo.
>
> Non è stato sempre così.
>
> Un tempo, le mie due donne si guerreggiavano per avermi tutta per loro, e in paese parlavano di me per via di Anita, che non si era sposata e che mi aveva avuta da Francesco mentre egli era in guerra.
>
> Non avevo ancor avuto il primo attacco d'asma, e i miei polmoni erano tali che potevo fare il do di petto, e tenerlo a lungo facendo vibrare i cristalli del lampadario. Ho cantato ancora, anche dopo l'asma, per molti anni, e ho smesso solo alla morte delle mie care donne, mia zia Peppina e mia madre Anita. Ho sognato che dormivano vicine su due lettini bianchi e ordinati e che io le svegliavo col mio canto, ma loro mi pregavano di fare silenzio perché erano stanche e volevano riposare ...
>
> Ora, finalmente, torna *il tempo delle fantasie e del mio canto di sirena senza coda*, ora che le mie due donne hanno lasciato il loro corpo terreno e sanno tutto di me e della mia vita.
>
> E io con loro. (PO 8–9; emphasis added)

(When Donna Peppina, who loved me more than anything else in the world, and for this stole me from my mother and always turned me against her, decided that I should study and become a 'big professor,' I was twelve and being in the world did not thrill me, because humanity throbs with desire and incontrollable and strong passions that I cannot feel and not even imagine and that, in the end, terrorize me.

Now that old age is coming, and I have ceased with inexplicable prematurity also to have my period, my shabby looks and the wrinkles that delay their appearance defend me more than the sloppy dresses that cover my body. Disguised as such, ageless and sexless, I finally laugh at the world.

It was not always so.

At one time, my two women would fight bravely to keep me all for themselves, and in the village people would talk of me because of Anita, who was unmarried and had me with Francesco while he was away at war.

I had not yet had my first asthma attack, and my lungs were such that I could do a high C from the chest, and keep it for a long time until the crystals of the chandelier would shake. I sang again, even after the asthma, for many years, and I only quit with the death of my two dear women, my aunt Peppina and my mother, Anita. I dreamt that they were asleep next to each other on two clean white beds, and that I would wake them up with my singing, but they begged me to be quiet as they were tired and wanted to rest ...

Now, finally, *the time of fancies and my stumpy-tailed mermaid's singing* come back; now that my two women have left their worldly bodies and know everything about me and my life.

And I with them.)

Such recollection becomes the hub of the images that follow the prologue in two intense stories, moulded out of the magmatic mixture of Southern fluids, passions, and tensions lived by others (or witnessed), and that have forever invalidated the felicitous outcome of a yearned-for *Futuro*. The future is now recognizable only from those fabulous (as unattainable) characteristics of an unreachable myth, which is re-evoked by the febrile activity of the writing women, particularly when the novelistic form gives way to an essaystic one to more aptly explain the level of alteration of the world Elisa and Chiara have created and live in.

Already in the prologue, the path designed by Chiara's writing is articulated along a series of memories that construct the physiognomy of her family, whose incongruity of character appears, at times, cruelly eviscerated, and at others seems to be mitigated. The element that mitigates Chiara's cruelty is her love for Anita and Francesco, for these wretched and unhappy parents whose names are so similar to those in Elisa's sad story, Anna and Francesco. Like Elisa, Chiara compiles a chronicle of facts, she writes of past childhoods and adolescences at an already adult age. She embarks on a breathless recitation of her mistakes, needless to say traceable in the family's sentimental 'sources.' These sources, which constitute her inspiration to write, are worsened by the suffocating society of the village from which she has isolated herself in the moment of meditation and creation. Chiara follows her predecessor Elisa in her desire for isolation, almost to the word:

> Nella casa dove sono rimasta, dopo che tutti se ne sono andati e finalmente si è fatto silenzio, mi trascino pigra e impolverata con i miei vecchi vestiti addosso, e le scatole arrampicate sui muri scoppiano di pezze prese nei mercatini sudati del venerdì.
>
> ... Hanno cercato di convincermi in molti a lasciare questa casa, perché è piccola e affogata e, quando mi viene l'asma, rischio sempre di morire davanti alla finestra aperta, ma io non dò ascolto a nessuno, e penso che è inutile preoccuparsi di ogni cosa: *la morte verrà quando verrà e nessuno ci potrà fare niente.* Mi porteranno via, per queste strette scale dei palazzi moderni, e avranno un gran da fare per svuotare tutto il ciarpame che è stato la mia vita. (PO 7; emphasis added)
>
> (In the house where I remained after everybody left and finally silence fell, I drag my lazy and dusted self with my old clothes on, and boxes piled up against the walls exploding with rags bought at the Friday sweaty fleamarkets.
>
> ... Many have tried to convince me to leave this house because it is small and oppressive and, when I get asthma, I always risk dying in front of the open window. But I do not listen to anybody, and I believe that it is pointless worrying about everything: *death will come when it will come, and nobody can prevent it.* They will take me away, by these narrow stairs of modern buildings, and will be quite busy at clearing out all the junk that amounts to my life.)

The weight of the Morantian text is apparent:

> Mentre per tanti anni le cose presenti o prossime m'apparvero remote, e quasi spente, m'accade adesso, nel silenzio della mia camera, d'afferrare voci e rumori sonanti in qualche stanza lontana del palazzo, e fin d'ascoltare dialoghi d'invisibili casigliani, o di gente in crocchio nella strada. Questi dialoghi mi raggiungono attraverso porte e muri, e sebben trattino per

lo piú d'argomenti insignificanti, acquistano nel mio cervello uno straordinario risalto. (MS 26)
(For years the things close to me seemed remote and almost lifeless, but now, in the silence of my room, I think I catch the sound even of distant voices and noises and hear invisible conversations between the tenants in the house or people in the street. These dialogues come through walls and although usually they are concerned with trivialities, in my thoughts they take on an extraordinary significance. [HL 14–15])

Both writing narrators unfold the thread of memories in a monastic silence – partly suggested by the appellation the narrator of *Menzogna e sortilegio* chooses for herself, '*la monaca* Elisa' – and a complete physical isolation. In spite of these two elements of segregation from the world, or, paradoxically, because of them, Elisa and Chiara are never really alone. As they have no ties with what should be their present, the two women are constantly accompanied by a crowd of *morts-vivants* who exercise their control, who urge and direct their writerly efforts, in a Pirandellian fashion. It is to the occult forces of memories that the women surrender, using the simile of a citadel besieged by assailants:

Infine, quando non c'è piú un punto della stanza e dell'orizzonte dove possa volgere lo sguardo senza che si facciano incontro con il carico delle loro storie, piango senza passione e senza furore, arresa ai miei ricordi come una cittadella ai propri assalitori.
Ci sono tutti: in questa casa senza aria e senza luce, io li riconosco uno a uno, anche quelli che non vidi mai neppure in una foto; e gli amici degli amici che si sono dati la voce, e popolano la carta da parati a fiori beige che ricopre i muri, e proiettano la loro ombra come in un grande cinema.
'Chiara, mi manda tua zia Peppina ... Chiara, ho conosciuto tua madre ... Chi sono io Chiara, mi conosci? ... Chiara ... Chiara ... Chiara ...'
Il bisbiglio cresce come un concerto di cicale d'agosto, in un attimo occupa tutta la stanza e io divento un fiore, un albero, un filo d'erba; o forse sono solo la nuda terra che hanno calpestato o l'acqua sorgiva che hanno bevuto.' (PO 9)
(At last, when there is not even a point in the room and on the horizon where I can look without their coming towards me with the weight of their stories, I cry with no passion and no fury, surrendering to my memories like a besieged citadel to its attackers.
Everybody is there: in this house with no air and no light, I recognize them one by one, even those I never met, not even in a picture; and distant

friends who called each other, and now crowd the flowered beige tapestry on the walls while projecting their shadow as in a large cinema.

'Chiara, your aunt Peppina sends me … Chiara, I knew your mother … Who am I Chiara, do you recognize me? … Chiara … Chiara … Chiara'

The whisper mounts as a concert of cicadas in August. In a moment it fills the entire room, and I become a flower, a tree, a blade of grass; or perhaps I am only the naked ground that others have trampled on, or the spring water that they have drunk.)

Chiara has been loved by her mother and she is profoundly aware of it, while Elisa is aware of the opposite, that Anna never fully loved her. Chiara and Elisa share, however, the ending of their stories. After a mild attempt at rebellion, vaguely comparable to those described by Chiara in the first part of her narrative, 'L'Audacia,' Elisa ends up by recording the chronicles of her parents. She records events, even those that occurred before her birth and adolescence, that lead her own life to be what it is today. She has no authentic knowledge of that period except through her *morts-vivants*' recollections, a distorted and surreal array of images in which mirrors play a fundamental role. And so, as a faithful *suddita*, as a faithful subject to her *morts-vivants*, Elisa listens and transcribes the memories of her parents in the hope of healing, while confessing her desire to be free from such slavery thanks to this last duty towards the dead, 'chi sa che col loro aiuto io non possa, finalmente, uscire da questa camera' (MS 29; 'Who knows if with their help I may not be able to finally leave this room,' HL 17). Instead, Chiara does not believe she holds the visionary powers Elisa declares herself to have. Further, Chiara does not nourish a febrile arroganсe to try to impose herself on the shadows crowding her room, as Elisa does. Chiara tries, however, to escape their influence and advice. But in vain, as her resistance to grow out of her family's memories is paralysing. Just like the trees in her street, Chiara does not grow:

> La sera mi siedo sul balconcino della camera da letto, che è stata quella di mia zia, e guardo sulla strada stretta e solitaria dove *anche* gli alberi non vogliono crescere. Cerco di respirare e di non farmi sorprendere dalle voci e di respingere le presenze che, prontamente, mi si animano attorno, attratte da un richiamo che origina in me, e, tuttavia, mi è sconosciuto. (PO 9; emphasis added)
> (In the evening I sit on the little balcony of my bedroom, which was my aunt's, and look on the narrow and solitary street where *also* the trees do not

want to grow. I try to breathe and not be surprised by the voices and I try to repel the presences who, suddenly, become animated around me. They seem to be attracted by a call that originates within me and yet is unknown to me.)

Crossing the threshold of isolation, the moment of separation from the world of she who is writing in an exasperated solipsism, has already taken place in the first part of *Passaggio in ombra*, entitled 'L'Audacia' (PO 11–161). As in *Menzogna e sortilegio*, we witness a profound, almost a theatrical severing of the story. Parts 1 and 2 of the same melodrama are being staged before us. The marker for this fracture in the discourse relating the story of the two heroines of the melodrama is represented by the blank pages between the first part, 'l'Audacia,' and the second one, 'Il Silenzio' (PO 163–266), which function like a curtain in a stage drama. It evokes virtually the staging of an opera, another thematic link to Morante's writing. The silence that surrounds Chiara is more easily noticeable already in the first part, when Chiara, already left to herself, narrates the facts of her childhood, the trauma of her birth, of her father's imprisonment, and of his abandonment. In doing so, Chiara engages a narrative that is inferior in time and length to that of Elisa's analogous 'racconto dei miei.' This last narrative sees its end in the well-known anaphoric-cataphoric hinge *fin qui/d'ora innanzi* (MS 434; 'until now/from now on,' HL 349).[51] Nonetheless, Chiara tries to reach the same dramatic effect.

In both novels, the *Erzählzeit*, the time of narration, displays a similar dilation of the history of the childhood of the protagonists-narrators, the *Erzählte Zeit*, or the time of the story. It does so to the point that the analepses will end up by swallowing the point of memorial emission. The reconstitution of this latter is to be obtained through the chronological reordering of the frequent analepses whose amplitude corresponds almost to the entirety of the narrated material. Of the present of both narrators we only know, in fact, the situation of isolation and presumed sloth. The narrated material is retraced in a nondescriptive 'present time' of the recording of past events in a geographical space evidently, as I already mentioned, muted from the original space of their childhood. In *Menzogna e sortilegio* the space is restricted to a Southern town, located in Elisa's 'triste mezzogiorno' (MS 40). In *Passaggio in ombra*, instead, the narrating 'I' explains the wandering, the vagabondage she underwent from the moment she left her birthplace:

> Ho vissuto in ogni città di questo paese e non ho potuto fermarmi mai, inseguita com'ero sempre dai mille mostri atroci della mia fantasia. Sono

andata pellegrina di strada in strada, di casa in casa, cambiando pure i bar dove mi piaceva prendere il caffè della mattina, perché non trovassero le mie tracce. Le tracce dei miei racconti di principessa esule su questa terra senza anima, dove i miei polmoni hanno trovato difficile perfino respirare. (PO 8)
(I have lived in every town of this country and I could never stop, chased as I was by the thousand fierce monsters of my fantasy. I went on a pilgrimage from street to street, from house to house, changing cafes where I liked having my morning coffee, so that they would not find my traces. The traces of my tales as exiled princess in this soulless land, where my lungs have found it difficult even to breathe.)

The time gone by of the characters' past in both novels is rich with deixes. This time is played against the other time, the present one that the act of writing – however less evident but no less essential to the understanding of the narrators' drama – intercepts. As Emanuella Scarano notes, since writing per se tends to establish a relationship with the world, Elisa too wants to establish a relationship with the readers. As the story is written, continues Scarano, it implies the recognition of the reality that is to be found outside the room where Elisa writes.[52] The frequent reference, by addressing a possible reader attests to a situation different from the initial one, of closeness and impossibility, of a narration staged only for the writing subject, who, in turn, now feels reasonably empowered by her own act. The two parts, the chronicle and the narrative of the parents, are marked by deixes such as *poi, allora, da allora*, often characterizing the enunciation in the narration. Spatio-temporal coordinates of *adesso* and *prima* enhance an apparent attempt at clarification in the present time of Chiara's chronicle, which opens up with a verb that exacts the act of reminiscing, 'Se ripenso' (PO 209; 'If I think again'). This sentence is evocative of Elisa's strategies for establishing the intricate tale of her family business. After the long section she claims to have written by dictation from her dead relatives, Elisa enters a 'lucid' state of insomnia, the lucidity of which is partly explained by the fact that she needs to interrogate her own *true* memory:

> Non udirete piú da me la voce molteplice della dormiente. Una lucida insonnia s'impadronisce di me, e io, nella camera taciturna e spopolata, altro non potrò interrogare d'ora innanzi che la mia vera memoria. Altro non potrò raccontare, cioè, se non le cose che vidi coi miei propri occhi, udii coi miei propri orecchi, e di cui mio padre e mia madre, nella loro diversa infamia, mi fecero confidente e testimone. (MS 434)

(You will no longer hear from me the many voices of sleep. A lucid insomnia has taken hold of me and, in my silent, deserted room, I can turn to nothing from now on but my own true memory. I shall not be able to relate anything but what I have seen with my own eyes, heard with my own ears, and those events of which my father and my mother, each acting under the impulse of his own passion, made me witness and confidante. [HL 348–9])

The two narratives follow in parallel fashion the eccentricities of the heroines' families. Most of all, they illustrate the desire for acceptance of the two young Southern women who are relegated to the space of their room. Elisa and Chiara both long for an existence which they – or their family for that matter – will never have. They cannot leave their room, or their apartment. Their life is now entirely within those suffocating walls. Their life, after all, was best described as 'ciarpame' by Chiara. Not even worth narrating, let alone living. Their role will remain that of melancholic mermaids who rely on their beautiful voice to enchant future readers.

Motifs and Techniques

The dense number of characters and the related interweaving of their existences in the story determine another series of intertextualities of *Passaggio in ombra* with *Menzogna e sortilegio*. Solitude and a difficult adolescent period do not allow those who are reminiscing to create characters whose lives and feelings have reached a balance.[53] Shady, indefinable, and erratic in their paths, the characters in *Passaggio in ombra* view in Chiara the exemplification of their own capriciousness, illness, and the typically Southern fatalistic approach to existence. No one, except Chiara's cousin Saverio, a bastard born of an act of violence, can escape the weight of their family's presence. Saverio, devoid of the encumbering weight of a family because of his own condition, is seemingly the master of himself. Young Chiara, after her abandonment by Saverio, a character patterned on Morante's Cugino Edoardo, will transform her supreme love into inextinguishable hatred, and passion will give in to abulia and sloth. Exactly like *Menzogna e sortilegio*'s Anna Massia (Elisa's mother), Chiara will no longer love anyone else. While accepting the Morantian theme of unrequited love, Chiara assimilates two characters of *Menzogna e sortilegio*, the mother with her folly for the cousin Edoardo and the daughter with her inability to enter the real world after the desolate years of her adolescence.

The Morantian moment of *smagamento*, that shift from adoration for someone – often a parental figure – that will, in turn, translate into disillusionment, increases the sense of closeness of these two literary sisters, Elisa and Chiara. It is this sense of *smagamento* that makes the utilization of space (or lack thereof) for the construction of both novels even more understandable. The descriptions of settings and of the closed atmosphere of the *quartiere* and the little town validate the reasons why Elisa and Chiara both remain enslaved to their sad past, which is reified in their respective and confining rooms. Destiny has relegated them there, to a room in which their affliction and the presence of their dead souls are sovereign. Far from being Isabella d'Este's *studiolo*, one in which she could write undisturbed because acutely conscious of her power outside the *studiolo*, this room-prison, however creative for Elisa and Chiara, remains nevertheless a psychological cell and not an exclusive niche for a woman.

The narrative construction happens almost always through indirect discourse, an instrument of writing in the shape of confession or complete exclusion of a voice outside the world constructed by Elisa and Chiara. Partly due to the rare presence of dialogued images, indirect discourse excludes rendition of the facts according to a point of view different from that of Elisa and Chiara. Facts are retrieved through the memory of the writing women, and their resurfacing amounts to a 'macchinosa tregenda' (MS 27; 'complicated world,' HL 13) of lies, as after the death of their parents, their memories transformed 'il loro drama piccolo-borghese in una leggenda' (MS 19; 'their middle-class drama into a legend,' HL 9) in which the two young women unearth a wealth of material to nourish their state of exaltation. On her account, Chiara records her own condition of cyclothymia: 'Il caso, o l'ineluttabile fatalità, mi hanno insegnato che la ragione è sconfitta dalla vita ben piú che la follia, e che questa, infine, è l'estrema difesa inviolabile dell'esistenza di ognuno' (PO 167) (Chance, or inescapable fatality, taught me that life defeats reason more than folly, and that this, lastly, is the extreme and untouchable defence for anyone's existence). The passages in which intertextuality becomes apparent are many, as the themes and techniques followed by Di Lascia in her noteworthy novel are very close to Morante's. This closeness in the rendition of the family saga is due to the function of the model text or canonical text that Morante's novel performs with respect to Di Lascia's. To this should be added the common attention to the novel as a genre that is inherently epistemological. Aside from similar treatments of themes and the role of the narrator in indirect discourse, we have – as we shall see in the following pages – the presence in both novels of an *Epistolario*, an epistolary exchange, on which, for different reasons, the outcome of both women depends. There exists a wide assimilation of lexicon,[54] titles of subchapters, even a similar utilization of rhetorical figures, and the use of capital letters in the imperatives[55] that each assumes for herself. Another apparent intertextual element is the use of the titles dividing the several chapters of the novel. *Menzogna e sortilegio*'s imposing body of pages, almost eight hundred, was published as a novel. However, Morante conceived of a novel that drastically differed from the ongoing literary narrative of her time, more inclined towards the dry, concise American prose of Ernest Hemingway that Elio Vittorini had imported with his famous *Americana* anthology in 1942. The novel was already, in 1948, prose against its own time; Morante conceived it in the garb of a feuilleton and wanted to keep the flavour of those old weekly publications of the turn of the century. It should also be mentioned that the very first novel by Morante, *Qualcuno bussa alla porta*, was in fact published as a weekly instalment in *I diritti della scuola* between 1935 and 1936. In fact, the titles in Morante's novel have an explanatory quality to suggest, as in feuilletons, the notion that from week to week readers would have known what was happening in the intricate story of this family and the love story between two cousins. Di Lascia's titles into which both parts of the novel are divided – for instance, 'Francesco rivede i parenti e prende una decisione' (PO 30), 'Una forestiera di cui nessuno si fida' (PO 33), 'Preparativi per la fiera. Una strana malattia' (PO 89), and 'Il segreto e un potente giuramento' (PO 141) – all keep the antiquated suggestiveness of Morante's titles, which is well understood by Di Lascia in her attempt to recreate the small-town atmosphere, one that Chiara describes to us as made up of gossip and rumours.

Di Lascia displays her most original traits in the story of Chiara and Saverio. 'Il Silenzio,' the second part of *Passaggio in ombra*, is a long recollection whose topic is the disillusion of love for the weak Cugino. This part appears in many ways to be a powerful dilation of the '*Cuginanza*' part in *Menzogna e sortilegio*; it actually functions as a counter-novel to Morante's text, as it depicts the tragic outcome of such passion. The capital 'C' is kept to evoke the character of cousin Saverio. The treatment of the precocious and unhappy love between the two cousins Chiara and Saverio is directly influenced by the story of Anna, Elisa's mother, and her cousin Edoardo, the 'Norman,' often referred to as the 'Cousin.' In spite of the evident memory of Anna's hallucinations in the novel of the Massia-Cerentano saga, though, Di Lascia finds different solutions. Chiara's falling in love with Saverio, lived by the *Erzähltes Ich* and narrated by a now juxtaposed *Erzählendes Ich*, is one of the most relevant innovations in the entire second part of the novel. Such innovation thus produces a twist in what would otherwise be thought of as a mere calque of Elisa's character and role in the story. It separates at this point Chiara's character from Morante's Elisa, 'monaca della menzogna' ('the nun of lies'). As the epithet says, Elisa is a nun; she has never experienced carnal love. She translates her mother's love for cousin Edoardo, internalizes it, and makes it her own. Elisa does so to understand her mother's fixation for the *Capriccio*, Anna's whim that Elisa – confined as she is – otherwise lives through only thanks to the maternal epistolary. Just as those letters were 'fake,' produced by Anna's febrile mind, so will Elisa live her love for her mother's cousin Edoardo. Anna's 'fake letters' are very important for the novel in that they constitute evidence and material for Elisa's current situation of creative illness. Garboli recalls, in fact, how the entire novel was inspired by, and born out of, the story of a blind lady whose son was killed, perhaps in Ethiopia. To keep the sad truth away from the blind lady, her relatives would write her false letters, making her believe they were her son's. Morante was deeply touched by the story, and novelized it in her book. In the novel Anna's reading of the fake letters to Edoardo's mother, Concetta, are important for rendering the notion of the hereditary disease of lies and spells cast on the entire Cerentano-Massia family.[56] The desire to write and imagine things is hereditary: Elisa *learns* how to write of her family condition by reading her mother's fake letters. She learns how to discern and analyse her mother's folly while simultaneously learning how to put their family story on a written page. Evidently, just like their neurosis, there is a genetic tendency in the Massia–De Salvi women to produce – and what's more to believe in – hallucinating stories in which they crown themselves *regine* (queens) of a world that does not exist. Anna Massia di Corullo, relative of the Norman aristocratic family to which Edoardo belongs, will write letters addressed to herself from Edoardo to please, simultaneously, herself and Donna Concetta, a mother who has gone crazy at the thought of her son's death. But Anna will not write consolatory letters. It could not be. The process of identification with the woman who is the addressee of those letters is complete. It is almost a cry for inspiration to her predecessor Elisa that Chiara expresses in *Passaggio in ombra*:

> Oh, trovare le parole per evocare la grande esiliata: colei che langue prigioniera in un punto segreto di ogni essere vivente, mentre noi ci

dibattiamo nel vicolo cieco del dolore! Oh, liberare dalle catene la nostra felicità! (PO 136)
(Oh, to find the words to evoke the great exile: she who languishes as a prisoner in a secret point of any living being, while we struggle in the dead-end alley of grief! Oh, to free our happiness from the chains!)

The 'riti incantati della MEMORIA e del FUTURO' (PO 266; 'enchanted rites of MEMORY and the FUTURE') emerge from the same desperate and magic silence that filled Elisa's pages in her chronicle and then the story of her family, from whose rich intertextuality Morante's world of the feuilleton and melodrama, of Proust's readings, Mozart, and Rimbaud, emerge today as they are re-evoked by another great anti-heroine, Chiara D'Auria:

> Il futuro non è la morte, poiché questa non ha bisogno di assensi per compiersi; il futuro, invece, è questo tempo incompiuto che ci aspetta, inesorabilmente simile a noi: a ciò che siamo stati, e a quello che non saremo. Esso scava le rughe che lo specchio rimanda, ed è minaccioso e potente; allo stesso modo non cessa mai di esercitare il suo richiamo e ci sfida con promesse e lusinghe, o ci minaccia col suo terrore incalcolabile. Io non ho alcuna intimità con il mio futuro, che mi coglie eternamente impreparata; i 'domani' di cui è fatto scavano dentro me un vortice di vuoto: come un abisso sul quale mi affaccio e che mi risucchia nella sua vertigine. Se ripenso alla mia vita, è stato sempre così; seppure le forme che ha assunto nella coscienza sono sembrate all'apparenza diverse, e perfino opposte.
>
> Per un certo tempo, nella giovinezza soprattutto, ho bruciato del fuoco che l'avvenire sconosciuto accende negli animi ingenui.
>
> Allora mi sembrava che il futuro fosse un pianeta imperscrutabile e che vi si potesse giungere solamente per malia o a opera di un sortilegio. Se piangevo, se i giorni mi venivano incontro dolorosi o inutili; se mi sembrava che non ci fosse niente ad attendermi lungo la strada, il futuro sfavillava dinanzi a me come un sole o come un disco volante. (PO 209)

(The future is not death, for this latter does not need approval to happen; instead, the future is this unfinished time awaiting us, so implacably similar to us; to what we have been, and to what we will never be. It digs up the wrinkles the mirror reflects back to us, it is threatening and powerful; and yet, it never ceases to exercise its appeal and it dares us with promises and flatteries, or it threatens us with its incalculable terror. I have no intimacy with my future, which finds me completely unprepared; the 'tomorrows' of which it is made plow inside me a vortex of void: like an abyss over which I look and that swallows me up in its vertigo. If I think back to my life, it has always been like this; even though the shapes that it took in my conscience seemed diverse in their appearance, even opposite.

For a while, during my youth above all, I burned with that fire that the unknown future ignites in innocent souls.

It then seemed that the future was an inscrutable planet and that one could get there only by magic or by spell. If I would cry, if the days would approach painful or useless; if I thought nothing was awaiting me along the road, the future would shine in front of me like a sun or like a flying disk.)

In Chiara's writing, the notion of a future time is deprived of any positive connotation. Our future is determined by what our past and present have been, and no escape is thus possible. There is no redemption, no religious sign for betterment. The only future she can expect is an undetermined time that fruitlessly *scava*, plows wrinkles in her face in the image the mirror returns of her. And yet, in the beginning, the future seemed to carry plenty of promises, of emotion for the unexpected. When she was young she longed for a future that would be accomplished by *sortilegio*, by a fantastic spell. Now she has abandoned that hope and opted for a future that holds no spells and for which she is no longer prepared. Even her menstrual blood has stopped, and she, just like a plant, is wilting. It is not coincidental that Chiara often likens her image to one belonging to the botanical world. She feels her life is not moved by passions, but only by the whispering of her *morts-vivants*. As such, it is not an existence moved by autonomous impetus. Retrieving to a pre-erotic stage, to a Morantian androgynous state – marked by the lack of menstruations – to a world unmoved by passions is Chiara's only chance of survival in the deterministic scheme of events that construct the plot of *Passaggio in ombra*.

Canonizing Morante

The necessity of an exquisitely Italian and female tradition that would function as intertextual reference for Di Lascia's *Familienroman* proves the flexibility of a renewed, and indeed hospitable, Italian literary canon, one that can be researched within a particular socio-cultural circuit for which a given text is valued, as it takes on curatorial and normative functions. Those very functions that I have always considered proper to Morante's work in my previous studies indeed find application in Di Lascia's novel. In summation, if we assume as lasting the weight of the Morantian novelistic 'cathedrals,' we are taking a productive path. Claiming uniqueness for somebody's work out of too much love, as Garboli did in Morante's case, cannot constitute a correct approach to literary history, nor help to trace Italian novelistic transformation.

The example offered by *Passaggio in ombra* defines only one, if very eloquent, step in the diachrony of the canonicity of Morante's work. Placed as my first case study of the literary process by which women authors entrust with their work their literary mothers, it is also the most revealing text of Morante's writerly signs and their lasting legacy. As her novels reveal, today more than ever, the ability to be meaningful within the Italian tradition, rereadings of her novels seem to have increased since 1995, the year of *Passaggio in ombra*'s publication. Reading and talking with other texts expresses a specific desire for interaction with those whose issues we share, of feeling the erotics of other authors' voices. As Carla Kaplan states, '[d]esire ... might allow us to listen to each other, through the mediation of the text, without assuming, as identification tends to do, that we already know what the other is saying. Second, incorporating a dialectic of desire and identification into a heterogenous rather than homogenous model of discursive communities opens a space in which concrete others can reveal their particularity, not only a place in which generalized others can affirm and confirm their similarities.'[57]

Come prima delle madri: Simona Vinci's Treatment of Morante's *Smagamento*

> Ma tu, mamita, aiutami. Come fanno le gatte coi loro piccoli nati male, tu rimàngiami. Accogli la mia deformità nella tua voragine pietosa.[58]
>
> La favola mammarola è stantia.[59]
>
> The mother is a big crocodile, and you find yourself in her mouth.[60]

Simona Vinci's novel *Come prima delle madri*[61] carries out a rereading of Elsa Morante's concept of *smagamento*. *Il mondo salvato dai ragazzini*, a hybrid work in which Morante's recurring topos of victims and perpetrators within dysfunctional families takes on the force of a classic myth, is an immediate reference for the topics that Vinci treats in her novel, while the title *Come prima delle madri* (also its epigraph) is a verse taken from this 1968 mélange by Morante.[62] The argument here is that Vinci not only appropriates Morante's notion of *smagamento*, but she problematizes it; she shows the zones of grey shades that make up the difficult relations children entertain with adults, particularly within the family, that will ultimately lead to their coming of age. Vinci insinuates a notion of evil that is far deeper than Morante's tones in *Il mondo salvato dai ragazzini*, and draws more from the abysmal pessimism characterizing the mother–child relationship in *Aracoeli*.

The Novel, the Roman Noir: *Ricoeur and the Notion of Emplotment*

Vinci wants to go back to a world that, as the title of the novel states, must be '*come prima delle madri*,' 'like before the mothers.' How can a world as such be articulated and even conceived? A world devoid of crime, a world before, 'prima' with respect to the 'crime' that is at the core of this novel, a blend of Oedipal novel and *roman noir*. According to Paul Ricoeur, emplotment suggests 'an integrating dynamism that draws a unified and complete story from a variety of incidents, in other words, that transforms this variety into a unified and complete story.'[63] It is in the novel genre that the definition lends itself to the most varied subversions. Ricoeur maintains that the novel, freeing itself from the rigid laws of interpretation of Aristotelian poetics, far from organizing an emplotment of uncomplicated understanding, can instead – particularly thanks to the system of characters – operate a sort of revolution of emplotment. In the contemporary novel, the modalities Ricoeur theorized for the expansion of the concept of emplotment are made particularly evident. More to the point, Vinci's novel presents itself as a novel of initiation in which the stream of consciousness and the necessary incompleteness of the main character dilate classic concepts of emplotment while simultaneously dilating the concept of action. Since the process of maturation and coming-of-age of the character defines the main plot, this novel partly follows the subgenre of the novel of initiation.[64]

In the *roman noir*, emplotment comes to be much more articulate than in a detective novel. The interaction between the notion of emplotment and the articulation of characters as seen by Paul Ricoeur provides further evidence for this textual analysis of *Come prima delle madri*. Vinci's novel adopts some of the modalities of the *noir* because they allow for presenting a particular milieu of immorality and sordid crime in which 'the detective risks his health if not his life'[65] within a novel of formation

(*Bildungsroman*) whose matrix is profoundly Morantian. Two elements regulate my reading of *Come prima delle madri*: these are, respectively, the fairy-tale-like construction of this novel of formation and the Morantian tenet that the world of children is undisturbed only until adults corrupt it by introducing the consciousness of sin. I want to discuss Vinci's need to go back to the original, her necessity to 'think the form' ('pensare la forma') in *Come prima delle madri* by looking at the intrinsic connections between literature and investigation, the intellectual curiosity that constructs investigation itself.

To investigate how children are forced to leave their world of dreams, one needs to 'tornare all'originale,'[66] go back to the original, urges Vinci, which she wants to do in this hybridized novel, hybridized not so much in its generic connotations as in its tones and modalities. According to Ricoeur, an expanded notion of action, parallel to the expansion of the notion of emplotment, envisions the 'moral transformation of characters, their growth and education, and their initiation into the complexity of moral and emotional existence.'[67] If seen in this way, action still pertains to the concept of emplotment. It is for Ricoeur more than just the behaviour of the characters producing changes visible in the situation, reversals of fortune, the 'external destiny' of people. Action amounts also to the internal movement towards self-growth and self-awareness. Ricoeur postulates that the simple notion of representing an already present reality is a formulation derived from an ill-advised abstraction of two moments from a continuous coordination. In turn, he proposes that mimesis be understood as a dialectic process that he traces through three moments, or phases. He develops the Aristotelian poetics and focuses on literary representation while discussing mimesis mainly as a narrative imitation of action: the inherent quality of the creation of a story is that the action lies right beneath it. For Ricoeur, mimesis depends first on the presence of actions – significant behaviour – to be represented. Actions are significant, or meaningful, because they refer to something beyond themselves – they are about something (*inter alia*, they are about their goals). Not surprisingly, for Ricoeur narrative emplotment constitutes the way in which we make sense of our being-in-time in the world.

The internalization of the events that construe the plot of the novel allows for Pietro's character development through the actual body of Vinci's novel. This process emphasizes the importance of self-reflection and psychological distancing by Pietro as his only possible means of escape from the family evil, mainly represented by the maternal character,

Tea. Representation, *trovare le cose nel fondo*, and finding the word for this representation signifies allowing for the deconstruction and decontextualization of representations (verbal ones, particularly) from the circumstances in which they were created. Self-reflection is described as a process model of recursive consciousness.[68] Pietro must see his own mother in a different manner in order to escape hell. How can he do so? In Vinci's novel all characters are doomed. It seems as if all these human beings are stained by original sin, and are unable to expunge it from their existence, not at any age. They appear to be moved, and to act, according to obscure forces, stained as they are by sins that are narrated as ineluctable facts, completely independent of their will. As Paul Ricoeur notes, sin indicates the consciousness of fault, and 'is not only the rupture of a relation; it is also the experience of a power that lays hold of man ... [S]in, too, is a "something," a "reality." Thus, we have to give an account at the same time of the preferment of a new symbolism and of the survival of the old under the direction of the new.'[69]

Sins intended as 'realities' are the original connections between the characters in the novel and in the great crimes of the mythological world. Great crimes in mythology prefigure the necessity of social institutions as founding elements of an ethical system to prevent the brutality of humankind. These crimes are thus 'needed,' necessary, so to speak. In the case of Vinci's novel, are the characters forming the emplotment perhaps affected by a Sadean form of evil? That is, are these characters evil merely because this is the true disposition of humankind, such that this kind of relation is a transgressive form of connection between the novel as a genre and the myth that comes to be evident in Vinci's text? Is this a reversal in the notion of myth/crime as we saw it in the past? And if this is the case, what are the pivotal instruments of such a bond? In my view, Vinci makes use of the modalities of the *noir* to construe the story of the initiation of Pietro in a dialogue with her literary mother, Elsa Morante.[70] In hybridizing the Oedipal novel of initiation with the modalities of the *noir*, as *Come prima delle madri*'s emplotment utilizes its elements, Vinci elaborates yet another subgenre for the traditional bourgeois family novel, which, in turn, makes the story of Pietro's coming-of-age very complex and disseminates meaning on multiple levels. What follows in an analysis of the interesting hybrid that Vinci makes of the novel of formation and the *noir*. The novel of formation in Vinci's text takes on the features of an Oedipal novel, since the protagonist's formation and entrance into adult life illustrates the revelation of his psychological enslavement to the mother. The main features of Morante's influence in Vinci's development of the son–mother relationship deal with the problematic intitiation of Pietro vis-à-vis Tea's teachings and, more generally, with the presence of sin in the mother's life that unquestionably moulds her son's.[71]

The Roman Noir

Tzvetan Todorov contends that the *roman noir* fuses the two stories of the detective novel, that of the crime, which in the detective novel has already been committed at the outset of the *fabula*, and that of the investigation, which instead composes the actual *noir*. In the *noir*, Todorov states, '[t]here is no story to guess, there is no mystery,'[72] as the reader follows the story step by step. Instead of diminishing the interest of the readers, the presence of the crime in the story of the investigation creates suspense (cause-effect) that is indissolubly tied with curiosity (effect-cause). The *noir*, even if (again as Todorov notes) does not necessarily compress the two stories of the detective novel into one, develops more analytical strata than the detective novel, investigates the causes of the crime, and does not look merely at its solution. Far richer than the detective novel in psychological complexities, the *noir* feeds itself and its entire plot on the causes of the immorality of the characters. Thus, the entire construction of the novel needs characters that are more developed and intricate than those of a detective novel; it cannot rely exclusively on the investigation of the crime. It is apparent that the *noir* makes the relationship between emplotment and the actions/thoughts/ethical system of the characters fundamental to the outcome of the entire text. For Ricoeur, the second expansion of the character at the expence of the emplotment happens precisely in the novel of initiation.[73]

These elements are present in the two parts composing the novel. There are two initiations to life (and sin) here: Pietro's and his mother Tea's. The epilogue ends both stories, as the mother's initiation to life and her son's develop in the direction of the gratuitousness of evil and the notion that we transmit to our children our own sense of despair. The first element retrieves in this novel the simplicity of fairy tales, which point the right way to children by showing cruel scenes of horror.[74] Vinci utilizes the fairy tale instead as it is: the linear – not baroque – introduction to a world in which horror is neither simulated nor artificial, but real, a constitutive part of what life is, so to speak, that presents itself in the most evident forms.

The other element in Vinci's novel, related to the previous one in a way, is the frailty of the Morantian notion of a world of *ragazzini* not yet disturbed by the knowledge of the world of adults, the latter considered immoral in its own very essence.[75] In *Come prima delle madri* Vinci tries a dialogue with Morante about the theme of childhood and traces the idealism and naivety in Morante's firm divarication of the two worlds of childhood/adulthood. However, Vinci's expressive style, unlike Morante's, does not possess any baroque nuances; she believes more in a dry writing, which leaves no space for reverie as in Morante, and actually declares the futility of it, since life, as it is, can only be already the theatre on which we stage our sadness. Before everything happened, we were clean, sinless; *we were integri*, as Morante writes:

> Eravamo integri, prima della Genesi; e può darsi che la cacciata dall'Eden vada intesa, nel senso occulto, per un gioco ambiguo e provocatorio: 'Avete mangiato il frutto *proibito*,' dice la sentenza del Signore, 'ma non quello *segreto* della vita, che io, Padrone del giardino, vi tengo nascosto, perché vi renderebbe uguali agli dei.'[76]
>
> (We were whole, before Genesis; and perhaps the expulsion from Eden must be understood, in its hidden meaning, as an ambiguous and provocatory game: 'You have eaten the *forbidden* fruit,' the Lord's command says, 'but not the *secret* fruit of life: that I, Master of the garden, keep hidden from you, because it would make you the equal of gods.')[77]

Knowledge and Sexuality Connection

Come prima delle madri reconnects predictably with the Morantian theme of maternity. According to Cesare Garboli, the theme of androgyny that he assimilates, rather questionably, to hermaphroditism, traverses the entirety of Morante's work, but is more openly stated and dealt with in *Alibi*. For Garboli, while the '[s]viluppo carnale di madre e figlio, inseparabili, stretti in una creatura sola' is quite evident in *Menzogna e sortilegio* ('the carnal bundle of mother and son, inseparable, is tied in one creature'), this particular novel presents maternity 'coi tratti perversi e deformi di una caricatura' ('with the perverse and deformed traits of a caricature').[78] Unlike Garboli, I think that if 'caricaturistic' might be the manner in which maternity is fashioned in Morante's works, one should not forget that we are dealing with a narrative depiction of maternity that is always written/described/interpreted by a scorned narrator, Elisa, Arturo, and Manuel. For instance, *Menzogna e sortilegio*'s narrator Elisa entertains a relationship to her mother that is tormented by many issues. Elisa-the-daughter sees maternity in the light of how her mother

Anna saw it – a frustrating, disheartening, and humiliating experience. In constructing the characters of Pietro and Tea and their interaction, Vinci accepts and elaborates the obscure side of motherhood, the very one that makes Garboli more incredulous about Morante's ability to be a 'mother' for women writers, and yet is one of the many gloomy glasses through which women and maternity are lived *and* represented, how the sense of oppression of mothers can be transmitted to their children, who, in turn, narrate their experience of it, invariably enveloped within the maternal experience. Every novel by Morante re-elaborates the Oedipal complex, as her novels deal with the notion of the *ragazzini* as sole warrantors of a world of illusion from which invariably follows actual knowledge of the world. But it is they who narrate and thus condemn their mothers (and fathers, as in the case of Arturo). Morante claims that salvation belongs to those who have never gone beyond the threshold of adolescence, because in that very phase, the beginning of maturity, *smagamento*, or the disillusionment that originates in our realizing that the person we love is not what we thought him or her to be, takes over, shading everything with dark tones.

The first part of Vinci's novel ends faithfully around the Morantian *diktat*. Pietro becomes painfully aware that his mother and his father, but particularly his beautiful mother, are not what he thought them to be at all. His mother's behaviour derives from motives that are hidden from him. They are dark and terrible, and it is Pietro's role to investigate his mother in order to understand his own behaviour. The *noir* modalities establish the itinerary that the reader must complete in order to grapple with what Pietro sees and tries to understand from the beginning to the end of the most difficult two years in his life. It is thanks to the *noir* overtones that the rich complex of themes in Vinci's novel, which count on the reading systems pertaining to this subgenre, on the expectations raised by readers who have competence in it, can effect an examination of the Morantian treatment of the difficult mother–child relationship. Something that begins with the birth of an individual other than us, and yet lives inside ourselves and takes the shape of nightmares.[79] In Pietro's life there is only space for nightmares, for terrifying images in which his subconscious compares Tea, his mother, to a Medusa, to a dreadful human being whose powers are the traditional patriarchal ones of castrating the man, her own child, until she dies: 'non era rimasto niente di vivo, da nessuna parte: Sua madre era morta' (CPM 10; 'nothing remained alive, anywhere. His mother was dead').

Far from drawing power from the myth of maternity, from the cliché of the longed-for maternity generally pictured by male writers, Morante (with the exception of Ida and Nunziatina) and Vinci examine maternity for what it often is: the procreation of unwanted children by mothers whose lives are restless and dissatisfied. Elisa and Pietro scrutinize their wretched mothers, and their writing about them is necessarily devoid of *humanitas*; it is implacable, and the result of their 'investigation' leads perforce to an ending that is much harder than what they expected. Also, Vinci's novel further develops what Morante had announced in her works: Vinci does not grace her characters with *pietas*, with the result that her novel will see a much crueller ending. Morantian *pietas* does not dilute the cruel traits of the discovery of the adult world by the child observing it, nor does parody ever enter the scheme of figures in Vinci's novel. Charged as it is with the notion that Evil is inherent in humankind, her novel expands on Morante's pessimistic treatment of motherhood.

Liberation from the Mother

A foggy, heavy, unbearable atmosphere defines Vinci's novel, marked as it is by events, by the setting of the civil war, and by the attitude of the protagonist. The stories of Pietro and his family and of the disappearance of his half-sister, Irina, are respectively recorded by various types of written texts. In addition to Pietro's reading of Irina's diary, which interrupts his own narration (CPM 157–69), we also read Tea's notebook, a text that begins and ends the second part of the novel (CPM 236–66). The *oscura stirpe*, the 'obscure stock' of Pietro's family, echoing the writing process of Elisa's family of *Menzogna e sortilegio*, dictates their story to Elisa in a fiction that their heir to this sinful world can accept or deny, as happened to Elisa with her mother's false letters. In her notebook, Tea speaks of the past, of her initiation to drugs, which was ignited by her desire to not think of what she had done out of ignorance and lust. This is an addiction that now forces Tea, so healthy when young, to stay 'a letto come una morta e quando si alza è solo per bere e farsi le punture' (CPM 129; 'in bed like she is dead and when she gets up it is merely to drink and get high'). Irina writes in her own notebook, as a *morte vivante* and symbol of a *memoria onnipotente*, of a memory of an age that precedes that defined by Pietro. Pietro, in turn, sees and records what happens in his present also when Irina, 'tante notti dopo, ha aperto la bocca ... E ha respirato la paura. La loro' (CPM 279; 'several nights afterwards has opened her mouth ... and has breathed fear. Theirs'). Not incidentally, Tea will declare in her notebook that the bond with her master, Kurt – a man who has facilitated her path to evil – has been something with no name that only fear could create, 'un legame che non ha nessun nome ... Tante cose insieme. Ho sempre paura di lui' (CPM 256; 'a bond that has no name ... Many things together. I am always afraid of him').

The elements of the *noir* emerge from a conflation of texts: from Irina's diary and Tea's notebook, from the omniscient narrator who intercedes for Pietro in the cruellest moments of his educational trajectory. They construct what in the beginning of the reading one could perhaps merely imagine. The certainties Pietro should have had as a child, those that remind of the CERTEZZE ASSOLUTE of Morante's Arturo; that world that Arturo thought to be perfect, and that would be defined by the island of Procida, cannot exist in this case, as it did not for him at the end of his formative two years. Arturo's world is one in which the myth is realized in an epic sense, or at least he tried to achieve it, lest the tragic intervention of parody dissolve and annul the sense of solemnity myth gives to stories. In Arturo's life, his mother's absence was not caused by a murder; at least this was not the mode in which his initiation was treated. The suspenseful thrill in Arturo's life derived more from learning of his father's true sexual orientation, and his weakness when dealing with love for his partners, than from an actual crime. A crime was committed, undoubtedly, but not of the sort we witness in Pietro's story of initiation to life. While Arturo leaves the island to go to war and thinks again of the island from *un'infinita distanza*, an endless distance, Pietro is still deep in his limited area of action, concerning that absence of memory for which, as Todorov states, 'no thriller is presented in the form of memoirs: there is no point reached where the narrator comprehends all past events, we do not even know if he will reach the end of the story alive.'[80] Pietro is left to decipher the enigma enveloping the maternal figure of Tea, as his own life – like Oedipus – depends on the solution of a riddle.

Unlike Arturo, Pietro does not appear to experience an infinite, endless time, the one used in the epic genre. He does not avail himself of a distance between the reminiscence – closed inside a box to be opened at ease according to the most varied reasons – and his own present.[81] Pietro cannot see his mother for what she was before her meeting with Léon: similar to a Morantian Nunziatina, all rosy-cheeked and unaware of the evil within herself. Pietro cannot know the maternal *prima*, the girl who Tea was before shooting a man without knowing what she was doing, before all the crimes she committed that now have elided any possibility for her son of seeing the light. In short, Tea has doomed Pietro to not see.

Unlike Pietro, and as Vinci's privileged readers, we read Tea's story in the second part of *Come prima delle madri*. The *noir* trajectory is more defined against the backdrop of the Italian civil war,[82] in which not the children, but the adults are actors of violence. Sexual relations among adults are described with dry, almost hyperrealistic details. The act of killing, dealing death, is treated just like sexual acts, with the same sharpness. In this, death and sex are united in the construction of a negative, nihilistic fresco on the impossibility of understanding how both heart and mind work. Eros and death are indissoluble in Vinci's novel, and we know it is the same in Morante's writing. When Elisa 'retells' the story of the night after the opera, in which her parents had sexual intercourse, there is the same notion that something was going rotten, that something that had nothing to do with eternal love, marital love, enduring love, was taking place. The world depicted by Vinci is articulated as an anti-model to the initiation of children into adult life. As in the fairy tales of the Brothers Grimm, everything one should *not* experience is narrated in full detail. Everything that should not be experienced, particularly in a family nucleus, is shown in all its forms of perversion, generating transgressive situations that problematize the concept of the family as an institution decreed as rule-giver for the individual. The rituals of initiation we read of in Vinci's 1997 *Dei bambini non si sa niente* continue. They now possess, however, a different matrix, much more mature, that finds its origin in the origins of ourselves, of who gave us birth in fear and guilt. And it does not let adults out of the children's world, as in *Dei bambini non si sa niente*, since guilt and fear are generated *prima* of Pietro's birth, *before* everything happened to him: from the mother to the son. The diegetic apparatus does not overlook adults: it must necessarily go through the maternal figure and traverse the motivations that led her to such immoral behaviour. The umbilical cord that wraps the child in its spirals like a genetic snake determines the passage of Original Sin from mother to son, a son who must find evidence of his own innocence as his only way out of such an enveloping, suffocating relationship. One, it should be remembered, that is not based on goodness and generosity, but on sin and guilt. Pietro's only way out of his desperate and insane love for Tea is to demonstrate that he is innocent.

In the structure of the novel, Vinci's choice of varying the points of view is rather effective, particularly in the case of the narrator. In the first part Pietro illustrates the transformation of his own world from an Eden of magic innocence in which 'esistono loro, lui, Pietro, e lei, mamma' (CPM 14–15; 'there exist only the two of them, Pietro and she, mummy') to the one he will delve into for his investigation, while in the second an omniscient narrator enters the stage. The shift in focalization and the changes in point of view prove to be critical in defining the origin of sin and guilt when Tea narrates her own story at seventeen. Indirect speech and the shift in point of view from Pietro to Tea, and in turn from Tea to Irina, as in cinematic shots and counter-shots, allow the protagonist, Pietro, to stay on two of the necessary levels for the *noir*: protagonist-observer of facts of which he makes an attentive selection, as is his right. Etymologically, the term 'crime' derives from *cernere*, 'to select.' Pietro is always being observed by the readers while he is himself looking at the case. Voyeuristically engaged, readers are allowed to do so thanks to another point of view, that of the onniscient extradiegetic narrator. The *gaze* turns upside down the sense of the Oedipal narration. It undoes the very premises, rediscovers the sense of the mother and of what has happened to her *before* Pietro's birth, how she herself was *before* she was a mother, *prima*. When we read the story of Tea before her sin, which shows her inclination to commit evil with no explanatory causes, the role of the novelistic hero is denied to Pietro, since, in spite of the fact that he is the little detective of this *noir*, he is netherless genetically tied to her. Pietro is not pure, he is not free from Tea's sin. His role in the novel is that of problematizing Morante's binary opposition between good and evil in her way of depicting *smagamento*.

In the construction of Tea's character, the three Jungian mothers are juxtaposed: the primitive, the Oedipal, and the oral all intervene to form an utterly unresolved motherly figure, one that does not acknowledge for herself, nor probably ever had, a maternal side. The issue of the mother's role in the construction of the individual is investigated both from Pietro's point of view and then in Tea's notebook, particularly in her days of pregnancy spent away from crowded Berlin and buried alive in the snow in a little house in Prussia. If the archetype is initially 'empty,' as Jung writes, if it amounts to nothing but to 'a *facultas praeformandi*,' which he describes as a possibility of representation that is given a priori, then the archetype can connote 'anything secret, hidden, dark; the abyss, the world of the dead, anything that devours, seduces, and poisons, that is terrifying and inescapable like fate.'[83] The historical example Jung chooses is that of the 'Virgin Mary, who is not only the Lord's mother, but also, according to medieval allegories, his cross.'[84]

Elisa's narrative of her wretched mother, Anna, in *Menzogna e sortilegio* destroys the myth of the *mater amabilis*. Anna is the other face of the image of the Madonna – *Nostra Signora Orientale* – an oriental Madonna whose 'cattivi pensieri le splendono intorno al capo come un'aureola' (MS 1: 665–6; 'unkind thoughts glow about her head like a halo'; HL 403). Elisa still remembers 'i desiderî turpi e disumani che la trafiggono paiono spade sante' (MS 1: 666 'the shameless and inhuman desires which obsess her are the marks of a saint'; HL 403). Like the Morantian Anna before her, Tea represents the anti-image of the mother in our literature. However, Tea's terrible thoughts are much more graphic than those written by Elisa's imaginative narration. From the Morantian character of Anna, Tea inherits and enhances the danger that a woman – when forced by the patriarchal system into her role of mother – represents for the psychological health of her children. In fact, the Madonna is a recurring motif in Vinci's novel; it serves almost to point us towards a Jungian reading of the novel. In Vinci's text, much is played on the polarity of this image, on the negative aspect of the Madonna, who denotes everything that is secret, hidden, and obscure. A painting depicting a marine Madonna hangs in Tea's bedroom. The presence of this painting in Tea's room defines the authorial strategy to utilize an ekphrastic process by which the subject of the painting could have disposed of its own autonomous and symbolic reason for being in the story. The *Mater amabilis*, as Jung notes, usually 'appears as a vessel of devotion, a source of wisdom and renewal.'[85] However, when Tea invites Pietro to sleep with her in her bedroom – 'Vieni, dormiamo. È da tanto che non dormi con me' (CPM 126; 'Come, let's sleep. It has been a long time since you last slept with me') – the child cannot help but notice that the symbolically charged 'crepa' ('crock') in the painting opens up, almost enveloping him. Pietro sees 'quel mondo incrostato di ghiaccio e sale che appare nel quadro enorme sulla parete di fronte prendere vita e venirgli incontro' (CPM 126; 'that world encrusted with ice and salt that appears in the enormous painting on the opposite wall becoming alive and greeting him'). And few pages further, '[l]a Madonna Marina gli sorride dalla sua grotta azzurra ... Gli occhi sono quelli da puttana di tutte le madonne' (CPM 127; 'the marine Madonna smiles at him from her blue grotto ... [H]er eyes are whore-like as in all madonnas'). The ambiguity in the depiction of the Madonna figure, paralleled with Tea, is made more evident by Pietro's reading of the painting. If entirely imaginary, the painting however takes its name from an area not far from Venice, where Pietro was in boarding school and where he first realizes his position of odd man out, of being a stranger and feeling a stranger among his peers.

As recalled earlier, the *noir* tones are used according to dictates that can be defined as Morantian since Morante's dream of the salvation of the body of *ragazzini*, one that should allow for their vulnerability, turns out to be vain and unobtainable.[86] Pietro's gaze is not a redeeming one, just as those of Morante's Manuel or Arturo are not. Pietro is the true son of his mother, a mother who understands that her body is not 'a good place' for a son, because she – stained by sin – is not a 'posto buono' (CPM 241; 'good place') to give birth to anybody. In fact, Tea names the child Pietro – stone – because she wishes for an incorruptible son, hard as a rock and invulnerable, a son 'ci camminano sopra gli insetti' (CPM 245; 'on which insects walk'), 'ci dormono contro gli animali' (CPM 245; 'animals sleep against it'), a son to call by this name because 'la pietra non cambia' (CPM 245; 'the stone does not change') because 'la pietra è una cosa buona. Una cosa che resiste' (CPM 245; 'the stone is a good thing. Something that lasts').[87]

The hybridized form created by the enmeshing of *noir* tones and the Oedipal novel makes it possible that the images of bodies – the body as a constant motif in Vinci's writing – link the world of the dead to that of forbidden love and the guilt of the living for which, as Morante writes, 'la memoria è peccato come la veggenza' ('memory is a sin like divination').[88] For Pietro, to make sense of the present through the past is a Hamletic impossibility. Hamlet, a character much loved by Morante, reappears in the character of Pietro, one of the several possibilities of hybridization that she theorized, as he is reminiscent of the radical Hobbesian opposition enemy/enemy in his coming of age.[89] According to Morante, 'la realtà ispira ripugnanza' ('reality repels')[90] in Hamlet, but Shakespeare's character does not find salvation in fiction and imagination, as in the first case she mentions, Don Quixote. In the end, rather than giving in to unreality, Hamlet 'sceglie di non essere' ('chooses not to be').[91] Still, 'not being' remains a decision. With respect to the mystery of his birth, Pietro, like Hamlet, acts as a detective in his own house where everybody is an enemy. Slowly, Pietro, within the time of the narration, acquires the knowledge that his family structure, far from being a normal one, is exclusively based on crime. Crime is not, then, as one would generally think, the element of disrupture of an initial situation reducible to the traditional sense of family ethics. It is not either, as in Roman law, a public crime that offends the social order and afflicts the entire community. Crime is the very structure upon which Pietro's birth and existence rest:

Anche lui lotta ogni giorno contro la sua falla, quella che gli impedirà di esercitare la volontà fino in fondo. Ha quasi tredici anni e già gli tocca trasportare ogni giorno quintali di sabbia per cercare di turare il piú a lungo possibile quel buco. Per tenerlo a bada e non permettergli di allargarsi a sua insaputa. Ogni giorno, lotta con un essere sconosciuto che gli vive dentro come un assassino, in agguato ...

La sua unica arma è quella sabbia finissima eppure cosí pesante da portare. La sua volontà è fatta di sabbia, e la sabbia, prima o poi crolla. (CPM 43–4) (He too fights every day against his hole [sin], which will prevent him from fully exercising his will. He is almost thirteen, and already has to carry every day tons of sand trying to stop the hole as long as possible. To keep it under control and to not let it get any bigger without his knowing. Every day, he fights with an unknown being that lives within him like an assassin, lying in wait ...

His only weapon is the sand, very fine and yet too heavy to carry. His will is made of sand, and sand, sooner or later, gives way.)

Dante's *Inferno* is quoted in Pietro's readings in his boarding school (which is likely in Venice, judging from the geographics of the text): 'Ei sono tra l'anime più nere / diverse colpe giù li grava al fondo / se tanto scendi, là li potrai vedere.'[92] Pietro's trajectory in the family inferno is marked by this *terzina*, drawing all evidence against his adored-damned mother while investigating fully 'the bottom of things.' As in a film *noir*, the narrative is open to constant interruptions, fragmented inserts in part allusive but never defined, sites in which the doubts of the reader are in tune with those of the child. Pietro learns to discern, to make distinctions, and to make himself invisible while carrying out his investigations. Pietro's desire to know his mother's secrets is essential for the very construction of the emplotment, because she is key to the *thriller*. He is afraid of 'tutte le cose che non capisce' (CPM 109; 'all the things that he does not understand'), '[gli] fanno paura quei due sul letto che dormono' ('is afraid of those two sleeping on the bed'), 'i soldati che scappano e si vanno a nascondere' (CPM 109; 'the soldiers fleeing'), 'gli stranieri' (109; 'the strangers'). Nina scares him by '[l]e cose che dice' (CPM 109; 'what she says'), and for 'quello che hanno fatto stanotte' (CPM 109; 'what they did that night'). Above all, above the soldiers, above Nina, 'sua madre gli fa paura' (CPM 109; 'his mother scares him'). Pietro, however, must investigate because 'il fetore di questa casa viene dalle fondamenta, ha impregnato i muri ... [u]na patina oleosa e puzzolente che aderisce a tutto quanto' (CPM 113; 'the stench of this house comes from the foundations, has impregnated the walls ... an oily and smelly patina that sticks to everything'). And so Pietro

> gira per la casa. Cammina a piedi nudi e sente freddo e ha paura di aver sognato tutto e paura anche di non aver sognato proprio niente ... [G]li viene in mente sua madre chiusa da piú di dodici ore in quella stanza con uno sconosciuto e si chiede perché e cosa fanno e cosa pensa lei e che cosa vuol dire questa storia. (CPM 108)
> (goes around the house. He walks barefooted and is cold and is afraid of having dreamt everything and is afraid also of not having dreamt anything at all ... [H]is mother, locked inside that room with a stranger for more than twelve hours, comes to his mind and he wonders why and what are they doing and what she is thinking and what this story means.)

Unlike Morante's children's basic inability to transform with their actions the irreversible path towards tragedy of their family, Vinci's novel proposes a transformation in the behaviour of his protagonist. Pietro actively pursues a transformation for his life. Pietro, in fact, decides – and this is Vinci's remarkable transformation with respect to the plots in which Morante envelops her children – to act upon what he feels are maternal wrongdoings. Pietro, more like his namesake in Bataille's *Ma mère*, searches for revenge against the forced *smagamento* to which his mother has pushed him. *Pietas* is not present in Vinci's universe and so, not even the delicate, problematic Pietro can escape the authorial law that nails him to his fate as a matricide – a fate that, as in a game of mirrors, Pietro reads on the *Resto del Carlino* even before the crime is committed. The death of his mother is already foretold. Pietro has been preparing the obituary for her for some time. Denouncing his mother to the partisans, Pietro thinks to free himself – once and for all – from that *falla*, that chasm that the sand cannot fill up. That curse under which he was born can be closed only if he denounces his mother. He will denounce her to the partisans for the only crime she did not actually commit, the death of Nina, the little girl found hanging from a tree with the sign *puttana* (whore).

Life in the family has been marred by the deviant personality of Tea. Pietro believes that his intervention in denouncing his mother will purify the family, or, rather, he believes that his own existence won't be marred by the sight of Tea's constant moral transgression. To the local partisans he will say, 'Mia madre è amica dei tedeschi. Non sta con voi' (CPM 322; 'My mother is a friend of the Germans. She is not on your side'). By denouncing her, Pietro believes he can retrieve the world as it should be 'before the mothers,' the world as it perhaps was in the Alps before Tea met Léon:

> Adesso, il mondo visibile era tutto quello che l'occhio riusciva a percepire. C'erano gli alberi, il cielo, l'acqua ghiacciata del fiume, gli avanzi di neve tra l'erba, la luna.
> E lui, il ragazzo, che camminava già sulla strada che aveva imboccato e non poteva guardare indietro. (CPM 323)
> (Now, the visible world was all his eye could perceive. There were trees, the sky, the frozen water of the river, the residues of the snow among the grass, the moon. And he, the boy, who was already walking down the road he had taken and could no longer look behind.)

In so doing, Pietro hopes the sand on which he has long walked will not take him to the bottom; he hopes that his mother's sins will not weigh on his shoulders and won't drag him to the abhorred place of darkness, *al fondo*, that place on which Vinci's *cattivismo* always lies. He decrees Tea's death: 'Io lo so chi è stato. È stata mia madre' (CPM 322; 'I know who did it. It was my mother'). With these words, Pietro seals the death of his mother. This charge concludes Pietro's trial of his mother in a reprise of the trials that Elsa Morante stages against her characters' mothers. The trial of the mother is a recurring theme in Morante's novels with a first-person narrator, *Menzogna e sortilegio* and *Aracoeli*. Pietro is a creature connected to Elisa and Manuel, the narrators and protagonists of the two novels, respectively. Because of too much love for their mothers, the two have never been able to conclude their dramatic trial with a final and clear sentence, such as the one that Pietro instead utters at the end of his adolescence – a destructive ending, no doubt, as Pietro, according to Morante's parameters, represents a modified version of the Hamlet character. He is the one to whom 'la realtà ispira ripugnanza, ma non trova salvezza, e alla fine sceglie di non essere' ('reality inspires repulsion, but does not find salvation, and in the end it chooses not to be').[93] His vindication, however, will end both his mother's and his own life. He goes beyond what Morante's children have done, in the direction of Bataille's Pierre. Mother and son, bound by sin, can no longer exist.[94] As Manuel writes in *Aracoeli*, 'C'è un patto di comunione carnale irrimediabile fra l'uccisore e il suo giustiziato. E nel mio bisogno d'amore, io godevo del suo gesto assassino come di una confidenza totale, una tenerezza' (Morante, *Aracoeli*, in *Opere*, 2: 1132;

'There is an irreparable pact of carnal communion between the killer and his victim. And in my need for love, I enjoyed his murderous act as a total intimacy, a tenderness,' *Aracoeli*, 71).

The theatre-like quality of the family texture – this horrible farce before the child's eyes – is conveyed by the heavy velvet curtains Pietro keeps looking at in his mother's room while describing his life inside the house. Everything inside the house is false, everything has been built to stage a recital of horror. This house evokes the terrifying fairy tales of the Brothers Grimm, but the little girls buried alive in there are close in authorial intent to Elisa in *Menzogna e sortilegio* because they demand to have their story told. This is the case with Irina, who leaves a notebook for this reason. But the caress of memory is not given to Pietro. He cannot escape or go further away from his mother, not until the time of the novel has elapsed. It is the matter of the novel that construes its *noir* aspect, as Todorov wrote. What differentiates Vinci's characters from the Morantian ones is their escape from the world of their parents. Pietro lives now with us: the *adesso* and not *prima*, an ana-cataphoric point that has also become a hallmark of Vinci's writing, ties him to his own present destiny. 'Per molto tempo ... per molto tempo. Per tutto il tempo ... Ma *ora*' (CPM 9, emphasis added; 'For a long time ... for a long time. For all time ... But *now*') is a time that takes into consideration only what Pietro is watching, what becomes true and real before his very eyes. If the Morantian Elisa reveals the fissure between the moment of the *racconto* dictated to her by the *morts-vivants* and the one in which she interrogates only her own 'vera memoria' (MS 2: 579; 'true memory,' HL 349), Pietro records what happens inside his family, but he does it in the time prescribed by the *noir*. And he cut the thread of Tea's life with cold deliberation (CPM 180).

Tea

The construction of Tea's character fits completely the code of the *noir*. Distant, sophisticated, addicted to drugs and sinful, Tea leads an existence not built upon the meanings society usually assigns to the term maternity. The character that theoretically sustains the entire economy of the *noir* is Tea, as her role as 'the mother' should eliminate any suspicion of her. Tea, however, *is* fatal. What does it mean to be fatal for a character in *Come prima delle madri*, which is neither a hard-boiled detective novel, a typical *noir*, nor a Hollywood film. The *femme fatale* is not the subject of power, but its carrier, for she is useful in the plot in making us wonder about knowledge and sexuality. She is a creation, that is, that allows for epistemological credibility and reliance. Tea's perversion thus appears execrable and absurd, because she is a *femme fatale* and mother at once. Tea is fatal because she is indeed deadly, since she is the assassin as she kills everybody, except Nina, whose death Pietro will decide to attribute to Tea chiefly because it is the only crime in the story that can be avenged. Pietro's denunciation confirms the existent connection with his mother. Tea is fatal because she 'represents the possibility of a libidinous satisfaction which cannot be contained by the symbolic Order and by the structure of family relations'.[95]

Faithful to her role, Tea must also kill Léon's daughter Irina, the daughter of the Law, who sees everything even when her eyes are closed. Irina *knows* Tea killed Pietro's father, Léon, who is also her own. Tea heard Irina's strangled cry while she was hitting Léon's face with a stone. Irina saw it all and, as a result, she must die. As a witness to Tea's crime, Irina's character works as a referent, as a sign of the Symbolic Order from which Tea is trying to escape in every way, and yet she is drowning and taking her son with her. The desire to know the secret of the woman's guilt is fundamentally sadistic and must also determine her punishment.[96] In accordance with the Law, Tea's guilt must be recognized. The first time, Tea killed for an unnamed desire, incomprehensible to her, and this is the way she will live henceforth.

Pietro's mother is a Medusean Tea, whose hair is compared to 'delle bisce morte' (CPM 12; 'dead snakes'). But since the snakes are dead, they are deprived of the deadly powers of the apotropaic Medusa. In fact, Tea is no longer a Medusa. She succumbs to a Perseus-Pietro, her son who is also the avenger once he discovers reality, because what he does now is done according to a reason, to a path of knowledge that, whatever it might have cost him, will not lead to the bottom, will not hopefully make him drown. Unlike Tea, who confesses in her notebook to not know why she does what she does, who claims that what happened and what she has done has taken place 'senza senso, senza che lo volesse davvero' (CPM 251; 'without sense, without her actually wanting it'), Pietro has a chance to not drown. Admitting to have also killed Léon, her only and true love, Tea denounces her lack of power before an evil that, far from excercising a cathartic power, indicates in her case only the misery of humans.

In Vinci the theme of a country divided in two, of the same blood symbolically divided in two, metaphorizes the shedding of blood in the mother–son relationsip in a complex ending to a personal tragedy. Pietro needs a separation from a mother-tiger, from a ferocious mother,

78   A Multitude of Women

and this will be a laceration marked not incidentally by the 1945 liberation of the country, the Motherland. Separation is implacable, atrocious, and physical, above all. Tea's end coincides with the end of the Civil War, a war that for Pietro is needed to put an end to an internal confict of his own multiple and unmediated desires towards the mother. The blood that will be shed in this case belongs to the *femme fatale*, to the devouring mother who wears a robe embroidered with a dragon figure, but it also belongs to Pietro, and as such it needs purification.[97] Tea is the *femme fatale* by definition, and Pietro watches her with his usual stone-like inflexibility (he is a *pietra*) while recording how 'le sue unghie laccate di rosso sono taglienti sulla pelle; lo sfiora, ma non lo abbraccia' (CPM 42; 'her red-lacquered nails are sharp on his skin; she brushes against him, but never hugs him'). Pietro is judgmental, and tries to find refuge from his mother's sin in the rigid ethic of children when he notes how 'la gente non ha da mangiare e sua madre sperpera fortune in mutande' (CPM 118; 'people are starving and his mother wastes a fortune on lingerie'); or when he shows his contempt for how Tea loves luxury and excess and wants to 'girare in abito da sera anche a dicembre in casa [sua]' (CPM 119; 'walk around with an evening gown even in December at home').

Perhaps Pietro has merely dreamt all this while he was in the boarding school in front of the *Isola dei Morti*; perhaps it was just one of his many nightmares. Pietro remains, nevertheless, alone, regardless of what level, what reading code we choose for the events of the story we have just read. Metaphorically speaking, Pietro remains isolated on a rock, like the tiny figure in Arnold Boecklin's *Die Toteninsel* of 1883. This is in fact the name in the novel that designates the island Pietro sees from the boarding school where Tea put him. Tea has exiled Pietro from their house, perhaps in an effort to defend her son from herself, from her own godlessness, from the awareness of the sin in which she lives; to avoid imposing on Pietro a life made of nightmares and horrendous rites. Pietro is destined to remain always alone as the small figure in Boecklin's painting whose stagnating atmosphere permeates the entire novel (CPM 29).

The Eden of the Proustian *vert paradis des amours infantines* no longer exists. It is an abyss, an eternal and boundless abyss, one of the Jungian symbols that designates the maternal figure. The child confers all the power on the maternal archetype set on a mythological backdrop and invests it with authority and numinosity, but only until the phase of disillusionment. At this stage, all the elements forming Pietro's world are turned upside-down, in a reversal of what seemed to be in the beginning, the beginning of his childhood, before he learned who his mother really was. According to Pietro, his mother is a 'Madonna bastarda' who does not alleviate pain but procures it. Tea exists only in the negative meaning of she who 'sorride il solito sorriso da troia' (CPM 105; 'smiles her usual whore-like smile'). His half-sister, Irina, had wisely warned him to close his eyes in order to not see all the ugly things (CPM 84), but she herself kept on seeing 'ugly things' even with her eyes closed. Pietro now knows that she was mistaken in her advice, because even with the eyes wide shut, 'restano le orecchie. Resta il cuore' (CPM 84; 'the ears remain, as does the heart').

In taking up the Morantian model (and challenge) of *Aracoeli* and *Il mondo salvato dai ragazzini*, Vinci successfully problematizes the binary opposition between good and evil proposed by Morante in the scheme of her characters and makes it an ambiguous business augmented by *noir* effects. Unlike Morante, who disengages children from the burden of the wretched world of adults, Vinci displays little mercy towards them. Without authorial *pietas* there cannot be a reversal of intention for Pietro. After his matricide, his most apparent evil action, Pietro is bound to remain deep down 'al fondo delle cose,' as in Dante's verses. Removing oneself from that abysmal place is an action Pietro can no longer perform.

From his mother Pietro has inherited fear. He is always afraid. In the Aristotelian tragedy, it is fear coupled with pity that effects the purgation of emotions and makes catharsis possible. If tragedy in the Aristotelian sense eliminates the evil afflicting human relations thanks to fear and pity, in Vinci's novel evil explodes in all its unspeakable violence. According to Aristotle's tenets, for the tragedy to unfold, agents must also possess certain qualities of character and thought. It is chiefly their action, however, that determines their final happiness, or the reverse. Here, the inability to reach happiness is, as noted earlier, motivated by the author's lack of *pietas* towards the main tragic agents of *Come prima delle madri*, Tea and Pietro. Hence, Vinci's novel appears to be an unfinished tragedy because, without *pietas*, it cannot contemplate either *catharsis* or *agnorisis* for Tea and Pietro. *Come prima delle madri* plays on the effect created by fear and only the *possibility* of mercy, two passions implicit in any human relation. Fear, enhanced by the dissolution of social ties, and mercy, a passion that inspires social relations, show how the excess of love, the 'overwhelming might of passion which puts one human being wholly at the mercy of another,' according to Jung,[98] can be actually a danger as immense as hatred, as in one of Morante's best-known theorems.

The dynamic interactions during war times between a mother who was too young and a child who grew up too quickly facilitates the equation that Vinci wants to make clear. Evil is taught to children by those they thought loved them, the most unexpected ones. The might of passion has put Pietro at the mercy of her mother, but evil is present in both; it has entered Pietro through the umbilical cord. Consequently, the child is not exempt from the awful game of excessive, if pernicious, love. The mirage of universal harmony will remain an inaccessible dream. The fruit taken away from Adam and Eve is forbidden *and* secret to humans. The depiction of familial relations[99] remains a problematic business that is not to be attributed merely to feminist readings of the family plots. The Morantian tenet about the uncorrupted world and the innocence of children, which Vinci seems to initially agree with in *Come prima delle madri*, is revealed to be an idealistic approach to the 'innocence' of nature and human beings.

The Prison-House of Marriage: Simone de Beauvoir and Elena Ferrante Discuss Abandonment

> Rovinare la vita di una donna non è forse l'ambizione di qualunque uomo?[100]
> That specific stone in the stomach pain when you lose something you haven't got round to valuing? Why is the measure of love loss?[101]

In her novel *I giorni dell'abbandono* Elena Ferrante offers a moment of complete clash with the literary mother she entrusts, Simone de Beauvoir, and her text *La femme rompue*.[102] The failed identification of the protagonist, Olga, with Monique at the end of her agony indicates how Ferrante the author, starting from a similar context of betrayal and helplessness for her protagonist, brings her 'version' of the story to a close. Unlike de Beauvoir's condemnation of Monique, Ferrante renegotiaties the terms of the prison confinement that Olga lived during her marriage up until her husband's abandonment. Using the space of the house as a political site for Olga, Ferrante deconstructs the behaviour exemplified by Monique's character. Beauvoir's own explanatory statements about the prescriptive passiveness of her character as a didactic anti-model did not sound convincing to Ferrante, just as they did not convince other readers of *La femme rompue*. In her daughter-text, Ferrante rereads Monique and her story, but especially rereads de Beauvoir's failure to perceive how by constructing with specific didactic purpose the character of Monique she did not anticipate the complete identification of so many women readers who, still today, suffer their partners' betrayal. De Beauvoir failed to see the intense disillusionment, anger, depression, and self-loathing that eventually lead to a (positive) departure of the woman from her former confinement.[103] Ferrante, though, also interrogates de Beauvoir's basic condescending mode in depicting Monique without compassion. And this is the striking difference Ferrante brings to the story, which could have otherwise been read, or misread, as an ordinary tale of a modern Medea in downtown Turin. In other words, with her powerful rereading Ferrante challenges the literary mother and her authority, showing how Sandra Gilbert's theories about a difficult literary daughteronomy can be reread when the texts of daughters do question the outcomes of the mother's texts. The prison-house of marriage and Olga's self-imposed 'house arrest'[104] thus receive different endings that depart from Beauvoir's text to arrive at geographically bound, societally explainable resolutions.

> Un pomeriggio d'aprile, subito dopo pranzo, mio marito mi annunciò che voleva lasciarmi. Lo fece mentre sparecchiavamo la tavola, i bambini litigavano come al solito nell'altra stanza, il cane sognava brontolando accanto al termosifone. Mi disse che era confuso, stava vivendo momenti di stanchezza, di insoddisfazione, forse di viltà. Parlò a lungo dei nostri quindici anni di matrimonio, dei figli, e ammise che non aveva nulla da rimproverare né a loro né a me ... Poi si assunse la colpa di tutto quello che stava accadendo e si chiuse con cautela la porta di casa alle spalle lasciandomi impietrita accanto al lavandino.[105]
>
> (One April afternoon, right after lunch, my husband announced that he wanted to leave me. He did it while we were clearing the table; the children were quarreling as usual in the next room, the dog was dreaming, growling beside the radiator. He told me he was confused, that he was having terrible moments of weariness, of dissatisfaction, perhaps of cowardice. He talked for a long time about our fifteen years of marriage, about the children, and admitted that he had nothing to reproach us with, neither them nor me ... Then he assumed the blame for everything that was happening and closed the front door carefully behind him, leaving me turned to stone beside the sink.)[106]

This is the rather cruel beginning of *I giorni dell'abbandono* by Elena Ferrante. I say rather cruel because in this novel tragedy happens casually – she 'didn't see it coming' – as the common English expression puts it. Into the humdrum everyday life of Italian homemaker Olga, while the children are quarrelling, her husband drops a bomb: he is leaving. Mario announces his abandonment as a matter-of-fact decision. His wife, turned to stone, remains frozen by the sink, incapable of uttering a single word. Olga thinks she knows him, she thinks she knows his 'quiet feelings' and his need for family rituals. She cannot believe he wants to leave her for good. She expresses the incredulity typical of one who is unwittingly passing from one stage of life to another, adrift beyond her own will and decision. She still believes that Mario must be going through 'uno dei quei momenti che si raccontano nei libri, quando un personaggio reagisce in modo occasionalmente eccessivo al normale scontento di vivere' (GA 8; 'one of those moments that you read in books, when a character reacts in an unexpectedly extreme way to the normal discontents of living,' DA 10). But this shift is seismic as Mario abandons her, and she abandons herself for an entire summer, just like Morante's Elisa and Di Lascia's Chiara before her did when confronted with *smagamento*, with their parents' betrayal.

I giorni dell'abbandono gives the tones of a Greek tragedy to a banal event. So, what are Olga's choices when faced with the quite telling element of her kitchen, the *sink*, when dealing with Mario leaving? She metonymically 'sinks in.' Olga's story, one of an abandoned thirty-eight-year-old woman during a rather gloomy summer in Turin, is the gripping account of a brief and painful journey from one stage to another in a woman's life. It is a psychological travel/travail forced upon her and her body, upon her 'situation.' This travail will eventually mean the re-conquering of an Olga she had long lost, while drawing renewed intellectual energies at the end of the summer. From being married to being separated, from living with somebody to facing life alone, from being fictitiously secure to being practically on the edge of madness, Olga gains certainty about her own strength and how much she can count on herself.

In considering Ferrante's novel, I focus mainly on three issues: (a) Italian women authors rewriting a female-authored text, here Simone de Beauvoir's *La femme rompue*, within a literary palimpsest in which male authority is not influential in its composition; (b) abandonment as a trope; and (c) linguistic and narrative techniques that signal a different stage in women's writing in which obedience to previous literary examples is no longer deemed necessary and female characters can afford to demonstrate their emotions without fear of sounding weak or impotent.

These topics interest me as examples of the ways in which tradition and originality work in writing palimpsests; of how authors deconstruct personal and/or historical myths; how they revisit the notion of authority on, and over, the female body; finally, how they strategically disseminate (new) meaning while appropriating *only* male jargon used in traditional patriarchal literature. Ferrante makes innovative use of all these territories to construct a realist novel, *I giorni dell'abbandono*, that functions as *pendant* and commentary on *La femme rompue*. Interestingly enough, it also works as a countertext to Ferrante's own previous novel, *L'amore molesto*,[107] in which Amalia – the protagonist's mother – abandons her husband rather than being abandoned. The situation in *L'amore molesto* is reversed with respect to *I giorni dell'abbandono*: Amalia leaves her husband with her three daughters. She also 'leaves' her reputation, while gaining a presumed freedom. Like the *poverella* in *I giorni dell'abbandono* to which a strikingly similar portrait connects her, she too drowns in the sea near Minturno. In *L'amore molesto* the focus is on the conventional treatment of the failed mother–daughter relationship in the juxtaposition of the two characters, which is only stressed and reconfirmed by the death of the first on the birthday of the daughter. In *I giorni dell'abbandono*, instead, Olga does not have a physical mother, but she has at least four literary and imaginative ones to deal with, and to these she will give honourable burial: Simone de Beauvoir the philosopher, Monique the passive Parisian homemaker, Elsa Morante the novelist of Southern families, and the suicidal *poverella*.

'Mythology is the very best school in the training of silence'.[108]
Rewriting a Tragedy

Until recently, rewriting a text often meant for a woman the process of rereading the text of a male author, thus positing her work in an uncertain position in which issues regarding her originality would almost inevitably reconfirm the genotext as the authoritative (and, needless to say, *better*) one.[109] In this process, the canonicity of the male author's authoritative text would be basically reinstated. In Ferrante's rereading of de Beauvoir's novella *La femme rompue*, I see a change in the palimpsest of texts that is virtually 'historic.' Let's use this term in the sense that this adjective represents a landmark innovation. Not only does Ferrante's manoeuvre exclude male models; Ferrante rewrites de Beauvoir's text without any of the fears that might accompany the rereading of an authoritative and successful woman's work. The new text is never 'innocent,' as Gérard Genette with Umberto Eco and Linda Hutcheon remind us, since it inevitably conduces to modifications of the hypotext. But gender can play an important role in these modifications, since, if it's true that it is the text to be read and rewritten, it is also true that the writing subject, as the gender-perspective of this literary action, is important in the interpretation/reception and (consequent) rewriting of the genotext.

Ferrante does not invoke de Beauvoir's text in order to elaborate on feminist theses, nor merely to re-establish its character's passiveness. Instead, Ferrante offers an analysis of the power of conventions and constraints that still linger for women in Italian society, the speculation that this is particularly a fact of life for women from the South, or for migrant women displaced in their new space, and she effectively rebels against de Beauvoir's openly stated authorial weight in forcing the readers' interpretation of her character. De Beauvoir wrote of her surprise at the lack of understanding by women readers of her tragic-allegoric construction of Monique. She could not, apparently, bear the fact that she had somewhat failed in projecting the image of the darkness for these women who, instead of benefiting from Monique's own blindness and didactically learning from her failure to reach emancipation from a situation of psychological subjection, all empathized with her.[110] While the philosopher de Beauvoir wanted to didactically explain how Monique arrived at such 'darkness,'[111] and use this image as a metaphor for the ontological ambiguity of existence, the exclusively novelist Ferrante pragmatically prefers to fictionalize the specific contradiction of women's situation. This split 'between freedom and alienation,' according to Toril Moi, 'is caused by the conflict between their status as free and autonomous human beings and the fact that they are socialized in a world in which men consistently cast them as Other to their One, as objects to their subjects.'[112]

In both her first two novels,[113] Ferrante's treatment of abandonment is tangible, the chaos is real, not allegorical, and there are no guidelines selected for women's betterment. In *I giorni dell'abbandono*, more clearly than in *L'amore molesto* – a novel in which many subtopics, the daughter–mother relationship being another salient theme, were enmeshed – Ferrante makes a precise statement in the choice of the text 'previous' to her own. She proves her concrete involvement with her own character – one born out of rebellion to those 'broken women.' Rather than de Beauvoir's philosophical detachment and contempt for Monique, in Ferrante's novel it is Olga's self-contradiction, or split, 'specific to women living under patriarchy'[114] that surfaces with all its linguistic, semantic, corporeal annexes.

In Ferrante's novel, from de Beauvoir's contempt, which, as we shall see, readers of *La femme rompue* generally do not share, Olga disengages herself. Consider the transmutation of de Beauvoir's preoccupation with the ideologies related to feminism and independence over the individuality of the character; Monique was not only Maurice's victim, she was also the *philosopher's victim*, and little hope is left for her at the end of the text. Ferrante is in full knowledge of the fact that women are not considered 'whole beings,' to speak in Moira Gatens's terms. Thus, ethical considerations pertain to Olga's role of complement, of 'appendage,' to Mario. Instead of despising Olga for her condition of societal 'imperfection,' as she emerges from culturization as an incomplete being,[115] Ferrante empathizes with her, avoiding victimization and condemnation and pragmatically looking for a position in society for her.

Self-enlightenment for Olga, though, occurs only after what de Beauvoir's Monique marks in her 'Monday, December 14 entry of *La femme rompue* as '[l]'affreuse descente au fond de la tristesse' (FR 203; 'the hideous descent into the abyss of sadness,' DW 205). *I giorni dell'abbandono* becomes the painful narrative of Olga's fall into the abyss. Nothing is spared her. Nothing is spared us readers, as well. The fall is useful, though, only when a cathartic moment follows. Upper-middle-bourgeois Monique, cornered in her suffocating Parisian apartment, is not given this chance or others. Perhaps not in an established feminist way, but in a way that we can understand as readers, Olga will succeed instead. The process of redemption and eventual resurrection/emancipation from Olga's abyss will be total, but not streamlined in a symbolic manner, since we will not be spared *any* blows. What is the significance of such a literary act in 2002? That biological and social conditioning is, and remains, a form of enslavement even now? That this too, like Morante's works, is a 'misogynist novel'?[116] My answer to both questions cannot be but negative, and I will explain my reasoning.

Ferrante's novel is one that 'mette in crisi,' puts into question women (and feminist) readers in its reading.[117] It entertains an active conversation with a previous text that has, in turn, a questionable treatment of an abandoned woman (even if with de Beauvoir's best intentions), but which feminist tradition has already distinguished as authoritative in its own right. We cannot overlook, in fact, that it is the protagonist's own French (female) teacher who gave her *La femme rompue* to read in 1978, back when she was attending high school with ideals of professional affirmation as a writer (GA 20; DA 21). Authority is transmitted still, but with a slightly different twist as it originates from yet another woman. It can be accepted and discussed and refuted within the same parameters in which it was conceived.

Medea and Abandonment: A Mediterranean Wife

A wife left by her husband for someone else is probably a daily happenstance, not to mention the stuff of melodrama and soap operas. How extraordinary can the ordinary story of Olga be? And why today do we need still to talk about stories like this? Wives abandoned by their husbands abound in literature as in real life. When speaking about abandoned wives in literature, though, it becomes difficult not to deal with myth, with the *Ur*–abandoned wife, Medea. The most famous of all these wives, Medea sees her tragic story repeated from time immemorial, from Euripides and Ovid to Corneille and Eugene O'Neill. It is not until Christa Wolf's version of the myth, however, that we see Medea's torment suddenly appearing in the garb of an 'everyday' life experience: being left by your beloved husband for another woman.[118] Wolf speaks often of the usefulness of myths to represent the present in the process called in German *Vergangenheitsbewältigung*, or 'the process of getting over the past.' She utilizes myth because 'it provides a model that's open enough to incorporate our own present experiences while giving us a distance from our subject that usually only time can make possible.' Also, Wolf claims that the inevitable presence of reality in myths makes them a perfect scene for examining the behaviour of 'ancient figures' in which 'people of the modern world' are recognizable while 'lifting from the banality of every day.'[119]

Wolf's statements apply to the banality of Olga's everyday life. Like Medea, Olga is a displaced woman with a displaced identity. She is an exile from Naples, living in Turin, where her husband studied engineering. She simply followed him after enduring sacrifices and hard times to let him finish his degree at the prestigious *Politecnico* and take up a job. Olga lives in a place where she can hardly be who she was in her youth. Because of her personal dislike for the strong display of emotions of which she was made the object during her youth, Olga has repressed her atavistic, Southern woman's pathos. Until that summer she has thus repressed her *Napolitanità* and has acquired manners that are not entirely her own in order to fit in with the mentality of the place and please her husband, Mario. Like Medea, Olga lives between two value systems, embodied by her homeland, Naples, and the Northern town of Turin, both capitals at one time, but of two entirely different reigns and relative cultures. In the transition from Colchis to the rich and advanced Corinth, from crime-ridden Naples to industrialized Turin, the situations appear to be strikingly similar. As in the case made by Wolf about Medea, Olga's boundary 'can easily become an abyss if the person in question isn't ready or able to conform to her new circumstances, which her hosts think of as superior to and more advanced than her older ones; though this doesn't necessarily mean they're more humane.'[120] In a sentimental diaspora, and in order to live with Mario, Olga has left her homeland, Naples, along with its noise and familiar sounds. In the strenuous process of 'conforming to her new circumstances' she has lost her power. Like Medea, she is a foreigner in another land, and she is just as passionate. They share a Mediterranean origin, a symbolic reference to passion in literature that should not go overlooked, and it should cause little surprise that, at times during the reading, we construct a parallel between these two figures.

When she left the South, Olga made a conscious decision to abandon it also intellectually. She has constructed a whole new set of behavioural patterns. Olga's traumatic memory of her Neapolitan background, one in which the South takes on a human condition, a state of mind, made of loud feelings and hurtful phrases,[121] prevented her from making the classic 'scenata' ('spectacle') of herself, five years before, when she witnessed a kiss between Mario and then teen-aged Carla. Also, now that, unbeknownst to Olga, Mario has left her for good, she refuses to give in to her *Napolitanità*. While she is in bed, flashbacks appear to the protagonist; other moments of dissatisfaction her husband has gone through begin to resurface. In fact, not *her* moments of dissatisfaction, of course, only Mario's emerge in her thoughts: once, when they were still dating, then another time five years earlier, when he had become reacquainted with Gina, a colleague from the Polytechnic school. On that occasion, Mario had started to do tutorial work with Carla, the daughter of his widowed friend. When Olga saw Carla one day kissing her husband on the lips rather than on the cheeks, she started worrying, realizing that the danger to her marriage was Carla, and not Gina. In an Italian version of *American Beauty*, the girl, according to the protagonist, was gauging the import of her own sexual power over men by the reaction of Mario, who 'la guardava come si guarda da una zona d'ombra una parete bianca su cui batte il sole' (GA 10; 'he looked at her as one looks from a gray area at a white wall struck by the sun,' DA 12). Initially, then, Olga tries to maintain an upper-class, subdued, rational behaviour that greatly resembles that of de Beauvoir's Monique:

> J'ai fini par céder. Puisque j'ai adopté une attitude compréhensive, conciliante, je dois m'y tenir. Ne pas le heurter de front. Si je lui gâche son

aventure, il l'embellira à distance, il aura des regrets. Si je lui permets de la vivre 'correctement' il s'en fatiguera vite. C'est ce qu'Isabelle m'a affirmé. Je me répète: 'Patience.' (FR 140)
('In the end I gave way. Since I have adopted an understanding, kindly attitude I must stick to it. No head-on collision with him. If I spoil his affair for him distance will make it seem charming – he will regret it. If I let him 'live it decently' he will soon get tired of it. That's what Isabelle assures me. I repeat to myself, *Patience*. [DW 142; emphasis in translation])

In accordance with her acquired Turinese role as wife of a professional, and rejecting the noise and verbal violence of her upbringing, Olga has opted for a behaviour that allows her to 'allungare il più possibile i [suoi] tempi di reazione riempiendoli di sguardi perplessi, sorrisi incerti' (GA 10; 'draw out as long as possible the time for reaction, filling it with puzzled looks, uncertain smiles,' DA 12). By delaying her reaction and display of grief, Olga had always hoped to defray the consequences of her instinctive passionate personality. Moving to the places – Turin, for one – where Mario's job would take them, she steadfastly learned how to keep that attitude permanently, using her self-control as a defence against unknown locals as much as the unwanted memory of traumatic scenes of her childhood, of those 'racconti femminili di sentimenti finiti, cosa succede quando colme d'amore si resta non più amate, senza niente'(GA 15; 'female stories of the end of love, what happens when the lover is no longer loved, is left with nothing,' DA 16). Reminding herself of how Mario came back to her that time five years before, in the heated and humid Turinese summer, Olga initially tells herself that '[e]ra solo una questione di giorni, poi tutto si sarebbe sistemato' (GA 12; '[i]t was only a matter of days, then everything would return to normal,' DA 13). Even now, Olga initially hopes to dilute and subdue the heart-wrenching pain of feeling abandoned. Illusion and dilution travel together in Olga's mental space.

In the days after Mario's abandonment, Olga colours her rare conversations with her husband with an 'affettuosa riflessività' (GA 15; 'affectionate thoughtfulness,' DA 16) in the old belief according to which wives must understand moments of malaise in the life of their husbands. De Beauvoir's Monique, in the beginning, does mental exercises to behave in this way. As her worst fears begin to solidify, Olga soon cultivates feelings of anguish and anger behind the calm posture that she imposes on her body. Figures from her rejected Neapolitan past, a past that she, like Delia before her, has not forgotten but wishes to forget, reappear, like the lady from her neighborhood. Both characters, Delia and Olga, Ferrante notes,

'Writing Is Always Playing with the Mother's Body'   89

have been built in similar ways.[122] Delia and Olga are both women who, since childhood, have exercised a self-reflexive version of what Ferrante calls 'la sorveglianza' (LF 113), a form of psychological 'surveillance' upon themselves and their own feelings. Indeed, these are women who have mastered self-control, the only weapon to come out of the *frantumaglia*, of that particular complex of moods, passion, and depression leading to a destructive despair. While the *poverella* did not exercise any *sorveglianza* upon herself, Olga will. The South comes back in full force through its reification in the figure of the poor abandoned lady, a lady who, according to Olga's mother, had lost all her body fluids, all her softness only to become 'secca come un'alice salata' (GA 15; 'as dry as a salted anchovy,' DA 16).[123] The poor lady had three children, and though sometimes laden with groceries, she was always generous with candies for little Olga. We are told that this lady had the looks of a woman who, although burdened with duties, was nevertheless happy with her work and with life in general. At some point, her husband leaves her for a woman from Pescara. The woman started crying every night. Everybody could hear her crying, a loud cry, a sort of 'rantolo che sfondava ad ariete le pareti' (GA 14; 'sobbing that broke through the walls like a battering ram,' DA 15), frightening little Olga. The abandonment of this woman soon became the talk of Olga's mother and her seamstresses while sewing, the woman having lost her name to become the 'poverella' (GA 15; 'that poor woman,' DA 14). Her grief disgusted Olga as a young girl to the point that, today, her controlled behaviour is partly due to the traumatic memory of that woman,[124] as she recalls that '[a]nche per via di quel ricordo, seguitai a comportarmi con Mario esibendo un'affettuosa riflessività' (GA 15; '[p]artly because of this memory, I continued to behave toward Mario with an affectionate thoughtfulness,' DA 16). Olga knows that Mario is trying to make her understand the necessity of breaking up their marriage, but she does not give in to his manipulative efforts, and her behaviour remains impassive for a while. One morning, though, the temptation of asking Mario, 'Ti sei innamorato di un'altra donna?' (GA 17; 'Are you in love with another woman?' DA 18) is too strong, and Olga is only impatient to hear him say so. But at the very moment when Mario's affirmative answer reaches her ears, it becomes impossible to keep any assumed posture. Olga loses control, her *sorveglianza* goes down the drain, and she emits guttural screams, as if the acquired values of her adult *benessere* would show all their artificiality in the face of Mario's abandonment. Now she is feeling 'in petto un dolore lungo che mi stava privando di ogni sentimento. Me ne resi conto quando mi accorsi che non avevo reazioni di fronte a ciò che gli stava succedendo' (GA 18; 'in my breast a protracted pain that was stripping away every feeling. I realized this when I noticed that I had no reaction to what was happening to him,' DA 19).

Unlike de Beauvoir's paralysed Monique, Olga realizes that a quick reaction might do her a lot of good: 'Dovevo reagire, dovevo organizzarmi. Non cedere, mi dissi, non precipitare in avanti' (GA 20; 'I had to react, had to take charge of myself. Don't give in, I said to myself, don't crash headlong,' DA 20). More to the point, 'Non fare come la poverella, non consumarti in lacrime. Evita di assomigliare alle donne in frantumi di un libro famoso della tua adolescenza' (GA 20; 'Don't act like the *poverella*, don't be consumed by tears. Don't be like the women destroyed of a famous book of your adolescence,' DA 20). With this dreaded image from her childhood, Olga alludes for the first time to the essential text for the construction of the present novel, *La femme rompue*:

> Ne rividi la copertina in ogni dettaglio. Me lo aveva imposto la mia insegnante di francese quando le avevo detto con troppa irruenza, con ingenua passione, che volevo fare la scrittrice, fu nel 1978, più di vent'anni fa ... Ma quando le avevo restituito il volume, mi era venuta la frase superba: queste donne sono stupide. Signore colte, di condizione agiata, si rompevano come ninnoli nelle mani dei loro uomini distratti. Mi erano sembrate sentimentalmente sciocche, io volevo essere diversa, *volevo scrivere storie di donne dalle molte risorse, donne di parole invincibili, non un manuale della moglie abbandonata con l'amore perduto in cima ai pensieri* ... E poi amavo la scrittura di chi ti fa affacciare da ogni rigo per guardare di sotto e sentire la vertigine della profondità, la nerezza dell'inferno ...
>
> Di quel libro dell'adolescenza mi vennero in mente le poche frasi che all'epoca avevo mandato a memoria: io sono pulita sono vera gioco a carte scoperte. No, mi dissi, erano affermazioni di deragliamento. Mettere sempre le virgole, tanto per cominciare, dovevo ricordarmene. Chi pronuncia parole così, ha già varcato la linea, sente la necessità dell'autoesaltazione e perciò si approssima allo smarrimento ...
>
> Via da me quelle immagini, quel linguaggio. *Via da me le donne spezzate.* Mentre Otto correva di qua e di là scegliendo con cura i luoghi dove urinare, sentii in ogni angolo del corpo i graffi dell'abbandono sessuale, *il pericolo di affogare nel disprezzo di me e nella nostalgia di lui.* (GA 20–1, 22, 23; emphasis added)

(I saw the cover again in every detail. My French teacher had assigned it when I told her too impetuously, with ingenuous passion, that I wanted to be a writer. It was 1978, more than twenty years earlier ... But when I gave her back the volume, I made an arrogant statement: these women are stupid. Cultured women, in comfortable circumstances, they broke like knick-knacks in the hands of their straying men. They seemed to me sentimental fools: I wanted to be different, *I wanted to write stories about women with resources, women of invincible words, not a manual for the abandoned wife with her lost love at the top of her thoughts* ... And then I loved the writers who made you look through every line, to gaze downward and feel the vertigo of the depths, the blackness of inferno ...

Of that book from my adolescence the few sentences I had memorized at the time came to mind: I am clean I am true I am playing with my cards on the table. No, I said to myself, those were affirmations of derailment. To begin with, I had better remember, always put in the commas. A person who utters such words has already crossed the line, feels the need for self-exaltation and therefore approaches confusion ...

Get rid of those images, that language. *Get rid of the women destroyed.* While Otto ran here and there, carefully choosing places to urinate, I felt over every inch of my body the scratches of sexual abandonment, *the danger of drowning in scorn for myself and nostalgia for him.* [DA 20–1, 22, 23; emphasis added])

By retrieving the memory of a book she loved but whose women she disapproved of for their weakness and lack of *sorveglianza*, Olga registers her reaction to *La femme rompue* and, by default, to Monique's bourgeois passiveness. Olga understands her, and is only too aware of her own dangerous likeness to Monique in that very moment. The danger of drowning in self-contempt like the *poverella* – and Amalia in *L'amore molesto* perhaps – is present, though, and she needs to react. Why do these women drown even if different forms of abandonment cause their psychological abyss?

Neapolitan (Plastic) Language

Ferrante's masterful narrative construction of Olga's split personality through the utilization of neo-standard Italian and Neapolitan dialect define the plastic possibilities of Italian language at their best. Neo-standard Italian and Neapolitan dialect register and compose two different Olgas living an intense state of suspension in the span of one summer. More than any other feature, the layering of language and dialect in Olga's indirect speech, in her useless silent dialogue with Mario and other characters, and particularly in her soliloquies, becomes the most convincing expressive tool of the novel. It shows in all its agility how Italian and dialect underscore her dramatic transformation. While Chiara in *Passaggio in ombra* spends one summer retrieving but not modifying the legacy of her past, Olga will, thus satisfying Ferrante's desire/necessity to transform de Beauvoir's ambiguous legacy. From controlled to obscene, careless, and rough, Olga's intense language[125] announces better than other elements (time and space, for instance) her change of state. Language is translated into literature, the one she is trying to retrieve in life through her vague recollections of high-school readings to find evidence of the fracture that has broken her heart. Speech functions as an instrument of reaction and empowerment against the fear of her growing sense of oddity before the succession of events. Olga is utterly aware of her position dangerously nearing those of Monique and the *poverella*. As we have seen, she previously held both as anti-models for the construction of her identity, one because she was too passive in her bourgeois attitude, the other because she was powerless in her passionate and tragic love for her husband. Far from being composed and semantically neutral, as Monique's language often appears to be even in the original French version, Olga's is entirely sexualized. The 'danger of drowning in self-contempt' becomes almost a sad reality for a while. While the feelings of abandonment might be the same as Monique's and the *poverella*'s, Olga can employ expressive tools to make her grief verbally tangible. The only image she can construct, however, is not the literary one she dreamt of during her high-school years. Her creativity is not related to her writing, but only to Mario making love with his new woman (GA 28; DA 27). The diary serves her as evidence of her madness, of her awareness that 'l'oscenità poteva levare faville di follia, se nasceva da una bocca controllata come la mia' (GA 22–3; 'obscenity could raise sparks of madness if it came from a mouth as controlled as mine,' DA 22). Classic semiotics assumes that, for discourse, meaning comes from the person to whom it is addressed. For a while, Olga will be speaking to no one. And during this rejection of discourse, Olga betrays her *diktat* of order and control, epitomized by her quiet voice, tones, and speech. Like Delia before her, Olga had decided to no longer admit the language of the mother, her dialect, that is, a language that is far from semiotic, and in which, as Giancarlo Lombardi recalls, 'so many arguments marked the life in the family.'[126] The first to change is Olga's discourse:

> Cominciai a cambiare. Nel giro di un mese persi l'abitudine di truccarmi con cura, passai da un *linguaggio elegante*, attento a non urtare il prossimo, a

un modo di esprimermi sempre sarcastico, interrotto da risate un po' sguaiate. Piano piano, malgrado la mia resistenza, cedetti anche al *linguaggio osceno.* (GA 27; emphasis added)
(I began to change. In the course of a month I lost the habit of putting on makeup carefully, I went from using a *refined language*, attentive to the feelings of others, to a sarcastic way of expressing myself, punctuated by coarse laughter. Slowly, in spite of my resistance, I also gave in *to obscenity*. [DA 26; emphasis added])

From a 'refined language' Olga's discourse begins to utilize one that is 'obscene' within one month of Mario's abandonment. Obscene language, if previously used by damned female characters, the traditional literary whores, the witches, the forsaken females, has not been considered a linguistic mimesis for the representation of the good married woman's character. Olga's language shifts to *pornolálos*, which would almost naturally appropriate a register traditionally the domain of male individuals of low rank. She deterritorializes hegemonic language, as a quiet, rational speech no longer fits her emotional state. Her linguistic terrorism is a need, not a choice, as she is trying to subvert a pre-constituted system of power, something very close to the Law of the Father. In so doing, Olga rejects temporarily also what were her female graces and virtues. Her enormous amount of sacrifice and time invested for the well-being of her husband, the 'breadwinner' of the family, has proved to be so wasted that she feels it right to reject her own sacred house-bound femininity in language, as in the looks she now projects, since these have been in turn rejected by Mario. Only in novels (written by men, usually) can women not request anything in return in a marriage! If Olga's self-control and femininity have been constructed with time, sacrifice, and wished-for distance from her home, her language now feels free to be as crude, rough, and hurtful as her wound.

Also Olga's biological body betrays her own *diktat.* Bodily reactions can hardly be controlled when one finds oneself under psychological and emotional pressure. If it's true, as de Beauvoir writes, that 'body is not a *thing*, it is a situation ... the instrument of our grasp upon the world, a limiting factor for our project,'[127] the lack of grasp of what is happening in her otherwise rather 'normal' life has the effect of creating an enormous pressure on Olga's body, an emotional volcano. Pressure plunges into the body, which reacts in turn by abandoning any cultural guard, any imposed societal behaviour. Her bodily reaction forces the change in her language, which, in turn, embodies her emotional wounds by losing control. Hers is '[n]ot a language of the desiring exchange of messages or objects that are transmitted in a social contract of communication and desire beyond want, but a language of want, of the fear that edges up to it and runs along its edges,' notes Julia Kristeva about the abject and language.[128] Her condition of *labilità* brings Olga to a split between thinking of Mario and trying to keep up with her house chores (GA 29; DA 26), those 'daily tasks' patriarchal wives repeat endlessly, that keep them from insanity as a sad anchor to everyday activity. Frantic and careless, Olga starts leading a crazy life in which things happen with no sense, and in its deconstructive nature, her language reflects her schizophrenia in dealing with her split and her attempt to reach an epistemology of the self through her experience. Her body undergoes actual physical malaise, which accompanies every action of her day and is worded with a crude lexicon, fitting and mimetic of Olga's situation:

> Sentii le palpebre pesanti, un mal di schiena, la voglia di piangere. Mi controllai gli slip, erano macchiati di sangue. Pronunciai una *brutta oscenità nel mio dialetto*, e con un tale scatto rabbioso della voce, che temetti che i bambini mi avessero sentito. Mi lavai ancora, mi cambiai. (GA 40; emphasis added)
> (My eyelids were heavy, my back ached, I wanted to cry. I looked at my underpants, they were stained with blood. I pronounced an *ugly obscenity in my dialect*, and with such an angry snap in my voice that I was afraid the children had heard me. I washed again, changed. [DA 38; emphasis added])

Olga retrieves 'obscenities from [her] dialect' in spite of herself. This uncalled-for use of obscenities seems to elicit a sense of freedom from all the behavioural enslavement of those years in which no dialect could be used, in which no arguments could be tolerated.[129] Olga has broken the system of sounds, images, perceptions, and movements that coordinated her existence. At this point, she has abandoned any modesty distinctive of the 'good wife,' and speaks[130] like the workers who change the lock to the door she significantly won't be able to open for one full day and night. After the locksmiths leave, after they tell her with allusive remarks how more delicate the new bolt is, and how she needs to pay attention to how she inserts the key in the bolt, Olga wonders on the meaning of their allusions to keys and bolts. The verb *chiavare*, literally *serrare, chiudere a chiave*,[131] has in Italian a rather clear and oft-used figurative sexual meaning. It is actually used more for its sexual meaning than for the specific notion locksmiths attach to it. Olga's imagery is far from Monique's bourgeois and almost asexual discourse, but the locksmiths' image is far too attractive for a ranting crazy lady who no longer has her lawfully wedded interlocutor. While Mario is gone forever, she remains with her fear of dealing with other male presences and erupts in a frenzy grounded in her mental wanderings about herself and her looks. Her speech is a highly charged one.[132] While tension builds up to the point of madness, when Olga is on the verge of throwing herself from the balcony of her Turinese apartment, the image of the *poverella* who drowned herself at Capo Miseno resurfaces 'rigida come una statua sepolcrale' (GA 47; 'stiff as a sepulchral statue,' DA 44')[133] from Olga's memory[134] to save her, 'per trattener [la] per un lembo della gonna' (GA 47; 'to grab [her] by the hem of [her] skirt,' DA 42).

There is also another connection between Olga and the poor lady, as for Olga, at an early age, writing became an instinctual need to circumvent the destiny of the *poverella*, while listening to her terrible fate under the table of her mother's workshop. Oral narratives are the ones by which Olga soon in life learns how not to be without a man. As with Isma, the narrating character in Assia Djebar's *A Sister to Scheherazade*,[135] Olga's first schooling was her mother's oral narratives along with those of her seamstresses. 'Cucire i panni addosso' in Italian means 'to gossip,' which in Olga's mother's workshop has taken a literal form: '[r]acconto e maldicenza e cucito: io ascoltavo' (GA 47: '[s]tories and gossip and sewing: I listened,' DA 44). While Assia Djebar's narrating character Isma would listen to gossips in the harem that she would eventually leave, but that her 'auditive memory' would never forget in order to retell the stories she heard and give freedom to women, Olga listened to these women underneath the sewing table, trying to do the opposite of Isma, trying to forget, as she innately knew they were marked by society. Neapolitan 'harems' would know more constrictions than the official ones.[136] Olga has memorized the phrases of those romantic tragedies, phrases that would signify the threshold between life and death, 'in bilico come un equilibrista' (GA 47; 'suspended like a tightrope walker,' DA 44). Trying to be true to the promise she made to herself, never to endure such a fate, meant also distancing herself from the image of abandoned women, of unhappy wives: 'away from me those broken women,' as Olga claims in the beginning.

The empty wanderings in the streets of Turin – a city that now looks like a fortress to Olga – are merely a feared situation in which she is now losing herself in spite of her efforts. Although she is lucidly trying not to repeat other abandoned women's path, her involuntary visual recollection brings her to repeat physically the wandering of displaced women, the breaking inside into pieces or, better, using the Neapolitan term Ferrante remembers from her mother's lexicon, the *frantumaglia* (LF 108), roughly a 'psychological shattering.' This is a word Ferrante's mother would use to express 'un malessere non altrimenti definibile' ('an indefinable sense of malaise); the word 'rimandava a una folla di cose eterogenee nella testa, detriti su un'acqua limacciosa del cervello' (LF 108; 'would remind her of a crowd of heterogenous things in her head, like debris on the slimy water of her brain'). As it happens to Olga in the novel, this *frantumaglia* is an inexplicable state of mind that Ferrante interprets as 'l'effetto del senso di perdita, quando si ha la certezza che tutto ciò che ci sembra stabile, duraturo, un ancoraggio per la nostra vita, andrà a unirsi a quel paesaggio di detriti che ci pare di vedere' (LF 109; 'the effect of the sense of loss when one reaches the certainty that everything that seems stable, lasting, an anchor for our life, will go to that landscape of debris that we think we are seeing'). She notes further, 'si può continuare nell'elenco ... [m]a nel caso è utile per spiegare che se dovessi dire cos'è il dolore per i miei due personaggi, direi solo: è affacciarsi sulla frantumaglia' (LF 109: 'one could go on in the list ... [b]ut in this case it is useful to explain that if I were to say what is grief for my characters, I would simply say: looking on the *frantumaglia*').

Frantumarsi, breaking into pieces, much more than *rompersi*, is the process we are witnessing in the novel. Just like the *poverella* before drowning, Olga is bound to wander, as she no longer has a place either outside or *inside* herself. Since her own husband has left the *apartment*, they have become *apart*, and she has psychologically *parted* from it, reconfirming the negative meaning one could give to the term *apartment*: being apart from the community, but also from your better half. That house, which until then was an extension of herself, becomes her prison, devoid of meaning: '[c]om'era inconcludente percorrere quella casa nota. Tutti i suoi spazi si erano mutati in piattaforme distanti, separate tra loro' (GA 139; 'how inconclusive it was to traverse that known house,' DA 125). Like Monique, who claims, 'Je ne reconnais plus l'appartement' (FR 152; 'I no longer recognize the apartment,' DW 153), Olga, too, finds the space traditionally allocated to her to be estranged from her now, no longer her extension, as it is *dis*-membered in its deconstructed levels. These levels constitute platforms in this abyss in which she feels herself drowning. From one platform to another – we can almost picture her while she jumps – Olga resists the temptation of drowning in de Beauvoir's 'darkness' of failed marital mutual understanding. The new bolt, however, makes this foreign space impossible to escape. Everything that witnessed her condition of married woman, as well as the chores traditionally attesting to her belonging to that status, now only means imprisonment. But how to react? She desperately tries to react to what she feels is her mental change of status, losing psychological balance, and sends imperious messages to her brain. 'Organizza le difese, conserva la tua interezza, non farti rompere come un soprammobile, non sei un ninnolo, nessuna donna è un ninnolo. La femme rompue, ah, rompue, rotta un cazzo. Il mio compito, pensavo, è dimostrare che si può restare sane. Dimostrarlo a me, a nessun altro' (GA 62-63; 'Organize your defenses, preserve your wholeness, don't let yourself break like an ornament, you're not a knickknack, no woman is a knickknack. *La femme rompue, ah, rompue*, the destroyed woman, destroyed, shit. My job, I thought, is to demonstrate that one can remain healthy. Demonstrate it to my self, no one else,' DA 57). 'Staying sane' while undergoing a breakdown has external evidence: she no longer recognizes herself. In a powerful *mise en abyme*,[137] she looks at her own image, and sees a woman, 'Sul momento non la riconobbi. Mi spaventai soltanto perché si era preso il mio cuore, che ora le batteva in petto' (GA 73; 'At that moment I did not recognize her. I was frightened because she had taken my heart, which was now beating in her chest,' DA 66).

In spite of all her promises, Olga now *is* the *poverella*. Her self is encumbered by all the relations she has established in life, not merely with Mario, but with her literary knowledge, represented by Monique's text, by the oral narratives of her childhood. Everything comes back to haunt Olga, and demonstrating to herself that 'she can remain sane' is quite a task. The *frantumaglia* encompasses several possible meanings, but they all define a profound state of disarray, of grief, and sadness, in which the loss of one's voice is fundamental to the following loss of identity:

> [P]ercepire con dolorosissima angoscia da quale folla di eterogenei leviamo, vivendo, la nostra voce e in quale folla di eterogenei essa è destinata a perdersi. Io, che a volte soffro della malattia di Olga ... me la rappresento soprattutto come un ronzio in crescendo e uno sfaldamento a vortice di materia viva e materia morta: uno sciame d'api in avvicinamento oltre le cime immobili degli alberi; il mulinello improvviso in un corso lento d'acqua. Ma è anche la parola adatta a ciò che sono convinta di aver visto da bambina, – o comunque durante quel tempo tutto inventato che da adulti chiamiamo infanzia, – poco prima che la lingua mi entrasse dentro e mi inoculasse un linguaggio: un'esplosione coloratissima di suoni ... O è solo un modo mio per dire l'angoscia di morte, il terrore che la capacità di

esprimermi si inceppi come per una paralisi degli organi fonatori e tutto quello che ho imparato a governare dal primo anno di vita a oggi fluttui per conto suo, gocciando via o sibilando da un corpo sempre più cosa, una sacca di cuoio che perde aria e liquidi. (LF 109–10).
([P]erceiving with terrible anguish from what crowd of heterogeneous individuals we raise our voice while living and in what crowd of heterogeneous individuals it is bound to vanish. I, who often suffer from Olga's illness ... picture it like a buzzing noise in a crescendo and a spiral-like crumbling of live and dead matter: a swarm of bees nearing us beyond the still tree tops; a sudden whirlpool in the water of a slow creek. But it is also the proper term for what I believe to have seen as a child – or at least during that made-up time that we adults call childhood – just before the tongue would enter and inoculate me with language: a colourful explosion of sounds ... Or, perhaps, this is the only way I can speak of the anguish of death, the terror that the ability to express myself can falter in a paralysis of the speech organs, and everything that I learned how to control since my first year of existence until now would float on its own, dripping or oozing away from a body that is, more and more, just a thing, a pocket of leather that lets out air and fluids]).

In Olga's view, Mario '[a]veva sommato finzione familiare a finzione coniugale a finzione sessuale per dar tempo alla sua viltà, per metterla sotto controllo, per trovare piano piano la forza di lasciarmi' (GA 77; 'had added family fiction to marital fiction to sexual fiction to give his cowardice time, to get it under control, to find, slowly, the strength to leave me,' DA 70). Adding fiction to fiction, Olga finds a new linguistic medium. She starts writing letters to Mario, similar to the letters Anna would write to her cousin Edoardo in *Menzogna e sortilegio*. The first act towards healing, towards resurfacing from the abyss, can be provided by writing. In the case of Morante's Anna, the letters represent instead the tool for her even deeper descent into the abyss of her neurosis; Anna will actually construct an entire world of lies for herself and her daughter, Elisa. Olga also starts writing letters, but to her husband. She struggles against his deceiving fictions of five years with her own fiction. These letters compose another form of narrative, another form of telling things to oneself, since they will never be sent. It is a form of self-analysis that could constitute an in-house remedy to Olga's impending madness. The content, though, builds a bridge between the unwanted stories of her childhood, or 'what as adults we call childhood' – those stories that actually brought Olga to writing ('Il bisogno di scrivere l'ho scoperto lì, sotto il tavolo, mentre giocavo' (GA 47; 'There under the table, while I played, I discovered the need to write,' DA 44) – and the present.

Perhaps it is only through the retelling of her story, through the use of Neapolitan, neo-standard Italian and the composite Italian of her letters, I would argue, that Olga can go back to her passion for writing. It is the *poverella* again who lends her the words in which to express her rage when Olga, while running from one office to another to pay bills (another woman's chore), sees Mario with his new woman, Carla, Gina's daughter. In the middle of posh downtown Turin, in via Pietro Micca, Olga strikes Mario from the back and describes her insane gesture with the same words she used earlier for the *poverella*'s rantings in the Neapolitan streets. Like the cry of the *poverella* who 'sfondava ad ariete' in the same fashion, Olga explains, '[g]li arrivai addosso alle spalle. Lo colpii come un'ariete [*sic*] con tutto il mio peso, lo scaraventai contro la vetrina, vi urtò con la faccia' (GA 77; 'I came up behind them. I struck him like a battering ram with all my weight, I shoved him against the glass, he hit it with his face,' DA 70). In this tragic encounter, Carla, young and beautiful prey of Mario/Jason, is wearing his grandmother's earrings, which Olga still calls 'hers.' Jewels are a traditional sign of male possession. After seeing Olga one time wearing those earrings, Mario took them from the house as a thief, only to give them to his new prey, Carla. Jewels and sexual property mean only one thing in Olga's eyes, and she spares no words for Carla who has stolen her husband and taken her earrings. 'Dammi quegli orecchini, dammi quegli orecchini. Volevo strapparglieli con tutto l'orecchio' (GA 78; 'Give me those earrings, give me those earrings. I wanted to rip them off of her, with the whole ear,' DA 71).

The economy of gift giving in exchange for obedience, sex, and wifely duties exposes in one paragraph the laws of the modern Italian family. Mario's grandmother's earrings are not merely a 'gift,' or perhaps they are not a gift at all, as 'for there to be a gift, *it is necessary* [il faut] that the donee not give back, amortize, reimburse, acquit himself, enter into a contract, and that he never contracted a debt.'[138] Those earrings reconfirm the symbolic and its process of 'exchange and of debt, the law or the order of circulation in which the gift gets annulled.'[139] This 'gift' is an exchange between the male and the female world, the tacit understanding of laws between parties in a contract. Like genes and husbands' last names, jewels (earrings, in this case) are passed from generation to generation, testimony to the newly reached different position of a woman in marriage. Olga reacts to her loss of the contract because those earrings meant the marriage with Mario,[140] meant belonging to

Mario's line, blood, family, and ultimately signified her entrance into a socio-economic world distant from her loathed Neapolitan one. Those earrings represent the most violent and visual evidence, almost a cliché, that, once and for all, Mario has passed onto another woman that condition Olga so much cherished. It is this knowledge that ultimately brings her to lose control of her imposed behaviour. Olga finally realizes that, once the fictitious status reached in society by marriage, one that ultimately determines also your language and behaviour, has been suppressed by external causes, a woman's action can be just as violent as any man's, if not more: 'Una donna può facilmente uccidere per strada' (GA 79; 'A woman can easily kill on the street,' DA 72). Olga now goes back to that ancestral and almost mythological pathos from the South she so loathed. All the limits and internal brakes are abandoned. The *poverella* is leading the situation for Olga.

Olga, however, realizes that women internalize men's needs because these necessities still signify their own existence and survival in society. Life becomes a reflexion of one's man's existence, a shadow behind a man's footprints. To love Mario and for her own survival, Olga has made herself love everything about him. Olga is jealous that Carla can arouse pleasure in Mario, but, on the other hand, there is nothing she can do: the earrings have been passed along to Carla, and with those jewels Mario has passed onto Carla also the right to make love and be taken care of. With those earrings, and Mario's sex, his name will likely soon become Carla's. While engaging in cruel sex with musician Carrano's encumbering weight on top, Olga sees multiple visions: the *poverella* as she goes back upstairs to her apartment, her husband's image. She finally goes to sleep with one phrase in mind, 'Amo mio marito e perciò tutto questo ha un senso' (GA 97; 'I love my husband and so all this has a meaning,' DA 88). She is still trying to hold on to something that gave order to her existence, or at least so she thought.

The next day, 4 August, is the worst day of the summer. While walking the dog still dressed in her robe, Olga actually crawls behind a tree and defecates like the last of the homeless. There is no control over her brain, which is working involuntarily. The traditional connection between the external world's stimuli and the body at the level of the cerebral cortex seems not to be functioning correctly, or perhaps it has finally started to act independent of any regulatory societal imposition. If not this is Olga herself, it is her own biological body, then, revolting against all those years in which she thought of beauty as a constant attempt at effacing corporeality. Olga wanted her husband to love her body, 'dimenticandosi di quello che si sa dei corpi' (GA 107; '[f]orgetful of what one knows of bodies,' DA 97) and offering instead the shape he liked best, '[il] desiderio che provava per me' (GA 116; 'the desire he felt for [her],' DA 105). Visions still occur: the *poverella* is sitting at Mario's desk while Olga tries to write. Her apparition lasts long enough for Olga to become breathless, and then vanishes. Olga calls up all her strength to react to that vision. After all, she no longer is the eight-year-old girl in Naples. The *poverella* tells her, 'Va' da Carrano' (GA 127; 'Go to Carrano,' DA 114). Like a figurine in a Christmas crèche, the *poverella* is represented by having a body in '*cartapesta*' (GA 141; 'papier maché,' DA 126), but she sits between Olga's now fragmented *spezzati*, 'profiles' – 'Si teneva in vita con le mie vene, le vedevo rosse, scoperte, umide, pulsanti' (GA 141; 'She was keeping herself alive with my veins, I saw them red, uncovered, wet, pulsing,' DA 126) – while writing in Olga's notebook. Olga is delirious; she is carrying on a dialogue with the *poverella*, that creature with a strong Neapolitan accent that, at this point in her life, is the only responding element. Nothing functions as before, she herself is no longer the human clock, the Hoffmann-like mechanical doll Olympia that Mario wanted for himself, a symbol of perfection she wanted to be identified with and in which she became a willing accomplice.[141]

Indicating the level of self-estrangement, there is a split in which Olga is no longer narrator-protagonist, but rather talks about herself in the third person ('l'Olga che voleva correre' *GA* 129; 'Olga who wanted to run,' DA 116) while feeling caged in her own house. As Moi writes, 'For the narcissistic subject, her ego or self is nothing but an alienated and idealized *image* of herself, another *alter ego* or double in danger in the world.'[142] While de Beauvoir's successful narcissistic woman thinks she is God, Olga identifies with the *poverella*, who is not incidentally the one seeking revenge for both women in this part of the novel. Only at the very end will Olga rescue herself and the *poverella*. For now the *poverella* is embodying Olga, who, in turn, is painfully aware of their juxtaposition in roles. The *poverella* is writing in Olga's notebook about Olga, but Olga, while looking at herself in the bathroom mirror, is also aware now of her two disjointed faces:

> Se io ero vissuta credendo di essere quell'Olga frontale, gli altri mi avevano sempre attribuito la saldatura mobile, incerta, dei due profili, un'immagine complessiva di cui non sapevo nulla. A Mario, a Mario soprattutto, a cui credevo di aver dato Olga, l'Olga dello specchio centrale, ora, in realtà, non sapevo nemmeno che faccia, che corpo avessi donato davvero. Lui mi

aveva *assemblata* sulla base di quei due lati mobili, scoordinati, sfuggenti, e chissà quale fisionomia mi aveva attribuito, chissà quale *montaggio* di me lo aveva fatto innamorare, quale invece gli era risultato ripugnante, disamorandolo. Io – rabbrividii – per Mario non ero mai stata Olga. I sensi, il senso della vita di lei – capii all'improvviso – erano stati soltanto un abbaglio di fine adolescenza, una mia illusione di stabilità. A partire da adesso, se volevo farcela, dovevo affidarmi a quei due profili, alla loro estraneità più che alla loro familiarità, e muovendo di lì restituirmi piano piano fiducia, rifarmi adulta.

... guardando bene nella mia mezza faccia di sinistra, nella fisiognomica cangiante dei lati segreti, riconobbi i tratti della poverella, mai avrei immaginato che avessimo tanti lati in comune. Il suo profilo ... si era acquattato in me chissà quando, era quello che ora offrivo allo specchio. (GA 138–9; emphasis added)

(If I had lived in the belief that I was the frontal Olga, others had always attributed to me the shifting, uncertain welding of the two profiles, an inclusive image that I knew nothing about. To Mario, to Mario above all, I thought I had given Olga, the Olga of the central mirror, and now, in reality, I didn't know which face, which body I had given him. He had assembled me on the basis of those two shifting, disjointed, ephemeral sides, and I don't know what physiognomy he had attributed to me, what montage of me had made him fall in love, what, on the other hand, had turned out to be repugnant to him, making him fall out of love. For Mario I – I shuddered – had never been Olga. The meanings, the meaning of her life – I suddenly understood – were only a dazzlement of late adolescence, my illusion of stability. Starting now, if I wanted to make it, I had to trust myself to those two profiles, to their strangeness rather than to their familiarity, and moving on from there very slowly restore confidence in myself, make myself adult.

... Looking hard into my half face on the left, at the changing physiognomy of the secret sides, I recognized the features of the *poverella* – never would I have imagined that we had so many elements in common. Her profile ... had been huddling in me for years, it was that which I now offered to the mirror. ([DA 123–4])

Unlike Monique, a character which de Beauvoir conceives as incapable of self-defence, 'cyborg-Olga' understands Mario has constructed her. She has become an automaton, an inhuman assemblage of body parts: she is broken in pieces like the *poverella*. Behind Olga there exist an infinite number of abandoned wives who lost their mind, with Medea at the head of the platoon. Olga dragged herself along for all those years, while building an existence in which the real and the fictive were constantly juxtaposing themselves, although never harmoniously, for the benefit of others. But as automatons in Cyborgia sometimes do, as in a Spielberg movie, Olga at a given point poses the question 'Who am I?' or like Anna Karenina, she asks, 'What am I doing?' to her own self. Only by departing from the image of the *poverella* can she undergo self-treatment. The search for her Self had begun unconsciously in the negative, and yet cathartic, simulacra that best fit her image and seemed to temporarily land on the fragile support of the papier-mâché *poverella* and her recollection. Olga and the *poverella* reify the notion of the Kristevian 'abject,' as they are something that is no longer alive and is not defined by anybody. If the father denies subjectivity, the cyborg goes back to kill him. In this case, cyborg-Olga will have to metaphorically kill both the memory of the cyborg's father, Mario, and the assembled character of the *poverella*/Monique, as she can no longer be represented by them. But Olga is not entirely a cyborg. Her *meridionalità* takes on the features of her on-going conversation with the *poverella*. It's herself in the mirror, but it's also the *poverella* seeking revenge and helping her to overcome this moment of hyper-identification with her. As Olga notes, 'Non c'è riproduzione tecnica che, fino a ora, sia riuscita a superare lo specchio e i sogni' (GA 137; 'There is no technical means of reproduction that, up to now, has managed to surpass the mirror and the dream,' DA 123). Olga and her body are deconstructed like a 'foresta di figure cubiste' (GA 145; 'forest of cubist figures,' DA 130), in which the only reality is her children: 'le mie creature vere nate dal mio corpo, questo corpo, ne avevo la responsabilità' (GA 145; 'those creatures were mine, my true creatures born from my body, this body, I was responsible for them,' DA 130). She does not kill them (well, almost), but she does not have to go as far as the inhuman crime of Medea, as she is not, finally, a misunderstood character. It is only the poor dog, Otto, that dies.

The value of motherhood should be reinstated with a positive connotation within the notion of corporeality. Now Olga sees her children as herself, and not merely as a reflection of the father, a production of Mario's genealogy; by watching them she restores her energy as she thinks of the immediate needs of her creatures: 'Perciò, con uno sforzo che mi costò una fatica al limite del sopportabile, mi levai in piedi. È necessario che mi riprenda, che capisca. *Riattivare subito i contatti* (GA 145, emphasis added; 'Therefore, with an effort that cost me a struggle to the limit of the bearable, I got to my feet. I have to take hold of myself, understand. *Get back in touch immediately*,' DA 130). Olga, the former woman-machine, has a body technologically constructed to react. Like an engine, it switches on again, and takes off. But the reaction can take place merely because her Southern background has reaffirmed itself in its entire passion-filled, problematic linguistic and behavioural context after this long period of exile in which her behaviour made her closer to being a mechanical cyborg. Her body has been infused with new life. After her obscene discourse, after the excruciating monologues, Olga is ready for her new existence. Like a Southern mechanical cyborg rising up before the 'Father,' in fact, she has reclaimed her life and goes to read again 'le pagine in cui Anna Karenina va verso la morte ... quelle che parlavano di donne spezzate. Leggevo e intanto mi sentivo al sicuro, non ero più come le signore di quelle pagine, non le sentivo come una voragine che mi risucchiava' (GA 207; 'the pages in which Anna Karenina goes toward her death ... the ones about women destroyed. I read and felt safe, I was no longer like those women, they no longer seemed a whirlpool sucking me in,' DA 183–4). Olga has retrieved her craft of writing, which is empowering, but only after the realization of what empowers – and defines – her. She has rewritten de Beauvoir's authorial-reading imposition of meaning onto poor Monique, who, in spite of being the author of her own diary, feels the constraints of de Beauvoir's intellectual thesis rooted in the text. Olga also rewrites the *poverella*'s tragic death at Capo Miseno, and has given a just burial to her. Both have found in Ferrante's text a place where they can be understood.

Ferrante's reading of de Beauvoir's novella is important in that it states in fiction what critic Toril Moi notes in 'Intentions as Effects,' one of her numerous works on de Beauvoir. Ferrante's 'misreading' of Monique's story attests to the failed effects of de Beauvoir's intentions. Without assuming necessarily that authorial intentions – clear statements made by the author – allow for authorial reading, Moi nevertheless notes that de Beauvoir intended to expose Monique's passivity to readers. Her intent, however, has failed owing to the presence of a 'series of other textual effects (to do with language, meaning, and epistemology) which necessarily undermine the authorial reading.'[143] While, as Moi maintains,[144] de Beauvoir's 'own reading is entirely plausible,' one should remember that it is Monique who is the author of her own diary. As such, she is 'the subject of her own act of enunciation, which is the writing of her diary.'[145] She is a writing subject. De Beauvoir claims that the husband Maurice's rationality is superior to Monique's world of contradictions. Unlike Noëllie, Maurice's new lover and an accomplished lawyer in her own right, Monique has constantly denied her own freedom, and puts her daughters before everything else. Monique does not conform, so to speak, to de Beauvoir's *diktat* about the importance of economic independence and not relying exclusively on what we can biologically perform, being a fit mother and wife and a reproducing machine. Moi sees in the 'continuous slippage of language and disintegration of knowledge ... a fundamental tension in de Beauvoir's work in general: the tension between her conviction that she has full epistemological control and her fear of slipping into the irrational chaos of the body and emotions.'[146] As a result of this tension, the construction of Monique's characters reveals at its fullest the 'unstable nature of knowledge,' perhaps the only thing the woman truly learns during her separation from the husband. De Beauvoir tries to force Monique into this flawed theoretical scheme. This was her intention in writing the novella and for how we should read it, in spite of her own assertions that she was categorical only in theoretical writings and 'free' in her fiction.[147] However, Monique's shuns de Beauvoir's rhetorical struggle between her condemnation of the character and her efforts to 'enact the very same delusions on the rhetorical level.'[148] The readers empathize with Monique, not with the writer, 'even ending up feeling cross with Beauvoir for placing Monique in such dire straits.'[149]

We are faced with what Moi calls a case of 'positive transference on to the character, negative on to the author.'[150] They both want to be loved, author and character, but it is impossible for the reader to love both. Ferrante rereads Monique's story and diary as Monique would want it read. De Beauvoir has Monique say, 'Comme tout devient compliqué dès qu'on commence à avoir des arrière-pensées!' (FR 181; 'How involved everything becomes as soon as one begins to have hidden motives!' WD 182). In order to gain self-enlightenment, Olga does not work at odds with her author and understands that Ferrante does not have – unlike de Beauvoir – 'hidden motives' for depicting Olga's grief. Quite the contrary: when the author realizes where Olga is going, she comes to rescue her and responds to her quest with empathy and courage. She does not 'exhaust her in afterthoughts,' but indicates a path through all her alienation. De Beauvoir saw alienation as 'transcendence attempting to turn itself into an object,' that characteristic motion by which, when we alienate 'ourselves in another thing or person, we deprive ourselves of the power to act for or by ourselves.'[151] I think for Olga there is hope at the end of her journey, as she is not deprived of her sense of transcendence. *I giorni dell'abbandono* does not condemn women's complicity in their own oppression and preservation of phallocentric discourse as de Beauvoir's text does, merely assuming that women's oppression was a mirror of ontological ambiguity. Ferrante's novel demonstrates instead how fragile knowledge of things can be, and that the danger of losing sight of oneself resides in our everyday banal lives as wives and women more generally. Only by unveiling the obvious can epistemology begin to work in a different direction, with no illusions, for women who do not theorize about themselves, but still wonder about their place in society. 'Ora so,' Olga says to Mario at the end of the novel, 'cos'è un vuoto di senso e cosa succede se riesci a tornare in superficie. Tu no, non lo sai. Tu al massimo hai lanciato uno sguardo di sotto, ti sei spaventato e hai turato la falla col corpo di Carla' (GA 208–9; 'Now I know what an absence of sense is and what happens if you manage to get back to the surface from it. You, you don't know. At most you glanced down, you got frightened, and you plugged up the hole with Carla's body,' DA 185). Olga is no longer afraid of her own determination. Far from accepting Simone de Beauvoir as her symbolic mother, thus dismantling one more time the statements by Garboli that I discussed earlier in this chapter, Ferrante reconfirms the re-emergence of the philosopher's role in identity studies and gender materialism, but as a intellectual mother to whom we can relate in the practice of writing a text. Respecting the mother signifies – as we said earlier – finding a new epistemological system in which our work can be inserted and conversing with texts that have something in common with our own. We criticize and then construct new works after the 'mother's works' and don't dismiss her writing as essentialist, passé, or insincere. Ferrante faces nevertheless the theoretical challenge of dealing with prescriptive – wished for – behaviour and the 'chaos of emotions.' 'S'affirmer comme sujet' in de Beauvoir's legacy might be difficult, but it is nevertheless possible when one has the literary and theoretical models to work with.

Seducing the Daughter

The power of Morante is the power of seduction that mothers exercise on their daughters. What daughter is not aware and jealous of the mother's ability to seduce? The same power that Garboli denies to Morante is, instead, that form of seduction that brought Di Lascia, Vinci, and Ferrante to measure their work against that of Morante – or de Beauvoir.

Also, if it's true that in her works Morante discusses the theme of maternity, she does so while looking at the dynamics between a fierce mother and a daughter who in the 'real world' might appear subdued and weak, but then vindicates again her right to express herself at the desk. These three 'daughters' of Elsa all bend Morante's legacy according to their own necessity for artistic expression. Di Lascia and Ferrante tell of experiences tied to the private in a narrative constantly swinging between the autobiographical and the fictional moment. Their fiction, born within a Southern atmosphere, always privileges the mother–daughter relationship as it develops in such a society while, in turn, presenting the social constructs of the South, often oppressive and confining. The mother–daughter relationship remains throughout their writing among their most in-depth analysed topics. Elena Ferrante accepts the challenge of reading a by-now classic feminist text, *La femme rompue* by Simone de Beauvoir. In her work, Ferrante brings together her deconstruction of *La femme rompue* and Southern prerogatives about families and women that are close to Morante's expressive form in *L'isola di Arturo* and, mostly, close to *Menzogna e sortilegio*. If Beauvoir's *La femme rompue* is hardly comparable to Morante's novels for its theoretical, almost didactic premises (never a part of Morante's poetics), Ferrante does not hesitate to challenge the French philosopher by transplanting Monique's situation into the treatment of the Southern abandoned wife. The result is even more innovative than Di Lascia's novel, as Ferrante opens up a discussion between very heterogenous texts – all authored by women – on women's condition in society. *I giorni dell'abbandono* represents a gripping hybrid of a *Familienroman* and a thriller that revisits the behavioural options offered to a wife by Southern society, while simultaneously working on the notion of language as a hegemonic tool versus dialect as the linguistic substratum that reveals our true inner self. Only when a balance is reached between these two expressive forms, will Olga consider herself truly healed of her existential malaise.

In every work Morante deals with the mother figure. Although she is certainly a source of life, a source of joy and connection to mother earth, the Morantian mother is also defined in her obscure side, the dark threat of death presented in all its terrifying powers.[152] Rather than being a contradiction in terms, Morante represented – better than other Italian women writers – the difficult relationship between mothers and children, one that is hardly determined by choice and freedom, but is, instead, confined to the realm of dependence and resentment: a master–slave relationship that has nothing to do with romanticized images of motherhood, and one that shies away from rhetoric and accepts in full the depth of mother–child suffocating love. In using the term 'Oedipal' when speaking of Vinci's novel, I intend it in the way Jacques Lacan – and later Julia Kristeva – revisited Freud's reading of the myth. In fact, what draws Vinci, Ferrante, and Di Lascia to Morante's complex narratives of motherly love/hate is the communal tenet that in the life of an individual, the maternal body and mind constitute the determining factors of his/her abjectness more than the confrontation with the father figure.

chapter 2

Of Fathers and Daughters, or the Italian Family Interrupted

The realist novel often avoids the elevated subject matter of tragedy in favour of the quotidian; the average, the commonplace, the middle classes and their daily struggles with the mean verities of everyday existence – these are the typical subject matters of realism. Until the advent of the Italian *giallo* of recent years, no melodrama, international conspiracies, aristocratic high life, and bizarre eccentrics made up the fabric of Italian novels. The Italian realist novel has often dealt with the fictionalization and narrativization of family by means of the banal verities accompanying conjugal love – or lack thereof. Often we read a realistic portrayal of the difficult Oedipal relationship existing between men and their mothers, perhaps the prevailing family relation in Italian narrative. But 'what happens to the sentimental family romance when a daughter *constructs* the novel?' wonders Lynda Zwinger.[1] This chapter responds to Zwinger's question with respect to those 'daughters' who wrote using the novel as a literary construct for family relations – particularly the one daughters entertain with their father. In fact, this chapter argues that a major thematic and structural shift has taken place within the Italian *Familienroman*. While the analysis of family relations remains largely a topic mirroring the actual issues at the core of Italian society, the contemporary family novel by women writers dealing with the father–daughter relationship has opened up new areas of reflection on the various forms of psychological dependence, identity formation, subjection to power and authority as *potestas*, and social construction that define the woman as a whole.

A Role Model for His Daughter's Novel

In *The Daughter's Seduction* Jane Gallop has metaphorized the father–daughter relationship, visible in many cultures, and not strictly Western.

Gallop views this relationship as parallel to the one between psychoanalysis and feminism, vastly studied at this point in English feminist literary criticism, particularly of Shakespearean works and nineteenth-century British novels.[2] In the Western novel the daughter's role is traditionally invested with all the qualities of patience, passiveness, resignation, and tolerance that make of her an indispensable element in the balance of passions and interests governing her family. Another form of the daughter's representation is the way in which the head of the family makes use of the wealth inherent in the daughter, namely, her beauty and grace.

In their treatment of this theme, Italian women writers make apparent that, far from being the element of solidarity within the members of a family that must prevail over more general social ties, familism is the knot that paralyses a woman's growth. When familism frames the woman's relationship with the father, the knot takes on even more problematic sexual, political, and ethical connotations.[3] At the core of these novels often lies the authorial attempt to analyse the ideological atrophy of a society – representing the public sphere – whose psychological tics and attachments to the space traditionally allocated to the family – representing the personal sphere – develop into a dysfunctional and disturbing element of the *Familienroman*. This represents an important shift in the traditional Italian novel, as it swerves from the rhetoric about a historic dependence of Italian men on their mothers' approval rather than on their fathers',[4] or (more frequently in cinema than in literature) the unresolved conflicts of the young Italian male with the father. It represents also a narrowing shift of the point of view by which women writers express a distinct change – not necessarily for the better – in the way they perceive themselves within both the family and Italian society. In fact, women writers narrow their system of novelistic characters to an often claustrophic one – the father–daughter dialogue – as a way to focus on their problematic relationship with a still prevalent patriarchal discourse in Italian society.

Writing about the powerlessness to distance oneself from the traumatic relationship with the father already creates in itself a point of arrival that is not entirely new to the writings of Italian women. As early as 1906, Sibilla Aleramo's autobiographical *Una donna* foreshadows Italian women's contemporary novelistic treatments of familism. The latter is a continuing theme in the treatment of the family structure in the novel while also unveiling how society heavily shapes and conditions the daughter's role in both the reality in which she lives and the literary representation of which she is the object. In Aleramo's novel, it is the Oedipal nature of the mother-father-daughter triangle and the consequences they will endure that underscore the psychological and traumatic growth of the writing subject. Aleramo brought to the fore the role of the paternal figure in the maturation process and subsequent development of the self-identity of her autobiographical fiction's protagonist. In Aleramo's muted focus, the father is the one that is partly to blame for the distance the protagonist takes from an overly passive mother who is weakened and reduced to folly by her relationship with a domineering husband. The daughter constructs this triangle, placing herself in antithesis to the mother figure, and refusing to align with the one who brought her into the world. Their conflictual relationship results in a sad and one-sided Oedipal competition in which the daughter thinks she is the sole deserving depository of the paternal affection. To gain her father's love and respect, the daughter engages in fervid activity in his factory, while her mother feels further suffocated by the gossip of the provincial town where they live. *Una donna*'s daughter does not succeed in limiting the power of her love for her father, as she is her mother's rival in this family triangle and incapable of seeing that a great deal of her mother's passivity is determined by an excess of love for her husband, and is not merely dictated by societal constrictions and the oppression of ritualistic forms of behaviour. Her folly results from the complex and destructive combination of love and the tyrannical power of patriarchal thought that paralyse her. Only later will the daughter advocate the rights of oppressed women unable to speak, as her mother was, and she will make amends for her unjustified contempt.

Sibilla Aleramo's *Una donna* represents merely one narrative – by now a female canonical model – upon which other writers structure their own vision of inequality vis-à-vis the old taboos that affected previous Italian female writers. In spite of the renegotiation with family models, though, the maternal figure still functions today consistently as an anti-model for the protagonist, stirring the narrating daughter to not follow what she perceives to be as her mother's path of total passivity and dependence on male behaviour while igniting a sense of rebellion for everything the mother tries to teach her in order to comply with men's rules. The father–daughter relationship in fiction strikes pessimistically at the image of the family, which far from being a serene and safe environment, is almost uniformly depicted as a disturbing nucleus in which women are indeed prevented from expressing themselves. The difficult ties between mother and daughter, all too often perceived as a biological and enslaving continuation of women's roles that the blessing/curse of procreation inevitably produces, are revealed to be only the first aspect a daughter examines in her life, while her relationship with her father comes after she has gathered strength from her own life experience outside the family. In shifting from treatment of the mother-daughter theme to the father-daughter one, the Italian novel by women suppresses the mother's character while emphasizing the conscious caesura between the world and the daughter's thorny and unresolved relationship with the father. Together with these two constant elements, women writers more frequently than not assign to the father figure the role of (negative) guide and teacher, making him responsible for their difficult entrance into adult society and their relationship with other men.

The daughter's novel deconstructing the encounter with the father, the first and determining male force in a woman's life, appears at a juncture of Italian women's writing that is less programmatically emancipatory than in the 1970s, or in the 1980s. It is not, however, a theme that appears multiplied in its treatment by chance, and there are several reasons for its rise. In a period in which issues linked to the complex relationship with the mother have been eviscerated and analysed in women's fiction – they have been, so to speak, 'literarily' acknowledged – the novel provides in all its modes and subgenres an ideal and hospitable space in which to perform an examination of masculine authority in a broader and more imminent sense. The female author can look to the other one who, like the mother, gave us life. The novel is now constructed from the perspective of a woman writer who is aware of the power writing grants her. Hers is often, but not always, a sympathetic way of presenting the daughter's thoughts, her weaknesses. In turn, the characterization of the daughter spurns the psychological constructions that encaged her in previous novels and instead suggests that the daughter's problems are the fault of her father. Masculine authority is thus often denied a positive role in the life of daughters. The relationship with the father is one that provides women with life but also enforces the rules that structure both their thinking about the domestic environment and the conceiving of the self in relation to the other. Whereas mothers often live still under the subjection of a patriarchal system – even if unwittingly – fathers have been until recently designated by Italian society to be their daughters' rulers, chiefly (and legally) by virtue of their surname, which binds their daughters from birth. Yet the father figure described in these novels does not always entail a biological connection. The daughter might have become one because of legal reasons, adoption or the second marriage of their mothers, whom they do not hesitate to blame for marrying these men. The father figure can also be that of a stepfather, or an adoptive father, someone who holds the dignity and responsibility that is given to such a title and name in the eyes of society. In all these cases, his presence is felt in the construction of the daughter's future existence, no matter the outcome.

Fathers constitute their daughters' first male model, as the daughters have entrusted them with all powers from a young age. Daughters have learned that the man in the house is also the figure of reference (and deference) in their relationship with the opposite sex. Consequently, daughters at an early age are made vulnerable and are traumatized by their fathers' behaviour in multiple ways. Whether the father stays with the daughter, and plays an active role in her life, or whether he abandons the household, he is the man on which the daughter will model her future interaction with other men. An entire existence depends on the very foundations fathers have laid for their daughters. Their abandonment, their betrayal, and their absence construct the identity of the daughters. In fact, this primary masculine figure appears in several of these novels juxtaposed with an individual with whom the female character begins an erotic relationship, often modelled on the daughter's initial inability to interact with the father. Awkwardness in expressing oneself with the father, which generates in turn the dependence on another man's approval, becomes a considerable challenge to the female protagonist and to her independence. The heroine of the story needs to struggle against not one, but two villains (at least) in her pursuit of independence and happiness.

Beginning in the mid-1990s, novels by Dacia Maraini,[5] Maria Rosa Cutrufelli, Margaret Mazzantini, Fleur Jaeggy, Anna Santoro, and Rossana Campo (the list could be longer) make up a rather expansive body of literary works that extol the importance of a gendered narrative approach to this fundamental relationship. In different ways and with different outcomes, these novels all make of the father–daughter relationship the key element in their narrative of self-discovery. In Fleur Jaeggy's *Proleterka*,[6] for instance, it is imperative for the daughter to assert her responsiveness to life by deconstructing her relationship with her defunct father. Throughout her life, the daughter-narrator reacted against her father's puppet-like asexual behaviour. Being moved by her passions, being able to feel that something moves also on the surface of her body, has been a priority, originating in a cruise on board the ship *Proleterka*. The daughter is constantly haunted by her fears of entertaining the same kind of apathetic behaviour that her father manifested through the years. To learn how to live after the pain of abandonment by any man in her life, she develops a personal theory of mourning through simulation. Another treatment of the father–daughter relationship marks Anna Santoro's novel *Pausa per rincorsa*.[7] Here as well, the father–daughter relationship is centred on loss, on the pain the daughter suffers in her unsuccessful relationships with her father and with another man, a disciple of her father, both of which were fundamental to her intellectual growth. For the woman, it becomes increasingly difficult to talk of her own father, but even more so to talk of her own neglectful and casual relation to him while he was alive. While she is closed in her shell of forced solitude despite, or because of, the deafening noise and colours of Naples, the phychological 'pause' takes over the gnawing demands of everyday life, and she can finally reflect upon the value of paternal words. The daughter observes the passing of time and how it has lacked that linear sense that she wished for. Time moves in spirals that force her to rethink, to consider the future that lies ahead of her. Her own future depends on that impetus necessary to go ahead, to continue to believe, 'cercare non solo la strada da fare ancora, ma le tracce della strada fatta. Bisogna cercare' (PPR 96; 'to look for not only the road to take still, but the trails of the road already taken. One needs looking').

Melancholia is not, however, the only chosen mode of expression for this topic. In Rossana Campo's *Sono pazza di te*,[8] for instance, the theme of the prodigal father resurfacing in his long-lost daughter's life is sustained textually by the use of the borderline farcical dialogue, a trademark of Campo's characters. In turn, this dialogue for once gives the father an opportunity to defend himself from his daughter's bitter memories and sarcastic remarks.

Though developing distinct outcomes, the narrations take place almost invariably in the first person, the use of which accentuates the autobiographical/confessional mode in the rendition of the events that led to the act of writing. The father–daughter relationship theme finds new linguistic forms, structure, and plot that vary modalities from text to text hybridizing several subgenres of the novel: the *Bildungsroman*, the epistolary novel, the detective novel, the travelogue, the confession, the diary, and memoirs. There are several plot forms shifting from the comic to the lyric, from the tragic to the didactic mode. The experimentation in these novels reveals the eclectic writing and thinking about the masculine figure that makes up the wealth produced by Italian women writers today. But it is the failure to comprehend the motives of their father's behaviour – hence the many recollections, in almost all these novels – that dominates these narratives of obsession and alienation.

Women writers who undertake the investigation of this relationship do so via the fictional treatment of a story that is, almost invariably, rooted in autobiographical traits with respect to the difficult encounter with the first 'other than the self,' the father, that first man in the life of every little girl since pre-Christian myths. The literary examples of the father–daughter relationship found in the work of Italian women writers demonstrate, nevertheless, that almost all myths are loci in which the contingencies of present times, in general banal, assume an ennobling connotation, while the myth returns, for a moment, to constitute what it was from the beginning, a human fact.[9] In the case of the mother and daughter, instead, the daughter's relationship (and narrative) moves on psychological tracks that are common to both, but on which the two female figures differ for the way they have acted and thought in life. The daughter's connection with the father, as recently expressed in the Italian novel, resolves bleakly into one in which love and understanding hardly construct a fruitful relationship. These stories of *patresfamilias* who abandon their families after swearing devotion to the Church and the Law, of fathers' domestic violence and abuse that determined the daughter's traumatic childhood, illustrate how the desirable daughter of the sentimental family romance is a male-authored character that needs to be problematized.

From the individual's difficulty at dealing with the father figure springs the authorial necessity for writing on this subject. The single unifying element that links these otherwise rather different novels within the wide array of women's literary production resides in the narrative rendition of a shared difficulty, almost a daughter's 'inability,' that is, to distance oneself from her own traumatic relationship with the father. The temporal pattern allocated to the depiction of such unstable relations develops according to orthodox Freudian temporal lapses. It takes time indeed to figure out what was one woman's relationship with the most important man in her life. Desires that should not be indulged, a constant need for approval that remains with daughters, these are some of the issues most frequently dealt with in postmodern novels about fathers and daughters. Though these narratives should not be 'grounded in the daughter's need for approval,'[10] some seem to fall back – at least in Italian literature – into the old patterns of psychological subjection that seem to regulate interior monologues. This until, in the end, we realize that these daughters, though recognizing the importance of their fathers, have chosen – at least in some cases – to live otherwise.

While the previous chapter illustrated the novels on literary and symbolic mothers, this chapter offers detailed readings of the modalities in which the father-daughter theme has been developed respectively in *La Dea dei baci*[11] by Ippolita Avalli, *Hot Line: Storia di un'ossessione*[12] by Francesca Mazzucato, and *Diario di Lo*[13] by Pia Pera. In Avalli's *La Dea dei baci* the theme of the paternal relationship with power and authority – and their abuse – creates a novel written in the first person about a Northern Italian orphan at the beginning of the 1960s. In the protagonist's case, departing from the identity that her community has decreed for the young girl must necessarily coincide with the separation from her adoptive father. In Mazzucato's *Hot Line: Storia di un'ossessione*, the protagonist does not thrive in creating a new identity for herself but, rather, remains anchored to a fictitious and temporary one that hardly suits her. Unlike the other two examples of daughters in novels analysed in this chapter, this daughter remains enslaved to the paternal power. Her attempts to rebel against the bourgeois system of her upbringing fail when she falls prey to yet another obsession, that for Gabriele, a casual encounter. Far from presenting the sort of androgynous world we see in Isabella Santacroce's *Destroy*[14] and *Luminal*,[15] Mazzucato's problematic relationship with the father figure exacts a clear notion of gender that, though partly a societal construction, does acknowledge the biological in it. Donna Haraway's suggestions that females should relate to the cyborg being and stop relying on organic nuclear families could be welcome in the situations Avalli, Mazzucato, and even Pera, present. As the cyborg breaks down the traditional humanist barriers – human versus animal, human versus machine, and physical versus non-physical[16] – we could perhaps see these daughters free, once and for all, from their post-childhood tribulations.

With respect to the notion of fathers' daughters, this chapter considers also the artistic lineage that daughters have chosen for their discussion of daughters' roles in society and in the development of the novel. In 1995 Pia Pera wrote *Diario di Lo*, a parodic reading of Vladimir Nabokov's *Lolita*, to see how elements of parody could be useful to a different and until then neglected point of view, that of Lolita rather than Professor Humbert's. For Pia Pera, *Lolita* represents at once a source of inspiration coupled with rebellion. *Diario di Lo*'s American publication led to an interesting and quite revealing display of sexual politics to Pera's detriment. *Diario di Lo* embodies a form of rewriting a text that modifies substantially how the protagonist lives her own story, one that is no longer bound to her stepfather's narrative. In *Diario di Lo*, the author attempts to liberate herself – adopting the mode of parody – from the figure of the father in an artistic sense, Nabokov, while freeing Lolita from the stereotyped figure of a nymphet with heart-shaped glasses to which her stepfather (and Stanley Kubrick's adaptation) had relegated her character in his memoirs. In Pera's novel, Lolita's narrative voice becomes fundamental to the presentation of her character, thus demonstrating how her very existence can depend on a muted point of view. Lolita-turned Dolly learns how to gain her voice and to speak on her own behalf. A double emancipation then: for the author, who rewrites a famous and scandalous novel according to her point of view; for the protagonist, Lolita-Dolly, who rewrites her own story made public thanks to the memoirs of her jailer-stepfather. In Avalli's, Mazzucato's, and Pera's works the novelists' authorial desire constructs a subjective journey into what until today has been an only occasionally traversed topic by critics: viewing the father–daughter relationship in the novel by daughters.

The Destruction of a Myth: Anorexia and Scapegoating in Ippolita Avalli's *La Dea dei baci*

Ippolita Avalli's own real-life events shape much of the matter of *La Dea dei baci*. It is from authentic material that a story of intense emotive display develops in this novel, in which Avalli began a trilogy continued in *Nascere non basta*, its second instalment, and in her most recent novel, *Mi manchi*.[17] The novel tells a sad fairy tale about a girl who once thought herself to be daddy's girl and is bitterly betrayed in her love. The magical effect of its intensely lyrical pages is not overshadowed by the grim disappointment with life and her father that the protagonist experiences. In *La Dea dei baci*'s thematic intertextuality with Avalli's previous novels, her readers find numerous elements that they will recognize: the Po valley landscapes, the friendship among children, gossip and rumours in the village, industrialization, the advent of television and cars, Italy resurrecting from the Second World War and entering the economic boom of the late 1950s and early 1960s. The novel's themes are the process of self-discovery, the loss of the mother, the relationship of the girl with the entity of a Catholic God, as well as with the father and with authority, and the constant idea of gratuitousness of sacrifice. In the foreground stands a lonely young girl who loves guitars and songs, while struggling for her own affirmation in a hostile environment.

In *La Dea dei baci*, Avalli confronts problems associated with the main character's identity via the protagonist Giovanna, a child that discovers in a hurtful way that she has been adopted. Her adoption from a Milanese orphanage will deny her integration into the small society of her adoptive parents. Quite the contrary. Adoption, in her case, will bring to the fore elements of hypocrisy, prejudice, and discrimination against those individuals who are external to the small community. What Giovanna – who later finds out her real name is Vera (which in Italian means at once 'true,' 'real,' and, finally, 'wedding ring') – discovers is, primarily, the broken pact of society with its children, as it does not provide them with a safe environment in which to grow; and, second, the broken pact between her putative father and herself. Finally, Giovanna realizes that being born is indeed not enough. Drawing unwittingly on Arthur Schopenhauer's warning at the core of his *The World as Will and Representation*,[18] to express, that is, a will by which we can assert ourselves, Giovanna-Vera attempts the affirmation of her own will to better represent herself when society fails to understand who she is.

Padania, O Beautiful

The main character of *La Dea dei baci* lives in prosperous Lombardy, a region dotted with big and powerful farms whose peasants live in tranquil and industrious economy. It is in the Lodigiano, this affluent and intensely Catholic part of Italy, that the sad adventures of the little girl Giovanna take place. After a childhood blessed by the presence of a wonderful mother figure, Luigina, a woman whose identity is built on a Catholic sense of piety and charity, Giovanna lives an existence that, as we will see, comes to be quite antithetical to the characteristic image of serenity that this geographic reference awakens within readers competent with Italian Catholic writers. Paradoxically, the tranquil scenery of the Po Valley, in whose descriptions as a nature of composed beauty by Avalli bring to mind Giuseppe Pellizza da Volpedo's majestic and yet contained views of the Lombard countryside, serves as a dramatic backdrop for the protagonist's journey/process through childhood and adolescence. *La Dea dei baci* presents itself as an anti-novel on Providence and on the tormented relationship that Northern Italian Catholics entertain with God.[19] More particularly, the novel eviscerates the troubled notion that God's divine laws must be respected. Rather, when placed in a condition of power, individuals corrupt the word of God, bending it through their control of its application in both the public and private spheres. It is a power, in the case of the clergy, that is based upon the right to be interpreters of the divine word and, in the case of fathers, on the natural/legal right towards their own children. Fatherly love, what is expected of the connection of adults with their children, is scrutinized in the novel when, instead of being nurturing and constructive, it becomes a juridical limitation for the latter. In this way, legal inadequacy results in the vilification and abuse of those who are made weak by age – the children – in their daily practices and feelings. Children are made incapable by those who hold the power – and assume it as an inalienable right – of assuring for yourself your own identity within society. Some individuals, like Giovanna-Vera, are forced to move out of their community, while others, like her fairy godmother, live in the belief of a justice located in the hereafter. Intrinsic to the discourse of the novel is the connection the author establishes between the two types of 'fathers,' the ones declared so by family ties and the priests who, in small towns, are unquestioned authorities and reference points for their parishioners. As it makes more stringent the opposite notion regarding the societal scapegoat, the notion of 'flock,' of those humans who rely on their pastor, is also quite central, as one cannot exist without the other.

Aside from the relationship with the father figure, the fundamental themes of the novel are the protagonist's relationship with God and with authority. In this cast of characters, in addition to the legal fathers, there are father figures who represent the Catholic Church, such as Don Bruno and the bishop to whom the little girl is sent after her tirade during Easter mass. The child feels dominated and martyred by their discourse up until the very moment she is able to find her own voice, though an erratic one. This inner, and until then, unknown, voice empowers her to express her own reticence in assuming untrue beliefs merely because they are taught as dogmatic tradition and the faith of the Catholic Church. The Catholic God, the supreme father, becomes the symbolic interlocutor for Giovanna as she searches for justice when she feels abandoned by her own father in the same way Jesus does by the Father. She searches for divine justice in order to pardon those who, like her father, have caused her unnecessary pain and made of her life a school of torture in which her identity has been shaped. Giovanna discovers that forgiveness cannot be granted without justice, particularly a divine one. Readers are left at the end to speculate whether divine justice exists or not. Nonetheless, *La Dea dei baci* is a novel of hope (but not in Manzoni's sense of the word), for it traces the footsteps of a young woman who succeeds by her own power, if not in finding happiness, at least in rejecting, and finally leaving, the place in which she spent her childhood and troubled adolescence. In the end, Giovanna-Vera goes to live in the city because there 'le ragazze possono portare i calzoni' (DB 37; 'girls can wear pants'). The metaphor of pants serves more to shed some irony on a tragic past that cannot be forgotten until there will be justice for Giovanna-Vera. Staying in that village after understanding the hypocrisy of her father is no longer possible. The two underwriters of the ancient pact of love and respect towards each other will sever it in front of authority (in the person of a *carabiniere*), and each will take his/her own way.

This novel of growth and formation depicts a difficult life apprenticeship in which the absence of love as an essential nutrient ignites the need for escape from a community that demonizes innocent children and turns them into sacrificial lambs for its own opportunism and hypocrisy. *La Dea dei baci* depicts a parable of the violence of good and evil, a negative fable about the girl's existence, in which Avalli eviscerates quite convincingly the notion of struggle with society that women in general entertain to ascertain their difference, biological and constructional. At the same time, her heroine will be successful in extricating herself both from the authority of the adoptive father, the so-called Law of the Father, and from his suffocating community. No longer will Giovanna be the collective scapegoat. She will depart from the identity that society had confined her role to be, and will indeed give re-birth to her new self. Fiction – intended as an agent of change – destabilizes and normalizes the myth, and turns it, as in the case of Ferrante's *I giorni dell'abbandono*, into a narrative of *ordinary tragedy*.

In the story of Giovanna-Vera, in the bitterness and squalor of the environment in which the protagonist lives, lyricism feeds itself on poetry,[20] the devastating poetry of childhood memories. Avalli writes an anti-Proustian text that excavates the trauma of youth in order to redefine the identity of the person who writes. This novel does not take form through the description and narration of involuntary memories, but through the logical and implacable process of an adult confronting the trauma of her youth; what made her the way she is in the *hic et nunc* of the narration. How Giovanna-Vera can construct her identity, coupled with the knowledge that she has been alienated from love after having known the one love her stepmother Luigina could give her, is the essence of this book. The novel describes hard life lessons, like those imposed at such a young age on the protagonist, which, in turn, set her on a particular path, due to bad teachers. This parable of Giovanna concerns a fundamental lesson: our active life can exist in private only if placed in relation with others. When others reject us, we must be able to move on and depart from the conditions in which our birth has initially put us, and find a new birth for, and by, ourselves. Here are analysed, for the most part, the fathers and their function in the turmoil that is the life of a daughter who, until the very end, is so engaged in love for the father that she refuses to see his errors and the lack of love in this first male figure. *La Dea dei baci* is a novel written in a clearly religious tone, if one understands by religious the complicated relationship that human beings entertain with the divine right and with the power that, for a longer time than one can remember, the Church has exercised, for both good and bad, over its followers. Religion is humans' relation to that which they regard as sacred or holy. The notion of sacrifice rejected by the author in this novel stems, just like the term, from that of what is sacred to the community. The notion of sacrifice is intrinsic to the notion of sacred, *sacer facere*.

The Ugly Fairy Tale, or 'Mom Goes to the Moon'

Fairy tales are stories that tell of miraculous and fantastic happenings. The main characters in fairy tales are often children who are in contact with supernatural creatures who help them through rough times. The sequence of functions within a fairy tale remains almost unvaried, as Vladimir Propp maintained in his *Morphology of the Folktale*.[21] The fairy tale that forms the structural canvas of *La Dea dei baci* could be understood as a perfect composition in accordance with Propp's theories. The characters construct the conventional tale sequence, the fairy adoptive mother – or magic helper – dies and leaves the poor child – the heroine – alone against all evil forces, particularly the stepmother, who is the 'villain' in the story.[22] At the end of the 'tale,' the heroine leaves as a 'seeker-heroine.'[23] And yet, though *La Dea dei baci* bases itself on the same functions and characters as a fairy tale would, the novel as a genre takes over the fairy-tale aspect of the text, particularly in the second part. Unlike the fairy tale, a genre that invariably presents shocking actions along the formation path of the heroine only to provide children with edifying teachings in the end, in a novel the sad end functions as the disillusioning, but necessary moment that makes us think on society's real (*veri*) happenings. The ending of this novel further confirms Frank Kermode's statement of the difference between myth and fiction:

'We have to distinguish between myths and fictions. Fictions can degenerate into myths whenever they are not consciously held to be fictive ... Myths are the agents of stability, fictions the agents of change.'[24]

A young girl, Giovanna, believes herself to be loved deeply by her parents. In the passing of only a few years, however, two distinct disasters take place: the loss of her adored fairy, delicate and enchanting, mother, Luigina, who, according to the little girl, 'goes to the moon,' and the subsequent, crude revelation that she was adopted. Giovanna-Vera is left without her mother at her birth and without her adoptive loving mother during her childhood. How can a novel with a title as dreamy as *La Dea dei baci* contain instead scabrous themes such as an abused childhood, even more destabilized by scenes of torture and sexual violence? How can one be drawn in, and tricked by, those inviting kisses that a goddess hinted to us in the text's fantastical title? Yet, it is in this brisk and crude reprise of the title that we find the magic of the book. It is in the initial enmeshing of novelistic and fairy-tale modes that its charm lies. As soon as we enter its world, we are greeted by a narrating voice that has not lost the gift of irony and offers to the reader, in her infinite wisdom, the tone of a fairy tale whose protagonist is modelled on the 'Little Match Girl' by Hans Christian Andersen:

> Allora: swissh! Ho acceso un fiammifero. Subito è comparsa la tavola imbandita, la grassa anatra arrosto con le posate conficcate nel costato. E dietro all'anatra chi c'era se non la mamma con le trecce sul petto che mi guardava sorridente? (DB 122)
> (Then: swish! I lit a match. Soon there appeared the prepared table, on it a fat roasted duck with cutlery stuck in its ribs. Behind the duck, who is it but my mother with her braids on her chest looking at me smiling?)

One of the reading levels of the novel is the brutal fairy tale in which witches are present – in the person of Giovanna's stepmother – and where fairies appear – one in actuality, her adoptive mother, Luigina. The elements could be those featured in fairy tales, but they morph in a concentric and hybrid scheme as they interweave with elements of the novel of formation and autobiographical fiction. In the chronological divisions of the traumatizing events that have articulated the childhood of the protagonist, the novel is enriched by numerous typical fairy-tale elements but does not hesitate to echo such classic epics as the *Iliad*, the *Odyssey*, and the *Aeneid*, often cited and explicitly compared to episodes in the life of Giovanna. The resulting effect is a poetry of displacement, of an Italian

Waste Land, whose objective correlatives deal with nature and animals, what Giovanna sees every day. This is a waste land from which we can depart to discover ourselves, whose symbolism is reduced to a minimal space. Giovanna is not peripatetic by nature, but she accepts this condition as inevitable. As in the case of Telemachus, for whom the *Odyssey* represents the journey to search for the father in the most literal sense, this novel represents for Giovanna a voyage taken in the search for her own roots in a society in which she is prevented from having a normal existence.

In truth, her parents are not her natural, but her adoptive parents. Luigina the fairy took her from an orphanage at very young age and brought her to their little town. At Luigina's death, Giovanna's father, perhaps forced by his own duties as Christian Democrat *sindaco*, the first citizen of his town, or by his desire for companionship, begins a courtship to Maria Bernini, the daughter of Lampo the sheepherder, also called the *accoppagnelli*, or the 'lambkiller,' by Giovanna. In the process, the father neglects his own daughter, who fears not being loved for something she has done to her father. Within a very short time, Giovanna's adoptive grandparents, Luigina's parents, secretly abandon the girl. She discovers them leaving like thieves at night, feeling guilty towards their deceased daughter Luigina for leaving her little girl. Subsequently, Giovanna discovers that they have gone to live with their son, Pale, near the Swiss border. In line with the most orthodox fairy-tale treatment, Giovanna-Vera's stepfather, now a widower, is not able to pry himself from spying on Maria's sculpture-like form.[25] He lives oblivious to all that Maria's body cannot give him. Like all sorceresses in fairy tales, she entices the poor girl with candies and sweet smiles, but reveals herself quickly to be the classic stepmother in full accordance with the unforgettable tradition of Cinderella and Snow White, along with a stream of lonely girls all left to a gloomy destiny. The little girl is now in the power of her young stepmother who left the convent – as Giovanna's father led her to believe – exclusively to look after her. In her naivety, Giovanna thinks that her stepmother, explicitly compared to the sorceress Circe – a literary figure always synonymous with enchantment and dangerous spells – is the one who brings her so much pain. It could not be otherwise. The memory of the meeting of her father's future wife, of forcing herself to visit her every day because 'Mi sembrava che andando dalla Maria ogni giorno, da sola, avrei smesso di sentire io che spariva da me stessa ogni volta che vi vedevo insieme' (DB 57, emphasis in original; 'I thought that by going to Maria every day, alone, I would have stopped feeling the "I" disappearing from myself every time I saw you two together'), lives in her like the knowledge of being the victim of a spell. The stepmother is a big, voluptuous python who tries to envelop Giovanna in her coils:

> Mi fissa con gli occhi scintillanti. Mi viene in mente l'illustrazione di un pitone sul libro di scienze. Sotto c'è un titolo: come mangiano i serpenti. Il mio serpente è giallo con le spire, la lingua biforcuta rossa e sta immobile, in attesa. Di fronte a lui c'è un pulcino. Neppure il pulcino si muove, benché tremi tutto. Sembra quasi che sappia quello che lo aspetta. Può solo stringersi nelle piume e tremare. Il pitone si limita a guardarlo. Non ho mica fretta sai, ho tutto il tempo che voglio, pare che gli dica con gli occhi gialli che non ti fanno entrare. (DB 60)
> (She stares at me with her scintillating eyes. She reminds me of an illustration of a python found in a science book. Under it one can read the caption: how serpents eat. My serpent is yellow with scales, a red bifurcated tongue, immobilized as it waits to strike. In front of him there is a chick. It doesn't even move, but trembles a lot. It seems almost as if it knows the fate that is awaiting it. It can do nothing but shiver inside its feathers and tremble. The python only watches it. I am not in a hurry, you know, I have all the time in the world, its yellow eyes seem to say that would not let you in).[26]

In the odyssey of Giovanna, Maria is a Circe who wounds both her and her father. Unlike Odysseus (and Giovanna), he does not want to escape from her spell. The man who he was once for Giovanna has forever died, and the girl evokes Odysseus when trying to flee Circe and avoid her spell by drinking the herb moly: 'Pensavo che oltre a essere un Dracula la Maria poteva anche essere una Circe e trasformarmi in un maiale come era capitato ai compagni di Ulisse' (DB 91; 'I thought that, in addition to being a Dracula, Maria could also be a Circe and transform me into a pig like she did with Odysseus's companions'). The stepmother is aware of the subliminal power the little girl exercises on her father and, in her peasant ignorance, openly manifests her contempt for Giovanna, while blaming her for her mother's death: 'Sta' pur certa che a me non mi farai diventare matta come la tua povera mamma che con te ci ha rimesso le penne' (DB 89; 'Rest assured that you will not drive me insane like you did your poor mother who gave up her last gasp for you'). The stepmother does everything she can to ensure that Giovanna goes through excruciating pain and grief. According to Maria – entrenched as she is in the bigoted education the nuns gave her – Giovanna is a 'bastard' and unworthy, therefore, of living in the same house with her and her future children. Her presence can pollute Maria's family. In the articulation of the relationship between Maria and Giovanna there is constant evidence of physical and verbal abuse; for any small misdemeanour Maria incites her husband to punish the girl, making her sleep under the stairs, locking the girl in the cellar by herself in the sole company of mice, terrifying her with blows. Maria mortifies Giovanna's body by sticking pins in her flesh when she uses her as a living human 'model' for her clients' clothes. The body, intended as 'the complex interplay of highly constructed social and symbolic forces ... a play of forces, a surface of intensities, pure simulacra without originals,'[27] is here merely a surface of painful intensities. Giovanna's body is mortified, vilified, and abused until she unwittingly enters the tunnel of anorexia.

The denying of food confirms the authority that nutrition – both material and moral – exercises as an inextricable principle that, when not adequately provided, undermines the individual's growth. Until Luigina's death, Giovanna is unaware that, in the eyes of the peasants composing her community, she was considered already stained by the guilt of being an illegitimate child and nameless girl. It is on this innocent child that the guilt of her unknown parents falls. It is as if the Original Sin had forever marred Giovanna, and a new baptism – thus a rebirth – is needed in order to purify her. During the years in which these events take place, the protagonist could neither clearly understand nor create a linkage between the paternal figure and the situation in which she lived, preferring instead to place responsibility for her condition in the hands of the wicked Maria. Raised in a society in which fatherhood is sacred and families are indissoluble, Giovanna has not been educated to question her father. An individual whom she loved so much could not treat her this way, and almost naturally she blames the 'other' woman, as she cannot see her father's flaws. Being afraid in one's own house cannot be permitted by a father we love so much, in fact, and Giovanna attributes to her stepmother the guilt of evil. Giovanna wonders, 'come si fa ad avere paura in casa propria?' (DB 34; 'how can one be afraid in one's own home')? Only now, in the narrative recapitulation of events, thanks to the temporal lapse that allows for further meditation, does the daughter understand her adoptive father's hypocrisy, his faults, his cruelty. Her father's blame for what was lost when Luigina died because of her has always hunted Giovanna. She is made vulnerable both by Luigina's loss and by her father's despicable giving in to the stepmother's pressure to get rid of this child. Giovanna's fictional situation brings to mind Rosi Braidotti's comments affirming – in line with Luce Irigaray – that the loss of the mother's body entails for the little girl a fundamental lack of primary narcissism as a scar of the wound due to separation. This originary loss also forecloses access to the mother as primary object of desire, thus depriving the female subject of *fundamental ontological grounds* for self-assurance. The little boy, on the other hand, is 'compensated' later for the loss of the mother by having his desire deferred to, and displaced to another woman. He may lose the original love object, but inherits the earth in return: men draw all sorts of advantages from their position of representatives of the phallic signifier. For the little girl, instead, there is only economic and symbolic misery.[28]

Lacking 'fundamental ontological grounds for self-assurance' means that Giovanna lacks her mother's imprint at an age at which she is hardly a subject. Internalizing the paternal refusal of her identity, as she makes him only too mindful of his departed wife and the promise he made Luigina never to abandon Giovanna that he now is fiercely trying to break, the protagonist expresses indignity with regard to her own situation. By internalizing her father's loathing and blame for the death of her mother, Giovanna practices the violence of her father on herself. Despite herself she reaches the most complete abjection. As a result of a protracted abuse, of which the prohibition of completing her studies is only one of many, Giovanna leaves the paternal home and liberates herself from the burden of an authority imposed without love. This she cannot accept. Giovanna leaves her village and goes in search of herself in the world. Departing, leaving her own community, signifies as well her own assumption of responsibility for the solitary journey, without a guide, without any support outside of that which she has chosen during the first agonizing period of her existence. We are faithful to that which is important for us, be it a much loved father or the poetry of Homer and Giovanni Pascoli.[29]

Anorexia and Anorissea

Feminine eating disorders have decreed the difficult relationship of women as individuals with a society that denies them the flexibility of their gender and identity, a gender that in the past has been designated as almost illegible in its demands. One question sums up the issue: Freud's '*Was will das Weib?*' alludes to the general unease that female illnesses instigated in male physicians. Looking at female illnesses and their treatment in society, it would seem as if disease becomes an oft-used representation of the feminine. 'In [its] double signifier of self-narrative and of social narrative,' then, illness 'asks to be read as a cultural affirmation, an affirmation of gender.'[30]

The subhead of this section contains the word *anorexia*, a term usually understood as the refusal of food given without love. The moral aberration, usually linked to the term coined in 1873 by William W. Gull as *anorexia nervosa*, was for a long time a space designated by authors to show how the potential created by this alimentary disorder was a coercive method in order to bring about the self and at the same time to exert a pressure on the Other than the self. As Jane Wood notes, in Gull's paper great importance was placed on the 'link he makes between the emaciation of the body and the "mental perversity" of the young female sufferers.'[31]

'Creative writers have been aware long before medical researchers of disorderly eating as a coercive tool to empower the self and simultaneously to exert pressure on others.'[32] Anorexia is ineluctably linked to the theme of the perils of childhood as well, as 'eating disorders are the outcome of profound conflicts between individuals and their parents and society.'[33] It is linked to that odyssey lived by individuals right up until the moment of fracture between their own future existence and the one in which their illness has declared their physical impossibility to live. Illness thus ties ontology and consumption to the consequences resulting from disobedience to the gods.[34] Anorexia also advances the notion of the inhuman consumption involved in cannibalism. A resolution of all this is offered in Christian terms, whereby the blood and flesh of Christ are offered in the form of the consecrated host and wine. Christians participate, on a symbolic level, that is, in the cannibalization of the human body of God.

In Giovanna's crippled existence, anorexia is induced by her parents' denial of food. She is given neither actual food nor love. The initial pain provoked by hunger plunges her into deep suffering; once the moment in which she realizes she is not treated as a human being passes, Giovanna begins her journey to madness through anorexia. She refuses the food left from the table for her since it is no longer necessary. Her hunger turns into knowledge that in turn becomes her sole refuge from her earthly hell. She can now see things clearly:

> Da quando mi era passata la fame, un bel giorno era sparita e non era più tornata, ero diventata magra, magrissima. Leggevo e il mondo intorno a me spariva. Mi chiamavano e non sentivo. Se queste erano le prove della mia cattiveria, ebbene, ero cattiva. Cattivissima. (DB 118)

(Since hunger had left me, one certain day it had disappeared never to come back again. I had become thin, very thin. As I would read the world around me would fade away. Someone would call me and I would not hear. If these were the indication of my bad behaviour, then, I was bad. Very bad.)

The self-loathing that Giovanna unveils in her recollection prompts a meditation on her self-imposed evilness. Paradoxically, her guilt rests on her own innocence within the community in which she lives, within this nuclear family to which she clearly represents an unwanted 'excess.'[35] Giovanna's sacrifice, her anorexia, is decreed by her own community and not decided by a conscious ideology of martyrdom. Her unitented questioning of the norms ('se queste erano le prove'; 'if this was the evidence') makes it possible that her loving attempt to adapt herself to the paternal will only takes her further away from the object of her wishes. Giovanna's unconscious refusal of masqueraded love, expressed by her incapacity to retain the little nourishment she is given, consigns her to evil. The little girl demonstrates the will, albeit still in an embryonic state, to violate the patriarchal *auctoritas*, to depart from that moment in which she is, like the local prostitute – the Goddess of Kisses, as Gioanna is accustomed to calling her – 'figlia di nessuno, di ENNE-ENNE' (DB 116 ; 'nobody's daugther, born of unnamed parents'). In addition to feeling like Odysseus, 'Nobody' that is, she now learns to be so also from a legal standpoint. If the father she loves so much, after all, is not her real father, but a man like all the others forced by appearances and by the environment to adopt a child, she wants to be nobody's daughter.

Giovanna is a living human being to whom the nourishment of love is denied. Neglected as if she was nobody, her illness exacts the notion of nothingness she has understood for herself. Through the peril of her existence, anorexia best interprets her sense of nothingness and of being nobody. Her personal odyssey, then, allows me to speak of her situation using a neologism, *anorissea*. She rewrites *Odissey* as a feminine anti-epic, by which I mean a living travail in which the lack of appetite – the travail of sentimental hunger – connotes Giovanna's true and real travel, or odyssey. In the process of self-starvation, partly induced by her stepmother in the case of Giovanna-Vera, there lies the firm will to leave behind what is unwanted by those we love. In the child's case, it amounts to herself. 'The practice of leaving the self' – Luisa Muraro states – 'leads to the undoing of the subject without undoing it in a myriad of uncoordinated instances.'[36] Such a practice, if applied to the female self, undoes all those relations that make her finally everything she desires to be and become. In particular:

> Il partire da sé non è un basarsi sul ruolo né sulla situazione, con quello che fanno vedere o credere, essere giusto e valido, ma risalire a, e muovere da un'esperienza, ossia da un vissuto vissuto, con tutto quello che ha di determinato, e da un vissuto ancora da vivere (il desiderio), mai l'uno senza l'altro. La pratica di partire da sé, ... è la scommessa di poter prendere le mosse dal luogo della nascita, con tutto quello che esso ha di dipendente, di pregiudicato ma anche di promettente, di nuovo, luogo di una divisione, di uno squilibrio, di una partizione che è una partenza, dove c'è sbilanciamento, struggimento, risentimento, insomma tutto quello che si innesca con quella «partenza» che crea la necessità dello scambio simbolico.[37]
> (Departing the self means not relying on the roles or the situation, with what is seen or believed to be right and valid. It means instead to trace, and move from an experience, from a lived lived, with all that has determined, and from a lived still to be lived (desire), never one without the other. The practice of leaving the self ... is the bet one makes to be able to take leave of the place of one's birth, with all that is dependent, prejudiced but also promising. Take leave of a place that is, again, the place of a division, of unbalance, of a partition that is a departure, where there is imbalance, torment, resentment, in short, all that that 'departure' ignited, that creates the necessity for the symbolic exchange.)

In order not to be cannibalized, the daughter will interpret the act of denying food as the act of departing from her family, sacrificing her own body to her love for the father. Only in this way can Giovanna-Vera exercise the practice of 'leaving the self.' Only by rising to the role of subject/complement in relations with the other – never as object – as Muraro seems to confirm in noting the necessity to highlight the 'fonte del pensare' ('source of thinking'), can Giovanna undo the 'già pensato e deciso' ('already thought and decided'):[38]

> [Q]uello che si scopre è il soggetto – me – non in posizione di soggetto ma di complemento: trovo me in relazione con altri, abitata da ricordi, mossa da desideri, trovo dunque desideri che mi muovono, ricordi che mi occupano, altre o altri che mi parlano o che addirittura parlano al mio posto, magari per contraddirmi![39]
> (What is discovered is the subject – me – not in the position of subject but as complement: I find me in relation to others, lived by memories, compelled by desires, I thus find desires that drive me, memories that consume me, others that speak to or for me, if only to contradict me!)

In Muraro's view, the deconstruction of the 'I' and the world endangers the sense of reality and the possibility of an alternative sense.[40] The traumatic awareness of being a sacrificial lamb presses down on Giovanna-Vera; this is one of the most difficult moments of her apprenticeship. However necessary, her awareness becomes one of the most enduring traits in this deconstruction of the Christian Democrat party of peasants in Padania as it was functioning at the time. The 'memories that consume her thoughts' are conspicuous.

Giovanna constructs a parallel between herself and the figure of Jesus Christ. In the Catholic religion, Jesus Christ represents the exalted son, a symbol of self-starvation as his forty days in the desert remind us, who continues to expound the theory of martyrdom and victimization of the individual by a society and by the fathers. In doing so, Giovanna-Vera exercises her own intellectual activity of self-discovery within one of the theoretical themes of René Girard. Without negating the importance of the figure of Christ, Girard situates the martyrdom of the Son of God in the realm of the practices consolidated for centuries with respect to the role of the sacrificial victim in society.[41]

Other Fathers

A corollary to one's own conquered individuality is the development of his/her awareness of the very authority that has imposed it on us. To accept the concept of authority without love, of pardon without justice, only because it was decreed and sanctioned by a document, sounds problematic. Paternal authority is forcibly revisited and discussed in *La Dea dei baci*. In fact, it appears as a long and multifaceted memory of the father, a life teacher whom the young girl won't forget, just as she can never forget the good teachers, for instance, the distinguished Professor Riboni. There are many fathers, and the blind Homer – via the teachings of Professor Riboni – is like a (good) father to Giovanna. Homer is the name that signifies culture for Giovanna; it signifies the emancipation from the condition of the sacrificial lamb into which she feels forced since the beginning pages of the novel. Homer is the author of the *Odyssey*, and Giovanna understands her own travel through life while reading of Odysseus's great courage and intelligence. Homer taught her not to be afraid to be considered 'Nobody,' but to use it as a tool to her own advantage. Much like her hero Odysseus, Giovanna knows how to draw out a life lesson from her journey of pain; a journey of no-return thanks to which a new life will begin for her. In Giovanna's life, there are no female models that are worthy of being followed. They cannot exist, as she lives in a suffocatingly traditionalist environment. She is, however, innately transgressive enough to be able to refer to them as models in her own travail. But hers is not a parody; it is an authentic and respectful homage that she pays to these men of patriarchal civilization. She refers to them as symbols of universal wisdom and suffering, not as 'male' models, making of their case a precedent for her own. Since she was not provided with female models for life, Giovanna creates upon these men's patterns her own. 'Jesus adopts the language of his interrogators, the language of rivals in the casting out of demons, in order to reveal the system of violence and the sacred.'[42]

Giovanna's teacher introduces the protagonist to the great classics of Italian literature. The parallel between her putative father and the other father figures who appear in her life constructs the path towards the leaving of the self of Giovanna. 'Leaving the self' is necessary for her ultimate purpose, that of conquering a space of independence. She must leave that very self that was originally made physical 'matter' through a maternal body only to be consequently disrupted by her loss. She was left to her master/persecutor playing the role of the beloved father. Aware of Girard's theories, we should not be surprised to read the daughter's declaration in which she literally worships her father like a god, a king, or a divinity in what could sound like a blasphemous mockery of the Creed, but which is one that Giovanna truly believes in as her love for her father will never expire: 'Io credo in te, papà, tu per me sei come Dio onnipotente, padre del cielo e della terra, di tutte le cose visibili e invisibili' (DB 80; 'I believe in you, father, you are for me like an almighty God, maker of heaven and earth, of all the things visible and invisible'). It is so because it is from the father's authority that everything derives.

Deconstructing one's own place signifies also knowing well the actual structure on which one's existence was based before the moment of departure. Giovanna, the daughter, seeks to explain first to herself the reasons for the paternal behaviour. How can your own father treat you like this? At the same time, she elaborates questions about her own identity while recovering the real memories of her childhood instead of those forced on her by others. Without openly condemning her own father, whom she will always love regardless of her final condemnation and separation, Giovanna tries to come to terms with her present identity, to which the continual and sadistic paternal abuse has contributed so much. The problem of paternity and of its refusal is twofold, insofar as the girl is an adopted daughter, not a natural one. Only with the act of the denial of the father as her sole authority, which she can no longer consider legitimate because it is unaccompanied by love that such a normative role must contain, the girl succeeds in feeling free. In other words, she succeeds in reconstructing her own identity and the memory of herself, indispensable for her to reach full adulthood. Only now, in the process of recalling the past, the young girl recognizes the unconsciously veiled nature of her own gaze towards the paternal lack in which hides the continual abuse to which she was subjected:[43]

> Ti sei accosciato davanti a me mettendomi le mani sulle spalle. Mi hai detto sottovoce: 'Son venuto a prenderti prima perché la mamma è morta. Guardami.' Ti ho guardato e i miei occhi si sono perduti nei tuoi. Credo di non averli più recuperati da allora. (DB 36)
> (You squatted near me, putting your hands on my shoulders. You whispered to me, 'I came to take you earlier because you mother died. Look at me.' I looked at you and my eyes drowned in yours. I believe I lost them since then.)

Sometimes fathers say to their daughters, 'You are the light of my eyes,' 'You are the apple of my eye.' Comparing their daughters to the wealth and gift of vision, fathers make manifest their child's intrinsic value and contribution to their life. The daughter, then, constructs in theory what corresponds to her father's most precious good. It is her intrinsic and exchangeable value – what she is 'worth' – that allows her father's society to take advantage of her, as the oft-quoted famous case of *Pride and Prejudice*'s Bennet sisters aptly demonstrates. Whereas among mothers and daughters a matrilineal heavy link of sacrifice and progress through sacrifice is created, among fathers and daughters the notion of sacrificing the daughter for the common good in relation to an archaic and certainly pre-Christian theme predominates. Alas, this 'common good' appears always to be seen in a masculine vein. The figure of Iphigenia remains what is possibly the most evident symbol of sacrifice of a daughter for the good of the collective, one that is perpetrated by a father without the blessing of her mother, Clytemnestra, who, in turn, will seek revenge for this unruly and bloody sacrifice.

Agnus Dei Qui Tollis Peccata Mundi

In the Catholic world, the most obvious reference to sacrifice is represented by the sacrificial lamb. The self-same symbol of Christ and of his sacrifice to liberate us from Original Sin, the lamb becomes in Avalli's novel a lacerating shout of protest against those who continue to abuse indefensible and good-natured creatures such as children. The trauma of abuse restricts itself to the field created by the symbology of the sacrificial lamb, reiterated in various ways since the beginning of the novel:

> Avevano ammassato gli agnelli da macellare nell'aia, vicino al fontanile. Faceva freddo e i loro musi fumavano. Il cortile era pieno di belati. Un gruppo di pecore faceva cerchio intorno ai piccoli che non capivano niente. Istupiditi dal freddo, cercavano il capezzolo. Ma le madri belavano di disperazione gonfiando l'aria di vapore.
>
> 'Non si può fare niente per gli agnelli. È la tradizione, è la Pasqua, per questo li ammazzano,' mi avevi spiegato. 'Ci sono casi in cui uccidere non è un'ingiustizia perché è un rito, dunque una necessità' ...
>
> 'Non si può salvargli la vita, sono predestinati.' (DB 13)
>
> (They gathered the lambs for the slaughter in the barnyard, near the trough. It was cold and their snouts blew vapours. The courtyard was full of bleating. A group of sheep made a circle around the little ones who did not understand a thing. Made stupid by the cold they looked for the nipple. But the mothers bleated of a desperation that filled the air with vapour ...
>
> 'Nothing can be done for the lambs. It is tradition, it is Easter, this is why they kill them,' you explained to me. 'There are cases in which killing is not an injustice because it is a rite, therefore a necessity ...
>
> 'No one can save them, they are predestined.')

'It is a rite, therefore a necessity': Giovanna understands how the innocence of the lambs is insufficient to save them from their destiny as decided by society. *Sacer facere*, 'to make something sacred,' is what they are doing to the lambs. According to the Church, then, it is not guilt that determines persecution, but the desire to make the innocent sacred. In *La Dea dei baci*, the community views are generally expressed via the characters of Torelli and Doriana, who – much like the chorus in classic tragedy – provide the background to both, Giovanna's indirect free speech and the narrative of her father's actions. As Torelli comments upon the events taking place in Giovanna's family, she also restores the parallel between children and lambs at the base of history and will say, 'I bambini sono innocenti. Sono gli agnelli del mondo' (DB 136; 'Children are innocent. They are the lambs of the world'). Indeed, children are the lambs of the world, and as such their sacrifice creates the archaic necessity to purify society. Easter lambs need to be killed; it is a ritual, therefore a necessity. They are not sacred, consecrated to the gods, that is, until they are killed. They are worthy of slaying, but not yet sacred. Giovanna, a killable lamb herself, cannot understand the meaning of this slaughter. What have these lambs done? She is a child, still ignorant of the importance of rites and rules and norms for a society that is still as connected to tradition and religion as the one in the Lodigiano. She wonders:

> Se Dio avesse voluto avrebbe potuto salvare quegli innocenti. 'Dio è troppo importante per certe cose,' diceva madre Rachele ... Ma se Dio era Dio avrebbe dovuto prendersi cura degli animali. Sa che gli agnelli non desiderano morire. Ma forse le cose non stavano così. Forse Dio non li sentiva.
>   Come faceva a sentirli se stava chiuso nel tabernacolo, un cofanetto tutto d'oro sull'altare? ...
>   Se Dio non parlava, se non mi faceva capire qualcosa di sé, come potevo credegli? E se non credevo, come potevo dire il rosario con gli altri la sera o cantilenare i salmi in chiesa? (DB 14)
> (If only God wanted to save those innocents he could save them. 'God is too important for some things,' Mother Rachel says ... But if God is God he should be able to take care of the animals. He knows that the lambs do not want to die. Yet, maybe God does not hear them.
>   'How could he hear them if he was closed up in the tabernacle, a golden case on the altar? ...
>   If God did not speak, if he did not make me understand something of himself, how could I believe in him? And if I did not believe, how could I say the rosary with the others at night or chant the psalms in church?')

It is this healthy, rational scrutiny of the unexplainable nature of rituals and of myths desired and consecrated by society that opens the horizons of the protagonist as a young girl. Giovanna is a lamb herself. She intuits she is going to be sacrificed. According to the distinction René Girard makes between the scapegoat *of* the text – the clearly visible theme – or *in* the text, her case belongs to the second, as the 'text acknowledges the scapegoat effect which does not control it.'[44] Giovanna's connection with the scapegoat mechanism is one that declares the 'truth of [her] persecution.'[45] Her adoption of male models for the account of her persecution follows her adoption of Jesus's starvation model when he felt abandoned by his Father. Far from being evidence of her acquiescence to the system, the daughter shows how she can narrate her story thanks to her learning, while the true persecutor, her father, lacks the cultural means to even begin to describe the story of the persecution. She takes advantage of previous scapegoat models to explain the mechanism of how her collectivity declared her to be a scapegoat and how she escaped from persecution. Giovanna-Vera knows she has been already considered an outcast by everyone in the small village at the moment in which her true identity as illegitimate daughter was discovered. Someone who does not belong to their community gave her away and Luigina the fairy took her under her wings, unfortunately not for long. Now Giovanna has no hesitation in publicly exposing herself to ridicule and contempt. She protests against the pre–Vatican II liturgical practices during Sunday high mass:

> Ho trascinato la sedia in mezzo alla navata centrale, scalza e a capo scoperto, tremando di sdegno e di fatica mentre intorno a me la gente nascondeva la faccia nei veli per soffocare la vergogna e il piacere dello scandalo ...
> 'La lasci stare,' ha tuonato il parroco. Da come mi guardava sembrava posseduto dal sacro fuoco. 'Sono il vostro pastore. Non sarò io a chiudere la porta in faccia a una pecorella smarrita. Cosa vuoi sapere, Giovanna? Parla!'
> 'Perché avete dimenticato Gesù?'
> 'Che intendi dire?'
> 'Gesù dava l'esempio con i fatti non con le parole. Voi siete bravi a predicare ma della gente non vi importa un fico secco. A voi interessano solo quelli che danno i soldi per la facciata della chiesa o per il campanile dell'Incoronata' ...
> 'Basta, Giovanna, devo riprendere a dire messa.'
> 'Sì, torna a dire messa. Tanto non è a noi che ti rivolgi. Ci dai le spalle, non vediamo niente di quello che fai. Non si capisce nemmeno quello che dici. Gesù amava il suo prossimo, parlava una lingua che tutti potevano capire'...
> Forse, come ai tempi della mamma, volevo che succedesse un miracolo, desideravo che Dio balenasse lo sguardo giù dal triangolo e dicesse al suo ministro: voltati, testone, se vuoi trovarmi non cercarmi accampato sulla pala dell'altare ma dentro il cuore sofferente di Giovanna, dentro le sue ferite, cercami nei suoi ematomi, nel suo sentimento di umiliazione che è di tutti i perseguitati e mi troverai.
> 'Hanno ragione a dire che sei matta, figliola. Però qui c'è dell'altro. Vedrò di parlarne al vescovo.' (DB 150–2)
> (I dragged my chair to the middle of the main nave, barefooted and no scarf on my head, trembling with disdain and fatigue while the people

around me hid their faces in their veils to hold back the shame and pleasure, of the scandal ...

'Leave her alone,' bellowed the priest. As he watched me, he seemed possessed by the holy fire. 'I am your pastor. I will not close the door in the face of a lost sheep. What do you want to know Giovanna? Speak!'

'Why have you forgotten Jesus?'

'What do you mean to say?'

'Jesus provided an example with words and deeds. You are wonderful at preaching, but you don't give a care about people. You are only interested in those who give money for the façade of the church or for the bell tower of the Crowned Madonna' ...

'That's enough Giovanna; I must get back to saying mass.'

'Yes, return to saying mass. It is not us that you address. You turn your back on us; we don't see anything that you do. No one can even understand what you say. Jesus loved his neighbour; he spoke a language that everyone could understand' ...

Maybe, just like when my mom was alive, I wanted a miracle to happen, I desired for God to look down from his triangle and say to his minister: turn around, blockhead, if you want to find me do not look for me camped out on the altar, but in the suffering heart of Giovanna, inside her wounds, look for me in her bruises, in her feelings of humiliation that are the same as all the persecuted ones and you will find me.

'They are right to say that you are crazy, my daughter. But here there is something else. I'll see about talking to the bishop.')

Giovanna wants to know why women have to wear a veil in church, why they cannot become priests (DB 151). She believes in a God of freedom, in a 'God of the women,' as Luisa Muraro writes. For Giovanna, as for Muraro, there exists a God that signifies freedom – the freedom to give women the possibility to vacillate and then rise to a painfully acquired freedom. In the end, the God of the women is neither a person, nor an entity, nor a substance: it is, according to Muraro, women's own expressive divine potentiality, a power.[46] God is the 'supreme potentiality,' an entity that is at once possibility for a new beginning and contextual content. If it is true, as the Vatican II document 'Sacrosanctum Concilium' affirms, that the council's own reason for being was based upon the desire 'to impart an ever increasing vigour to the Christian life of the faithful; to adapt more suitably to the needs of our own times those institutions which are subject to change; to foster whatever can promote union among all who believe in Christ,'[47] it is hard to argue that the protagonist, a young girl who feels so close to Christ in her passion and her torments most human, intuitively understands that the celebrant turning his back on the people gathered for mass cannot lead to genuine faith, but only fear. In fact, such a posture inspires in the faithful ones the fear of a God who is too distant from them; of a God who did not listen to his child and abandoned him, instead. She questions the God in which she has been taught to believe. This is neither a God of the women, nor of the oppressed. This is why Giovanna unconsciously anticipates the rules dictated by the Vatican council.

The form of collective mimeticism will not take her to physical sacrifice, but ties will be forever severed from community. The scene set in the church at high mass is very dramatic, as Giovanna's presence in the church signals her inevitable exodus from the community and connects the public epilogue of her story within the community with the private epilogue in which she will bid farewell to her previous existence. Before the final and dramatically charged talk with the Maresciallo in which both father and daughter decree legal separation from each other, Giovanna severs herself religiously from the adoptive father, from her priest, and from any form of religious oppression with this public scandal. Only after this moment will she also sever her legal ties with her adoptive father. She is certainly not a juridical miscreant, as the separation takes place by mutual agreement. And yet, for Giovanna the paternal figure remains relevant in that special teaching he gave her before and after the advent of the stepmother, before and after the advent of a muted relationship no longer based on love but on hatred and lack of respect. He was her teacher, master, and tyrant:

> Eppure, tu che non mi hai dato la vita mi hai dato un insegnamento che la vale: riconoscere il proprio stato di necessità interiore, corrispondergli, dargli spazio, voce, anteporlo a tutto. In negativo, me ne davi l'esempio. In negativo, sei stato un maestro autentico. La tua ferocia mi insegnava a non tirarmi indietro, a piantare a fondo il coltello nella carne, a tenervelo conficcato e a rimestare nella ferita aperta per far sgorgare sempre nuovo sangue.
> Credevo di aver ben appreso la lezione.
> Credevo e non sbagliavo: ho messo anni a capire che il tuo insegnamento lo praticavo soprattutto su di me. (DB 167)
> (Really, you that did not give me life but did give me an important lesson: the ability to recognize one's own state of internal need, to talk with it, to give it space, voice, and to put it before all. You gave me an example on the negative. On the negative, you have been a true teacher. Your ferocity has

taught me to not pull myself back, but to plant a knife deeply in the flesh, to hold it in and to turn it in the open wound in order to always bring new blood to the surface.

I thought I learned this lesson well.

I thought I did and I was not wrong; It took me years to understand that, for the most part, I practised your teaching on myself.)

Giovanna is not awed into obedience any longer, as she has mastered the pedagogic teachings of her father, thus making coterminous the paternal with the pedagogic.[48]

The brutality of this image, of that 'knife planted in the flesh,' brings us, one more time, to the image of sacrifice. According to Girard, sacrificial children do not belong to society; in other words, they have no links to it.[49] In the case of Giovanna, it is her very illegitimacy, the terrible sin she carries since birth, that makes possible for her the use of violence without retaliation towards the behaviour of her adoptive father, as it would have otherwise been unnatural in a relation determined not only by a paper contract but also by blood.

Her fairy godmother – Luigina – having gone to the moon, her grandparents having left, and Don Bruno sent on a mission to Brazil,[50] the protagonist is left alone to defend herself from her persecutor/tyrant. Paradoxically, her father, the one who should protect her from adversity, as her legal guardian, is instead her own persecutor. Indeed, fleeing from her guardian becomes the only way for Giovanna to become '*Vera*' and to escape her destiny as a sacrificial victim. In *La Dea dei baci*, the sacrificial victim is a daughter, in line with the mythology and the Greek tragedies Giovanna loves so much. The Freudian explanation of the mechanism of the expiatory victim as the foundation of every cultural order, or of any modern work, not demystified in *Totem and Taboo*, can be useful in reading this novel as an emancipatory and not traditional one in its approach to issues of self-awareness. In Freud's theory, however, the prohibition against killing one's own father is at the base of a societal system on which the first of the commandments found in Moses' tables rests, together with the prohibition of incest. Freud notes that 'since taboos are mainly expressed in prohibitions, the underlying presence of a *positive* current of desire may occur to us as something quite obvious and calling for no lengthy proofs based on the analogy of the neuroses. For, after all, there is no need to prohibit something that no one desires to do, and a thing that is forbidden with the greatest emphasis must be a thing that is desired.'[51]

The Gospel of Luke is the text chosen by René Girard to exemplify the notion of the expiatory lamb, the scapegoat. In it, the evangelist Luke collects all possible evidence for the scapegoat Jesus Christ – Girard notes – as the drama of Christ is needed 'to present the perspective of a victim dedicated to the rejection of the illusions of the persecutors.'[52] In the Gospels Girard finds the 'increasing ability to identify the underlying scapegoat mechanisms,'[53] which can no longer be operable when understood. 'Persecutors' – maintains Girard – 'always believe in the excellence of their cause, but in reality they hate without a cause. The absence of a cause in the accusation (*ad causam*) is never seen by the persecutors.'[54] The Gospel of Luke serves as another text from which Avalli draws much inspiration. Its function is that of constituting an anti-text for Giovanna-Vera's tirade in the church. This is an operation contrary to that which Luke laid out in the Gospel, one that I do not hesitate to define as the 'Passion of Giovanna-Vera.' The desperate love that ties the young girl to her father, the daughter's first man, opposes Girard's contention that 'usually, the unfortunate victim turns to hate those who hate him'[55] in that the protagonist collects a set of evidence against herself, and not against the father. She seeks to free her persecutor, establishing a cause, a justification for paternal behaviour. She rebels, however, at the absence of a real cause for the persecution to which she has been subjected by her father; she rebels against the incongruity of the collective system of persecution in her village. Love in the face of her father makes her pitiless towards herself, but only for as long as Giovanna remains in the collective. It is only by leaving that she can refuse her own role as victim *sine causa*. Separating herself from the group that has chosen her as the scapegoat signifies also her rebirth, leaving behind the collective dynamics that have forced her into the role of victim. Looking back, Vera writes about her father:

> Ti reputavi dalla parte della ragione. Usavi le maniere forti per inculcarmi il bene. Educarmi al rispetto dei Comandamenti. Non mi hai mai chiesto come la pensavo io. Per me il Dio degli Eserciti e della Santa inquisizione era un perverso. Ci aveva dato un comandamento impossibile da rispettare. *Ama il prossimo tuo come te stesso*. Com'è possibile amare qualcuno come se stessi se – come diceva persino don Bruno, un suo ministro – una vita intera non basta a sapere chi siamo? (DB 97; emphasis in original)
> (You held yourself on the side of reason; you used strong means to teach me the right way, to educate me in the way of the Commandments. You never asked me what I thought about it. For me the God of the Crusades

and the Holy Inquisition was a pervert. He gave to us a commandment impossible to respect: *Love thy neighbor as thyself.* How is it possible to love somebody like you love yourself if, as even Don Bruno, one of his ministers, says, an entire life is not enough to know who we are?)

The problem of the construction of identity as women and as adults is in strict dependence on the old relationship with the first man, the father. The awareness of paternal hypocrisy makes a way for itself in Giovanna: 'Professavi il Credo scacciando dalla tua mente l'immagine di questa ragazzina picchiata che non riusciva a costruire uno scudo col quale difendersi dal tuo diritto di farle male' (DB 96; 'You professed the Creed, clearing from your mind the image of this abused little girl who was unable to create a shield with which to defend herself from your right to hurt her').

The 'right' to do evil is invalidated the moment that the protagonist goes away from the community that has decreed the father as the legitimate executor of such a right. In Giovanna's case, to be a child of nobody ('ENNE ENNE') signifies and entails the beginning of a journey to the discovery of herself, Odyssea. ('Nobody' – *nessuno* – is what Odysseus calls himself when faced with the monstrous Cyclops.) Inevitably Giovanna wonders, 'Com'è possible essere figli di nessuno? Nessuno è figlio di nessuno' (DB 121; 'How is it possible to be nobody's child? Nobody is nobody's child'). Giovanna indeed feels she is nobody's daughter and a non-existing body for her putative father. Even to be born means in her case to be born from nothing. Giovanna's rebirth from a persecution whose mechanisms have been painfully understood will destine her to salvation.[56] Like Odysseus, the young girl refuses to adapt to the norms imposed by society for understanding her own identity, however double, of Giovanna and of Vera. She decides to pass on to action, to a so-called active life. To separate her Self from the father in a Lacanian sense, she needs to create herself from herself and move to a different community that does not decree her sacrifice:

[W]ith each birth something uniquely new comes into the world. With respect to this somebody who is unique it can be truly said that nobody was there before. If action as beginning corresponds to the fact of birth, if it is the actualization of the human condition of natality, then speech corresponds to the fact of distinctiveness and is the actualization of the human condition of plurality, that is, of living as a distinct and unique being among equals.[57]

The analysis of her relationship with her father is related another moment central to her path to liberation: after the scene in church, which in the novel suggests the first and very public separation of Giovanna from her community, she must see annulled the legal and juridical sanction between her and her putative father. Declaring her ties annulled, Giovanna avoids the sacrificial slaughter to which lambs are predestined by society. She must withdraw, however, from every juridical responsibility that ties her as daughter to her persecutor – her father. Giovanna makes a powerful statement. After her penultimate meeting with her father and the *carabinieri*, Giovanna is now officially only Vera for the whole world, and she finally asserts: 'La carta che avevamo firmato era in pratica un atto di morte reciproca' (DB 210; 'The paper that we signed was in actuality an act of reciprocal death'). To be born to the rediscovery of the self in an act that declares the death of both parts signifies renewing the possibility for Vera of aspiring to a real life. Action in her case corresponds to a creative act, writing and publishing poetry, an endeavour that justly honours the courage of this daughter who continues to see the father as the executor of persecution. With her creative action Vera aims for the destruction of that old world of hypocrisy so as to reconfirm her new word:

È finita, ho pensato.
Vi avevo sepolto nel passato. Avevo abbassato la saracinesca. Tu, e i vivi che mi avevano fatto soffrire non ne sareste più usciti. Solo i miei morti sarebbero venuti con me. Era finita. (DB 211)
(It's over, I thought.
I buried you all in the past. I lowered the shutter. You and the living ones who made me suffer would never escape again from there. Only my dead ones would come with me. It was over.)

The violence of psychopathological relationships is not fatal but is never resolved or ended.[58] Giovanna, nevertheless, has defined a new form for the *ius humanum* in which her relationship to her father (and the society of which he was the major, the sovereign of the little town) must end. According to Giorgio Agamben, sacredness is 'the originary form of implication of the naked life in the political-juridical order.'[59] The relation of the *homo sacer* to the sovereign constructs the notion of life as a referent to his sovereign decision. The *mulier sacra*, Giovanna, reinvents her relation to her sovereign. She refuses the original imposition of the political bind with the sovereign. Better, she performs what is called *terminum exarare*; she cancels the ancient borders between her father's authority and her (non-existing) one. The *verberatio parentis*, the violence of the son against the parent, is now the violence of the daughter against the father. By erasing the ancient prohibition of transgressing fatherly authority, Giovanna can finally leave and obtain the miracle of a rebirth. It is in the transgression of a norm, however horrible, yet traditionally part of society's rituals, that she can see her own life included in the new order. The first part of Giovanna-Vera's existential journey is drawing to an end. Purposefully retrieved for one more final assessment in this novel, the act of lowering the shutter that closes the window of an unwanted past, or Muraro's 'lived lived,' makes the necessity for Vera's isolation and departure more apparent. It is only 'moving from an experience,' as Muraro writes, 'from a lived-lived,' that Giovanna-Vera can distance herself from her 'place of birth.' In the process of undertaking this intense journey of pain, Giovanna will know how to understand, to draw a lesson from it. It is only, as Arendt comments, by contravening the law of mortality by exercising the law of action that we can begin something new. Human beings, Arendt states, 'are not born in order to die but in order to begin ... Thus action, seen from the viewpoint of the automatic processes which seem to determine the course of the world, looks like a miracle.'[60] Indeed, the act of severance from her bad teachers is the little miracle Giovanna makes for her own existence.

A Dutiful Daughter: Francesca Mazzucato's *Hot Line: Storia di un'ossessione*

An exploration for the father–daughter relationship in novels written by Italian female authors shows how these texts often continue to reveal 'the daughter's need for approval from a paternal, or even a paternalized, source of unspoken desire.'[61] Making the relationship with her father the main theme of her novel is a significant step forward for the Italian literary daughter, because it enhances the complexity of paternity and paternal function versus the father figure, too often perceived merely as a metaphor of patriarchal society by feminist theory and philosophy.[62] In Francesca Mazzucato's 1996 *Hot Line: Storia di un'ossessione*[63] the attempts to adjust to a much-hoped-for revision of the father–daughter relationship by feminist critics proves to be a painful if necessary task of uncertain solution for the female protagonist.

When literally (and literarily) dealing with her own father figure, the Italian daughter's attitude is much less transgressive and more contradictory than the prescriptive one theorized by other daughters in Anglo-American critical studies.[64] The daughter's attitude remains bound to childhood traumas and recollections. Unlike in Giovanna-Vera's story, reminiscence of the past in *Hot Line* is not conductive to any departure from the system in which those traumas occurred. Daughter Lorena's existence remains fully permeated by the traumatic and never resolved relationship with and loss of her father. In short, Lorena is paralysed by the past when trying to face the future, and she cannot leave the self except for fleeting masquerades and incursions into other female roles, like the phone-sex caller. In a way, Lorena represents many literary daughters, their vulnerability to loss, and the difficult task of mourning that follows. The bleak conclusion of this novel finds its sequel in Mazzucato's later novel *Web Cam*,[65] where the daughter's vulnerability, particularly her corporeal vulnerability, is only confirmed with respect to loss. If one was hopeful the author would extricate more meanings from her protagonist's existence other than full gratification in sex, this is not the case.

The Economies of Pain

When *Hot Line: Storia di un'ossessione* was first published, perhaps owing to the heavy marketing barrage that would greatly rely, for its promotion, more on the transgressive contents of the novel than on the melancholy and unhappiness traversing the text, it struck me positively as the manifesto of a healthy, almost redeeming transgression that owed much to previous books on the subject of pornography as liberating. A good girl with a solid upper-middle-class education, the protagonist, Lorena, works for a publishing house as a translator. She could be considered almost the portrait of the dutiful intellectual daughter depicted in Simone de Beauvoir's *Mémoirs d'une jeune fille rangée*. Of course, this perception vanishes when Lorena decides to go into the phone-sex business as her secret night job. However, Lorena does not enter the business of selling human flesh at a cheap price, a business for which many feel disdain and wish for its demise. Her job is to deliver verbal, vocal sex that she sells to needy and mostly alienated Italian men. The particular nature of Lorena's job, her independence, her casual sexual encounters, her virtual sex with subsequent descriptions of orgasm and masturbation, all seemed quite provocative and thematically innovative, at least for an Italian novel. In *Hot Line*, the business whose ads fill cheap pulp magazines picturing well-endowed women with a phone number just below their breast appeared at first to empower this intellectual and well-educated young woman. Talking about such a burning issue in narrative fiction was the equivalent of an ideological and liberating exercise in power that would show intellectual feminist progress and emancipation in Italian literary expression. This 'daughter's text' could almost convince readers it was a narrative she created to skew and demystify society-imposed roles. The daughter's narrative was trying to re-organize 'an important subject/object/family position separation – affecting not only gender, but parent position: she takes on herself both father and mother, both masculine and feminine, which is also what hysterics do. Hysteria and endogamy make an uncanny mess of generational and patrilineal articulations and taxonomies, the generic and genderic (and fictional) stabilities of story and desire.'[66]

Appropriation of one's own body, then, instead of enduring misery and consumerism at one's own cost could have been the key to understanding *Hot Line* in its disturbing desire of the father. After my first superficial response to and understanding of the novel, however, I felt it became increasingly problematic for one to consider *Hot Line* as a 'feminist heterosexual erotic narrative.'[67] The more I tried to see it as a liberating book, such as the work of Kathy Acker in which the leading question is what pornography brings as signifier (especially for women), the more I came to recognize how intricate its discursive underpinnings really were, and how, instead, the melancholic and 'sentimental daughter' was to constantly resurface in this dark tale.

On the one hand, *Hot Line* does contain some of the changes we witness in other contemporary Italian women's writings, a sense of verbal openness about women's eroticism that exacts a genuine desire to verbally 'codificare la presunta oscenità delle donne' (HL 18; 'codify the presumed obscenity of women'). Nothing of the sort was considered practicable in Italian literature until recently. *Hot Line* comes across like a novel that wishes to trouble gendered familial positions; it does a good job 'of affecting not only gender, but parent position,' as Zwinger writes.[68] On the other hand, and more dangerously, *Hot Line* remains unquestionably a heterosexual erotic narrative from which the categorizing adjective 'feminist' should be deleted, since it is ill fitted to the discourse of obsession and psychological subjection the writing unveils. This is a novel of self-discovery, patterned like a journey into the belly of the protagonist's existence while its narrator speaks freely of perversion and obsession by means of confession, her own as well as those of her callers. Its erotic undertones are deceiving and misleading because the protagonist's daughterly apprenticeship has not been successfully accomplished.

It is partially for this reason that *Hot Line*'s analysis has a place in this chapter. No mapping of a daughter's discourse could be complete without the agonizing manifestation of her difficulty in severing the ties with the father figure, no matter how transgressive the novel might be. Daughterly disavowal of the father – a wished-for *Verleugnung* – will not take place entirely. Unlike in the case of *La Dea dei baci*'s Giovanna, this daughter will not manage to sever herself and start anew. Melancholy is the strategy set for her story,[69] as her discourse obeys the law of the dynamics between mourning and libido.

The front jacket flap of *Hot Line* poses the following question (roughly translated): 'Is there really a connection between the choice of a problematic job and the morbid affection for a forever remote father?[70] Trying to arouse the curiosity of the reader by connecting the adjective 'morbid' to the noun 'father,' as if the title by itself was not already enough, can be a good way to attract buyers. I chose to take up the challenge implicit in this intriguing sentence, and I began my analysis with this very question. Indeed, this is a novel in which the broken promise of fatherly eternal love and faithfulness exacerbates the whole issue behind daughterly love. Unrequited love for the father and the daughter's regret for his broken promise of eternal love and devotion to his women turn out to be the underlying modalitie of Lorena's traumatic living condition, as she constantly experiences her own unworthiness for love while drowning in a nihilistic display of eroticism, self-eroticism, and solitude. She feels unfit for an enduring love. Her own failure to have satisfactory relationships her entire adult life and the decision to undertake the experiment of an odd job for a 'dutiful daughter' as a phone-sex operator appear to stem from her failed relation, or lack thereof, with her father. The articulation of this relation confines the daughter to the time of childhood, in much the same garb of a terrible fascination with the body of the father that Nadia Fusini describes in *La bocca più di tutto mi piaceva*.[71] As incest constitutes the taboo central to the birth of modern Western culture, it leads to not only the mother–son relation, but the father–daughter one as well. In Lorena's case, the mesmerizing effect produced by her father's intermittent presence in her life, her *attaccamento morboso* (HL 14; 'morbid attachment') to him, prevents her from ever maturing and building adult relationships with other men. If there exists anything about adulthood she grapples with, it is perhaps the ability to be hurtful with the means appropriate to adults, such as sex. Sexual proximity in exchange for love might not be a good way to solve one's traumatic childhood.

Psychoanalytical criticism focuses on the intensity with which themes are presented in the text, while it also questions some of the most current feminist revisions of Freud's analyses. As previously noted, Lorena's narration of her present life is interspersed with recollections of moments of her childhood that she spent with her father. Such episodes function as concentric waves that frame moments of Lorena's present existence. Even the rhapsodic and subsequent relation Lorena entertains with other men is ensnared with the one she had and still has with her father. When Lorena meets a man, Gabriele, in an encounter in which erotic tension builds much of the otherwise aleatory relation, her sense of estrangement from the father figure, surge of melancholia, and the relative incapability of mourning the loss of what she never actually had overwhelm any action with respect to the new man. More to the point, the unhappy story of obsession with Gabriele is an emblematic, directly related re-enactment of Lorena's obsession for her father.

The enmeshing of these two stories, the one with the father and that with Gabriele, illustrates the replicable nature of the primordial relationship with the father, replicable because it was never consummated and is limited to a libido of fetishistic nature that results in nothing but the daughter's melancholy.[72] Sigmund Freud stated in 'Mourning and Melancholia' that 'successful mourning' occurred in an individual who was able to exchange one object for another[73] after a latency period. In Lorena's case, we could advance the notion that the father could be exchanged with Gabriele to accomplish mourning. The protagonist will not succeed, however, in either attempt at departing from such losses, and that is why Lorena is the melancholic daughter who cannot manage to *actually* transfer her libido to another object in order to overcome her initial loss.[74] As Judith Butler reminds us, though, we are not looking for a 'full substitutability'[75] of the lost person, as this is not something to strive for. However, it is correct to say that, right when we think we might have overcome the sense of loss from our relationship by beginning another one, recurring patterns in the way we relate to others begin to assert themselves. Entrenched as we are in old behavioural patterns, this new relation ends up by making us realize only more acutely the loss of the other. As Freud notes, we have internalized the loss, and made it part of ourselves as melancholia, by transforming normal mourning into a pathological one. Instead of taking its due course, mourning has now shaped itself into the form of self-reproach, 'to the effect that the mourner himself is to blame for the loss of the loved object.'[76] No mourning can thus be perfected.

As in most classic studies of the feminine Oedipus Complex, Lorena represents the dutiful daughter who would do anything for her father,[77] or to regain his love, which Freud considered to be the lacking object the daughter thought she once had and then lost. Lorena fails to succeed in the process of mourning, thus leaving readers with few of the *signs of hopefulness* that Freud had optimistically theorized. Contrary to what Freud anticipated in his seminal 'The Dissolution of Oedipus Complex,'[78] Lorena does not at all overcome the feminine version of the complex. After feminist readings and rereadings of Freud's theories mediated via Melanie Klein, Joan Riviere, Jacques Lacan, and more recently Judith Butler, it becomes very difficult to substantiate 'exactly' what we can do with this essay of Freud. We are left to wonder if its tenets are at all applicable to complex individuals who enact the father–daughter relationship in a world where the notion of gender is so drastically changed in its understanding. As Freud himself was eager to admit, there are limitations to some of his studies on the Oedipus Complex. What remains unquestionable even today is that 'the little girl likes to regard herself as that which her father loves above all else'[79] and the subsequent re-staging of the trauma she undergoes upon the recognition that, essentially, in order to grow up, 'she has to endure a harsh punishment from him and is cast out of her fool's paradise.'[80] In Lorena's case, these two moments will be constantly intertwined and inextricable from her endurance in the obsession for another man, Gabriele, via the self-loathing that takes her as far as getting the job in Modena. Far from finding the forced closure Freud mentions as 'normal' in little girls growing up, the re-staging of her trauma will become for Lorena a recurring thought turned into a lifelong obsession.

Lorena X. and Dora K.

Hot Line's heterosexual discourse illustrates Lorena's behaviour to be almost another case of study for Freud. Although it is devoid of any lesbian component, we are tempted to regard it as a 'Dora K. sequel.'[81] In presenting us with her confession, Lorena does study her own case of obsessive neurosis; if not a story about self-esteem, *Hot Line* is at least about self-awareness. The 'Lorena X' case is unveiled. The novel functions like a working-through rendition of the events, one that fails to be 'in progress,' however, as it never 'becomes.' *Hot Line* limits itself to examining all the steps Lorena takes in order to make herself less vulnerable to the lack – her father's absence. Lorena's story is one in which Freud's variation of Napoleon's pronouncement 'anatomy is (absolutely) destiny'[82] ought to be provocatively interpreted in the most essentialist manner in that it reveals its suffocating ineluctability, since the outcome of all this won't be the 'normal' desire for procreation Freud found so categorical in women. If their sexual orientation is heterosexual, women can't escape their destiny as daughters; they can't escape their first love, their father. Contrary to what Freud wrote, after the actualization of the inevitable moment of disappointment at the father's breaking of the promise he made to Lorena as a little girl, she will never gain self-worth. In spite of all her transgressive camouflage, Lorena accepts her destiny as the sentimental/dutiful daughter in the sense that she does not overcome her lack and move on with her life. In a tragic but fruitful way, this was the path Giovanna-Vera managed to find for herself. This ontogenetic view is compatible, Freud notes, with the phylogenetic one that envisions this stage as a possible one in everybody's life. In the case of the little girl, however, Freud dismisses any trouble about the recognition that she will never gain what she lacks. 'The essential difference [between boy and girl] thus comes about that the girl accepts castration as an accomplished fact, whereas the boy fears the possibility of his occurrence.'[83] In the case of Lorena, the 'loss of love' of the father, one that should eventually facilitate the growth of the little girl vis-à-vis that of the boy – deeply engaged in his fear of castration – will not act in this manner. It will eventually become her unwanted, unresolved, destiny, offered to the readers *as is*.

'Lorena' is not the protagonist's real name; it is a fictional name she uses for her secret identity when speaking with her clients at night. It is a name that inevitably reminds us, linked as we are to our own *hic et nunc*, of Lorena Bobbitt and her husband's actual eviration (or castration, as Freud would always use this term instead while meaning eviration).[84] 'Lorena,' as Claire Kahane notes, is 'a virtual anagram' of Leonor or 'Lioness.' The suggestions such a name ignites make it only plausible that Lorena-the-Lioness could avenge herself and her mother for the desertion they both suffered by the father. She could finally break free of the sorrow caused by that broken promise her father made to her never to leave her. Further, if decapitation is the equivalent of castration, as Freud theorizes in 'Medusa's Head,'[85] Lorena could finally claim vindication for her mother's and her own masochistic passiveness. It is the lack of a female economy of desire that promotes female rage.⁸⁶ Kahane argues that, in Freud's and Klein's conceptualization, 'it is the mother,' the

> ambivalently constructed other who bears at the same time the traces of self, who is the primal object of this unconscious rage and desire – an object, moreover whose value potentially rivals that of the phallus, and whose loss within a patriarchal symbolic order is made analogous to castration. The analogy returns us to the overdetermined trope of castration at the heart of psychoanalysis and to knife-wielding, castrating women – the mythical Judith as well as the more prosaic Lorena Bobbitt.⁸⁷

Obsession derives from the Latin verb *obsidere*, 'to put under siege.'⁸⁸ She who is obsessed is constantly under the psychological siege of her loss. In *Hot Line* the psychological siege of her father's object becomes the focal obstacle to Lorena's adult life. It creates a paramount obstruction to her fulfilment as an individual. Her loss is textually exemplified repeatedly in both Lorena's second, illicit job and in her sense of unworthiness of anybody's love that partially drives her choice to become a sex caller. Lorena knows the difference between a recurring thought and an obsession: 'L'ossessione non si toglie dalla testa, rimane nella testa e nel cuore e fa male, fa male ogni volta che ci si pensa, cioè ogni giorno. Non appena la mente è sgombra si intrufola e ci prospetta giustificazioni improbabili' (HL 72; 'Obsession never leaves you, it remains in your head and heart and hurts. It hurts every time that one thinks about it, that is, everyday. As soon as the mind is clear it slips right into and offers unlikely justifications'). It is Lorena's basic inability to mourn the loss of her father that turns her grief into the pathological state of obsession, and situates her in an economy of melancholy in which the 'subject persists in his or her narcissistic identification with the lost object.'⁸⁹

The lack of compliance in *Hot Line* to the temporal limitation of Lorena's mourning period for her presumed lack as provided in Freud's studies also constructs the lack of the protagonist's self-esteem. This long-standing stage only prolongs her desire not to enter the sameness of her mother, and yet there is no actual split from the father's lack. The two parental figures collapse into her unresolved fixation, almost repeating verbatim the situation theorized in Zwinger's study. Had Lorena's mourning been framed within a 'reasonable,' quantifiable time – assuming this term has a meaning aside from sterile medical wording – a regular lapse of time like the one accorded by Freudian parameters, her personal grief could have passed on as admissible, even justifiable. It would have entered with full rights the category of 'normal.' Lorena could have entered adult life as expected, and her transgressive act of phone-sex operator could have in turn become an actual form of transgression. In the protracted time that goes from childhood to adulthood, this feeling of loss, reified in the most literal loss of the father, becomes instead what the book says right from the title: an obsession devoid of transgression, as Lorena will never trans-pass mentally her family apartment's threshold. Her confession mirrors quite faithfully Freud's assessment of the melancholic:

> The melancholic displays something else besides that which is lacking in mourning – an extraordinary diminution in self-regard, an impoverishment of his ego on a grand scale. In mourning it is the world which has become poor and empty; in melancholia it is the ego itself. The patient represents his ego to us as worthless, incapable of any achievement and morally despicable; he reproaches himself, vilifies himself and expects to be cast out and punished ... He really is as lacking in interest and as incapable of love and achievement as he says.[90]

Work, relationships, her geographical situatedness, everything in Lorena's life seems to entrap her in this tale of obsession that, in turn, provokes perennial melancholy. Sexual issues, concerns regarding actual autonomy ('non ho fantasie di dominio, caso mai di sottomissione,' HL 26; 'I do not fancy any domineering dreams, perhaps some of submission'), and eating disorders become intertwined in the reminiscence of a difficult adolescence, of Lorena's female *Erziehungsroman*. Crushed between the power of the Catholic Church, an institution in which her mother blindly believes to the point of sending the daughter to serve mass, and the *Feste dell'Unità* (the Communist Party popular gatherings to which her father would invariably take her as a child), Lorena illustrates her growing up as passively living through, and by, the traditional poles of power in Emilia-Romagna. The Church is represented by the rite of the mass where the child assists the parish priest in administering Holy Communion, a sacrament of which her only memory remains the number of mouths wide open Lorena would see ('quante bocche,' HL 26; 'how many mouths').[91] Unlike in the case of Giovanna-Vera, there is no act of protest against the passive role she had in the mass, only the recollection. The Communist Party is reified by the famous tradition of the *Feste dell'Unità*. One *Festa*, in particular, is constantly brought to mind, the one at which her father promised her never to leave her mother: 'Io e la mamma non ci separeremo mai' (HL 14; 'your mother and I will never separate'). Her father's broken promise is forever entangled in one of the sources of power that Lorena rejects. The loci of the Church in Bologna and the *Festa dell'Unità* are evidence of the polarization of secular and religious powers through which Emilia's airtight patriarchal system runs society. They are two key places in the destiny of the daughter, as *Hot Line*, in its complete passiveness to the system, exposes both institutions for their suffocating roles in the education of women. Her father's word, representing his infallibility in the eyes of the daughter, has been desecrated by his own acts. By not keeping faith with his promise, the world his daughter believed in has crumbled under his sin. Paradise is lost.

As a lawyer, the father utilizes words skilfully, playing games with them that hold no veracity. His own profession actually entitles him to play with signifiers. Such a job, thanks to a millennial-long stereotyping in Western literature and theatre, only elicits the deceptiveness of the father's discourse, which now shifts towards the private in mystifying his daughter for his own benefit. The construction of discourse continues according to the law of the father, while matrilineal history appears to be interrupted. In the novel, the recollection of a scene in the Bologna courthouse works to explain the patriarchal discourse that the establishment made official. Lorena's mother is forced into an undesired separation while her lawyer, 'Z.,' pleasantly chats with his colleague, her husband and counterpart in the separation case ('Ridevano e si davano delle pacche sulle spalle,' HL 53; 'They were laughing and slapping each other on the back'). The father's discourse appears to be firmly rooted within Italian society, as even in one of the most progressive parts of the country, Emilia-Romagna, the habits of patriarchy are stifling. The act of the lawyer politely opening the door to his client, the former wife of his colleague, Lorena's father, only draws out the hypocrisy implicit in such gestures. Politeness as empty etiquette shows a lack of respect for the woman who is incapable of actions that could achieve her emancipation.

The explicit bonding among the 'boys' caught playing their usual power game in a place that is familiar to them (the courthouse) is reminiscent of the initial statement Lorena makes about her estrangement from any form of bonding with boys as a child. As a young girl, her decision to not bond with her mother, her lack of compassion for her, her personal resistance to understanding her, find a commentary in the Freudian notion that '[i]nvariably the child regards castration in the first instance as a misfortune peculiar to herself; only later does she realize that it extends to certain other children and at length to certain adults. When the universality of this negative character of her sex dawns upon her, womanhood, and with it also her mother, suffers a heavy loss of credit in her eyes.'[92] It is hardly a surprise that Lorena holds her mother partly responsible for the abandonment of the father since, as Freud notes in his analyses, 'girls hold their mother responsible for their lack of a penis and do not forgive her for their being thus put at disadvantage.'[93] As for Lorena, her awareness of female sexuality (her descriptions of solitary pleasure and the sexual education needed to achieve such pleasure introduce the actual story of her obsession) fails to grant her the power of organizing an economy of desire exclusively defined by female criteria:

> Prima ero come divisa tra la percezione istintiva di un corpo, il mio, che da solo poteva accendersi al piacere, e il buio, il niente, l'ignoranza assoluta, la finzione. Non sapevo a chi chiedere consiglio : gli uomini, i ragazzi nel loro universo spiccio parlano di masturbazione, ... noi forse non troviamo le parole. (HL 3)
> (Before I was divided between the instinctual perception of a body, mine, that could ignite pleasure by itself, and the darkness, the nothing, absolute ignorance, pretence. I did not know to whom to turn for advice: men, boys in their brisk (no-nonsense) world talk about masturbation, ... perhaps we don't find the words.)

In the end, the nearness to the other theorized by Luce Irigaray works against Lorena's capability at gaining control of herself, even as an adult. In this post-Freudian story, the (gendered) roles appear to remain intact. Man is active, woman is passive; there's nothing new, except for what Lorena does at night: 'lavoro in un telefono erotico e sono anch'io una sex-worker anche se mi occupo di una forma di sesso virtuale che i miei amici francesi chiamano "masturbation sophistiquée"' (HL 7; 'I work in the phone-sex business and I am a sex-worker even if I deal with a form of virtual sex that my French friends have termed "masturbation sophistiquée"'). In this self-analysed story of 'Lorena X,' the roles remain the same as in Dora's analysis by Freud. According to tradition, the father speaks while his daughter listens. In her illicit job, Lorena listens while sex is being spoken. Perhaps this is her only bitter-sweet revenge; the very one that, in fact, initially prompted me into thinking of this as a progressive tale, only to comprehend fully the implications of

Lorena's choice later. In speaking of her new line of work, Lorena confesses to her readers that she has not said anything to her parents:

> Non sanno che lavoro al telefono già da un mese, vorrei raccontarlo a entrambi, vorrei scandalizzarli, chiamarli testimoni della mia trasgressione, ma non è il momento : sono diventati cosí rari questi pranzi insieme, anni fa erano frequenti e io non mi accorgevo di tenerci tanto, è una unità un po' ipocrita, forzata, ma siamo tutti insieme, posso vedere la nuca di mio padre che guida, i capelli radi sulla fronte e piú folti ai lati, il sorriso, il sorriso che a volte sfugge, diventa svagato, la mamma è imbarazzata e lo vedo il suo imbarazzo, cerca di contenerlo, ma si nota, è un imbarazzo misto a un sentimento di pena.
>
> Non ho molti ricordi del periodo che ha preceduto la separazione, il momento in cui iniziò questo dolore sordo, questa litania di morte che mi porto sempre dietro. (HL 19)

(They do not know that I have already been working via the phone for a month, I want to tell them both everything, I want to embarrass them, to make them witnesses of my transgression, but it is not the right time: the moments when we have lunch together have become so rare, years ago they were so frequent and I did not realize we were so close to each other. It is a unity a little hypocritical and forced, but we are all together. I can see the nape of my father's neck as he drives, his hair thinning in the front and thick on the sides, his smile, a smile that at times is fleeting, becomes absent-minded. My mother is embarrassed, and although she tries to hide it, I notice it. It is an embarrassment mixed with a feeling of pain.

I do not have many memories of the period before the separation, the moment in which this deaf pain began, this death-like litany that I always carry with me.)

Modena

Although from Bologna, Lorena has chosen to work in Modena, a nearby town, near the train station. Modena is the town that reminds Lorena of her bourgeois Saturday meals with the father at Fini's, one of the culinary bastions of the opulent Italian bourgeoisie. The location of the restaurant could partly signify the decision of Lorena to undertake her porn-calling, even for a few months, in the very city where Fini is located, Modena. Confined to tradition, and driven probably by habit, the father has been taking Lorena and her mother to eat at the lavish Fini restaurant also after to the dissolution of the marriage, a ceremony that still takes place, in fact, years after their separation. In the novel, the Fini restaurant functions also as a synecdoche of gluttony. While the incestuous relationship becomes metaphorized into a culinary speech, one that is consumed in front of the mother, Lorena recalls the first time she saw her father naked. Watching the nape of her father's neck while he drives along the Emilia road to Modena, while she sits as an obedient daughter in the back of the car as she always has for as long as she can remember, re-evokes in Lorena the first time she saw her father's nudity *and* his voice: a scene that – in both elements composing it, the body and the voice of the father – triggers her memory, never leaves her alone, and reveals her unaccomplished task of severing from the father figure. The concentric waves of the past keep modulating the present with a rippling effect:

> Sento la voce di mio padre che parla con la nonna in cucina, e basta l'eco a rassicurarmi. Guardo dalla finestra: lui si alza e comincia a salire le scale. Va a fare la doccia nel bagno al secondo piano, penso. Corro in casa, lo seguo a distanza. Riesco a vederlo di spalle mentre si toglie l'accappatoio ed entra nella doccia, una vecchia doccia con una tenda di plastica. Quella parte del suo corpo cosí segreta, indecente, la prima nudità maschile, la trovo bella ... L'acqua sul suo corpo, scrosci d'acqua sul quel corpo caldo, profumato ...
>
> Perché vedo la sua nuca solo in rare occasioni e non mi viene neanche il gesto cosí familiare di fargli una carezza? (Una carezza sulla nuca, oppure un bacio). (HL 20)

(I hear my father's voice talking to my grandmother, and its echo is enough to reassure me. I look at the window: he gets up and begins to go up the stairs. He goes to take a shower in the second-floor bathroom, I think. I run into the house, I follow him at distance. I manage to see his shoulders while he is taking off his robe and enters the shower, an old shower with a plastic curtain. That part of the body so secret, indecent, the first male nudity, I find it beautiful ... The water on his body, the water roars on that warm, scented body ...

Why do I see the nape of his neck only on rare occasions and the familiar gesture of caressing never occurs to me? (A caress on his neck, or a kiss).

The scenes of traumatic recollections of meals spent with her father at Fini's in Modena are juxtaposed with the telling of Lorena's present existence of sex operator shuttling between Bologna and Modena. In the brief twenty-minute train ride from Bologna to Modena, Lorena endlessly retraces her trauma as a cruel practice on herself, to be better fit psychologically to listen to the callers' confessions later in that town that ties her to her father and her childhood. She can constantly re-enact the trauma.

She rides the train with the African prostitutes as if she were in her father's car, looking at the nape of his neck. Even though she shares the train with the prostitutes, Lorena's commuting holds a rather different purpose. She is paid to listen to sexual confessions, which always begin with the specific request for the writing of money necessary to get a "conversation" started with clients. Lorena lets her clients speak as they want while they in turn find in her "active" passivity a true *jouissance* in the Lacanian and literal meaning of the word. In Mazzucato's tale of obsession, the structure of feminine sexuality is connected with the knowledge that it has been constructed in accordance with male-oriented patterns of pleasure. The protagonist constantly plays with them, even though the results at the end of each call are only small bittersweet victories. Though bittersweet, it is through this process of listening to others that she becomes aware of the reasons for her own melancholy and her basic apathy, except where her father's need is concerned:

> La vita quotidiana qui al telefono è costellata di urgenze e io le osservo come spettatrice ... Io non vivo mai necessità assolute, qualcuna relativa legata a singoli momenti e situazioni, di brevissima durata. Tutto mi è sempre parso perfettamente intercambiabile. (HL 25)
> (Daily life on the phone is a constellation of urgencies that I observe like a viewer ... I do not ever live absolute necessities, something relatively linked to single moments and situations, usually of a very brief duration. Everything has always seemed to me perfectly interchangeable.)

Lorena is aware of the dynamics of female pleasure. She is also profoundly aware of the construction of female sexuality as it is given under patriarchal terms; otherwise she could hardly perform the task of pleasing men. Pretending a complacent orgasm for those men who desperately needed 'modalità fisse di piacere' (HL 18; encoded ways of pleasure') was what Lorena developed before landing her temp job in Modena. She thought 'di non meritare di godere' (HL 18; 'not to deserve pleasure'). This is true until she gets her job in Modena, which I originally read as an empowering activity in its fullness. As she deemed herself undeserving of experiencing pleasure, her true life now takes place at night in Modena, where *abisso notturno* or 'nocturnal abyss' signifies both the abyss of the voices she hears and the plunging into a sexual orgasm that is not feigned, 'Ho un desiderio di fluidità e limpidezza che provo solo sui treni, al telefono, perdendomi' (HL 31; 'I have a

156   A Multitude of Women

desire for fluidity and clarity that I feel only on the train, on the telephone, losing myself'). This desire '[è] un piacero strano, condivisible con una voce ma non condiviso con un corpo, quindi un piacere autoreferenziale, sofisticato, primitivo su cui è proiettata l'ombra dei muri dell'ufficio, l'ombra dell'inquietudine che mi ha portato a lavorare in questo telefono' (HL 38; 'is a strange pleasure that is shared with a voice but not with a body, thus a self-referential pleasure, sophisticated, and primitive, on which the shadow of the office walls is projected; the very shadow of restlessness that led me to work in this phone').

Lorena retells the first memory of solitary sexual pleasure (HL 4), where 'la fantasia' takes over and in which 'si evita l'infinita pena che spesso accompagna i congiungimenti carnali' (HL 16; 'one shuns the infinite pain that often comes with carnal relations'); a solitary pleasure in which she can be 'come un uomo, finalmente, senza un uomo' (HL 5; 'like a man, finally without a man'). She reaches jouissance by herself, while affirming Lacan's assumption that 'woman not being-whole' has a 'supplementary jouissance compared to what the phallic function designates by way of jouissance.[94]

The knowledge Lorena has gained serves the purpose of making her revenge effective, and wherever possible more effective than it ever could be by manipulating male fetishism by phone. The sad aspect of parodying the remake of male pornographic discourse – that is, the traditional notion of pornography as used by women for men's pleasure – is similarly visible in Francesca Mazzucato's inverted use of one particular part of the female body to mime the essence of pornography. Her form of prostitution prevents her from having an actual encounter with the other; it leaves only her voice. However, Lorena's form of selling sex is physical since she utilizes a part of her body (her voice) in order to feign arousal and interact with the male. 'The pornography addict cannot sustain the body as a whole and so takes it to pieces, so that he can deal with just one fragment at a time; it is with these fragments that he entertains himself and passes his time.'[95] Out of the possible *pieces*, the voice is what Mazzucato's character opts for to represent her separation from her bourgeois Father's system. She voices that body that has been completely erased and ultimately betrayed by the patriarchal system.

Confession as an Obsessive Form

Lorena confesses to us. *To acknowledge* is the root (Latin) meaning of this verb. Jeremy Tambling argues that confession needs to be discussed from three aspects: what kind of knowledge is produced by confession, sexuality as a topic in confession, and how the demand to speak is related to the production of narrative. What is the role of confession in the production of Lorena's narrative? Is she confessing that her own act of listening to aroused males via the phone alleviates her restlessness? 'Sapere di consumare la mia inaudita transgressione è un po' come punirlo' (HL 22; 'To be aware of consummating my unprecedented transgression is a bit like punishing him'), Lorena states. We need not wonder about who the 'him' might be. It is interesting, however, that the 'audible' part of one's body comes again in that adjective, *inaudito* – 'unheard of,' quite literally. There is the audible part that Lorena takes always into consideration, even when confessing to us her crime of being a porn-caller, and thus quite 'audible.' *Belle de jour,* Luis Buñuel's famous film of 1966, in which Catherine Deneuve played the role of a bourgeois Parisian, Sévérine, who prostitutes in the afternoon while her husband, Pierre, is at the hospital working long hours, constitutes a cinematic antecedent for *Hot Line.* Like the film, the novel concerns a young bourgeois woman who chooses an unworthy way of behaviour out of protest, or out of too much love for a man. In Sévérine's case, it was an oppressive feeling of love for her own husband, while in Lorena's it is a protest against her own father's abandonment *and* too much love, as well.

The traumatic memory of how her father left her as a child and her mother, after a nightmarish twenty-four hours of phone calls for his lover, led the protagonist into seeking vengeance as a grown-up by utilizing the same 'means' by which she lost the father to this unknown woman: the phone. She can produce and arouse desire over the phone with her voice. With her father having left them for another woman who constantly solicited him by the phone, what Lorena chooses to use for her pornography cannot be any visible part of her body; it clearly has to be her voice. Her audible part that has never been listened to, which in the novel becomes a *pharmakon* for Italian men on the verge of male hysteria owing to the de-legitimization of their masculinity, is now her only tool. By possessing and utilizing her voice (which is pure *phone,* as she does not feel herself to be a subject of desire in any relationship), she exercises, at her leisure, a form of authority over others.[96] The *phone,* as in the telephone calls, is something Lorena has transformed into her bitter business of living. Selling only this 'part of the body' is what arouses the male pornographers. According to Luce Irigaray, touching and not seeing defines women's way to pleasure. The 'voice' is not a vehicle of her father; only the act of touching could be. She is, therefore, no object of desire unless she desires to be one, and tries in this fashion to delete her sense of rejection.

Male fetishism becomes a part of the game. Clients ask her how she is dressed, how she looks (HL 14–15), and she fills that fissure between the visible and the knowable with a masquerade. Questions about her dress invariably lead her to a list and description of the most obvious pieces of clothing she imagines might arouse her callers and they might want to imagine her wearing. What they cannot see must be imagined as they would like it to appear in order to reach arousal.[97] The lack of differentiation Joan Rivière describes between womanliness and masquerade as a woman that lasts until the female individual has grown aware of this construction, caught as an important moment in the formation of her identity, reverberates in Lorena's reaction to her new awareness. Her sense of lack-turned-into-loss – which makes Freud's distinction ever thinner and closer to Klein's – becomes understandable the very moment in which she comprehends that she had never had the love of the father from the start. She now has to demonstrate full awareness of the game she is playing, of how she is manipulating men's fetishism. She needs to perceive a manner to avenge her own sense of indeterminacy in this exploitation, even when refusing to assume the role of dominatrix in the conversations, as she prefers to leave such a job to her colleague 'Marilyn.' She is not needed by anybody, and yet she mourns the lack. Again, let's not forget that she is not exposing herself; she is not really dressed in flashy clothes and garters, as she describes to her callers. This masquerade is as virtual as her calls. It is a deliberate manipulation of the imaginary desires of men turned into a form of intellectual revenge.

In spite of all this, I contend that it is precisely her melancholic mood, her initial confusion between loss and lack, that reveals the limits of her chosen transgression, and thus it is merely a pretended transgression and not a joyous one. As Slavoj Žižek states, in today's world, 'transgression itself is appropriated, solicited even, by the dominant institutions, the predominant opinion as a rule presents itself as a subversive transgression.'[98] The significance of her job loses any claim of actual transgression as it is constantly subverted by the confession by Lorena of a tale of impossible love for the object-father who, far from being lost, has really never been hers. As Žižek claims, it all results in a melancholy that 'is not simply the attachment to the lost object but the attachment to the very original gesture of its loss.'[99]

My analysis of the (failed) transgression that Lorena attempts to commit as a means to overcome her melancholy could be completed if we did not have other elements of the novel that further my thesis about Lorena's desire as power and obsession for the father turning into a flawed behavioural pattern. The truth of the matter is that although the book claims to be the story of one obsession, it is in reality the story of two obsessions 'for the price of one,' as marketers say. Lorena cannot get rid of her father's ghost, a ghost that determines her ability to eat certain foods instead of others, to claim vengeance and temporarily abandon a decent job in a publishing house in order to sell her voice to anonymous caller. A ghost, particularly, that moulds her entire subsequent relationship with the other man with whom she falls in love and about whom we are presented with the alternate narrative: Gabriele, a client, and her obsession for him. Her basic lack of self-worth will be conducive only of disappointing relations in which unrequited love will take over any other feeling.

Second Obsession: Gabriele

Since Lorena comes from a broken family, the father-daughter-mother triangle is broken, disseminating meaning through her life. Fragments of it are scattered everywhere. Its original unity and coherence, a sort of Holy Trinity, loses any chance of reaffirmation with the entrance of the third woman.[100] Out of this lack, the ghost of her father determines her new obsession for Gabriele, a man whom, like her father, she will never have:

> The melancholic still displays the metaphysical yearning for another absolute reality beyond our ordinary reality subjected to temporal decay and corruption; the only way out of this predicament is thus to take an ordinary, sensual material object (say, the beloved woman) and elevate it into the absolute. The melancholic subject thus elevates the object of his longing into an inconsistent composite of a corporal absolute; however, since this object is subject to decay, one can possess it unconditionally only insofar as it is lost, in its loss.[101]

Lorena's obsession with Gabriele acts as a continuation and expansion of her original obsession with the father. The original obsession becomes also the obstacle to a fulfilment of her desire, to a fulfilment of the urgency she finally feels for him. 'Posso giocare anch'io con la mia urgenza, pensavo che per me non ci fosse nulla di necessario, invece no, invece no' (HL 40; 'I too can play with my urgency. I thought that there was nothing else necessary, instead no, instead no'). A moment of hope emerges from the well of inertia Lorena has plunged into since her casual encounter with the man. The practicalities of sexual consumption, the money order to be made out in order to receive phone sex, Lorena's own awareness that her life is not at all what she projected but something that she endures as she endures the company of the commuting Nigerian prostitutes on the train from Bologna to Modena, do not save her from this painful encounter with Gabriele. His voice has a 'lieve accento bolognese, tenero, familiare' (HL 36; 'soft, tender, familiar Bolognese accent') that quickly makes us think of her father's accent, her father's voice. Lorena finds it simple to talk with Gabriele of the 'increscioso e spesso imbarazzante dolore che ci provocano le persone che amiamo, e non è strano parlare di morte e di dolore dopo un orgasmo al telefono, perché è stato un piacere doloroso, che mi fa ancora male' (HL 37; 'regrettable and often embarrassing pain that people we love provoke in us, and it's not out of the ordinary to talk about death and pain after a phone orgasm, because it has been a painful pleasure, which still hurts'). Lorena is no longer acting; she cannot transgress her obsession with the father figure that is now replicated by Gabriele's familiar voice. 'Mi lascio andare, non è la solita routine di parole scontate: lo intuisco subito quasi sgomenta' (HL 36; 'I let myself go, this is not the usual routine of trite words: I sense it immediately, almost frightened'). Effectively, Gabriele's voice becomes another obsession (HL 40), and we know what is going to happen next. We are bound to see Lorena dealing, once again, with the father image.[102] Why is she bound, for instance, to perform only oral sex on Gabriele? A statement such as 'Non potevo immaginare che si potesse desiderare in modo cosí doloroso' (HL 76; 'I could not imagine that one could desire in such a painful way') unquestionably directs us to dealing with the issue of pain. As female rage, pain, and anger are often repressed, they nevertheless leave only 'phantasms of emptiness' in their place, and void replaces rage. 'The only way to possess an object that we never had, that was from the very outset lost,' Žižek continues, 'is to treat an object that we fully possess as if this object is already lost.[103] Gabriele is there, Lorena meets him and desires him, and yet she deals with this new love as if it were already lost.[104] It is not by chance that Lorena recognizes that the only tie to Gabriele was indeed 'il dolore che ci provocano le persone che amiamo' (HL 37; 'the grief that people we love provoke in us').

In her fourth novel, *Web Cam*, Mazzucato deals once more with the paradox of melancholy as she presented it in her first novel. In *Web Cam*

Lorena's attempts at coming to terms with Gabriele's ghost so as to finally terminate the circle of obsession in which she moves will in turn make of her, after being the subject of a love obsession, only the object of a highly dangerous one with the dark overtones of a thriller. If we think how promisingly liberating *Hot Line* appeared to readers, the approach to the issue in *Web Cam* hardly reveals a step forward. Feeling the void of having lost someone that you thought you once had becomes a constant regret: something that she never had and never will be hers, whether it is her father or Gabriele. There was never an actual relationship between Lorena and her father, but merely a daughter's unhappy sentimental subjection. By trying to recreate the same interaction with Gabriele, one that is doomed to fail, she does not overcome her melancholia, but only augments her sense of personal loss and decrease in self-esteem. Hers is a trauma that is everlasting and, therefore, never fully resolved, not even after the orthodox Freudian temporal latency period that patients affected by traumatic events usually experience before they can utter a narrative of the trauma.

The different milieu, the Bolognese affluent professional high bourgeoisie versus the Padanian agrarian type, makes an enormous difference in the different kinds of 'kicks' fathers will give their daughters, literal in the case of Giovanna, figurative in the case of Lorena. It is the outcome, what the daughters both do with their lives, that draws the drastically diverse paths their narratives will follow. Whereas in *La Dea dei baci* one witnesses the daughter's parting from the father figure, with a clear annihilation of ties, both legal and social, that result in Giovanna's act of *terminum exarare*, in *Hot Line*, instead, the separation between daughter and father remains clouded by melancholy for time past that the daughter still cherishes, when she thought she was her daddy's (bourgeois) good little girl. Whereas the civil and social contracts between Giovanna and her father are severed, even if under duress, the one of Lorena with her father continues. Nothing becomes disengaged. Though Lorena's act of writing does not offer a redeeming ending to her fatherly love, it remains indisputable that, in order to become an 'active' individual in Arendt's sense of the term, daughters have to be cast out of their fathers' paradise. Yet the lack of the father is still there.

Of Artistic Fathers: Pia Pera, *Lolita*, and Her Diary, or the Power of Rereading a Text

> Curiously enough one cannot read a book: one can only reread it. A good reader, a major reader, an active and creative reader is a re-reader.[105]

> Between the age limits of nine and fourteen there occur maidens who, to certain bewitched travelers, twice or many times older than they, reveal their true nature which is not human, but nymphic (that is, demoniac); and these chosen creatures I propose to designate as 'nymphets.'[106]

The final part of this chapter addresses issues specifically connected with the artistic relation daughters entertain with fathers. More particularly, what do Italian women novelists do at the end of the twentieth century with their reading of male authors? Is it just another form of imitation of models or do they position their work with respect to that of their fathers in a different – but non-essentialistic – way? What strategies of postmodernism do they use to comment in a literary form upon questionable depictions of the woman in all stages of her experience? As explained in the case of Giovanna-Vera, the use of fatherly figures was not a parodic one, as she could not have the emotional distance to operate in that manner. She was, however, able to convert them to her own needs and make of the scapegoating mechanism a structure for deconstruction from within the very social and ideological setting of her suffocating setting, the Po Valley, with the Christian Democrat's shield indicating a *Libertas* that for her came only with leaving the town.

For some, such as Pia Pera, the author of the third novel I examine in this chapter, the answer relies instead on the skilful employment of rereading[107] patriarchal texts. In *Diario di Lo*, Pera's rereading can be considered a 'fruitful' utilization of parody to be recognized not as the 'key element' of postmodernism, but to be used as a venue for her own criticism (and) playfulness to overrun explicit misuses of female characters. Writing involves reading, and good writing necessarily involves the act of rereading. Homage is unquestionably an element of rereading, even when, as in Pera's case, the desire to revisit Nabokov's patriarchal use of fiction and rhetoric looms large. Far from ignoring literary fathers, literary daughters engage in a discussion with their texts that, in my view, is more fruitful than simply longing for the perfect relationship with the father figure. Paternalism abounds in literature, and it's difficult to ignore it. Better to make (useful) fun of it.

Limiting the Ethos of Parody

Lolita is a self-reflexive novel; it is a work on the art of making a novel. Extremely metanarrative in its outcome, it constitutes one of the most brilliant examples of the use of double coding, anticipating its vast application during postmodernism. In its exasperated consciousness to be an example of literature that ontologically folds onto itself – searching in its sublimation for its own real essence – Nabokov's narcissistic text lends itself to the authorial desire of retracing and criticizing signifiers of a social reality through its parodic writing.

Nabokov's novel *Lolita* resonated as 'a grenade exploded in the mid-50s,'[108] and its resonance can still be heard in recent events. Forty years after the controversial explosion of the *Lolita* grenade, Italian writer Pia Pera published *Diario di Lo*, a parodic rewriting of *Lolita*. What interests me most about *Diario di Lo* is not only Pera's intent to deconstruct Nabokov's novel in all its elements: the seductive power of a nymphet; the need for seduction of a European decadent aesthete such as Professor Humbert; Lolita's mother, Charlotte Haze – a gullible widow hungry for European good taste and culture. More to the point, I am intrigued by Pera's systematic dismantling of the values hidden in Nabokov's writing, exemplified by the writing about a girl whose credibility before the readers depends entirely on an expatriate professor's judgmental and begrudging pen, the pen of a middle-aged professor of literature whose exasperated aestheticism borders on authentic illness. Pera juxtaposes other values with those of the professor. These values, chiefly Lo's freedom to behave mischievously, think independently, and wish for emancipation from her suitor, are equally questionable from an ethical standpoint for their results. Just like Nabokov, Pera was not concerned with giving an ethical spin to her story.[109] Pera's deconstruction aimed at revealing a female subjectivity willingly overlooked by Lo's creator, Humbert Humbert. Pera's understanding of the heroine is a postfeminist one that critiques Nabokov's outrageous depiction of this female child. Her rewriting of the story empowers the character of Lo as she changes from a mere, though manipulative, object of desire, to being the very writing subject. The story that the entomologist denied, that of a chrysalis becoming a butterfly, is hence narrated by Lo this time.

The Lawsuit

On 10 October 1998 the *New York Times* Arts section devoted a good deal of attention – quite unusual for an Italian writer – to Pia Pera. The columns concerning Pera, however, did not discuss her narrative merits, but a lawsuit over copyright infringement and the limits of artistic borrowing that Vladimir Nabokov's son, Dmitri, filed against the American publisher Farrar, Straus, & Giroux, which had 'dared' to buy the rights for the English translation of Pera's *Diario di Lo* – to be published in America as *Lo's Diary*. Why such sudden fame for Pera and why a lawsuit? *Diario di Lo* was yet another parody of *Lolita*,[110] but Nabokov's son Dmitri did not like his father's art to be challenged in such a manner. His legal action against Farrar, Straus, & Giroux and his lawyer's accusations against Pia Pera of 'aesthetic and literary vampirism'[111] are emblematic of how artistic sons do not receive their fathers' intellectual legacy, just their financial one. Dmitri seemed to not have fully grasped the basis for his father's own theories concerning the art of novel writing. This dutiful son might not have been aware of the difference between the use of parody[112] and plagiarism *tout court*.[113] Without copyright issues looming large in the story, Nabokov's son would have hardly written the gratuitously condescending preface to *Lo's Diary* in its English translation. Mockingly carrying the same title, 'On a Book Entitled *Lo's Diary*,' as his father's postface to *Lolita*, 'On a Book entitled *Lolita*,' Dmitri Nabokov tells *his* version of the story. In his rendition of the events, author Pia Pera 'decided to seek inspiration, fortune, and fame from a book called *Lolita*' without 'a figurative knock on [Dmitri's] family door in Ithaca or Montreux.'[114] Dmitri further wonders:

> Are writers to strive for mediocrity lest their works similarly enter the 'common consciousness?' Are icons of popular culture – *Star Wars* perhaps – to be made subject to plundering by free riders because they have entered the common consciousness? The *Post* urged me to 'rethink' my stance, asking whether books like Madam Pera's 'can truly do the original anything but homage?' By ignoring the fact that homage to *Lolita* can be and has been paid with bona fide licenses, the question seems naïve.[115]

There is very little to argue about concerning paying homage to previous texts.[116] The case about *Lolita* was settled in an original way,[117] although detrimental to Pera's novel, which suffered furthermore from a rather dull translation that American reviewers bashed.[118] It is perhaps out of a desire for justice for her frustration with the American press that I decided to take on a study of this interesting novel dealing with stepfathers, stepdaughters, literary fathers, and literary daughters. The present study underscores a parallel path for both textual changes and a conceptualization of literature that is extremely conscious of its gendered nature. Its consciousness is manifested by the woman author's interest in texts that need to be revisited, not so much out of a sense of aesthetics (also), but because women as readers – or rereaders – can no longer unconditionally surrender to seeing their existence pictured in a paternalistic and condescending manner. Metamorphoses of the text are deemed necessary at this point, and we see how Pera appropriates the genre of parody to make her case and Lolita's.

Lolita *and Whose Parody?*

Postmodernist theories have greatly expanded the codes regarding the retrieval, the rereading, and rewriting of a novelistic text. Postmodernism utilizes interpretive keys that conceive – even favour, when one accepts the influence of postmodern tenets in a 'positive' way – the development of a novel genre as a literary medium in constant transformation. Its emerging texts will, in turn, re-evaluate the generic properties of the texts they reread. Calling upon Jacques Derrida's theorizations on the authority of the written over the aural, Giulio Ferroni speaks of the predominance of the word of one who is no longer there over he/she who is now reading it.[119] Ferroni mentions the notion of re-appropriation of 'physical traces,' which he assimilates in turn to 'graphic signs.' Rather than on actual authors, the evolution of the genre depends on the permanence of these 'signs.' The historical importance of the novel – more than for other genres – relies on the authority of previous writings over future ones, as textual authority transmits signs to be re-contextualized in yet another society. The authority of these signs then emerges from their impact upon the formation of other written texts. New texts produce a literariness that is able to depict its muted transnational and transhistorical situation, all set on the background of the 'other' written text(s). The re-evaluation of a previous text tends not to an avant-gardistic and antinomic research of the 'new' per se, but, rather – if we accept the 'positive' aspect of postmodernism[120] – to a jocose and skilful re-employment of previous structures and codes. The new text carves its sign upon the previous text, forming a writing whose scope (among others) is that of generating a palimpsest of innovative modalities. Originality does not stand alone, but comes in the company of the texts against which we measure incoming texts.[121]

Parody in the Novel

The novel is rooted in historical and geographical time more than poetry, for instance, and yet the paradox of its 'reality' as a fictional state independent of its concrete situatedness still exists. In the exercise of re-appropriation constituting and igniting the evolution of the novel by women writers, it is fair to discuss briefly how postmodernism deploys parody. Parody, as it stands, is a literary mode that fuses creation with criticism without restricting its employment to a text that could be considered just a mere satire. In its transposition of the hypotext, parody receives therefore also interpretive modalities, and makes the new text never 'innocent,' as we are reminded by Genette, as it inevitably is conducive to modifications of the hypotext.[122] Pastiche, parody, and metatextuality all constitute authorial interventions concurring in the typologically innovative spirit of *Diario di Lo.*[123] According to Linda Hutcheon, parody is 'both a personal act of supersession and an inscription of literary-historical continuity'[124] in which separating the pragmatics of the narrative strategies from formal structures becomes laborious. 'While the act and form of parody are those of incorporation,' Hutcheon suggests, 'its function is one of separation and contrast' and 'it is this doubleness of *both* form and pragmatic effect or ethos that makes parody an important mode of modern self-reflexivity in literature.'[125] In her statements, differing (separating/contrasting) from the previous text would seem the way to construct originality, not plagiarism. Genette basically states the same, including the parodic genre in the 'transformation' of hypotexts, whereas caricature and, above all, pastiche go under the label of 'imitation.'[126]

In Giulio Ferroni's more expansive notion of a posteriori writing, the predominance of the written attests to the evidence of a continuum and indefinable intervention a posteriori of the written upon the word, reworked within new cultural entities and realities that redefine the semantics of the previous codes in a colloquium between texts that can, and do, generate often useful *querelles*. As we know, the rewritings of texts within the realm of a literary history refuse geographical limitations. 'Keepers and pursuers of life beyond death'[127] abound, no matter the period in which we are living and reading. In my view, however, the weight of an author depends on the authority of his/her writing more than on his/her own image. Thus, we construct future texts based on the written word of the author rather than on his/her image. The re-evaluation of literary authority finds its ideal space not in the avant-gardistic and antinomic research of the 'new,' but, rather, in the deployment in the new text of structures and thematics previously utilized, which thus carves the sign of the new text upon the preceding one. Its writing subverts the previous treatment while re-asserting the import of the Genettian hypotext to the means of its present process in-being. It contributes to a palimpsest of innovative modalities while disseminating meaning; it gives 'a different configuration of content.'[128] The originality of rewriting resides, however, in the re-utilization of topics and characters according to the interests that the given hypotext exercises in the determined social and political need of the moment in question. This is also why parody can often be found in texts enmeshed with satire, not made easily discernible from it. Their coexistence can still take place, though with the firm understanding that, as Linda Hutcheon notes, while the first is an 'intramural' entity – eminently literary – the second is 'extramural' – social.[129] Hutcheon states that satire aims at ridiculing its target, while parody concurrently pays homage to it. An author can eternally make the choice – in virtue of a right called free expression – to reconnect with the discourse another author embedded in his/her narrative. He/she might be attracted by a thesis to debunk rather than by mere stylistic exercise, as one of the concepts central to historiography – that of linear progress – is indiscernibly linked to the logic or analogical repetitions of the images of the past. In my view, the audacity demonstrated by the author in entertaining an active conversation between his/her text and previous authoritative texts shows the necessity for both a revision of the novelistic structure chosen to represent similar actions in a parodic undertone,[130] as they are now framed within different ideological conjunctures; and a revision of those (past) ideological conjunctures that made that text possible and are now deemed obsolete by some. A different – however playful and ironic – employment of novelistic techniques has the merit of changing a great deal in the message readers are left with in the end.

In our time, the acts of rereading for women authors often signify dealing with the rereading of female characters who they feel have been mistreated. The 'mistreatment' of the female character, or heroine, is something worth considering, particularly in the light of the several daughter–father relationships we see at work in *Lo's Diary*. My reading of Pia Pera's novel illustrates aptly the properties connected to the theoretical notions on parody, genre legacy, and 'posthumous' transformation as elaborated by Ferroni and de Lauretis.[131] The (gendered) rearrangement of the semantic universe takes its literary shape by means of the meaning(ful) dispersion and dissemination of previous texts.[132]

Diario di Lo encloses the personal story of the protagonist, beginning again from the unfinished (and willingly ambiguous) account given to us by Humbert Humbert, the writer of his memoirs, without granting any merit to he who, after all, had led Lolita-Lo to her act of writing. It is not a continuation of the story, or a so called 'spinoff.' It is not even a memoir, as it deals with the publication of the verso of the same story that Humbert had laid out in his manuscript written with the collaboration with John Ray. The beginning of *Diario di Lo*, enhanced in its apparent prefatory function by the use of italics (just as in *Lolita*), presents the character of Nabokov's nymphet, now a fully grown woman, going to the famous publishing house that originally published the text, Olympia Press, after its publication was forbidden in the United States. Diegetically retracing the path of her persecutor-lover's journey, Dolores Maze Schlegel – Lo claims this is her real name[133] – demands remedies in a long conversation with the psychologist John Ray, living in Paris as of October 1995. The author's characterization of Dolly as an object of presumed seductive passivity damaged her as an individual, turning her youthful beauty into a silly and prematurely dead 'former' nymphet. From being powerless at the attacks of the old satyr, Pera's protagonist takes important steps to show her own will and represents it quite aptly in her diary.

A Perceptual Haze?

Dolly can, interestingly enough, only do so now because she finally lives in a privileged condition. Certainly privileged, for, in speaking of herself, she is now the intradiegetic narrator, charged with telling John Ray how the events actually transpired in those two years of her past:

> 'Già...,' sorrise la signora Schlegel accavallando le ginocchia luccicanti di peluria dorata. 'Ma non si preoccupi, quella che avete pubblicato voi è una *storia assai inventata*, non voglio togliere nulla al suo autore, o *forse lui la vedeva così*' continuò senza smettere di masticare una gomma alla menta, per poi aggiungere, con occhi radiosi di scherno: 'A parte la mia morte e poche altre sciocchezze ... Magari vorrà dare un'occhiata *alle mie impressioni di allora*. Sono sicuramente meno letterarie.' (DL 7; emphasis added)
>
> ('Yes,' Mrs. Schlegel said, smiling. She crossed her legs, which glistened with a golden down. 'But don't worry, what you published was a completely *made-up story* – not to take anything away from the author. Or maybe that was *the way he saw it*.' She was chewing a piece of mint gum. Then, her eyes radiant with mockery, she added: 'Apart from my death and some other nonsense ... Maybe you'd take a look at *my own impressions of that time*. They're definitely less literary.' [LD 1; emphasis added])

The damage for which Dolly claims revenge, while chewing her trademark peppermint gum, consists of having been denied a 'normal' ending; of having been denied an everyday existence. The stain of being a 'Lolita' will always cloud her existence. According to Dolly, Humbert's narrative was a made-up story; things were recounted the way he saw them; and, though his writing was indeed crafted and furbished, Dolly's impressions at the time will clear her position with the public and deliver her from what – at this point – we all believe to have been a rather unjust and untimely death. The conversation between Mrs Maze Schlegel and John Ray is pivotal for our reading of *Lo's Diary* because it sets the parameters of this parodic text. This is a diary of impressions recorded at the time in which events actually occurred – and not memoirs, a genre that implies the act of writing at a later date. The choice of the change in writing genre appears to be logical, since (a) the genre chosen by Humbert Humbert, that of memoirs, could have seemed inadequate for a twelve-year-old girl, as relatively uneducated and decisively rebellious as Dolores Maze Schlegel; (b) in the collective perception, the adoption of this genre fully corresponds to the type of testimony that a young girl could leave of herself.

A corollary of these two points is that it would have been technically very unlikely for Lo to adopt the memorialistic genre, which presupposes a completely different kind of culture and social background, and belongs instead – needless to say – to *Monsieur le Professeur*. We should constantly be mindful of the fact that Lo composes her gasping narrations at an age located between twelve and fourteen, a period fully revealed in the 'chaos of little notes' composing her diary. This chaotic rendition of a 'love story,' which finally appears just as Lo jotted it down, rejects Humbert's opinion of her in terms of a 'disgustingly conventional little girl' (LO 148). Humbert, even in his alienating medical condition, wrote instead in the present of his past, chiselling out the analepses of his love for Lolita in the memories of a model solipsist, and that is how he constructs his own identity. The irony and subtlety demonstrated by Humbert make up for the lack of subjective and spiritual elements in the novel. Humbert, indeed a true idealist in his solipsism, considers the nymphet as an indispensable 'accessory' for the description of his sexual pleasure, and reported in the memoir that 'Lolita had been safely solipsized' (LO 60). Made aware in her adulthood of the misuse of her persona, Lo becomes consumed by rebellion for having been narrated/ill-judged in her most intimate traits in a story that deprives her of a true – or, at the very least, of her own – perspective. Lo is especially hurt by the arbitrariness of Humbert's authorial choices with regard to the values eventually ascribed to her character, while so many others were taken away from her existence before the readers. What role did she willingly play in this story of incest and dependence that finally brought her seducer to a full crisis of personality and to his internment in an asylum? Dolly had all the (textual) freedom to retrace her own story. As the narrator of *Lolita* himself admits, he 'simply did not know a thing about [his] darling's mind' (LO 286). Nor did he care, as he baulked at any real responsibility for the little Lolita.[134] Luckily, this very ignorance of the child's mind and blindness to her perceptive gaze gives involuntary permission to Dolly to retell things the way she saw them.

In its practice of critical re-appropriation of narrative, linguistic, and rhetorical codes, in fact, *Diario di Lo* does not merely revisit Lolita's myth. Nor does it revisit the process by which Nabokov's book materialized the mythical search for eternal youth of a man morbidly attached to a green image of life such as the one enclosed in female pre-adolescents. This is, instead, a search that goes beyond the crystallization of the myth of eternal youth in the figure of the nymph. In Dolly's writing, which can no longer hold the memorialistic structure of its intertextual model, and instead has to transform itself in a frantic diary – that of Lo – the practices pertaining to this form of writing are put under scrutiny by the female writer performing the operation of writing. Hence, Pera's authorial intention proposes – as Dolly does – the demise of a male myth compatibly with the means offered by a 'different perspective' (precisely, the one Dmitri Nabokov's lawyer was joking about.) This shift in perspective appears to be the inevitable consequence of what brought Dolly–Mrs Schlegel–Lo to resolve – a decision shared by her empiric author – to collect her own incoherently assembled writings and give them to a publisher out of a sense of personal justice. The difference between her seducer's and Mrs Schlegel's perspective reverberates in this statement: '*o forse lui la vedeva così*' (DL 7; 'or maybe that was the way he saw it,' LD 1). He saw the entire 'thing' differently, this aside from Dolly's more limited literary ambitions compared with those of her seducer, as alluded to by the initial scraps that preceded the diary. We connect this shift in perspective and writing genre with the notion of parodic transformation (in a novel) as a social act, as it reveals the social changes in both audiences and readership and the negotiations that the reading of a text undergoes. *Diario di Lo*'s parodic alteration is as it should be. In her own rereading/rewriting process, Pera also establishes theoretical constructs more attuned with the ideological context in which she is located as a writer and as a woman. It is a consequential construct from a generative point of view, because the second text simply could not exist without the first one, for a reaction needs an action in order to be occur. Also, the relation between the hypotext and the emerging text is essential in the assessment of both the social and the ideological transformations that have taken place during post-feminism, as it concerns women's freedom of expression. In this postmodern conception of *imitatio*, Pera does not look at the text merely for its stylistic merits, or simply to present it in a frequently utilized satiric mode, but rather she charges her parody of *Lolita* with profound ideological implications by transforming the content by using the same strategies as the book, thus unwittingly following the precept according to which the elements selected provide the understanding of the social and cultural implications of a genre. What differs makes up the meaning. More to the point, it is her rendition of 'Dolly's psyche,' something that Humbert admitted not knowing, as we have seen, that introduces other cultural signifiers that, in turn, transform the pre-existing codes of reading as previously introduced by the Russian writer. Moreover, the shift of the reader's interest from the *professeur* to his 'disciple' and her relation with eroticism is vital. And we give in to her charms when we hear her voice[135] finally speaking her story.[136]

Just like *Lolita*'s, so also *Diario di Lo*'s narrative discourse is articulated in a first-person narrative, but this time it is hers. By destabilizing known characteristics of poignant scenes in *Lolita*, then later shifting the point of view and moving the perspective onto Dolly, Pera consciously deconstructs Nabokov's text *while* playing by his rules. This is another aspect of the predictable need for evolution expressed by a text when it adopts – in the parodic use of a previous one – a different genre. Destabilization of the previous text's 'message' defines the authorial revisitation on three parallel axes in their relationship with the pre-adolescent character: the character itself, the author, and the narrator. Narrative discourse thus becomes the *matter* itself of the criticism exercised upon the hypotext by the emerging text, as the latter constructs the whole spectrum of signifiers. The reason, though, for this closeness between texts is not motivated by a predictable discussion based on generic transformation. It relies also on the diverse matter. What comes to the foreground in *Lo's Diary* is Lo's sexual drive and her curiosity vis-à-vis Humbert's. In *Diario di Lo*, Lo is empowered by her own logos as well as her own gaze. The focalizing eye of the famous sofa scene is hers while her voice records it – most importantly – in the *precise* moment in which it is taking place:

Così niente gita al lago, benissimo, allora vado nello studio di Hummie, che per un po' continua a scrivere facendo finta di non sentirmi, finché mi piazzo sulle sue ginocchia e gli spazzolo la faccia coi miei capelli caldi di sole, restiamo fermi, io guardo il foglio, lui lo copre con un libro facendo finta di niente e poi lento lento mi si avvicina, io aspetto di vedere che fa, magari mi bacia, o qualcosa del genere, ma mi sembra troppo presto, troppo presto per ora, poi sento crescermi dentro una voglia cocente di stringermi a lui, sentire il suo morbido – ha una pelle liscia come seta – ma questo non si fa, mi dico, non è da donna che vuole godersi i suoi meritati trionfi, cosa darei per rannicchiarmi contro il suo petto, ma non cedere non cedere non cedere, mi ripeto ma sto cedendo, muoio dalla voglia, ci sono quasi, meno male che da giù Céleste grida alla mamma di un topo morto trovato in cantina. Io corro via a rotta di collo, lascio Hummie *seduto alla sua stupida scrivania, pieno di voglie irrealizzate,* perché c'era arrivato quasi! Vorrei tanto sapere come farà a non baciare la terra su cui cammino, adesso. Ha la faccia tutta sfocata dal desiderio ... Diavolo! Cosa aspetta mia madre a sposarselo? (DL 118-19; emphasis added)
(So, no trip to the lake, fine, then I'll go to Hummie's study. For a while he goes on writing, pretending not to hear me, until I sit myself down on his knees and I brush his face with my sun-warmed hair. We're just sitting there, not moving, I glance at the page, and he covers it with a book, as if by chance. Then slowly he leans closer to me, and I wait to see what he's going to do – maybe he'll kiss me, or something – but it's too soon, too soon for now; I feel a burning desire to press myself against him, feel his softness – his skin is smooth as silk – but no, I say to myself, that's not done, not by the woman who wants to enjoy her well-deserved triumph. What I wouldn't do to nestle against his chest ... Don't give in, I repeat, don't give in, but I am giving in, I am dying with longing, I'm almost gone, but luckily from downstairs Céleste shouts to Mom that she's found a dead mouse in the cellar. I scram, leaving Hummie sitting at his stupid desk full of unrealized desires, because he nearly made it! Now I'd like to know how he'll manage not to kiss the ground I walk on. His face is blurry with desire ... Hell. How long can my mother put off marrying him?) (LD 91-2)

In *Diario di Lo*, the girl *runs the show* to the point that she wonders when her mom is ever going to marry the professor, providing her with the chance for further erotic exercise. All the while he keeps writing, quite oblivious of her thoughts (as usual), 'sitting at his stupid desk full of unrealized desires.' Humbert did not seduce Lolita. Granted. His real crime was not seducing Lolita, but undermining her brains. Daughters who tell and *are* the story they are narrating question the very stable separation between the subject and the object in the family positioning. This happens regardless of whether the focus of their writing is their relationship with the mother or with the father. Their acting upon their family's dysfunctional situation affects the entire staging of the novel.

In the literary counter-shot of the sofa scene we just read, we are presented with an entirely 'thinking' character: Lo's sexual drive manifests 'seeds of adult energy and sexuality'[137] that further justify her refusal to die of childbirth coupled with her desire to finally talk. In Pera's text, narrative discourse modifies itself into a web of dialogues, opening up the stuffy and suffocating atmosphere of Humbert's prison cell, where he was in fact drafting his memoirs. The Sadean passion and deforming myth for forbidden love for youth now leaves room for an open critique and mockery of the aesthetic tics of the *étranger* appalled and yet incurably seduced by American middle-class shallowness's best production: little girls like Lolita, and big monsters like her mother.[138] All these elements culminate in the declaration of, in Nabokov's opinion, an indiscriminate supremacy of art above any other element of judgment. Pera, by contrast, continues to analyse Lolita-Dolly's character rendition and makes a decision. Her task is to grant justice, *rendere giustizia*,[139] to characters who have been neglected or ill judged by the same author who re-vindicates their birth, de-throning old kings and putting on the throne (so to speak) those who had been the jesters until then, even in a paradoxical respect for the text of which the author – Pera in this instance – composed the parody.[140] Emblematic of Pera's authorial intentions is a dialogue between Lo and her faithful Céleste, the 'colored maid' of Nabokov's *Lolita* (LO 36), a life teacher, and the only female image actually perceived as a guide for the young girl – aside from Aunt Nora. A new subjectivity, the search for the self, emerges from Lo's conversations with Céleste:

> 'E da dove verrebbe quest'altra personalità?'
> 'Oh, non lo so davvero, mica facile da spiegare, comunque la personalità che non è la propria non va, bisogna trovare quella vera.'
> 'E cosa ne è della personalità che non è la propria, si restituisce al mittente?'
> 'No, una personalità che non è la propria non è proprio di nessuno, è una personalità che non avrebbe dovuto mai esserci, è uno sbaglio'
> 'Vuoi dire che quella personalità viene uccisa? Come quando si perde un bambino?'

174 A Multitude of Women

'No, è diverso: a perdere un bambino non si fa nascere qualcuno che altrimenti poteva vivere come te e me, liberarsi di una personalità finta è sbarazzarsi di qualcosa che non esiste.'
'Ma se non esiste che bisogno c'è di liberarsene?'
... Céleste finisce di stirare il mio vestito a quadretti, sta zitta un bel po', poi mi dice: 'È difficile da spiegare, ma ci sono delle cose che non esistono ma fanno più male di quelle che esistono. Come gli incubi: sono solo dei sogni, eppure quando vengono si urla e si sta male. Se uno si trova una personalità che non è la sua, è come se sognasse invece di vivere.' (DL 92–3)

('And where does this other personality come from?'
'Oh, I don't really know. It's not easy to explain, but the personality that isn't your own isn't right, so you have to find the true one.'
'And do you return the part of the personality that isn't your own to whoever sent it?'
'No, a personality that isn't your own isn't really anyone's, it's a personality that should have never existed, it's a mistake.'
'You mean that that personality is killed? Like when you lose a baby?'
'No, it's different: when you loose a baby someone isn't born who otherwise would live like you and me; to be free of a false personality is to get rid of something that does not exist.'
'But if it doesn't exist why do you have to be free of it?'
... Céleste finishes ironing my checked dress, and she's quiet for a while, then she says: 'It's hard to explain. There are things that don't exist but do more harm than those that do. Like nightmares: they're only dreams, and yet when you have them you scream and feel bad. If you have a personality that's not your own, it's like dreaming instead of living.' [LD 70]).

As in the case of the sofa scene, a literary counter-shot to *Lolita*'s shot, Pera systematically utilizes Nabokov's novel's most famous passages to turn upside-down Nabokov's world and construct for her Dolly a new identity as a present to bestow upon the shattered image of the child Lolita – now adult and disillusioned with life. Her rereading is based on the very same techniques proposed by *Lolita*, namely, the revelation and the concealing of the male narrative voice; the ridiculing of the obvious, which in *Lo's Diary* is mainly represented by her ironic and disenchanted recording of Humbert's erotic and perverse desire. Her recording undermines the solipsist's image that, as Leona Toker notes, continues unvaried in its interpretation and justification by the many male scholars of Nabokov's work.[141] In Pera's text, Lo and her story are narrated and revisited in a feminine/feminist key as an attempt to debunk the stereotype of Lolita, as the erasure of her own voice was wanted by the man who wrote about her, making her 'infamous,' but did not make her speak her mind. Lolita appears as a character, in fact, only in function of Humbert Humbert's depraved fantasies, while her lines in the story are very few. The book title already underscored the link between the two different topics, *Lolita or, The Confession of a White Widowed Male*. The story of the nymphet Lolita becomes in essence that of her persecutor – the 'white widowed male.' A peculiar persecutor – it should be noted – since, in telling of her he is actually composing an apology for himself, while pretending understanding and forgiveness for his misdeeds from the jury (his narratees), thanks to a presumed 'objective' rendition of the events: 'I want my learned readers to participate in the scene I am about to replay; I want them to examine its every detail and see for themselves how careful, how chaste, the whole wine-sweet event is if viewed with what my lawyer has called, in a private talk we have had, "impartial sympathy." So let us get started. I have a difficult job before me' (LO 57). 'Impartial sympathy' also requires the belief that a reciprocal attraction was taking place between a young girl and a particular type of adult male, as it is specified a few pages earlier by the drafter of these memoirs. Our sophisticated, debauched expatriate invokes our impartiality in judging him. He even pretends to erase his own crime by using the evidence of a latent immorality in Lolita as his defence, since, as Humbert continues to state, his stepdaughter was not a virgin long before their 'encounter.' In virtue of a common, and very misguiding, etymological origin of the lemmas nymph and nymphomaniac, the professor wishes to acquit himself from all the accusations, placing – as frequently happens in real life – much of the responsibility on the child's erotic drive.[142] He reconfirms the urging of desire for the 'diverse' because the pedophile wants to be readmitted to the group of conformists, whatever the rule might be. In his narrative, Humbert, for exculpatory reasons perhaps, was adamant about Lolita's role in the whole story, noting that 'it was she who seduced me' (LO 132), and adding later (again an apologetic remark) that, just like Lolita, 'Sade's Justine was twelve at the start' (LO 276). Lolita, however, is fully aware that the professor's attentions signify only one possible thing, incest: '"The word is incest,"' as she notes at page 119 of Nabokov's novel.

In the introduction to the 'scandalous confession of a white widowed male,' *Lolita*'s preface, John Ray remarks that Humbert 'had often stressed in his own books and lectures' that '"offensive" is frequently but a synonym for "unusual"; and a great work of art is of course always original, and thus by its very nature should come as a more or less shocking surprise' (LO 5). Ray could have not used better words to describe Humbert's aim for his act. Not only does the prefacer give an inevitable moralistic cue, he also introduces the possibility of measuring a text's originality against others', this in accordance with the concept by which all texts must be measured, checked, and scrutinized.[143]

Pia Pera accepts the challenge. As reported in the interview for the *New York Times*, Pera believes that 'all that [she] did was to accept Nabokov's invitation to a literary tennis match, that ... has a long and well-established tradition behind it.' Aside from this 'legitimation' of Pera's actions, Nabokov's novel presents itself as an unusual acknowledgment-in-disavowal of morals, of admiration for masters of the novel, like Edgar Allan Poe and his poem 'Annabel Lee,' or Mérimée's *Carmen*, to which is not foreign, but rather essential, an intense mockery of the very same influences we discover in Nabokov's novel. The canonical treatment of desire in narrative, though, if revealing of the reciprocal attraction nymph-entomologist, relies also on an image of the male who, struck by a traumatic experience in youth, conceives the female image – Annabel, Valeria, Lolita and her mother – as a passive object of his desire, in accordance with the traditional 'prey-hunter' binaries. And this is stated in spite of his calculated use of her previous experience before the jury to deter eventual accusations about his conduct. It is a passive female image of desire, and, despite all his declarations at the end of his memoirs, Dolly signifies for Humbert Humbert only what society indicates with her name nowadays, that is, a 'Lolita.'

In Pera's work, there are many factors conveying originality in the reprise of *Lolita*, as we see how the thesis of the seducer is deconstructed so as to demystify, once and for all, the idea of a passive complicity between the seducer and the seduced. An attentive variation of the linguistic code thus also grants Lo control of desire in language, limits the power of the seducer, and deconstructs discourse to the point that she is the seductress, the baby–*femme fatale* rather than the seduced twelve-year-old baby girl. She wanted the prerogative to be seduced, and was very happy to be considered a *femme fatale* in the making! Indirect speech is carefully utilized to relieve once and forever Dolly's character of the qualms of Nabokov's stereotype that also concerns Stanley Kubrick's *Lolita*'s heart-shaped glasses through which her gaze transfixes the pedophile.

Dolly's new narrative role as first-person narrator and the change in the narrative mode by which she gives her side of the story and details her torrid affair with *le professeur* in *Diario di Lo* are a conduit for establishing the game rules of an apparently specific Girardian triangle. The most traditional triangle of mimetic desire, without any fears of misrepresentation, is the one that Lo will eventually form with Humbert Guibert and Filthy, while underscoring the latent homosexuality in both characters. The characteristics of mediation proper to the novel are also revisited as they generate an interesting twist on the Girardian scheme, since the object of desire is describing the other two's fixation on her. And more. This intense parody of *Lolita* produces one desiring subject and two desired objects; the desiring subject, this time, is the female; in the previous triangle of the hypotext *Lolita*, Lo-Humbert-Quilty, the girl was the desired object. From being an object of mediation, Lolita transforms herself into a subject of desire; from a nymphet into a butterfly, inversely to what Nabokov's text allowed her to do. At the end of his confession, Humbert proclaims: 'Had I come before myself, I would have given Humbert at least thirty-five years for rape, and dismissed the rest of the charges. But even so, Dolly Schiller will probably survive me by many years. The following decision I make with all the legal impact and support of a signed testament: *I wish this memoir to be published only when Lolita is no longer alive.*' (LO 308-9; emphasis added). The death motif could not be excluded from the construction of this triangle, and it's only fitting that the most frequented poetic imagery of death in *Lolita* is 'Annabel Lee' by Edgar Allan Poe, for Nabokov greatly admired Poe's romantic heroine. He juxtaposed his discussion on the death penalty with the aesthetics of a dead woman, as 'the death of a beautiful woman is, unquestionably the most poetical topic in the world.'[144] Lolita no longer exists in her entomological connotation of 'nymphet.' She is dead, then, according to what remains of her in the memoirs of the professor, also conveniently deceased from a thrombosis on the eve of the trial. In *Diario di Lo*, instead, she reveals to us her love story for her sophisticated stepdad, who, far from dead, has nice meals in Parisian restaurants with John Ray. The technical conclusion would appear then to be the death of Lolita as seen in Nabokov's novel. Lolita is forced to die in childbirth – delivering a stillborn girl – for a twofold reason: she can no longer claim any rights on Humbert and his version of their story, since fame, if death would not catch also our very literate pervert, could already be there, waiting for him outside the mental asylum; her character would continue the traditional international male novelistic rendition of the corrupted woman who has to be an 'unfit mother,' like Anna Karenina, Emma Bovary, Nora, and so on. We discover that the death assigned to Lolita also secures silence over a story whose celebrity must be unencumbered by moral scruples, as its Vintage book cover calls it 'the only convincing love story of the century.' As Lo sees it, it seems to have been a rather different thing altogether: 'Non sono io che penso le cose sporche, sono le cose sporche che pensano me' (DL 343; 'I'm not the one who thinks dirty things, it's the dirty things that think me'; LD 275). With this statement, Dolly attests to the fact that the romantic myth of the child has faded to give way to a simulated world transmitted via the media, which suggests intents and promotes acts that have nothing to do with the world of childhood but everything to do with that of celluloid: American consumerism at large, and pedophiles by default.

Pera, once more, resists the novel by changing its ending. Dolly/Lo's death would not fit with the altered perspective in which her novel is structured. Instead of being 'lived' by the two men, Humbert and Quilty, Dolly/Lo outlives them both. She *speaks* instead of *being spoken* about. She simply has to. And her husband is deaf. Without the cruelty of punishing Guibert more than he himself did, there is the twist we were expecting for the mechanism of irony so essential to parody to be reintegrated into the story, in a further homage to the law of Master Nabokov. Preventing her own character from dying, with her own authority, Lo questions the authority of the man who gave her a literary birth. And death, of course.

Denial and reaffirmation of the value and authority of the written word travel on parallel lines in *Diario di Lo*, generating a game that lasts the time of its reading and, perhaps, a little longer. The authorial desire to suppress a mere female character generates also the character's desire in a narrative path that is ludic, but not only such, as it illustrates Lo's wish to avoid saving Humbert:

'Ti piace la storia della sirenetta?'
'Mi piace la morale.'
'Sarebbe?'
'Non salvare mai un uomo.' (DL 233)
('Do you like the story of the little mermaid?'
'I like the moral of the story'
'What's that?'
'Never save a man.') (LD 186)

From the text emerges a narrator-protagonist who is fully responsible for her actions, who has a voice that is not pure *phone* but actual speech, and therefore is authoritarian in the assertion of her will. More than

Francesca Mazzucato's seemingly transgressive porn-caller daughter Lorena, who in the end remains acquiescent and subjugated to her father's ruling. After an adolescence marked by someone who would speak for her comes the moment of Lo's return in the tennis match with artistic fathers, the 'fathers of the Novel.' The emblematic deafness of her husband and child represents yet more male silence against her incongruous – however truthful – block of notes. In the eyes of John Ray, her 'little pieces of multicoloured paper' are comparable to some 'prisoner's messages.' Being the matter of which Lo's diary is made, it also composes the subtext of violence 'on her part.' To write means not only, as Nabokov said, to rewrite, but also to write something new. Lo has looked through the keyhole of her *Professeur*'s literary door in order to affirm the discovery of her own discourse. While not denying the master's teachings, she nevertheless reveals a muted sensitivity. Lastly, Dolly/Lo manifests an active desire to participate in the story. Rather than portraying the fixations and perversions imposed by a male author upon female characters, Lolita can finally expose them while showing no victimization on her part. Mirroring this shift is one of the three epigraphs Pera chose for her novel, a poem by Anna Achmatova. This is an ironic intertextual response to Humbert on the inspiring nymphets of Dante and Petrarch, Beatrice and Laura,[145] and, of course, of him, the great *professeur*:

È Bice capace, come Dante, di poetare,
o Laura di cantare il fuoco dell'amore?
Ho insegnato alle donne a parlare ...
E ora, Dio mio, chi le farà stare zitte? (DL 5)
(What if Dante's Beatrice were a poet
and Laura could sing of love's flame?
I encouraged women to speak ...
My God, if only I could stop them now!) (LD xi)

For Italian women today, writing literary fiction takes on the responsibility and the understanding of the manner in which such artistic action can be accomplished while also looking at the characters' system from the point of view of a woman whose gaze has been necessarily transformed by history, life, and public and private events. A gaze of which feminist studies are only too conscious. Thinking of novels such as *Diario di Lo* as banal rewrites or plagiarisms, as Nabokov's son so vehemently stated about Pera's work, is naive. Indeed, when we think of what kind of literary operation Pia Pera has put herself into in giving justice to Lolita (but not making a saint out of her character), one of the most beloved, and yet problematic, literary creatures of the past fifty years while the monster pedophile indulged the sympathy of all readers,[146] we also understand the threshold that Italian women writers have trespassed. On the wave of, or independent of, other women's artistic actions – like Jean Rhys's rewriting of *Jane Eyre* – Italian women writers have engaged in (I would dare say, with some success indeed)[147] a difficult enterprise, since to parody non-relevant texts can be understood but to reread *Lolita* is a scandal. That Nabokov's son wrote the preface to the American translation of *Lo's Diary*, this without giving Pera the benefit of the promised postface, says quite a bit about the publishing world and how it purposely vilifies women's talents or brilliant minds as soon as they leave their bordered space, often framed by the 'women's literature' sign.[148] Finally, as Hutcheon notes, parody does not merely involve textual comparison and a race to see who scores the most points in all this display of irony, humour, and literary innuendo. The structural identity of the text, Hutcheon claims, relies on the decoding as recognition, interpretation, and new encoding.[149] If these daughters threaten male literary icons who have built their careers on subtle and exquisitely decadent perversions, if in short they manage to create a parodic 'difference' with the chosen hypotext, they are doomed and 'punished,' even if with a futile review based on a questionable translation of the original. Women have been taught how to speak, alas, and Humbert knew this about Lolita when he wrote: 'I knew I had fallen in love with Lolita forever; but I also knew she would not be forever Lolita' (LO 65). Indeed, he was right. Now she is Dolly, and we need to learn how to listen to her.

chapter 3

Italian Sexual Patho-Politics Revisited

This chapter of *A Multitude of Women* addresses the literary representation of sexual politics in the past decade. In fact, the theoretical engagement of Italian feminist philosophers and thinkers with the issue of gender as a social and political construct in the debate on the sex/gender issue of the 1990s went hand in hand with a profound transformation in women's novelistic narratives. Almost at the same pace as, but disconnected from, theoretical groups such as Diotima, several Italian women writers have investigated in their fiction what Rosi Braidotti calls 'the specific ways of knowing of the human flesh' in a narrative form.[1] Corporeal identity has pervasively shaped women writers' investigation of eroticism and the flow of sexualities, both the normative ones and those contested – formerly known as 'perverse' forms of sexuality – while revisiting the abortion theme and women's freedom in a sexuality unbound from societal constrictions. What has been called in this book the *hybrid* phase, or the fourth one in women writers' production, has developed a 'body' of writing that is drastically different from those of the first three phases. As in the cases already presented in chapters 1 and 2, several of the novels that appeared from the mid-1990s onward are evidence of their authors' wish to discuss the female protagonist's relationship with her body and her sexuality without a veil of modesty. The change in ethics and in society at large with respect to women's issues has influenced women writers' outlook on their representation of thematics regarding the female body and its sexuality; oppression is linked to sexuality, but so is the pleasure derived by the power that sex – and the practice of sex – may infuse in women. All of this has had powerful resonance in these women's narratives and carries important corollaries.

Sexuality as a topos in fictional narrative elucidates other aspects of women's position in Italian society. Conventional novelistic issues such as family and marriage appear now conjoined to issues of gender construction or the rebuttal of the gender that society forced upon women from a young age. When a woman author sexualizes the page, when she genders it, the novel can no longer assume, or tolerate – without apt justification – the presence of *sventurate* or *poverelle*, 'unlucky' passive characters. Granted, not all characters in today's novels are liberated, emancipated, and conscious of their rights. Elena Ferrante's *poverella* in *I giorni dell'abbandono* is just one of the possible examples with a cause for her presence in the novel. As the realist novel favours the mirroring of societal idiosyncrasies, female characters might still experience an existence that is a set of tribulations. And yet these characters are unlikely to be presented in the same perspective as Alessandro Manzoni did with the illustrious example of poor Gertrude. It is our own subjectivity as readers that has undergone drastic changes, thus transforming the modalities of our identification with the character in keeping with how contemporary authors envisage their creatures. It is also unlikely, however, that we will get the pale hint of sexuality we were used to reading in Elsa Morante's and Natalia Ginzburg's prose. As seen in the previous chapter with Francesca Mazzucato's novel *Hot Line: Storia di un'ossessione*, many boundaries have been eliminated in the treatment of the body in novelistic writing. In the 1990s, the 'pale shade of sex,' as I call the modest reminders of a sexual life for the protagonists of writers such as Morante and Ginzburg, has reshaped itself into a profoundly theoretical battle site, which finds its ideal container in the novel. The frame of the novel offers a locus in which characters propose and experience what theorists discuss. As in the case of Pia Pera's Dolly, characters – which embody ideas – often represent the most obvious formal contribution to the construction of the 'novel of feminist theory.'

The novel as a genre has always paralleled and explored current debates in the society of its time. In the case of the discussion on the body and on the notions of sex and gender, which, after a full decade of segregation, have been again re-composed in a more fruitful manner, the Italian novel has manifested the generic powers of making the debate on sexuality and gender roles apparent to a vast majority of readers.

Sexuality in America is often regarded more in terms of social rights, as Rosi Braidotti does not fail to note. While these rights allow free expression outside the norms for the individual, the connection of sexuality with rights ultimately stigmatizes sexuality, as it subjects it to yet another set of rules. This connection gives in to conservative thinking, reinforced by current Christian fundamentalist ethics, to such an extent that in the 1990s sexual harassment became a bed rock of feminist struggles in lieu of pornography.² This understanding and treatment of sexuality defies the very scope of a free sexuality. Instead of being freed by their own arguments, women find themselves locked in a logic that serves the puritanical *diktats* of politicians involved in problematic crusades against sex and women rights. It is difficult not to agree with Braidotti when she argues that sexuality, if seen only in terms of sexual harassment, and not as a healthy site of analysis and of empowerment, undermines feminist studies. The most apparent threat from this understanding of sexuality seen only in 'legal terms' is that it returns the spotlight to issues of order and regulation while confining, once again, the import of literature produced by women writers to a limited space. This interpretation of sexuality produces dogmatic positions and represses artistic (aside from the mere political) modalities and innovative uses of the field of 'sexuality' for women thinkers, artists, and academics at large. Further, re-inscribing sexuality within feminism in the United States has often been left to lesbian groups, to all 'other voices,' as a result producing a problematic and incomplete equation sexuality/ transgression.³

The 'queering' of Italian texts successfully deconstructs many grand narratives in their seemingly monolithic message – or, rather, helps to analyse the creation of narratives that do not follow unity and tradition, but favour fragmentation and experimentation. Queering both literary and the analytical work has opened new and more complex fields of critical discourse on the symbolic inscription of heterosexuality. This chapter on the patho-politics of sexuality follows a Continental line of thought in tune with Braidotti's, particularly her fluctuating concept of the sexual subject. According to Braidotti, one of the objectives of feminist practice today is to 'overthrow the pejorative, oppressive connotations that are built not only into the notion of difference, but also into the dialectics of Self and Other ... as now a She might no longer be a She, but a subject-in-progress, a mutant ... a post-Woman embodied subject cast in female morphology who has already undergone an essential metamorphosis.'⁴

As such, sexuality cannot stray from the notion of gender and gendered identies as political *and* material constructs, a radical change in feminist criticism. Indeed, problematizing the 'matter of bodies may entail an initial loss of epistemological certainty, but a loss of certainty is not the same as political nihilism,'⁵ and produces, instead, productive transformations on how we think of sexuality.

Sexuality as a social and symbolic, material and semiotic institution is singled out as the primary location of power, in a complex manner which encompasses both macro and micro-relations. Sexual difference – the sexualized bipolarity, is merely a social implementation of the political economy of sexualized identities, which is another word for power in both its negative or repressive (*potestas*) and positive or empowering (*potentia*) meaning.[6]

Further, Braidotti contends that the centrality to the constitution of the subject of sexuality and sexual difference makes it arduous to eradicate them by merely reversing socially enforced roles. She argues instead for the enactment of 'metamorphoses.' On a similar note, American philosopher Judith Butler discusses the undoing of restrictively normative conceptions of sexual and gendered life. She defines the kinds of '*reorganization* of sexual norms' that are legally and culturally crucial in order to accommodate and understand the needs of people who live 'sexually and affectively outside the marriage bond or in kin relations to the side of marriage.'[7] Braidotti's concept of 'metamorphosis' and Butler's idea of 'reorganization' seem to overlap in that both authors indicate the theoretical step to break free from a construction of gender and sexuality that is obsolete at this point in human history and yet still socially validated in practice, particularly from a legal standpoint. As Butler states, gender studies' assigned task is that of learning the distinction between restrictive norms and those that 'permit people to breathe, to desire, to love and to live.'[8]

Some contemporary Italian writers have been fortunate enough to have even circumvented the long-standing problem of Italian literature – the lack of erotic writing.[9] This subgenre, though successful in writers such as Anaïs Nin and others in France, is a form rarely evidenced in Italian literature. Sexuality is a valid space for discourse and, more generally, for self-discovery in writing; it has proved necessary for a re-discussion of the perspective through which writers see their identity, sexual preference, and gender construction, as well as Italian society's formidable conservative structure. In the works of new Italian writers, sexuality and eroticism become a space for reinventing the modes in which a story concerning two individuals, regardless of their sexual orientation, can be told to readers, thus reconfirming the by-now established notion that the body is indeed a space defining experience. Female sexuality is often proposed as an active moment in which porn, erotic writing, and sex *tout court* can be reworked, understood, and enjoyed by women readers.

Closer to my own subject, though, is the following question. Where can one situate Italian writers who define sexuality also/still within a heterosexual form of discourse? They queer the discourse, but not entirely. Their 'writing on the body' does not reach the tones of Jeanette Winterson's explicitly homosexual prose, for instance. How can one begin to find categories of critical analysis that can include work by these writers? This chapter illustrates sexuality, norms, and societal rules as important thematic features/sites of protest and rupture in the contemporary Italian novel by women in the work of Dacia Maraini and Melania Mazzucco, two very dissimilar writers whose novels best depict the literary field as an ideological space. The treatment of abortion, maternity, reproductive choice, and sexual difference adds new sites of intellectual and theoretical struggle to the themes traditionally left unspoken by Italian male novelists, namely, the father–daughter relationship and incest,[10] the mother–daughter relationship, lesbianism, and different forms of female pleasure. While there are no inherently 'female' themes in the novel genre, in women's novels there is, nevertheless, frequent analysis of female sexuality (and its constraints) that needs a detailed examination. For Dacia Maraini, the constant and never contradictory definition of abortion and the consequent right of a woman to giving life – though with pain and endurance – acts as a unifying theme for her characters. In her novels, sexuality is consistently discussed along with women's reproductive rights, one of the most politicized aspects of sexuality, even and especially in recent years.

In Melania Mazzucco's novel *Il bacio della Medusa*,[11] lesbianism is regarded as a complex site for a deeper understanding of Italian society at the beginning of the twentieth century. The treatment of perverse desire in this novel demonstrates the awareness that sexual identity cannot be confined and limited by societal constructions that consider lesbianism an irregular path to sexual fulfilment, a problematic notion of sexuality that results in a lack of lesbian literary criticism and reconfirms the heteronormative framework of much of Italian Women's Studies[12] and, more in general, Italian literary studies. In both Maraini and Mazzucco, the social aspect of the literary assumes an integrative role in the artists' perception of a woman's world, one in which sexuality still signifies subjection to laws that are inconsistent with a more fragmented interpretation of the terms woman, gender, sexuality, and sexual rights. Ethical – aside from aesthetic – concern appears to model the otherwise very distinct texts of Mazzucco and Maraini, as they share a common effort at discussing questionable practices of Italian society. Their novels are case studies of an on-going debate in which female writers also show their engagement with issues that are familiar to feminist academics, while expanding them in a more lyrical and suggestive manner for their readers. In this way, the formal literary apparatus comes to be an ideal forum for the rhetorics of representation of a multitude of women's needs for the twenty-first century.

Dacia Maraini and the Politics of Choice

> Somebody who should have been born is gone.
> Yes, woman, such logic will lead to loss without death. Or say
> what you meant,
> you coward ... this baby that I bleed[13]

In reference to the relationship between political theory and practice, Luce Irigaray stated that 'it is not possible to give so-called university courses without being concerned with women's freedom as regards the rights to contraception and, if necessary, abortion.' Irigaray also pointed out many other rights that need to be gained, namely, 'identity, work, love (especially sexual), relationships to children, and culture.[14] Irigaray's thoughts on emancipation define the need for a university curriculum to mirror and debate what happens to women in society. Those passages that movingly depict the dramatic moment of a woman's decision to give up a life over which a woman has absolute power, especially when this choice becomes an imperative, are the focus of this present investigation, for the way in which Maraini's narrative voice bears witness to this feminine experience in her life-writing narratives and essays. In fact, such works give an ethical significance to her aesthetic pursuits. The analysis of the images of abortion in Maraini's narrative is informed by her strong political message about personal freedom despite any ideology, and establishes the author's coherence in her statements, whether in fiction or through other documents.[15]

Abortion has always been an issue and a motif in Maraini's writing, long before her programmatic engagement with the feminist claims of the 1970s. Maraini discussed abortion in autobiographical novels,[16] poems, or plays (e.g., *La donna perfetta*, *Lettere a Marina*, *Il treno per Helsinki*). All the fictional works reveal personal experience that is also scrutinized within non-fictional contexts such as dialogues, letters, and essays (e.g., *Storia di Piera*, 'Lettera sull'aborto'). Maraini's outwardly fictional narratives, and her openly autobiographical non-fictional works present co-extensiveness between the writer and her subject matter, a co-extensiveness that blurs the boundaries between *auto* and *fictio*. In exploring the issue of abortion as represented in Maraini's narratives and in her latest 'Lettera sull'aborto,'[17] I intend to define a certain literary/autobiographical connection rather than merely focusing on the socio-political situation in which Maraini's writings are clearly embedded. The first part of the chapter illustrates the ways in which a writer and feminist activist[18] such as Dacia Maraini has accomplished the creative research of giving shape to the sorrows, the decision processes, and the constrictions that surround the material experience of getting an abortion, and finally how she represents the arduous decision that leads a woman to eliminate what some see as 'life' from within her.

Un clandestino a bordo: *Sexual Politics in Dacia Maraini's Narrative*

Much has been said about Maraini's engagement in public life in Italy, where, since the 1970s, she has been present in the struggles for women's rights, those involving ethical and social issues especially. Maraini's political aesthetics[19] are a most representative example of what *letteratura al femminile* ('literature in the feminine') meant in Italy at the time, a literature in which the gender issues that society faces occupy most of the narrative space. The specific purpose of this aesthetics might be considered, in Sharon Wood's words, that of 'challenging women to change.'[20] Indeed, the literary works of Maraini have been substantially indissoluble from her engagement in the Italian women's movement. As is well known, her attempt to revisit androcentric Italian society permeates her work entirely and encompasses several genres of writing. In general, Maraini adopts the narrative genre that Rita Felski defines as the 'feminist realist novel of self-discovery,' a text that 'traces a clear developmental plot in which the heroine moves from a state of alienation to a discovery of female identity through a process of separation from male-defined values.'[21] The protagonists of Maraini's novels all undergo such a psychological journey, while the search for female emancipation is fictionalized in various techniques and strategies through the reworking of already existing literary types to fit the needs of feminist personal and political beliefs. In the Italian political arena, roughly composed of a conservative/Catholic side and a liberal/secular one, abortion – and its regulating law 194, promulgated in 1978 – represents still today a highly politicized issue.[22] The debate focused on a woman's personal responsibility in making a choice for herself, a personal issue that becomes political when brought to the political stage. As the *Manifesto di rivolta femminile* claimed back in 1970, 'the first reason for resentment against society' for women still lies 'in being forced to face maternity as a dilemma.' Feminists at that time saw society and its laws' 'refusal of the freedom of abortion' as part 'of the global denial of woman's autonomy.'[23] Apart from the ways the issue is still constructed today socially and politically, for a woman – still today – abortion also fundamentally means physical pain, emotional distress, psychological torture, and ultimately, a devastating sense of loss, even when the foetus is unwanted.

In 1996 the then-director of *Nuovi argomenti*, Enzo Siciliano, asked Maraini to write her opinion on the issue of abortion. The result was 'Lettera sull'aborto.' Maraini's letter is intertextually mindful of, and inevitably different from, the famous Oriana Fallaci's *Lettera a un bambino mai nato*.[24] Fallaci deals with a woman's dilemma of having to choose between having a baby and having a career, with all the negative and positive implications of each option. Maraini wrote her letter in her sixties when, with her fertile years behind her, she could speak of her condition in a very pragmatic way. The ghostly image of her unborn child is what brings together abortion and loss, pregnancy and loss, in her prose. Unlike Fallaci's *Lettera a un bambino mai nato*, structured as a conversation between an unborn child and its mother that reveals all of the woman's weaknesses, fears, and ambitions, Maraini's 'Lettera sull'aborto' is an appeal to women who want motherhood but want it redesigned in different terms. It invites a serious reconsideration of women's position in society, in view of what 'having rights' really signifies for a person of the female gender.

Maraini's letter reiterates the problematics of a woman's choice to terminate a life. But she discusses the issue of reproductive choice as well as a woman's need and right to be a mother, the latter being a decision that holds the same importance as the one of deliberately giving up one's reproductive potential in the name of other very relevant rights. With touching yet disenchanted words, Maraini defends both rights, that of being a mother and that of getting an abortion. Among the factors leading to a woman's choice to abort, she underscores the importance attributed to our body, and the fact that women in Italy still belong to an androcentric and capitalist society, where being pregnant is still perceived as an obstacle to achieving independence, a career, and a measure of control over our bodies. As feminist theory has taught us, abortion establishes a fundamental interrelation between what we could consider the personal and the political, between the 'I' and the 'we.' In fact, personal decisions and choices do reflect what we consider the political sphere, a place where a person must be granted certain 'rights' to direct his/her life in one or another way. Maraini's feminist claims and her struggle for the abortion law form the 'political' aspect of her fictional and autobiographical work. Yet there is also another, very distinct aspect that must be considered: her fictionalization of personal pain and psychological suffering experienced at the time of abortion. This more subjective mode of Maraini's involvement seemingly departs from her desire to obtain justice for all the women she met in her years of militancy. It is made apparent in her literary pieces on abortion, where a more lyrical vein sustains the weaving of the narrative. Those passages are directly drawn from personal experience and a recollection of past events and show the difference between personal and political choice. Choice is personal, but so is suffering: when a woman who desires motherhood is denied this option, or denies it to herself, a large component of pain enters the game of 'rights.' The choice must go to women, as only deciding – desiring – to be a mother can be conducive to a 'successful maternal experience.'[25]

More specifically, I base my argument on the considerable importance that the autobiographical experience holds in Maraini's literary representations of abortion. Proofs of this are the lexical similarities between the 'Lettera sull'aborto' and her previous fictional texts, which include descriptions of the actual experience of loss and of the 'eternal' pact between a mother and her child, which are complemented by actual narrative images of a baby floating in the mother's womb. On several occasions Maraini's experience of her own 'therapeutic abortion' (an involuntary interruption of pregnancy due to health causes) is brought in as authentic material for a literary representation. In my analysis, I present these materials to stress the fact that historical reality is indiscernible from Maraini's literary creation. It is not coincidental that, in her narrative, abortion starts as a motif with *L'età del malessere*,[26] and with the exception of *La vacanza*[27] (written soon after the writer experienced her own first abortion), it remains one of Maraini's leading thematics.

I must discuss now the actual term *abortion*. The *Random House Dictionary* gives two distinct terms to define the act of losing a baby, 'abortion' and 'miscarriage.'[28] Abortion, 'also called voluntary abortion,' is 'the removal of an embryo or fetus from the uterus in order to end a pregnancy.' Miscarriage, 'also called spontaneous abortion,' is 'the expulsion of a fetus before it is viable, esp. between the third and seventh months of pregnancy; spontaneous abortion.' With *abortion* the adjective used – voluntary

– implies that the woman's will interferes with the birth of the foetus, while miscarriage is strictly used to describe children unwittingly lost by the bearing mother because of situations that do not depend on her own will (illness, accidents, etc.), thus stressing the concept of an act that took place 'spontaneously' with no violence done on the foetus. This lexical distinction – abortion as a voluntary action, miscarriage as a spontaneous one – is quite telling about how people think about the decision of a woman to not procreate. 'Miscarriage' means not carried properly, so an accident happened on the way to reproduction. In Italian, for instance, only one signifier covers both semantic areas: in using the word *aborto* one can mean something medically needed, something spontaneously occurring, or the actually reasoned 'choice' of not continuing a gestation, the 'voluntary' act of terminating an unwanted pregnancy. Depending on the situation, the noun *aborto* is accompanied by different terms: *terapeutico* ('therapeutic'), *spontaneo* ('spontaneous'), or *provocato* ('provoked').[29] One would imagine that the lack of a specific distinction between the two concepts would make a major difference in the relevant decisions, laws, and social mores. Yet, just as in the case of Zingarelli's Italian dictionary, in the way Maraini's narrative reinterprets women's suffering, this distinction is blurred and seems to lose strength. Whether the woman has decided on the loss (thus making it 'voluntary') or the loss occurs against her will, for medical reasons, pain is basically portrayed in the same fashion, as the knowledge of a loss does not mean the actual oblivion of that which has been lost. Mourning is always latent. As in the case of Mazzucato's father figure, such representations of loss tend to prevail in spite of the programmatic stand that articulates the different female characters portrayed by Maraini.[30] Loss exists in spite of the strong public position Maraini always took in terms of abortion choice. Yet, Maraini's narrative representations of abortion changed according to parallel mutations taking place in Italian society as the issue became increasingly public and new measures were being tried to prevent further problems with the design of the new law 194.

As first presented in *L'età del malessere*, abortion is a completely forbidden act caused by male lack of consideration for the character Enrica, and imposed on her by her lover. In *Donna in guerra*,[31] abortion becomes a necessary instrument of independence for Vannina, who must abort her child because its birth would tie her up with an oppressive husband. Unlike Enrica, Vannina is not abandoned by her man: she is the one to leave Giacinto by killing his potential progeny (through her abortion), but in the process of ensuring her human rights as a person she also gives up her own right to become a mother. Vannina refuses to be a container[32] for Giacinto's seed. She gives up a role attributed to woman since the beginning of societal organization, and rejects maternity when its social significance finally becomes clear to her, which happens especially through the voice of Giacinto, a voice symbolically defined as 'paterna, autoritaria.'[33] Giacinto offers a male objectified outlook on woman and her position in society.[34] One way the novel denounces women's oppression is by exposing the false premise of masculine ideology, the notion that a childless woman is 'unnatural.'[35]

Abortion is, again, the topic of the theatrical work *La donna perfetta*,[36] written in the same years as *Donna in guerra*. Here, though, self-discovery does not enter the trajectory of Maraini's character. Nina is a victim of society, but the issue of abortion is deprived of any emancipatory solution; abortion and its motivations are pictured more in the manner of Enrica's experience in *L'età del malessere* than in that of Vannina's newly discovered condition as a person reconfiguring herself. In her anti-mimetic representation of the story of Nina – a young woman who aborts a child by her student boyfriend and later dies from uncontrolled bleeding (where physical blood is another 'loss') – Maraini investigates the behavioural models and societal patterns that produce women like Nina. The main character of this apologia is a young woman whose subtly masochistic behaviour is shared, according to the author, by many women who still live in complete subordination to men. Yet, the lack of alternative models that we experienced in Enrica's story is now filled by the presence of Christa, a German friend who helps Nina in her Calvary. As Christa is a foreigner, her different views on male–female relations are entirely 'justified' with respect to Nina's complete subservience to Italian societal repressive mores.

After the most political and engaged period of her career, Maraini reconsiders abortion's psychological rather its socio-ideological implications. In her most overtly autobiographical fictional period, from the early 1980s to the end of that decade, on several occasions and in several genres, Maraini explores her recollection of an authentic experience, the therapeutic abortion she suffered in the early 1960s, which caused her separation from her husband and constitutes the topic of the recollection narrative in the novels *Lettere a Marina*[37] and *Il treno per Helsinki*.[38] It was already also explicitly mentioned in *Storia di Piera*, as the author's counterpart to Piera degli Esposti's history of nine abortions.[39] Because of the personal suffering in the tragic experience of having to have her foetus taken out of her womb, in those years Maraini's narrative focused more on the self and the motif of self-confession. It dealt primarily with the concept of loss rather than focusing on the issue of choice and the fairness of the law. Indeed, in that particular circumstance, Maraini's abortion was not a choice. Her choice would definitely have been that of keeping this much-desired blue-eyed baby, which is clearly indicated by the way in which the female characters of those years desperately fancy their children. Bianca's recollections of the moment of her loss, in *Lettere a Marina*, and even more so Armida, in the highly autobiographical *Il treno per Helsinki*, are far from being aligned with Vannina's choice and her *presa di coscienza* rendered explicit by her abortion. In conformity with the pattern of self-discovery of the feminist realist novel, Vannina's choice is a declaration of power, of acknowledgment of the self. However, Bianca and Armida acquire a new knowledge from their common experience. They learn that the significance of their lives is not in another person. Ultimately, they realize that this lesson has a high cost, which thus anticipates Maraini's current understanding, that 'L'aborto è dolore e impotenza fatta azione ... la divinizzazione del nulla,' (LA 24; 'abortion is grief and impotence turned into action [... is] making a god out of nothing,' LA2 12).

Lettere a Marina is chiefly a novel about redefining love, including erotic love, between women. Rita Felski theorizes this kind of narrative as conducive to the process of self-discovery, since the other woman mirrors the protagonist of the story.

> The figure of a female friend or lover invariably plays a symbolically important role in the protagonist's development. This transference of allegiance from a heterosexual relationship to one of intimacy between women involves overcoming the negative value which women have been conditioned to place upon their own sex; the recognition of the other woman serves a symbolic function as an affirmation of self, of gendered identity.[40]

The topic of self-discovery is enhanced by Bianca's frequent flashbacks to her childhood in a strict boarding school, where she learned about masturbation and lesbian love. Self-discovery as the beginning of a new life is articulated by her difficult attempts to write the novel she plans to finish, in a sort of 'multiple beginnings,' as theorized by Genette. Through her letters to Marina, Bianca offers an almost self-conscious parallel between biological and artistic conception. *Lettere a Marina* is also about abortion; either freely decided or medically necessary, Bianca's act of interrupting her pregnancy is never presented really as a choice. Rather, it is a necessity suffered by a woman who has either been deprived of her decision to procreate or is physically unable to continue her pregnancy. Indeed, in this epistolary novel, both cases are presented. The first is brought in tangentially by the character of Basilia, who was raped by her own father,[41] and thus, as incest survivor, anticipates the Marianna Ucrìa of a more recent Maraini novel.[42] Basilia's case presents incest as a prevalent and legitimate cause of abortion. The second instance of abortion in *Lettere a Marina* occurs when Bianca tells Marina of her own. The protagonist brings a sense of loss to the topic, which also anticipates the one found in 'Lettera sull'aborto' and stands in contrast to Basilia's reaction to the tragic rape:

> Forse qualche altro giorno e ce l'avrebbe fatta. Tu non sai come si muoveva questo figlio dentro le *cupole* fresche del mio ventre. Aveva i muscoli di un nuotatore era un atleta. Si voltava e rivoltava su se stesso faceva dei capitomboli dei salti mortali da lasciare il fiato sospeso.[43]
> (Perhaps another time and he would have made it. You can't imagine how this son stirred beneath the wide *dome* of my belly. He was an athlete with the muscles of a swimmer and all on his own he made headlong jumps that took my breath away.)[44]

But sorrow overcomes hope when the death of the foetus is revealed to Bianca:

> Poi una mattina ho smesso di sentirlo ... Mi acconciavo ad andarmene senza un sospiro non me ne importava più niente delle cose buone e belle che mi aspettavano fuori non me ne importava niente di niente. Ero appagata di me di lui ... Nel momento che ho scelto di morire mi sono lasciata andare l'utero si è ammorbidito ha permesso che sgusciasse fuori prima la testa e poi le spalle e poi il torso di un bellissimo bambino dagli *occhi azzurri* spalancati morti ... Sotto le fasce strettissime sentivo ancora i piedi minuscoli dell'*atleta* che si puntavano per spiccare il salto op, op! nella grande volta *azzurra* del mio utero indolenzito mio figlio faceva volteggi e *acrobazie*. Io lo seguivo con l'occhio interno che hanno le madri un occhio ardito e attento da falco guerresco e trattenevo il fiato quando si librava nel vuoto per un attimo prima di afferrarsi alla corda volante per poi lasciarsi cadere con delicatezza sul pavimento sanguigno.[45]
> (Then one morning I stopped feeling him at all ... I would forsake without a sigh all the good and beautiful things awaiting me outside where nothing mattered to me any more nothing at all. With my son I had fulfilled myself and now I could surrender myself to death ... At that moment when I chose

to die I let myself go and my uterus softened just enough to allow the head to slip out then the shoulders and then the body of a very beautiful baby with *blue eyes wide* open in death ... Beneath the tight bandages I felt tiny *athlete's* feet pushing off to take a flying leap up! up! in the great *blue* vault of my numbed belly as my son did his *acrobatic turns*. I followed him with the interior eye that mothers have the warlike and watchful eye of a falcon and I held my breath when he poised himself for a moment in the vault before he seized the swinging cord to let himself gently on the blood-stained floor.)[46]

Reminiscent of the same autobiographical experience is another passage in *Il treno per Helsinki* when Armida, pregnant with her husband's baby, loses her child. It uses almost the same lexicon as *Lettere a Marina*, almost the same descriptions; certainly the same immense sadness is evoked in the narrative mimesis of the abortion scene. Armida's recollection expands into many facts left untold in *Lettere*, thus further magnifying the bases of the resemblance with Maraini's personal experience. Background details are supplied, such as the announcement of her pregnancy, and her departure from the public hospital in Rome caused by her manipulative mother-in-law. Afterward, we witness Armida's disappointment in herself (a feeling shared by most women) for not being able to carry a baby, and her sense of defeat in witnessing the uncomplicated natural birth of Zaira's child. The personal aspect of Maraini's experience in Armida's recollection is almost obsessive when it comes to the description of the 'celestial baby';[47] the guessing of the baby's sex with a hair and a ring is repeated in both novels. In *Il treno* the secret pact between the woman and her own life, and the evident similitude of the foetus to an 'acrobat' or to an 'athlete,' are vividly described, almost in the same words as in *Lettere a Marina*:

> I muscoli si sono irrigiditi nell'ultimo abbraccio del figlio amante che vuole fare della mia *cupola* una tomba moriamo insieme lui ed io per quel patto d'amore che ci lega contro tutti io mi arrendo al suo possesso e lui si avvinghia a me mortalmente ... Poi crollo nel sonno. I muscoli si allentano lasciando che il figlio venga rapito da mani professionali che senza neanche una carezza lo gettano nel secchio della spazzatura. Poi mi dicono che era un maschio come aveva detto Gesuina aveva gli *occhi azzurri* ed era robusto e sorridente. Il *piccolo acrobata* si è rotto l'osso del collo e si è rifiutato alla famiglia per sempre.[48]
> (My muscles go rigid in the last embrace with my lover son who has decided to make my *dome* into his tomb. We are both of us dying in a love pact that welds us together against the world. He possesses me. I surrender myself into

his possession. He clings to me. He embraces me in the agony of death ... Then I collapse into sleep. My muscles relax so that my son can be snatched from me by expert hands. Without even a caress they throw him into the refuse bucket. Then they tell me he was a boy just as Gesuina had predicted that he had *blue* eyes and that he was smiling and sturdy. The little *acrobat* has broken his collar-bone and has fled from the family for ever.)[49]

In those years, the persistent fictionalization of a personal occurrence, that of the unwanted abortion, as we see in *Il treno per Helsinki*, remains a paradigm of Maraini's writing. The pact between herself and the child remains intact, as do the lemmas chosen to repeat the mother-child love story over and over again. In this ballad, a blue-eyed *acrobata* or *atleta* is a boy happily playing in his mother's metaphoric 'blue dome.' But motherly protection will not be enough: he will not jump into life, and thus the pact is broken. Once again the woman is denied motherhood on her terms; she is left alone to her life, to her responsibilities. In osmosis between author and character, Armida tells Paolo about her determination not to have children anymore, which is what Maraini also apparently chose. The legacy of Maraini's experience and her engagement in the feminist groups provides corroborating evidence of this osmosis, thanks to Maraini's clear vision of what abortion really means to a woman: a painful but sometimes necessary choice, a difficult issue to understand, especially for those who do not experience it.

Voci *and* Un clandestino a bordo

For many militant feminists, the 1990s brought the bitter realization that women's entrance into society's structures did not undermine its androcentrism. At this time, Maraini re-proposed the view of abortion as an act imposed on woman by the phallocentric order. After millennia, women still decide to resort to the oldest and saddest (not to mention most dangerous) decision. We give up our own lives, breaking up what Maraini calls *patto d'amore*, a pact of love established between women and their foetus, for a strange, and yet at times mandatory, kind of 'survival law.' I call it a strange 'survival law' since many abortions in Italy today are not always motivated by economic necessities. On the contrary, it is not unusual that, in certain classes, abortions are often determined by a woman's desire for success, for a career beyond the traditional role of caregiver, a goal that has always been of great importance to Maraini.[50] The writer's message is that a woman's option to refuse to give life is a choice that must be guaranteed politically and legally. Yet, Maraini asks, what is the price women pay for this kind of choice in a male social order? This is a line of thought that Maraini has consistently taken and has convincingly argued in several recent interviews.

Though belonging to different genres, the essay *Un clandestino a bordo*[51] and the detective novel *Voci*[52] are parallel and complement each other in their intent and scope. *Voci* is a novel about a mysterious murder that is loosely based on a real case. The plot revolves around the intricate relations between the members of the murdered woman's family and the narrator's efforts at self-discovery. After the murder of her mysterious and beautiful neighbour Angela Bari, Michela Canova, a radio journalist, begins a series of investigations of unsolved murders of women whose voices still demand to be heard. Through these investigations the truth about many people emerges. Angela's death is instrumental to unveiling the real tragedy behind the woman's family: as adolescents, she and her sister Ludovica were forced by their stepfather, Glauco, to participate in incestuous and brutal relations that lasted for years. Only after Angela's murder will the unbalanced sense of conspiracy that ruled Angela's and Ludovica's lives surface, as will their habit of defending themselves against men. In a confession to Michela, Ludovica finally admits to her darkest secrets and to the fact that their mother knew about the rape and domestic violence.

> 'Era come se mia madre mi avesse fatto capire che quello era il sacrificio necessario per tenerlo in famiglia, per mantenere la sua protezione, la sua benevolenza. Era un sacrificio non detto, occulto e segreto ai suoi stessi occhi, oscuro come la più oscura delle notti ... Ma noi tenevamo la bocca ben cucita, non lasciavamo trapelare niente di niente, per proteggerlo e proteggere la mamma ... Mi consideravo morta per me e per gli altri ... e accettavo questa morte come l'olocausto necessario per tenere la famiglia unita : la sola cosa che si salvasse nel naufragio orribile dei sentimenti; che responsabilità per una bambina!'[53]
>
> ('It was as if my mother had wanted me to understand that this sacrifice was necessary to keep him in the family, to keep his protection, his benevolences. It was a sacrifice never spoken of, hidden and secret, dark as the darkest of nights ... but we kept our mouths shut, not letting anything seep out, in order to protect him and our mother ... I saw myself as dead, to myself and other people ... and I accepted this death as a necessary sacrifice to keep the family united, the only thing that could save the horrible shipwreck of feeling – what a responsibility for a child!')[54]

The abuse perpetrated upon the sisters by the stepfather is shown to have continued beyond adolescence, and to have extended to other men in their lives, to husbands, pimps, even men who sincerely loved them.

These issues are especially privileged in the passages where the narration deals with the abortion experience. A case in point is Ludovica, the surviving sister, who, in order to conceal the shared tragedy of incest experienced in their youth, does not hesitate to lie and invent a different culprit for the abortion Angela underwent as an adolescent. The story of an abortion caused by Glauco, the incestuous stepfather, was the source of Angela's insecurity. As amateur investigator Michela will later discover that Angela slowly lost control of her own life, becoming estranged from her family, after this abortion of her stepfather's child. Such dynamics reconfirm the relationship of dependence (mental and physical) to which women are subjected in youth and which we are later unable to overcome, thus explaining the difficulty of 'making choices' for ourselves. But the matter becomes even more tangled for Michela as, while in Florence, she finds out from the mother of the two women that Ludovica, and not Angela, was the sister who had been hospitalized for an abortion. When Michela confronts Ludovica she replies by explaining the blurred limits of the relationship with her sister. The enmeshment of the two sisters in the events of each other's lives, the confusion arising from Ludovica's conflicting narrations, and her love/hatred for Angela, is all a cover-up for the narrative of rape and incest perpetrated by their stepfather. This is an event that has literally destroyed both lives, more literally so in the case of Angela. In *Voci*, then, and against Judith Wilt's theorization,[55] abortion in narrative does not function as a medium to subvert the plot. I suggest, instead, that its fictional treatment follows the traditional path of passiveness and the fear women suffer, stressing the physical aspect of abortion rather than its means of subversion. In the novel, such a pattern is eloquently suggested in Ludovica's lines, when she tells Michela about her mother's admission of her obvious knowledge of the father's unremitting incestuous rape. As in a Greek myth, the father will kill his daughter. It is a tragedy indeed. In the case of *Voci*, there exists no possibility for maternal choice: the girls are victims of incest and the stepfather sees abortion for both, aged eleven and fourteen respectively, as the only solution to his problem. Here, the love for the father, such a frequent theme in Maraini's writing, is taken to its extreme consequences with the reiteration of a master-slave emplotment. The plot of this novel does not entail any maternal loss. And there is no desire for a continuing female genealogy, since the reproduction of a self would be inconceivable for these characters that have no self-esteem. There is only concealment of guilt, a sexual guilt in relation to society. Abortion is again an act of violence perpetrated by men against impotent women, as Maraini represented in *L'età del malessere*. In these novels abortion, originally a woman's private responsibility, is treated as an ethical concern whose discussion must involve the analysis of problems concerning the behaviour of a society as a whole, including both women and men.

Even if Maraini's argument might provoke controversial interpretations, I suggest that, in her mature period, namely, after *Marianna Ucrìa*, Maraini does not contradict her previous statements about abortion as a writer or as an activist. Indeed, although Maraini's entire novelistic production has always possessed an evident programmatic stance, in her latest works a stronger necessity to deliver reflections on abortion surfaces, making non-fictional writing almost a mandatory decision. In *Un clandestino a bordo*, published two years after *Voci*, Maraini revisits a non-fictional map of the female body, this time unrestricted by the actual motivations for the loss of life within the womb, be it abortion or miscarriage. To voice her analytical argument, Maraini chooses a genre more suitable than the novel. The first part of *Un clandestino a bordo*, 'Lettera sull'aborto,' is a long reflection on one of the most important struggles for women's liberation, the issue of maternal choice. Unlike in the case of Fallaci's *Lettera a un bambino mai nato*, in which the journalist was addressing an unborn child, Maraini's letter addresses an adult intellectual, Enzo Siciliano, inviting him to take a stance in this debate. The text is followed by a series of shorter essays. Maraini favoured this genre over the novelistic, and therefore fictional writing, for its highly effective rhetoric. In this context, the female writer can more openly and pragmatically examine the issue and propose it to the reading public, since no distracting narrative structure is at play. In remembering her own experience, Maraini notes:

> L'aborto può essere attivo e passivo. Si può volere la liberazione del proprio ventre da un intruso e si può volere che l'intruso rimanga, disperatamente rimanga con noi.
> E a quel punto, improvvisamente ho scoperto che stavo pensando al bambino non nato come al clandestino della nave di Conrad che viene accolto dal capitano nel suo battello. (LA 10)
> (The loss of a fetus can be both active and passive. We can want the liberation of our womb from an intruder, and we can want the intruder to remain, desperately want for him to remain with us.

At that point I suddenly discovered that I was thinking of the unborn child as the stowaway on Conrad's ship who is welcomed on board by the captain.) (LA2 4)

In this text Maraini utilizes a trope deployed by Joseph Conrad in his story *The Secret Sharer*[56] as a rhetorical tool to explain the moral choice a woman faces during pregnancy. Utilizing the metaphors of the vessel[57] for the mother and of the stowaway for the foetus, Maraini creates a very effective discursive space for the vicissitudes of pregnant women. She focuses on their obligation to decide, in one way or another, about our own moral existence as well as about someone's life. As Maraini contends, a sense of innate familiarity between the mother and the foetus is established immediately. The foetus is our own life within ourselves, and we know who is in our *vessel*. The secret of this pact belongs only to the two interdependent beings. It is a further development of the 'pact' between Armida and her baby fictionally explained in *Il treno per Helsinki*, and between Bianca and her baby in *Lettere a Marina*, of the secret between mother and child that remains such and precedes reason.[58] Maraini reiterates the physical and psychological suffering that the decision, and the allegedly 'free' choice, to get an abortion bring into a woman's life.

With the passing of the euphoria of the feminist years, many feminists of the second wave such as Maraini have realized that this 'choice' is always related to a woman's need to rid herself of a cumbersome weight that could put her future at risk in a world where androcentrism is still both dominating and pervasive. According to Maraini, this phenomenon is particularly evident in those female subjects whose lives are part of industrialized and advanced Western societies, since the 'desiderio di aborto comincia lì dove comincia il benessere' (LA 23; 'wish to have abortion starts with the advent of prosperity'; LA2 11). Maraini reminds us that abortion is not simply the decision to terminate a life because of all the above-mentioned reasons. In some cases, the clandestine passenger is forced to 'get off' the boat, the uterus-cradle in which he has lived until then, to leave a mother who does not want to let go of him because of her feelings of betrayal concerning the love pact she established with her foetus at the outset of her pregnancy. In those cases, suffering is pervasive, and taking one's life becomes an option. The Italian language's use of the signifier *aborto* to cover the two English semantic areas of 'abortion' and 'miscarriage' also leads to a lack of lexical distinction that facilitates Maraini's job. In Italian, attributing the responsibility to the mother simply corresponds to the act of adding the qualifier 'voluntary' to the noun *aborto*. The wide spectrum of images of *loss* in Maraini's narrative refers both to abortion and to miscarriage, thus inscribing the notion of activity and passivity with respect to abortion into the cultural, legal, and symbolic discursive space. The captain in Conrad's story represents the mind of the woman who accepts the stowaway, facing the danger of wrecking his ship in order to save him. But what if s/he did not save him? Maraini wonders,

> Cosa può succedere che impedisca al capitano di pescare dal mare il suo doppio? sarà la paura di riconoscersi in quel corpo nudo e bisognoso di cure? o l'orrore di vedersi replicato in un altro, come dentro 'uno specchio scuro e immenso'? (LA 17).
>
> (What could exist that would stop the captain from fishing his double from the sea? Could it be the fear of recognizing himself in that naked body that needs care, or the horror of seeing oneself replicated in another, as in a 'somber and immense mirror'?) (LA2 8)

Maraini suggests that it is dangerous to speak of liberation in connection with abortion. It is with this concept that she struggles when she speaks of leaving a child behind. Are women more liberated after an abortion? Is what Marina Warner claimed true, that in the area of motherhood women's authority is uncontested and that it is demonstrated in Medea's tragedy?[59] Adriana Cavarero reads a representation of feminine power in the Demeter myth:

> The myth says in fact that maternal power is the full power both to generate and not to generate: she does not have to generate, but she has generated already and she can generate again. This is because she carries in her womb the past and future infinity of human existence, as well as nothingness in the future sense of 'no longer.' And right here lies the deepest meaning of the feminine 'secret' of life, which archaic cultures attribute to the Great Mother: to generate is an exclusively female experience, but it is not an automatic and obligatory process where women are mere vehicles.[60]

Reproductive powers, maternity, and the ability and willingness to procreate are some of the few terrains where women's decision power should be exercised without recrimination on anybody's side. Also, as Rosi Braidotti plainly puts it, women's reproductive power is constantly being put at stake by modern reproductive technology, since 'contemporary bio-technology displaces women by making procreation a high-tech affair.'[61] Maraini echoes Warner's considerations on women's reproductive power, although she notes that 'si tratta di un potere che ha perso la sua vera essenza, ma che rimane nell'ombra come il mito di una forza recondita e vitale' (LA 8; 'It is a power that has lost its true force, but that remains in the shadows like the myth of a concealed and vital strength,' LA2 9). This kind of power strikes back at women like a boomerang[62] and does not take them far, because children quickly become a difficult burden to carry. Regardless of the theories that claim that gender, unlike sex, is a social construct, gender discrimination is still rampant in the work place. As Maraini alerts us, women pay a very high price for freedom from reproductive obligations:

> L'aborto sembra essere il luogo maledetto dell'impotenza storica femminile. Lì dove si rappresenta la perdita ripetuta del controllo sulla riproduzione della specie.
> L'aborto è dolore e impotenza fatta azione. È l'autoconsacrazione di una sconfitta storica bruciante e terribile che si esprime in un gesto brutale contro se stesse e il figlio che si è concepito ... Le donne, più sono bistrattate, disprezzate, tenute ai margini e più sentono il bisogno di provare, in modo tortuoso, disperatamente masochistico e rischioso, quel potere che la storia dei padri ha cancellato dalla loro vita. (LA 24)
> (Historically, abortion seems to be the damned realm of age-old female impotence. It represents the repeated loss of control over the reproduction of the species. Abortion is grief and impotence turned into action. It is the self-consecration of a defeat – a burning and terrible historical defeat that finds expression in a brutal gesture against oneself and the conceived child. For the women who practice it, abortion is a sign of malaise and of war against oneself ... The more women are mistreated, scorned, relegated to the margins of society, the more they feel the need to demonstrate, in a tortuous, desperately masochistic and risky way, that power that the history of the fathers has obliterated from their lives.) (LA2 12–13)

For women, the experience of abortion is inevitably linked to the other side of the coin, to reproduction and the act of giving birth, and becoming a mother. Indeed, for Maraini it is impossible to speak about abortion independently of maternity, as the physical concavity of the empty womb must necessarily be integrated with the convexity of a pregnant belly. Maraini's fictional narrative affirms this interdependence first. Later, the author's letter to Siciliano openly exposes it in all its implications. Abortion necessarily evokes motherhood, with the implied act of rejection or acceptance of the 'clandestine' passenger women carry in our wombs. Maraini states such inevitable complementary properties of the two concepts:

> Sarà perché per me l'aborto è stato soprattutto un esproprio, qualcosa di non voluto e non aspettato che ha spezzato in me una attesa felice, che non si è mai conclusa con un incontro, l'incontro con l'altro da me. Il clandestino a bordo della mia nave è scomparso prematuramente nel buio della notte senza lasciare una traccia, un nome, un ricordo.
> Oppure sarà perché in realtà non si può parlare di aborto senza parlare di maternità. Sono legati l'uno all'altra come gemelli siamesi: l'uno la faccia al sole, l'altra la faccia all'ombra dello stesso astro rotolante nell'universo femminile. (LA 20).
>
> (Maybe because, for me, losing a fetus was, above all, an act of expropriation, something neither desired nor expected, that terminated a happy expectancy in me, that never ended in a meeting – the meeting with that other being from me. The stowaway on my ship disappeared prematurely in the darkness of the night without leaving a trace, a name, a memory.
> Or maybe it is because in fact one cannot talk about abortion without talking about motherhood. They are linked to each other like two Siamese twins: one facing the sun, the other in the shadow of the same heavenly body orbiting in the female universe.) (LA2 10)

The border between abortion and miscarriage become even more blurred when abortion is so blatantly counterbalanced to motherhood. What really matters in Maraini's letter, which is completely devoid of political rhetoric, is not how and why a child was lost, but the loss in itself, the fact that a woman has been deprived of her own life, of the *re*-union with the self represented by her fetus. This realization is what, in 1996, at age sixty, inevitably caused Maraini to speak of loss in connection with abortion and of life in connection with motherhood, even though she spent years conducting pro-choice campaigns in the working-class Roman suburbs, where she worked with culturally deprived women who desperately needed to give up their cumbersome 'authority of motherhood.' By losing a child, by giving up the pact with the unborn, a woman loses yet one more chance to discover her identity, and she does so in obedience to laws that are not hers, that do not belong to her body, *al suo corpo*.

Maraini shares with Simone de Beauvoir many of the views on pregnancy and abortion of the controversial but still seminal *The Second Sex*.

A common ground between the two writers is established as they emphasize contraception rather than establishing the fairness of abortion. Another is the interdependence between pregnancy and abortion, which de Beauvoir qualifies as always an 'especially desperate remedy.'[63] Well before Maraini and other Italian feminists, de Beauvoir indicated that for women abortion is an issue[64] fraught with social problems, and like Maraini, she argued that for a woman an abortion is always a difficult and hard choice:

> In her heart she often repudiates the interruption of pregnancy which she is seeking to obtain. She is divided against herself. Her natural tendency can well be to have the baby whose birth she is undertaking to prevent; even if she has no positive desire for maternity, she still feels uneasy about the dubious act she is engaged in. For if it is not true that abortion is murder, it still cannot be considered in the same light as a mere contraceptive technique; an event has taken place that is a definite beginning, the progress of which is to be stopped.[65]

In the same fashion as Maraini and other feminists, de Beauvoir formulates specific accusations of the hypocritical attitude of society abhorring the representation, as much as the problematic presence, of the abortion, in respect, then, to the children, unwittingly protagonists of all sorts of abuse. Maraini's reflections also mirror the considerations on abortion and on the actual meaning of the term 'right' that Diane Elam presents in *Deconstruction and Feminism*. There is danger in utilizing the term 'rights,' created by male subjects, which is observant of categories that do not reflect what women's rights might be and 'is always an appeal to a certain *description* of the human as more human than other descriptions.'[66] Elam reconsiders how 'rights' actually construct the political subjects who are entitled to those 'rights,' and states further:

> Indeed, to continue arguing in terms of rights may well be anti-feminist. An abortion is each woman's choice. To seek to enshrine it as a 'right' risks neglecting the sentiments of the woman who chooses not to have an abortion, or who has an abortion and regrets it, or who has or doesn't have an abortion and can't decide whether she did the right thing. An abortion, that is, is not like a vote. You don't use it to express yourself, to feel one with yourself. Abortion is no more or less natural than sex – and feminists know how the notion of 'conjugal rights' has served to enshrine marital rape for centuries in the West.[67]

In Elam's view the meaning of 'rights' in politics seems to always turn out to be based on universal notions of male subjectivity. On different ideological premises, Mary O'Brien also detects a certain inconsistency and deficiency in the definition of 'life' and 'rights,' 'Neither pregnancy nor abortions are rights, but are existential choices related to the *historical* relations of reproduction which patriarchs pretend are not historical but natural.'[68] Maraini's letter is an open invitation to rethink the natural sources of the term 'difference' with an open mind, rather than an alignment with outmoded essentialisms. The author confirms that women's 'forms,' that our 'discourses,' are strictly related to our embodiment, and are not a simple reflection of our social roles. Regardless of how many individual women choose to become parents, women ought to voice their needs as birth-givers and mothers, and these needs must become socially acceptable. Essentially, what Maraini always theorized about abortion, both as a writer and as a feminist activist, is the noncontradictory necessity for Italian women to break the all-encompassing internalized Catholic prohibition on contraceptives.[69] In her more constructed, more engaged narrative, in her theatrical works, and most notably in 'Lettera sull'aborto,' Maraini suggests that sexual players need to undergo a process of maturation in order to use contraceptives in a more responsible way, which could prevent pregnancy and, consequently, abortion. Only as women gradually generate a new concept of sexual life can a truer *diritto alla sessualità* be claimed that will enable us to transform the world and give it a new symbolic order in accord with women's rhythms: a world, that is, as Judith Butler hopes, in which a true 'reorganization' can take place also with respect to reproduction and prevention. More recently, in one of her latest interviews, Dacia Maraini consistently reinforced her opinion on abortion:

> Non credo che sia una conquista e nemmeno una bandiera da tirare su con trionfalismo ... L'aborto è un non senso, un'arma disperata e autolesiva, una violenza sul corpo della donna e di riflesso su quello del nascituro, comunque una sconfitta e una lacerazione.[70]
> (I don't think it is a conquest and even less a flag of triumph. Abortion is a non-sense, a desperate and self-destructive weapon on the woman's body and by default also on the newborn, always a defeat and a laceration.)

On law 40/2004, on artificial insemination, Dacia Maraini argues again against laws that prevent women from asserting their rights of being mothers:

Questa è una legge che fa indignare soprattutto le donne perché è sulla loro pelle che è stato deciso cosa fare e cosa non fare. Dunque, adesso è ancora più importante battersi per la riuscita del referendum. I diritti vanno difesi sempre, non sono acquisiti una volta per tutte.[71]
(This is a law that especially angers women, as everything has been decided about their body. Now, more than ever, it is important to fight for the outcome of the referendum. Rights must be defended always; they have not been conquered forever.)

The story goes back to centuries of womanhood under patriarchy, where the female body functioned as a system for the reproduction of the male. Something is inherently wrong with considering a person only as a birth-giver. Even though in the generative process women are blessed with the choice to give humankind reproduction, not being able to look at her child is, for a mother, still terribly painful. To borrow Joseph Conrad's lines, '[t]o make you hear, to make you feel it is before all to make you see.' Women who have experienced pregnancy and abortion can physically understand this. Maraini, as a writer, makes all women *see* this experience. She possesses an incredible ability to make women see what they should have seen from the beginning. Maraini's paratactic style of writing makes deliberate use of a simple lexicon and syntax, but her conclusions are far from simplistic. Throughout her works she maintains that, although abortion is an indispensable right in a society that values women's contributions, it nevertheless constitutes a dramatic moment of subjection to needs that might be foreign to the woman involved.

In her revisionist effort Maraini hardly betrays feminist beliefs when restating the *natural* necessity of becoming a mother for a woman in 'Lettera sull'aborto.' Men have used women's natural desire for mothering to subject them to a symbolic patriarchal order that sees only its own advantage in that desire,[72] and therefore has always exercised rights over the reproductive powers of women. However, these findings cannot possibly prevent women from giving birth, especially now that the goals of economic independence and professional development are about to be reached. Maraini seems to say that surrendering our choice of motherhood in the name of equality would be evidence of weakness on our part. As seen from her perspective, in feminist politics abortion no longer entails self-determination. Rather, it prevents women from exploring new avenues for self-discovery. Judith Butler claims that 'feminists who criticize technologies for effectively replacing the maternal body with a patriarchal apparatus must nevertheless contend with the enhanced autonomy that those technologies have provided for women.'[73] I would also argue that, as with any other aspect of sexuality, artificial insemination is yet one more political site, one in which the power of women must come to terms with the dangerous politicization of the very act.[74] Losing this power means losing our right to sexuality in many ways. According to Butler what matters is not to 'extend the "right to life" to any and all people who want to make this claim on behalf of mute embryos, but rather to understand how the "viability" of a woman's life depends upon an exercise of bodily autonomy and on social conditions that enable that autonomy.'[75] The collaborative exchange between 'bodily autonomy' – or right for the woman to choose – and the 'social conditions that enable that autonomy' hoped for by Butler synthesize Maraini's ongoing effort to re-discuss life, the right to life, and women's sexuality in her work. Since rights and women's right to choose can quickly be overturned – or merely be 'misnomers,' as Butler writes[76] – one should never forget that women must still be *donne in guerra*, even when being at war signifies renewing their personal pact with life and giving life. When women think of themselves as vessels of another individual's life, the underlying question for their choice should be when and how they want to exercise such lasting power, as the connection between women and their creations is an everlasting one.

Perverse Desire and the Reversal of Medusa's Gaze in Melania Mazzucco's *Il bacio della Medusa*

> quando mi riconosco, resto immobile a fissar me stessa,
> come se mirassi una medusa[77]
> E chi la guarda la Gorgone? Tutti si scostano, sgattaiolano, non vedono,
> sperano di cavarsela. Deve afferrarti per farsi fissare, la Gorgone, ma
> non ha braccia. Non sarà quella che mi pietrifica, non me.[78]

Because of their very nature, literary works imply the presence of readers (implied and/or empirical) whose assigned task is to complete – at every reading – the works' meaning. This relationship between the text and the reader feeds into the notion that one individual cannot struggle for her/himself alone in search of a meaningful reading/reception/interpretation, but needs 'to enter a collective work in which one's own status as a subject must, for democratic reasons, become disoriented, exposed to what it does not know.'[79] Literature can, therefore, provide individuals with this sense of 'collective work,' for its texts present a forum in which the examination of societal values and the investigation of identities take place regularly. Since the publication of Sigmund Freud's works, literature has also been used as a rhetorical means to explain the complex relations between the known and the unknown elements of human existence. The discourse of literature, like that of myth, can be likened to psychoanalytic discourse, for both are directly and structurally connected to the representation of trauma and other mental disorders. Literary discourse offers numerous ways to extricate meaning from psychoanalysis showing modes useful to the presentation of 'the complex relation between knowing and not knowing.'[80] One of the possible ways of interaction existing between psychoanalytic and literary discourses resides in the ability of the latter to present traumatic experiences of various kinds in the stratified utterance of the narrative discourse linked to trauma. In this manner, literary discourse fully assumes responsibility for its role in committing trauma to the painful journey of ascent to the surface of the human being, since its story, 'the narrative of a belated experience, far from telling of an escape from reality – the escape from a death, or from its referential force – rather attests to its endless impact on life.'[81] Judith Butler notes how psychoanalytic discourse has often contributed to establishing the notion of a 'primary sexual difference' in only one – and a rather limitative aspect – of its functions. The other function that Butler mentions, and more cogent to my study, looks at psychoanalytic discourse as a 'critique of cultural adaptation as well as a theory of understanding the ways in which sexuality fails to conform to the social norms by which it is regulated.'[82]

The process of interaction between literature and psychoanalysis, far from limiting itself to the cold exposition of clinical case studies – presented in Melania Mazzucco's *Il bacio della Medusa* in the form of homosexual hysteria, childhood traumas, and alienation – constructs the political and aesthetic value of this work as well. By political we understand the role by which literature can express the ineffable and offer the gift of the word to those who endured silence and will, in turn, become *politikon zoon*. A social animal should have, in fact, a voice to represent its own identity. The elements constituting sexual difference and our own existence as Other with respect to the norms established by society can be investigated to reveal the ways in which they actually *differ* from the established norm. As such, the artificially imposed norm circumscribing the sphere of humankind needs to undergo scrutiny.

Melania Mazzucco's literary discourse finds great power in the conflation of myth and psychoanalysis to support the author's personal message about the freedom of loving another subject that society has unnecessarily cast as Other. *Il bacio della Medusa* entails a discussion of the subversive behaviour of the two protagonists – Norma and Medusa – culminating in the difficult realization that being in (physical) love with each other is forbidden by norms and as such, this love *should be* impossible to pursue. Rather than limiting the novelistic treatment to telling of the 'affair,' Mazzucco looks at the future of Norma and Medusa in a hopeful and open manner, to a prosperous human contentment that finally arrives for both unhappy creatures. The promising manner is formally suggested in the novel by the articulation of postmodernist multiple, open endings that oppose – even with a happy ending by the sea – strict condemnations of lesbian love.

My exegesis illustrates passages contained in both the first and second parts of this complex, self-reflexive novel as they reverse and defeat the falsely 'authentic' medical assumptions of the *Controromanzo*.[83] Mazzucco's construction of the novel attests to a firmer confirmation of Freud's essays of his findings on the problematic relationship between neurosis and perversion and places them within the frame of her novel. Confuting the law of medical discourse and juxtaposing hypotheses to novelistic discourse proves to be an invaluable formidable postmodernist weapon to critique sexual identity as constructed in turn-of-the-century bigoted Italy. Moreover, the treatment of female homosexuality and the problem of sexual diversity, when framed by the historical context of the then recent Italian unification, gives an interesting spin to the story depicted in *Il bacio della Medusa*. The *mise en jeu* of archetypes and fears that have been linked for centuries with the female image illustrates quite aptly how sexuality has become a site for adjustment and reconfiguration of the woman's position in Italian society. Mazzucco's rereading of the Medusa myth offers suggestive narrative instances for a commentary on the latency of the psychoanalytical unknown, on the reception and comprehension of trauma of different sorts, and on René Girard's notion of 'sacrificial suitability.'[84]

The issue of desire coupled with the problem of perversion that can also, but is not limited to, signify homosexuality, comes to join the discourse of trauma rooted in the maternal image, one of the underlying themes of the novel. In the reality of her absence, the maternal figure, a source of grief and loss for both protagonists of the novel, is reciprocally searched for, and substituted with the existence of the other. Their reciprocal search confirms the perennial impact that the trauma of maternal absence and of childhood episodes connected with such absence has on children. For the two protagonists, both of whom had been living with the consequences of their respective childhood traumas, the encounter with the other – forming the couple – provokes a subsequent legitimate rebellion against societal constrictions and mores and against psychological and literal dependence produced by communitarian laws. The critique of suffocating social codes that do not allow for any form of diversity in the construction of the 'woman' gender, the composition of alternative endings to the one prescribed by society for transgressive women are at the core of Mazzucco's novel.

The Kiss of the Medusa Woman or Medusa's Pathological Desires

In their seminal study on female literary imagination, *The Madwoman in the Attic*, Sandra Gilbert and Susan Gubar note how in nineteenth-century literature 'even the most apparently conservative and decorous women writers create fiercely independent characters who seek to destroy all the patriarchal structures which both their authors and their authors' submissive heroines seem to accept as inevitable.'[85] The enduring creation of 'fiercely independent' characters as a fictional means to overrule patriarchal structures, the authorial entrustment with one's own work of a 'monster woman' to propose or live differently from what is socially acceptable (though not to the same extent) is also present in the Italian novel by women. Such a phenomenon, which could be defined as a form of deconstruction from within, takes place in the narration of women as characters to be perceived as the 'author's double' who 'reject the submissive silences of domesticity' and 'seek the power of self-articulation.'[86] In this sense, monstrous creatures like the Gorgons, when utilized in female literature, do come with an entirely different reading than the radical misreading provided by patriarchal poetics.

Questioning the terrible powers of Medusa is an operation that, in revisiting the myth of the Gorgon, this time seen not as a terrible object but as a transgressive desiring subject, retrieves pre-existing notions of the extraordinary powers – adversarial to men – of the Gorgon. In fact, in a pre-Olympian time, Medusa was considered to be the serpent-goddess of the Amazons. She represented women's wisdom, and her snakes were symbols of this wisdom. She was the giver of life and death, and the giver of rebirth and immortality, as testified by her presence on the pediment of Artemis's temple in Corfu. In Mazzucco's novel, the locution *il bacio della Medusa* organizes the entire textual exegesis in an antithetical position, vis-à-vis the mythological belief of the Olympian Medusa, and recuperates the pre-Olympian notion of the gentle girl Medusa who dared the gods as she kissed a boy in Athena's temple. Mazzucco's position is one that envisages women's attraction for Medusa. Not necessarily and not always, in fact, are women 'repelled by Medusa, but sometimes empower [them]selves by identifying with her ... Whether she functions as an image of aversion or of empowerment, Medusa clearly evokes powerful emotional responses.'[87]

In this female-authored novel, the revisited image of the Medusa myth engenders feelings other than those typically brought about in men when they stare at her freezing eyes in literary texts.[88] It is the exercise of pressure by the community that takes love away from Norma, not the gazing of Medusa. The system constructing the medical-legal writings functions within the text as an alternative to the sacrifice practised by primitive society. The presence of the *pharmakon* constructs, therefore, a *public vendetta* that ostracizes those who are diverse, in a duplicitous way, like Norma and Medusa. These women are different in their homosexuality, as well in their *qualità di straniere* ('foreign quality') or *condizione servile* ('servile condition'), both of which respond to the demands that are required of the 'ideal sacrificial victim.'[89] The gaze exchanged by the two women originates perverse desire and foreshadows the power of Medusian Eros transmitted to Norma.[90] In a textual confirmation of the opinions expressed by Susan Bowers, Mazzucco's Norma and Medusa provoke – in being ideal *pharmakoi* (remedies) – a violent desire to defend conservative values on the part of the community, insofar as they represent 'the intense power of female eroticism' shared by 'millions of women condemned as witches.' Witches, just like Medusa, construct the generative fulcrum of hate for women in a society dominated by men'[91] as they represent – among many other things – the danger of the senses. The outcome is the drama of self-love that the Lacanian Law of the Father has always denied – and yet is ignited by a patriarchal society that considers not only Medusa, but Norma as well, to be *outsiders*. Neither woman conforms to the expectations of society embodied by the Turinese arch-conservative setting that serves as the social moralistic backdrop for this postmodern melodrama. With partial success, this society attempts to destroy this communion of souls through the exercise of the medical-juridical written power, clearly a patriarchal voice.

Being a lesbian was probably likened to monstrosity during the reign of King Umberto I of the House of Savoy. In her intricate story with

Medusa, Norma is a woman who embodies a 'non-masculine lesbian' typology.[92] She is one of the two female characters for whom Mazzucco needs to construct an emblematic – symbolic and not metaphoric – situation where the need for love of the woman is not elided by the Gorgon's gaze, but actually awakened by it. The subversion of norms – even those prescribed by by-now conventional readings of lesbian characters such as Maraini's 1981 *Lettere a Marina* – Mazzucco operates in her novel confirms the paradox marked by the representation of Medusa – a famous female monster of patriarchal mythology – caught in the 'impossible' moment of giving a kiss. This paradox is made evident in the novel's locution in the title, 'the kiss of the Medusa,' in which both nouns appear charged with the role of destroying the significance traditionally attributed to the Gorgon's gaze, her apotropaic powers, that is. The more traditionally held belief about Medusa is connected to her apotropaic gaze that made impossible not only physical contact with the Gorgon, but even holding her gaze. The kiss engages the characters more actively than the gaze had been able to do. If Medusa's gaze turns men into stone, her kiss will awaken her lover. In the fairy tale, a popular form of myth, the actant – the character whose role is that of awakening the sleeping beauty – is 'gendered in the masculine.' In *Morphology of the Folktale*,[93] Vladimir Propp states, however, that what matters is not 'who' does the action – the gender, that is, of the character performing it – but the function in itself. *Il bacio della Medusa* subverts indisputably such assumptions, while showing – among other things – the limits of Propp's analysis when utilized in a narrative constructed by a woman's point of view.

Hélène Cixous's seminal 'The Laugh of the Medusa' (*'Le rire de la Méduse'*) envisions the possibility of reading the myth of the slain Medusa as a different and empowering one. Cixous does so from a diverging, ironic perspective that reconsiders this myth along with the proposition of her notion of *écriture féminine*.[94] Medusa is for Cixous the pre-Olympian nymph, related more to Hesiod's tale than to Ovid's. It is in pre-Olympian time, in fact, that Cixous situates inventiveness and creativity, in the lost space of the mother that we need to retrieve to see our path. In Ovid's story, instead, it is Perseus who becomes famous, while Medusa is relegated to her role as a monstrous female, an enemy to male integrity and, ultimately, to his safety, such that it is apparent, from thereon, that 'the history of women's images in Western culture is the history of an attempt to defuse the power of female eros.'[95]

In Teresa de Lauretis's *The Practice of Love: Lesbian Sexuality and Perverse Desire*, all theories connected with perverse desire are revisited in an engaging discussion with previous feminist criticism written in opposition to Freud's interpretation of sexuality. Freud's tendency was to always consider perverse desire in an ambiguous, but still androcentric, manner. De Lauretis traces feminists' interest back to the 'thin seduction' that Freud's work's inherent ambiguity exercised on women, since in his writings women finally saw themselves as desiring subjects, vis-à-vis the old notion of being desired ones.[96] De Lauretis activates Freudian theories on perverse desire by operating a necessary and implicit rotation of the initial perspective from which Freud had proposed them. She eliminates a priori the image of the desiring woman as hysteric subject and uncovers instead the path of perverse desire as separate from the *Sexualtrieb*,[97] or sexual drive. In doing so, de Lauretis constructs a general and yet very specific model for a conceptualization of lesbianism.[98]

In my reading of the novel, the deregulation of perverse desire is associated with the feminist rereading of the mythical *topos* of Medusa – yet another famous monstrous woman – as it confirms that 'for women artists to transform Medusa from what she has been deemed by males into Aphrodite/Medusa, the embodiment of the female Eros with which women can identify, is to re-possess themselves, to liberate their bodies and their mind from the patriarchy.'[99] Mazzucco's particular take on Medusa's apotropaic gaze problematizes the ways in which lesbian desire was regarded at the time in which the novel is set. Medusa's gaze is apotropaic only for those who cannot see the unknown and for those who repudiate it in fear of deregulating societal norms.

A Young (Freudian) Bride

Norma's romance in *Il bacio della Medusa* begins in 1905. This is a deceitful incipit, as hers appears to be the 'normal' story of a young girl who gets married to an elegant widower who takes her away from a humble condition and dependence on her brother. She is a Florentine girl who spends her time diligently studying philology at the university; she is nicknamed *Mouche* ('fly') by everybody except her Piedmontese fiancé, who simply refuses to call her *Mosca*. She is beautiful and chaste. Upon Norma's arrival in Turin, it is apparent that she is a foreigner among the Piedmontese, who do not accept the young bride from Florence as one of them. The unification of the country is still too recent – a mere twenty-five years – and, under the Savoy flag of the Counts Argentero, Norma 'parlava un italiano da accademico della Crusca, evitava il francese, sprezzava i dialetti, non capiva il torinese' (BM 37; 'spoke an academic Italian, avoided

French, had a disdain for dialects, and did not understand Turinese'), all terrible flaws in the austere and conservative Turin of the time.

What could be the endearing story of a young and tender bride, of her honeymoon to Paris, a city that readily embraces Norma's innocent and sincere carnal knowledge,[100] reveals instead all the trials a young woman is subjected to when she is put in an environment that hardly suits her. When a character is not docile, this forcing upon her of societal mores will, in turn, exacerbate her dormant 'transgressiveness.' Misled by their literary competence, readers are inclined to believe in a novel that follows conventional (male) patterns of narrative and theme. Identifying with the characters that seem to be drawn from a traditional melodrama, readers are slowly enveloped into a complex web of readings that articulate the subversive treatment of turn-of-the-century novelistic motifs: the marriage, the honeymoon (we only need to remember George Eliot's ironic and disappointing wedding journey to Rome of *Middlemarch*'s protagonist, Dorothea Brooke), and a woman's place in the family. With them soon comes the realization that Norma does not hypocritically respond to laws imposed by heterosexual society, as her education is based on a culture that practises sincerity and scientific curiosity with respect to life rather than a sullen obedience to the rigid tradition of passiveness – sexual, and not only – imposed upon the bourgeois woman. Unlike Eliot's Dorothea Brooke, however, Norma is sexually active and not afraid of her own sexuality. She has successfully survived the traumatic moment of the ritualistic passage from virginity into fuller life as a woman. Norma understands – with tones that are cognizant of Paolo Mantegazza's writings – the oppressive and often insincere role played by sexuality in a marital union.[101] She does not reject it nor does she passively accept it. Quite the contrary, she discovers the physicality of the act of deflowering not to be as cruel as the flower images in Catullus's poem let her believe.[102]

By a strange coincidence, 1905 is also the year of publication of Sigmund Freud's 'Three Essays on the Theory of Sexuality,' which discuss the issue of sexual normalcy. Teresa de Lauretis's study of Freud's essays in *The Practice of Love* reconfirms the import of his approach to the analysis of so-called perversions. In particular, de Lauretis extols the ambiguity within the very lines of those writings, for they could encourage a more flexible interpretation of female sexuality and sexual drive. She reiterates the degree of freedom that Freud's studies female sexuality have meant to feminist studies on sex, sexual behaviour, and normative conceptions of human nature more generally.

In his analysis of the relationship between sexual drive and sexual object, Freud affirms the independence of the first – *Sexualartrieb* – with respect to the second. He takes a stance against the notion of sexuality understood in terms of pathology. Both Teresa de Lauretis and Jonathan Dollimore find in Freud's statements some ambiguities,[103] further advanced in his conclusions. What matters, though – as de Lauretis recognizes in Freud – is the characterization of sexuality in terms of its swerving from the 'norm.' Swerving from the norm can no longer be interpreted in terms of 'abnormal,' but rather is merely the expression of a sexual activity 'other' than, and yet intrinsic to, the norm, as it follows a different path towards pleasure. If seen in this way, perversion is only one of the possible signifiers for sexual drive. Such reorganization of this concept allows for a specific theory of perverse desire, drawn to characterize the dynamics connected with female homosexual desire. Freud's theory also limits the validity of theoretical praxis, both the feminist one and the psychoanalytical one of a more traditional stance. The negative Freudian theory of perversion becomes thus a form of revision of sexuality out of necessity. Perversion is the expression and rediscovery of an original intensity of a being usually repressed in his/her sexuality.[104]

In studying Freud's theories on perverse desire, de Lauretis embraces Dollimore's thesis that there is a paradox outlined in them that allows for perversion to be such only when intrinsic to normalcy – 'being integral to just those things it threatens'[105] – thus making its disturbing presence within the realm of norm its most 'shattering effect.' De Lauretis's reading sees a normal sexuality as the one that signifies the mediating capacity of the ego – intended as a body-ego – to establish 'incessant material negotiations' among 'the pressures coming from the external world,' 'those coming from the internal world, from the id's instinctual and narcissistic drives,' and those coming 'from their representatives, the superego.'[106] Compromises that are not necessarily fulfilling for all individuals involved are thus perforce created. 'Normal' behaviour, in its bracketed use, requires the notion of a sexuality that recognizes the validity of compromises, one that can accurately mirror that part of society that promotes such rules as indispensable to the civil order. Furthermore, 'normal' behaviour must also be willing to perform the same rituals that construct the scaffolding of pleasure according to the laws that this society promulgates. To sum up, all these activities proceed towards procreation, as it is the norm and rule society expects human beings to follow. As Freud describes it, 'sexual activity is perverse if it has given up the aim of reproduction and pursues the attainment of pleasure as an aim independent of it.'[107] De Lauretis does not analyse perverse desire as a pathology of desire, but rather as a non-heterosexual desire, or even better yet, as a non-normatively heterosexual desire. Perverse desire deregulates society and opens spaces of understanding for a multitude of sexual behaviours.

Turning Medusa's Head *Upside Down: Mantegazza, Florence, and Norma*

At the turn of the past century, ethno-anthropological studies were fundamental to the process of modernization of Western society. In Italy, Paolo Mantegazza was an ordinary professor of anthropology at the University of Florence – the same university where Mazzucco's Norma studies Romance philology – and where her father, a much-revered and feared professor, is a fictional colleague of the illustrious anthropologist. Mantegazza's Darwinian studies have greatly influenced the opinion of Italian upper-bourgeois classes, and much of his work opened new paths to the notion of a female sexuality within the Italian collective imaginary. There was the revelation, limited to the enlightened bourgeoisie, of sexual behaviours strictly pertinent to the female body, not generated by male desire. The female body, thanks to Mantegazza's findings, revealed itself to be not as passive as is assumed by the Catholic Church's precepts, but instead quite active. Needless to say, Mantegazza's scandalous findings would lead to his dismissal from his post at the University of Florence, but his relevant role in the discovery and learning of human behaviours, particularly those linked to sexual relations, will remain unmatched for a long time in conservative Italian circles.

In introducing the English translation of Mantegazza's *The Sexual Relations of Mankind*, Victor Robinson writes about the 'Apostle of the state of hygiene in Italy,' the 'pioneer sexologist': 'When Mantegazza wrote about love, he could not be calm. For everywhere he saw sex, the source of the profoundest of human emotions, bringing tragedy instead of happiness to mankind.'[108] This kind of amiable speculation on the personality of the famous anthropologist notwithstanding, there is a paradox in Mantegazza's work that – in the economy of our study – has similar consequences to Freud's oft-cited 'ambiguity.'[109] Like Darwin, Mantegazza also travelled among Australian Aborigines, as well as in Asia and the Americas. Mantegazza talks freely of sexual perversions in his work, composing a precise nomenclature based on centuries-old abnormal behaviours. He does so by utilizing, as Freud does, classical examples from ancient Greece's male homosexuality[110] and the one practised in Rome, while availing himself of the most recent anthropological discoveries rooted in

Darwinism. According to Mantegazza, sexual (female) perversion, such as lesbianism was then considered, 'brings with it domestic unhappiness; and it behoves the married man to keep a sharp eye out for these strange and hidden manifestations of lasciviousness, which, taken in the beginning, may be dominated and overcome by physiologic love.'[111] The contradictory nature of Mantegazza's research on female perversion, which further corroborates the uneasiness of post-Unification Italy in dealing with non-procreative sexuality, emerges almost constantly in his theories. The more Mantegazza tries to convey the importance of women's *jouissance* the more he denounces – and warns their husbands about – the danger of their pleasure. In addition to this contradiction, Mantegazza claims it is impossible to give a precise definition of the threshold between physiological sex and pathological sex.[112]

His theories on female pleasure, on the impossibility of setting boundaries for what is to be considered normal or not, are subsequent to the categorical distinctions he made on the typologies of pleasure explained in his *Fisiologia del piacere*. In this book the physiological pleasures are presented as being clearly separated from the pathological ones. The former are 'conformi alle leggi ordinarie dell'organismo'[113] ('in conformity to the ordinary laws of the living organism') – therefore responding to the needs of man – while the latter 'costituiscono sempre una deformità o una malattia'[114] ('always constitute a deformity or illness'). The second typology includes the subsequent categorization of the 'congiungimento tra persone dello stesso sesso'[115] ('sexual union between same-sex people). Two women who practise sex together reach 'un godimento spasmodico che raggiunge spesso il parossismo. I piaceri venerei fra donne snervano, sfibrano e riescono deleteri per l'organismo' ('a spasmodic pleasure that reaches paroxysm. Venereal pleasure between women debilitates them, wears them out, and is dangerous for the organism').[116] Solitary pleasure can be practised, but pleasure exchanged between women is, basically, dangerous. In her treatment of sexual perversions, de Lauretis seems to adopt Mantegazza's scientific views, but devoid this time of the moralistic attitude shown by the Florentine scientist. Deregulating means especially finding previous shady areas of thought that call for being dismantled and understood in their deeper tones. It would almost seem as if de Lauretis had read Mantegazza's findings in order to establish the criteria that organize non-normative sexual practices, among which female homosexuality is only one. Far from being pathological or physiological, sexuality is neither innate nor acquired, but 'dynamically (re)structured by forms of fantasy private and public, conscious and unconscious, which are culturally available and historically specific.'[117]

Mantegazza concludes the theme of *tribadismo*, though, with eloquent words of admiration for the young woman who can avoid such *nefasti sviluppi* ('nefarious developments'),[118] stressing instead the necessity of a normal and 'honest' sexual growth. In so doing, he ultimately reconfirms the social condemnation so patent in *Il bacio della Medusa*. If not with his findings, then certainly with his commentaries, Paolo Mantegazza subscribes to the firm categories of division into which his contemporary Cesare Lombroso, the Turinese scientist and father of criminology, had divided the typology of women in his studies. His study on women shows even more than Mantegazza's work the (dangerous) sign of the times. Lombroso's *La donna delinquente* (*Criminal Woman*) – companion text to *L'uomo delinquente* (*Criminal Man*) – is the social, ethical, and ideological document of an era in which the desire for keeping the woman as an inferior human being could still be corroborated by the sciences without fear of criticism. Claiming the validity of science through the data he collected, Lombroso could afford to make observations of a more general nature, being firmly convinced that 'at the present time, the moral sciences are interwoven, or rather, fused with the natural sciences.'[119]

At the time, ethics and physiology would thus go hand in hand. If today Lombroso's analyses appear ambiguous (not to say offensive) and likely to be rebutted, during his time the positive echo was large. Once Italy was unified, politicians, scientists, and intellectuals were trying to form a common identity for Italians. Given the position of the Piedmontese themselves as winners of a long struggle for independence and unification, it seemed that the identity that Italians should assume was theirs. Illiteracy rates were lower in the Savoy regions and *pro capite* income was the highest. In short, it soon became clear that theirs was the identity upon which being Italian should be modelled in the near future. By the same token, for Lombroso it was necessary to draw the model for the 'normal' woman to set against the data that previous scientists had collected on tribes. Without studying the normal, law-abiding woman, it would have otherwise been difficult if not 'impossible [for Lombroso] to determine where the normal state ends and the pathological begins.'[120] Opposing the normal woman to female offenders, divided into prostitutes and criminals by bringing in reasons of physiological difference, and of science more generally, Lombroso could expeditiously spread his theory, for there was the need for a 'model' for the female identity in the newly unified country, and as a consequence all anomalies had to be excluded. Lombroso likens the woman to the child for her physiognomy,[121] and distances her from the man, since she is not as fully intellectually developed. Skulls of female offenders show – according to Lombroso – the measures of the criminal woman. Phrenology becomes a tool to distinguish those who are deterministically led to crime by birth. And so it applies to categorizing women. While Mantegazza was very encouraging of women and their minds (but not their bodily desires), Lombroso's faith in women's inferiority was adamant: 'Woman is a male of arrested development.'[122]

In many respects, one of the protagonists in this novel, the Florentine Norma, has all the attributes of the normal, law-abiding woman, and yet her personality surpasses that threshold between the normal and the pathological both sexually and morally. Norma is 'different,' as she cannot conform to any of the categorizations Lombroso expressed in his study. Neither entirely 'normal' nor entirely 'criminal' or 'prostitute,' Norma was a woman tormented in her growth, in her marriage to Felice, and in her love for Medusa. Her sexual behaviour never conforms to what Lombroso and Mantegazza would suggest for the normal woman of the United Kingdom of Italy. Their findings make manifest the clash between scientific findings and their moralistic interpretation of male scientists who, even when recognizing the widespread lesbianism among female subjects who were not necessarily criminals, nevertheless condemn such sexual praxis.[123]

Mazzucco's novel can be read as an allegory for struggle between sexual desire and love as prescribed by authoritative norms and the non-norm, between conforming to and differing from established social practices; irregularity in terms of sexual practices at the beginning of the twentieth century was used as one more imposition upon Italian women. According to Butler,

> the norm governs intelligibility, allows for certain kinds of practices and action to become recognizable as such, imposing a grid of legibility on the social and defining the parameters of what will and will not appear within the domain of the social. The question of what it is to be outside the norm poses a paradox for thinking, for if the norm renders the social field intelligible and normalizes that field for us, then being outside the norm is in some sense being defined still in relation to it. To be not quite masculine or not quite feminine is still to be understood exclusively in terms of one's relationship to the 'quite masculine' and the 'quite feminine.'[124]

Being still related to the norm, non-normal sexuality can be related to the history of madness in its attempt at liberation (and repression) of the individual within society. When liberated, non-normal sexuality, 'far from suppressing the action of norms, on the contrary reinforces it.'[125] Gender production is another form of regulatory power, but hardly any longer in heterosexual terms. My own logic brings me to read Butler's take on this issue, as I see her point on power and deregulation of gender, but I follow de Lauretis's analysis to better understand the defiance and resistance in the character of Norma, the Piedmontese 'Norm,' and the drama of not finding any 'place' for female lovers in Savoy's Italy. Refiguring sexual gender in terms of social conditioning, as an *in-*position on the woman, means understanding what was layered upon the original sexual drive of an individual by society. 'Defiance and resistance,' writes de Lauretis, 'are the specific problems, and the symptoms, of female homosexuality, what makes it perverse and such that, unlike neurosis and hysteria, psychoanalysis is impotent to alter it.'[126]

Norma and the Normal Woman

The resistance of Dora K. to her father in the eponymous Freudian case of 1923 bears a resemblance to Norma's existence in Mazzucco's novel. Before her 1905 marriage to Conte Argentero, Norma would never have dreamed of her current sexual fullness – unthinkable to her – since 'non aveva neanche preso in considerazione l'idea d'interessare, piacere mai e poi mai, ad un uomo' (BM 31; 'she did not even take into consideration the idea that a man could be interested and like her').[127] After the wedding and the simultaneous actualization of heterosexual eros, her husband's jealousy isolates Norma in the family hunting lodge near the French border. In fact, Norma has shown a wonderful but rather awkward predisposition for lust, and Felice worries, just as Mantegazza warned all Italian men to remain alert in such cases. Norma never rejected Felice during the honeymoon, her behaviour being utterly unusual for a woman *bien née*. In short, she shows none of the signs of the sexual behaviour expected in a normal woman, such as the one described by anthropologist Giuseppe Sergi in a letter to Cesare Lombroso,

> The normal woman loves to be courted and adored by man but gives in *like a victim* to his sexual wishes. I know of several ladies who become frigid and fastidious when their husbands approach, even though they love them

greatly; some insist that girls who hope for pleasure in marriage find trouble instead. Everyone knows that women need a lot of stimulus before they *succumb to sexual pleasure*; without such measures, the woman will remain cold, neither giving nor receiving satisfaction. It is well known that many inferior races have adopted measures that seem like torments to excite their women; the men submit to painful operations to have the measures at their disposal. This gives us empirical confirmation of the lesser sensitivity of women, even women of the humblest grade.[128]

Substantiated by statements such as this one by Sergi, Lombroso's conclusions of the 'Senses and the Psyche of Woman' chapter state that even normal women *feel* less, just as they think less than men. Even Aristotle is brought in with his maxim 'Nihil est in intellectu quod prius non fuerit in sensu.'[129] Apparently, there is little one can do, as the woman's 'dullness to pain is Darwinian, not ordained by God.'[130] In Norma's attitude, ambiguity is a constant parameter that impedes and proscribes statements regarding her normalcy or deviation. Hers is surely a distinct personality that is trying not to succumb to any of the oppressive societal impositions made upon Italian women at the time, some of which carried the arrogant belief that these were scientific statements. Ethical statements, made only after 'scientific' studies on collected data, could be taken as proof of the 'criminality' of a woman. And Norma will be one of them.

Although secretly loving her attitude and promptness to sexual activity, aroused but also frightened by Norma's inclination to pleasure, Felice incarcerates his young bride in a lodge in the Piedmontese Alps. Her incarceration is the result of an ulterior attempt by patriarchal authority to confine a woman who is 'diverse.' This is merely the beginning of Norma's descent towards the mental internment at the end of her journey of self-discovery, as it should be in the logic of the panopticon. The non-Turinese Norma is frequently seized by 'strange fits' of inexplicable cause. Shortly after her marriage it appears evident how displaced she is in an almost-Victorian society in which there is only one possible ideal for a woman of her class: the innocent and chaste one, a form of mental chastity a wife should hold *even* after physical union with the future father of her children. As indicated by the embroidery on some nightgowns of the period that invokes God's clemency for such impure acts, the reproductive aspect of sex is the only permissible one for a woman of her standing. Not only must sexuality be limited to the goal of reproduction, but 'sexuality and maternity are incompatible.'[131] The young bride spends her days in the atrocious company of her sisters-in-law, whom she dubs *le Arpie* (BM

76; 'the Harpies'), Emanuela above all. The latter is a spinster, a fervid believer of Mantegazza's doctrines who is appalled by Norma's strangeness. Not only does Emanuela dislike Norma because she is not Piedmontese and noble, but more tellingly because Emanuela can sense that feel for lust hidden by Norma's celestial features (BM 37).

The only diversion for Norma from the profound boredom in the Alpine Stura Valley where the hunting lodge is located is the reading of the two local newspapers, the reactionary, *Lo Stendardo*, Conte Argentero's usual reading, and *Il Corriere Subalpino*, a more liberal publication to which she has subscribed. Remote from all sites of her previous interests, particularly her beloved studies, sitting in the fog of her existence – a fog that forebodes her advancing myopia – one news story catches her attention: '*Al tribunale militare di Berlino è cominciato ieri un sensazionale processo. I soliti ufficiali tedeschi omosessuali*' (BM 64, emphasis in original; '*at the military courthouse in Berlin a sensational trial has begun. The usual homosexual German officers*'). A little while later, Norma goes back with her thoughts, collected by an attentive narrator, to that awkward locution, '*I soliti ufficiali tedeschi omosessuali*':

> Che vorrà dire? Si chiese. Nel vocabolario italiano, che conosceva piuttosto bene e che consultava volentieri, alcune parole meritavano una definizione scarna, un'etimologia grecizzante netta e accertata ma un significato concreto piuttosto nebuloso. (BM 74)
> (What could that mean? She wondered. In the Italian dictionary, which she knew rather well and consulted gladly, some words deserved a scant definition, an ascertained and clear Greek etymology but with a concrete meaning that was rather foggy.)

The unequivocal etymology does not lead, though, to an explanation that enlightens her as to the meaning of that term, which, in spite of the Greek and Latin Norma studied in Florence, is entirely obscure to her. Why is the closed-doors trial of German soldiers placed at the beginning of the novel (why are they defined as *soliti* by the reporter who seems to know the whole affair far better than the protagonist could ever know)? The Italian reporter, assured and certain of his own heterosexuality – and by default, normalcy – a citizen of the Kingdom of Italy, is a member of the very community that finds Norma odd. The officers are German *and* homosexual. According to the phrasing used by the nationalistic reporter, deviation is constructed as *their* norm. Norma then begins her own process of discovery by trying to find meaning in a word that she should know in theory, as she studied its prefix, but in practice does not 'get.' Just as she knew the act of defloration in theory through Catullus without knowing it in its actuality, she tries to guess now at that word that sounds familiar, and yet obscure.

The insertion of this article in this part of the novel is a key for reading the story to come, a harbinger of what the protagonist will go through next. Norma throws the newspapers in the stove, where they become a 'palla di fuoco che ... portava in sé i segni della nevrastenia delle donne non più in fiore e delle parole che non trovano posto nel vocabolario del Tommaseo' (BM 75; 'a fireball that ... carried with it the symptoms of neurasthenia of women no longer young and of words which do not find their place in Tommaseo's dictionary'). The anxiety that such reading conveys to Norma for the feeling of indecency she senses, as she cannot find this word in Tommaseo's book – a sort of linguistic bible for the Florentine woman – introduces one of the most important scenes in the novel.

In fact, this scene illustrates the intuition of Norma for a desire unknown to her until then. The scene marks the entrance on the Argentero property of the lantern operator Mundin and his granddaughter, Madlenin-Medusa. Norma is an integral *part* of the Argentero property; with her foreignness she constitutes the most complex part to be governed. Her duplicitous and latent difference is what makes her the most precious and the most difficult element at once of the otherwise solid Argentero fortune. Although her husband does not hesitate to call her 'his best investment,' we know how much that investment will cost him in the end. In the most theatrical sense of the term, the scene is staged as if the curtains were rising on the living room of the family hunting lodge. A lantern reifies the ambiguity of the scene. The lantern, evocative symbol of a life spent through a glass, reverberates with past existence.

> At Combray, ... my bedroom again became the fixed and painful point of my preoccupations. They had indeed hit upon the idea, to distract me on the evenings when they found me looking too unhappy, of giving me a magic lantern, which, while awaiting the dinner hour, they would set on top of my lamp; and, after the fashion of the first architects and master glaziers of the Gothic age, it replaced the opacity of the walls with impalpable iridescences, supernatural multicolored apparitions, where legends were depicted as in a wavering, momentary stained-glass window. But my sadness was only increased by this since the mere change in lighting destroyed the

familiarity which my room had acquired for me and which, except for the torment of going to bed, had made tolerable to me.[132]

The Proustian overlapping of images that Mundin's magic lantern produces embodies also the overlapping levels of Countess Argentero's unconscious thoughts. The shades of the lantern create the effect that Norma, no longer Countess Argentero, retrieves the Mouche she once was. Norma

> non aveva più visto una lanterna magica, da allora non ne aveva mai avuto la voglia. La associava al buio, alla solitudine, allo smarrimento, alla sensazione di essere stata abbandonata. (BM 92)
> (had not seen a magic lantern for a long time, she had not felt like seeing one ever since. She associated it with darkness, with solitude, with a sense of dismay, with the feeling of having been abandoned.)

Through her involuntary reveries into the past, Norma discovers that these squabbles and secrets testify to deeper impulses. Motionless, Norma cannot act out her desires for this little girl who is about to enter – perhaps forever – her life. Torn by passion and social reserve, thrown off by the unexpected forms her desire is about to take, Norma feels the surge of her yearning, this in spite of her own fears of becoming like her mother, the 'nymphomanic' Hélène. Mazzucco is queering a turn-of-the-century story in a postmodern novel that shifts layers of bisexual romantic longing by showing human emotions elevated to metaphysical inquiry (and vice versa). This is a queer reading that opposes society itself, as it questions the social foundations on which the 'impossibility' of this story is built. Swerving backgrounds, lighting effects, tiered images construct Norma's complex mind. Along with the magic lantern re-emerges the childhood trauma of her mother's nymphomania. In a painful flashback moment, Norma, now back to being Mouche, re-evokes her mother, Hélène, in one of her betrayals. This reminiscence is related to the image of cinema as a silent, dark cave of her mind in which Norma explores past events that she quickly learns to fear any time they resurface. Hatred for Hélène's mendacity towards her beloved father, disgust for her inclination to lust, these are some of the reasons for Norma's perennial silence and her fear of being left alone, particularly in the company of men.

The image of her mother is re-evoked by Mundin's lantern; the fatal woman appears before Norma like 'un ectoplasma sfolgorante, riemerso dal passato' (BM 93; 'a blazing ectoplasm, resurfaced from the past').

Norma's contradictory love and hatred for this most beautiful mother reignites grief and suffering (BM 90-3). From the unconscious recollection brought forth by the lantern, suffering at the remembered and lost maternal body,[133] emerges Norma's sense of gratitude towards Mundin. In a free-indirect speech and shift from the third-person narration about her story, Norma unearths her bewilderment at having given Mundin much more than he asked for his performance: 'Lo compenso per avermi restituito l'unico ricordo che avrei voluto perdere, lo indennizzo perché non avrei mai dovuto invitarlo?' (BM 98; 'I pay him for having given back to me the only memory I would have liked to have lost, I compensate him because I should have never invited him?'). The knowledge that she does not own her destiny is paralleled only by the same lack of free will so patent in the little girl (BM 103). Shaken from her lethargy by the lice's attacking Medusa's head, Norma decides to give her a bath, taken by an irresistible impulse partly determined by a disquieting feeling of familiarity with this girl's body (BM 103), as 'stanotte le pareva che mosche, formiche, pidocchi e meduse fossero una cosa sola' (BM 98; 'tonight it seemed like flies, ants, lice, and medusas were one thing'). Her unexpected and enormous reaction before the adolescent's *acerba perfezione* (BM 109; 'unripe perfection') is paralysing:

> Norma non riusciva a scuotersi: era paralizzata da una sensazione di inevitabilità, come un presentimento. Subiva la presenza di Medusa, e la realtà del bagno reso turchesco dalla temperatura smottava, franava, liquefatta. Si sentiva spettatrice di se stessa – la realtà sembrava una scena già nota, conosceva già questa ragazzina rasata, aveva perfino l'impressione di avere già visto quello che stava vedendo ... L'avrebbe sfiorata, quasi con timore, e poi toccata, con naturalezza; l'avrebbe insaponata, detersa, sfregata, lisciata, lavata, massaggiata, asciugata ... Tutto si consumò in un istante, ma un istante lunghissimo, atemporale. (BM 110)
> (Norma could not shake herself: ... she was paralysed by a sensation of inevitability, like a foreboding. She was subject to Medusa's presence, and the reality of the bath made turquoise by the temperature was slipping, sloughing, liquefied. She was a spectator to her self – reality seemed a scene already known, she already knew this shaven girl, she even had the impression of having already seen what she was watching ... She would have brushed against her, almost in fear, and then she would have touched her, with simplicity; she would had soaped her, cleansed her, smoothed her, massaged her, dried her ... Everything was consumed in an instant, a very long, timeless one.)

The reaction of a young woman such as Norma, who herself has relatively recently emerged from adolescence, appears enormous and unjustified. It is a reaction that, in the narrative rendition of the scene, appears to be enhanced by the ichnography linked to the photography of the time. A reference is made to a fixed image, blocked in the mind by those laws of physics that allow for that process to take place. Medusa *enters* the eyes of Norma, penetrates her soul, and arrives at her heart. Norma's attempts at protecting herself from this intoxication are in vain:

> Per proteggersi da tanta invadenza, con istintiva discrezione, Norma chiuse gli occhi e voltò la testa: ma scoprì empiricamente che, a dispetto delle intenzioni del pudore, la legge della persistenza delle immagini sulla retina possiede un'infallibilità scientifica. Giacché la retina dell'occhio trattiene un'impressione per una frazione di secondo dopo che l'immagine che l'ha prodotta è stata rimossa, nel buio delle sue palpebre serrate sopravvisse quella sagoma nuda e indecente di acerba perfezione. (BM 109)
> (To protect herself from such invasion, Norma, with an instinctive discretion, closed her eyes and turned her head: yet she empirically discovered that, despite of her modesty's intentions, the law of the persistent images imprinted on her retina possesses a scientific infallibility. Because the eye's retina fixes an impression for a fraction of a second after the image that produced it is removed, that nude and indecent silhouette of immature perfection survived in the dark of her closed eyelids).

In the light of this moment, the scene of the bath takes on a different significance, as we are slipping towards what Mantegazza could not explain, the slippage from 'physiologic' sexual drive to 'pathologic' perversion. How could this be?

Perverse desire, a non-normative one rather than a specific pathology, is affirmed in this act of intimacy between the two protagonists. What Norma intuitively thought while reading the article on the German homosexual officers has now materialized via this symbolic baptism of both characters. The seduction of a genital nature of the maternal caress usually given to a child is now perceived within a lesbian dimension that, in turn, produces long-lasting effects on the adult, Norma, as well as on the child, Medusa.

> Vedeva solo la nipote del mago della lanterna magica tutta nuova al tocco delle sue mani; come nel caleidoscopio, per un'incomprensibile magia, un'immagine trapassa in un'altra, così nella sua testa si rimescolavano in

sequenza disordinata fotogrammi di rinascita e agnizione, o forse solo di una sconosciuta serenità: il pulcino con i capelli corti e gli occhi grandi che rompeva il guscio dell'indifferenza ... l'orsa leccatrice di Virgilio, allegoria efficace che, chissà perché, in quegli attimi sospesi continuava ad aggirarsi alla periferia della sua coscienza. (BM 112)
(She saw only the niece of the wizard of the magic lantern very new to the touch of her hands; as in a kaleidoscope, due to an incomprehensible magic, an image changed into another, so did the images in her head mix themselves into a disordered sequence of photos of rebirth and revelation, or maybe only of an unknown serenity: the chick with short hair and big eyes that breaks the shell of indifference ... the licking bear of Virgil, an efficacious analogy that, who knows why, in those moments of suspense continued to wander at the periphery of her consciousness.)

Seduction is not merely seen as a 'fantasmatic place.'[134] It is now articulated in a process of total reversibility between subject and object, a liberating process in which objectification of the desired person is no longer possible or desirable. Unconsciously, Norma and Medusa are both already desiring-desired *subjects*.

This scene is a key one as it marks the elimination of the threshold between the desiring subject and the desired object seen in the activation of an internal transformation of its terms. In other words, it is here that both individuals become desiring subjects. Mazzucco's postmodern reorganization makes it necessary to take into serious consideration that 'the impossibility of "subject and desire" cannot be ascribed to homosexuality, which is precisely the displacement of the paternal signifier and the circumvention of the law that would bar the female subject's access to the female body.'[135] Even more so, the scene shows Mazzucco's revision of the representation of the love relationship, one that is 'universale, che si disinteressa del sesso, dell'età, del periodo' (BM 140; 'universal, which disregards sex, age, period'). Perversion in lesbian love should thus be understood as *being* the same as the structure of the novel, as *entering* into the novel's structure, as its treatment deconstructs a traditional interpretive mode. Perversion destabilizes meaning, and the novel is its best wrapping.

This encounter between the two outcasts has fatal consequences. Later, Medusa returns to the valley after her two-year journey of initiation spent with the lanternist Peru in France. Medusa is hired by the *Signora*, despite all the gossip in the village about Madlenin-Medusa, 'Medusa la Franzesa, Medusa delle marmotte, la putan' (BM 187;

'Medusa the French, Medusa of the marmots, the whore'). Medusa is a temptress, and Norma succumbs to her ways. *Das Unheimliche*, the uncanny, is present in the mask of Medusa-Madlenin, in something as domestic as a servant in whose eyes the *Signora* mirrors herself[136] and gives in to her repressed pleasure. The *Signora* and Medusa share a common destiny. So, again, what is Medusa's role?

The Forbidden Gaze

The grotesque paradox of the Olympian Medusa is the juxtaposition of her extraordinary beauty and her horror, which is represented by the writhing serpents on her head and her power to petrify. In his unfinished essay 'Medusa's Head,' Sigmund Freud found a psychoanalytical definition of the ways in which men are terrified by the dangerous and inaccessible power of Medusa's gaze. He defines the power of the Gorgon's gaze in the following terms: 'The sight of Medusa's head makes the spectator stiff with terror, turns him to stone. Observe here that we have the same origin from the castration complex and the same transformation of affect! For becoming stiff means an erection. Thus in the original situation, it offers consolation to the spectator: he is still in possession of a penis, and the stiffening reassures him of the fact.'[137] While admitting a dual effect of Medusa's power, Freud's finding also makes apparent that such a notion of sexuality is always perceived and described only in male terms.[138] Freud seems to exclude arbitrarily the insurgence of desire in a female observer of Medusa's head, even if the very same essay recalls Medusa's face as appearing on the shield of a female goddess Athena.[139] Rediscovering Medusa's powers in a pre-Olympian way, such as Mazzucco's reading does, can help in discussing lesbian love as a liberating non-normative notion of love.[140] As Bowers notes, 'The same image that has been used to oppress women can also help to set women free.'[141]

In this perspective, Medusa terrifies and turns men away (or kills them) for they cannot phallicize the female. Men, though instinctively envious of female sexuality, do not recognize a part of their own complex sexual nature. Not knowing themselves, they must kill the Gorgon.[142] Such destiny does not touch women, as they are seduced but not petrified by her power, in which they mirror one another. The two fortresses of female power according to the patriarchal society, marriage and procreation, are thus annulled in the passion with which Norma and Medusa consume each other's gaze. Medusa's apotropaic gaze does not take life away from Norma, it infuses her with a new one, as Norma conceives and creates a love novel for her maid and lover. Paraphrasing a passage by Jane Gallop about Leclerc's comment on Johannes Vermeer's *The Love Letter,* Norma not only is a woman, she is a *Signora.*[143] In the rereading of the Hegelian master/slave dynamics, while the *Signora* is also the subject of the narrative picture along with the maid, precisely as in the Vermeer painting, the maid is Medusa, the woman with whom she is in love. And the maid's smile is reassuring, for it allows the *Signora* to work at her writing.[144]

Deconstructing and going beyond the Freudian *stiffening,*[145] a hypothesis that would lead to fetishism (woman-fetish) as an indispensable element to prevent the terrifying effect of the Gorgon's gaze, Mazzucco's Medusa is configured by a different frame of mind. She makes Norma fall in love with the Gorgon, constructing a logic of desire that is transgressive because it is generated and dictated by laws contrasting those regulating male desire. Norma does not fear Medusa while the two women discover each other's bodies in the sanctuary where Norma inscribes their names in the guest book. Medusa's hand, with the wound caused by the marmot, re-emerges in Norma's memories. In her supreme unhappiness brought on by the fate of her daughter Angelica, born without a brain, as in a dream, 'scoprì l'inconsistenza del corpo della Medusa, e la fragilità delle sue ossa di ragazza, e lasciò che Medusa scoprisse l'abbondanza della sua carne di donna' (BM 228; 'it discovered the inconsistency of Medusa's body, the fragility of her young bones, and allowed Medusa to discover her abundant womanly flesh'). The sense of corporeality continues to prevail over the sense of the word so much so that it justifies the frequent utilization of *frei erlebte Rede,* a technique reminiscent, in particular, of Arthur Schnitzler's *Fräulein Else*[146] and also *Traumnovelle.*[147] The corporeality prevails as well because of the inability of the world to express the signifier of the ineffable and sublime, to express that desire for which, in the physical love scene, 'il pensiero scomparve nella coscienza, divenne azione ancor prima che se ne rendesse conto: Norma non fuggì e non le chiese più di lasciarla sola' (BM 325; 'thought disappeared from consciousness, became action again before she realized it: Norma did not flee and did not ask her any more to leave her alone'). The 'transfiguration of Medusa in the contemplative dress,' that *méduser,* the French verb[148] recalled by Norma, with its ability to 'stupify and dazzle,' takes away the word, but Norma and Medusa flee the power of Thanatos through that of Eros. In the case of Norma, who attempts to draft her own romance novel written specifically for Medusa, silence is the only way possible to maintain and manage creation, the work of art, *ex-stasis*, of nature's incomprehensible, artistic form for a common language from which the two women are invariably excluded. The Schnitzlerian condition of *Mittelbewusstsein* in which Norma seems to lead her existence – suspended between word and silence – remains the most apt to articulate her thoughts and her writing.

How and in what direction can we reread the myth of Medusa at this stage of the novel? Are we in the presence of a symbolic order of the mother that exorcizes male traditions of Medusa the 'monster woman'? Not completely, in my view. We can, however, bring in a reference to the practice of entrustment (*affidamento*) that Luisa Muraro theorizes as a way to enlighten the complex relationship between the two protagonists. Aside from their respective states of alienation, Norma and Medusa are both orphans and live in different ways the abjection of their own mothers. In Norma's case, her perversion is almost inherited from her mother Hélène, and is further transformed and deformed by her lesbian love for Medusa. Implicit in Judith Butler's theory on the mat(t)er, is that the '"mother" in question in this originary loss is in fact the site and the object of homosexual love.'[149] For Medusa corresponds to a total submission towards her *Signora*. Norma and Medusa lack the language taught to us by our mothers. The gaze allows them to escape the real world, 'in the extreme region of a mortal spell, in the *Todesansucht* in which the "I" darkly dissolves itself.'[150] Together, they rediscover their own identity, leaving the self and searching for a reciprocal mediation, to retrieve the maternal figure, in that practice of entrustment deriving from the Hegelian *Sittlichkeit*.[151]

According to such practice, can we believe that Norma functions as a guide to Medusa? I feel that the opposite takes place. Furthermore, I am convinced that they establish autonomy in their relationship. It is, after all, the eternal problem of love: that of creating autonomy that can defeat the desire to trust somebody with our love, to *make us* in the name of love. In the practice of entrustment there exists a positive foundation: that of ensuring a new ethical order, from which the woman can re-establish thresholds. Entrusting oneself to someone else, however, means to rely on someone else at any given point. The 'convergence' of biological and cultural, which Toril Moi brilliantly explains in her reading of Freud's famous phrase *die Anatomie ist das Schicksal*, 'Anatomy is destiny,' determines the drive that pushes us to be others.[152]

Norma's literary ambition constructs an entirely new path of desire, in which l'*Estero*, France, the Riviera, but above all the sea, become the means for the two women to realize their journey of self-discovery. Maria Zambrano unequivocally connects the sea to the duplicitous Medusan image of the hermaphrodite invertebrate and the beauty of the Gorgon in that they embody the 'belleza ambigua, prometedora del fruto final del Oceáno insondable.'[153] Zambrano distinguishes the image of the mirror that captures the appearance of the real from the Logos of the sea in the hope that all that is created and that is natural gives us the word, 'su logos recondito o celosamente guardado,'[154] that escapes rationalization. The sea, then, is the *locus amoenus after* the known spaces where it is possible 'ritrovare il già da tempo cercato' (BM 361; 'to find again what had been, for a long time, searched for').

As only Medusas can do, they *become* the sea, as their gelatinous nature allows them to inhabit the water without obstacles. Each mirrors the other to find once again knowledge of the self through each other. As in Italian (and in Spanish), the term *medusa*, because of its semantic polyvalence, holds also in French the power to refer both to the Gorgon myth and to the invertebrate hermaphrodite – the image of the marine Medusa – an organism in which male and female sexual organs coexist. Aside from recalling the image of the orchid of the Proustian metaphor of 'doing cattleya' to which Swann and Odette hinted for the sexual act, *les mauves orchidées de la mer*, the homophony *mer/mère*, sea/mother, brings back the maternal discourse to the equation, the Medusa's life inside the maternal sea, unfortunately *insondable*, as Zambrano suggests. The homophony *mer/mère* also recalls the absence of the maternal image, which the two protagonists symbolically search for during their forbidden holiday at the beach on the Côte d'Azure. This is a voyage to their pre-natal past, a baptism in which their bodies will meet in their declaration of a communal fate. This is a voyage in which the concepts of mother and lover will blur into the endless convergence of Medusa and the sea. In Proust's *Recherche*, homo-female characters – Céleste and Albertine – live out their encounters in proximity to the sea. The sea – an amniotic liquid – is an aid in the articulation of their own Logos in their search for happiness-identity: it is in the sea that they can escape from their initial trauma of losing the mother. Unlike the male Proustian character, caught by panic at the sight of the Mother/Medusa, as this would mean the loss of his individuality, female characters do not panic. As Elizabeth Viti notes, 'Women loving women, his females appear to prefer *direct* access to the Mother, only available through another female body.'[155] Mazzucco's characters embrace the Proustian absence of ambiguity about lesbian characters. Further, in this hypothetical ending, Norma and Medusa no longer live in fear, as it is their own sexual diversity, their lesbian 'perversion,' that protects them.

Norma and Medusa share the search for a definitive solution to their traumatic existence, hoping to reconnect themselves to the umbilical cord that Oedipal characters try to sever. The two women replace adolescent fear with a consciousness of their own sexuality. The Elysian maternal image has taken on, for each lover, the semblance of the lover's beloved face. The practice of love, that is, the actualization of homosexual desire, protects from the obsession of difference:

> La sua bocca era assetata dal caldo e da un'emozione intensa, la certezza che quello fosse il luogo e che proprio lei fosse la persona cui Norma voleva mostrarlo. Anzi, di più, la certezza suprema di essere la prima persona cui l'avesse mostrato. Non c'è altro, c'è tutto, è tutto qui, è questo il punto in cui tout se tient, laddove tutto torna e si rivela, e il futuro nasce dalla liberazione del passato, la spirale, la spirale, è qui il segreto, infiniti giri intorno a un punto, e il cerchio è sciolto dalla prigionia, è stato liberato, pensava Norma. Barbara Medusa mi sei cara, come il sole sulla bianca roccia? Barbara Medusa mi sei cara come la notte nella buia stanza. Cercavo chi mi somiglia, e trovo te, che nel letto mi aspetti. Barbaro amore tu sei del mio paese. (BM 361)
>
> (Her mouth was dry from the heat and from an intense emotion, the certainty that this was the place and that she really was the person to whom Norma wanted to show it. Even more, the supreme certainty of being the first person to whom she would show it. There is nothing else, everything is here, this is the point in which tout se tient, where everything makes sense and reveals itself, and the future is born from the liberation from the past, the spiral, the spiral, here is the secret, infinite circling around a point, and the circle searched for is freed from prison, it was freed, Norma thought. Barbara Medusa, you are dear to me, like the sun on the white rocks. Barbara Medusa, you are dear to me like the night in a dark room. I searched for someone like me and I found you, that await me in your bed. Barbara, my love, you are my home.)

In Mazzucco's novel, the revolution of the patriarchal law justifies the presumed death of Norma's mother, Hélène. Her sexual 'defect' makes her unworthy. By the same token, the elision from society of Norma takes place by the elision of her own wedding: the juridical writing of her wedding contract will be forever deleted[156] by the Sacra Rota in July 1917, while her forced segregation in the Regio Manicomio of Turin seals the end of her public story. The condemnation of the medical diagnosis is of a holistic nature: it responds to all criteria by which people are judged in society. Therefore, nothing can be done to rescue Norma from her confinement. Norma will be denied an existence, as her marriage to Count Felice Argentero is annulled. What is worse, mental illness will seal her away from her Medusa forever. With Norma confined in the Regio Manicomio, Medusa will migrate to Paris, as this is the destiny of many restless Italians who find no place in their country. Expatriates, as we know, abound in our literature.

Sexuality as Liberating Matter

In their works, writers Dacia Maraini and Melania Mazzucco measure themselves and their ability to produce an imagery that richly contributes to a more varied Italian novelistic panorama that – as I argued in the introduction – only too often sees critics devote their research to male authors, segregating still today women's authored production to the realm of the 'romance.' Maraini's and Mazzucco's literary efforts conjoin male traditional texts and female antecedents to construct aesthetic texts where an emancipatory component is necessarily present but no longer prevails. Their protagonists earn their ground in their tormented relationships with love for the child and duty to remain true to themselves and their identity; with the institution of marriage and family; with a notion of sexuality not envisioned by societal norms and their subsequent coping with the uncertainties connected to their transformed, multifaceted role in society. Above all, and always, their characters deal with the unresolved relationships with the father and mother figures that affect their own identity construction. Since awareness begins with the body, from the ascent of bodily sensations that, in turn, become elements of knowledge and politics, it is hardly a surprise that women writers choose to write about sexuality and sexual politics to affirm awareness. It is through the acceptance of their body and of instinct that characters learn how to see their original community from different standpoints that will not necessarily follow the Law of the Father or that of the Mother, but will serve to indicate intellectual independence for the Italian woman writer.

Teresa de Lauretis's suggestive analysis of Sigmund Freud's (and partly Jacques Lacan's) writings on perverse sexuality in *The Practice of Love: Lesbian Sexuality and Perverse Desire* has been an indispensable instrument for my work on Melania Mazzucco's Medusa, the beautiful woman whose hair is made of terrifying snakes. Mazzucco's title appropriately frames the innovative quality intrinsic to the interaction of fictional writing with psychoanalytic theory, as it is the author's desire to deconstruct the traditionally held notion of female identity in contemporary post-Unification Italy while looking to the Gorgon's myth for a lesbian love story between Norma and Medusa. Placing her love between two women at the beginning of the twentieth century, Mazzucco utilized the topic of perversion and lesbian sexuality to tell us yet another story of displacement and confinement. Authentic details of life in post-Unification Piedmont comment upon the strong moral ties – almost Puritanical – that would certainly not allow for such forms of love. Nevertheless, Mazzucco's novel demonstrates how 'a feminine text cannot fail to be more than subversive. It is volcanic; as it is written brings about an upheaval of the old property crust, carrier of masculine investments; there is no other way.'[157]

Subversion is demonstrated in the authors' re-discussion of the literary stereotypes on the domesticity of love and the suffocated sexuality of women as it unmasks the societal structures that instrumentalize women's 'febbre invincibile dell'istinto' (BM 450; 'invincible fever of the instinct') apparent. Like Butler's speaking subjet, the protagonists of Maraini's and Mazzucco's novels realize that 'If I am always constituted by norms that are not of my making, then I have to understand the ways in which that constitution takes place ... Sexuality is never fully captured by any regulation ... It can exceed regulation.'[158] Maraini's and Mazzucco's writings make manifest the desire to explore female sexuality, not to the benefit of sexual pleasure, but – much more fruitfully – on behalf of all women so they can depart from obsolete and counterproductive notions of what sexuality should amount to.[159] Sexuality is by nature a rather displaced, unregulated matter that takes norms into consideration, but that exceeds them as our own individual characteristics take over what the collective thinking might assume and establish. In the case of sexuality, then, the personal takes over the public. While utilizing different rhetorical figures, whether in Maraini's more traditionally plotted novels or in Mazzucco's quite postmodernist approach to plot linearity and other narrative strategies, these works nevertheless manage to demonstrate the power of women's writings to bring forward what troubles us immensely. But that invariably should happen: departing from someone else's norm and constructing our own. After all, myths are stories we tell ourselves to surmount our fears, and novels are what makes the myths change into everyday life, once again.

Conclusions

Drawing a map of female novelistic expression over the past decade was arduous from the outset, and I realized the further dangers that could derive from confining women novelists to their 'territory.' The overall scope of this book is a demonstration of women's writing, which, while early on committed to mainly male canonical models, has slowly slid towards what, at this point in literary history, one might comfortably define as other women writers' canonical texts. In fact, the thematics and the articulation of contemporary novels can no longer justify or find sufficient a palimpsest that is exclusively male. The uncontested influence of women-authored texts such as Elsa Morante's or Simone de Beauvoir's comes, for instance, coupled with the rereading of important texts by men such as Nabokov. Indeed, in this *hybrid* phase some of the most interesting novelistic juxtapositions of literary tradition and hypotheses of reworking the tradition have emerged. However, at this point there is no such thing as a strictly female topic. Simona Vinci's depiction of the Second World War's desolation that sets the background for the protagonist's own desolation is a reworking of many a neorealist work. Nevertheless, Vinci weaves a complex, intertextual narrative, rich with layers that are undoubtly in tune with her own fascination with the world of children, of which, as Duras says, 'we know nothing.' Because of the undoing of our own notions of femininity and masculinity, as Mazzucco's *Il bacio della Medusa* aptly illustrates, we need a form of criticism that reacts more flexibly to what writers are trying to tell us about what 'style' means for them. Again, it is the reading we do that makes a text a 'novel,' something 'new,' that is, by which we can refigure the period we are living in and make sense of it. It is a dialogue we establish with the writer. But if the writer makes his/her assertions with a monolithic voice, there is no longer any space left for me as a critic to comment and examine how he/she is speaking of this reality.

A Multitude of Women revolves also around the possibility of rereading the construction of 'woman' and familism in their novelistic transformations. Family plots in women's novels today are not necessarily humourless, clichéd, or ideologically motivated. These negative attributes often ascribed to feminism's critique of the family have left room for a diversified way of feminizing the familial space that is neither myopic nor reductive, but actually focused on new analyses of relations. The relationship with the mother, with the father – be he a biological, adoptive, or literary one; the relationship that women entertain with their own often instrumentalized sexuality, while writing and trying to find a vantage point that best represents *them*: they all constitute an all-encompassing problem that needs recognition as an attempt to deconstruct values considered, and handed on to readers as, a given.

'A mother is only brought unlimited satisfaction by her relation to a son; this is altogether the most perfect, the most free from ambivalence of all human relationships.'[1] In my study, I have dealt particularly with the compelling, and yet ambivalent, relationship between literary mothers, of which the influence of Elsa Morante's writing on Mariateresa Di Lascia, Elena Ferrante, and Simona Vinci constitutes only one example. My readings suggest that their characters, family sagas, and even the ever-transient position they assign their narrators need analysis for an appreciation of the suggestive presence of women in the novel as projected by women novelists, one that no longer suffers from the 'fear of the literary mother.'[2] While not always openly dealing with issues of philosophy and ethics, women writers propose a literary revisitation of some of the tenets on which modern Western civilization is based, namely, the very position of oppressed individuals, particularly women and children, within its orbit, as based on a common conceptualization of human action in the terms perceived by Hannah Arendt in *The Human Condition*. In the case of Ferrante's second novel, *I giorni dell'abbandono*, the achieved bourgeois condition of Olga, in fact, cannot be compared to the already established one of Monique, the daughter of a doctor in affluent Paris, and the novel reinterprets conjugal abandonment, showing how vain the bourgeois life is if a woman limits herself to decorating her *living room* and not to rethinking her life. Morante's anti-heroines deserved justice, and Ferrante and Vinci rewrote Morantian stories with a new – and necessary – twist.

I could not finish without touching briefly upon the much-discussed topic of violence in contemporary women's novels. If we are to accept

Georges Bataille's notion of the word, evil emerges constantly from the world of adults; it appears to be the inevitable cancer that will eventually disturb and pollute the world of childhood. In turn, childhood and adolescence are forever marred by sin. It is perhaps this aspect that puts Simona Vinci's work more in tune with Morante's novels, as a dark, gloomy quality of the word childhood emerges from her stories. Unlike in Morante's works, Vinci's children's everyday life is portrayed with splatter and bloody details, with a great display of violence, and with images that make readers aware of the unavoidable element of evil in human nature. The banality of evil, to use Hannah Arendt's famous expression, is right before our eyes, and often within our own families, where we are witnessing an implosion of violence. Regardless of our personal beliefs, evil becomes the most telling element for society in explaining the degree of rupture of the very structures we once believed would create stability and order. Vinci's *cattivismo*[3] exists with substantial and more nuanced differences from Morante's *smagamento* that derive mainly from the reasons that evil manifests itself. Vinci seems to subscribe to a Bataillan sense of evil in the way this dark side of human nature is often situated within family relations. This form of evil is neither automatized nor drawn from the visual images offered by everyday *cronaca*. Vinci's *cattivismo* is made more complex by a permanence of sadistic attention towards the body of whoever lives near the protagonists. *Cattivismo* lies at the bottom of things, *al fondo delle cose*, as she said, not on the surface of videogames. Evil is not concentrated on velocity and the commercialization of products. Indeed, Vinci's *cattivismo* is more profound than any other interpretation of evil we see in today's Italian literature. The problematics her texts generate assume proportions that are much wider, much deeper than those that other works of fictional literature propound in the depiction of disquieting families. As Vinci maintains, for her it is important 'dimenticare l'ossessione di un mondo in forma di parole e tornare all'originale: la forma, quella che è lì, evidente per tutti' ('to forget the obsession of a world in the shape of words and go back to the original: the form, the one that is there, obvious to everyone').[4]

This book has not sought aesthetic validation per se for the novels analysed, as it is apparent that few works can actually appeal to and interest all, and 'resonate' at all times. Interest in a text is always localized and temporally framed. The shapes by which we recover/depict the substance with the word, though, vary a great deal. Using Simona Vinci's words, what was of value here was to search those literary shapes *dal fondo*, from the bottom to the top, as they need constant evaluation and consideration.

The task of artists – novelists in the case of my study – is (more than ever) a twofold one. Novelists are at once 'inheritors' and 'originators' of the literary genre they have chosen.[5] The implicit pact that novelists make with earlier authors about their enterprise, what they will do in their texts in reconsidering the validity of former works and how they offer them a reply in novelistic form, must account for the assimilation of matters that are mobile by nature, namely, social realities and subjectivity. While love, happiness, death, and family are eternal themes, the ways in which novelists depict them – through style, characters, setting, point of view – often communicate opposing views from those that the earlier texts presented. To follow unilaterally the footsteps of older 'fathers' or 'mothers' of the novel becomes inadequate, particularly when authors are trying to offer a muted, multilateral, and more fragmented point of view than what was offered before. As Sandra Gilbert states, the literary daughter must deal with a 'conundrum,' with the patriarchal that lies in every literary (female) precursor when she 'achieves her greatest strength.'[6] As such, women writers know that they must deal with influences and examples that force them to be, in George Eliot's words, 'foundress[es] of nothing,' for 'human culture, says the literary mother, is bound to rules which make it possible for the woman to speak but which oblige her to speak of her own powerlessness.'[7] Italian women writers have long learned how to incorporate in their writing both the tradition of (artistic) powerlessness and the ability to subvert it with new epistemological tools.

Binary oppositions are as obsolete in theory as in practice, for they are not conducive to the understanding that only by undoing gender also in literature – that is to say, by reformulating an idea of sexual difference as a multi-layered notion – can we realize the changes we are all living through. What would be auspicious is a pluralistic approach that takes into account the contribution of both 'fathers' and 'mothers' to attempts to grapple with the representation of societal issues in the construction of the contemporary novel. Needless to say, all this reorganization should happen with the clear understanding that the first and foremost task of the novel is always that of presenting an insightful portrait of relationships between individuals and society along with all the issues – technical and theoretical – that such a deceivingly simple goal inevitably brings.

The mechanisms of reading, rereading, and rewriting that help to construct the relationship between the novels of women writers and the texts they have inherited – be they 'motherly' or 'fatherly' – are always at work in Italian women's writers' novels. Their choice is no longer restricted to a canonical male point of view or to an inspiring mother whom the woman writer has entrusted with her filial artistic respect. Dacia Maraini, for instance, has stated that she has five mothers and a grandmother, and many fathers.[8] In the case of women novelists, I tend to believe that their world is much more composite – rhyzomatic, to use Deleuze's widely cited term – than one would think, as they rely not only on a male tradition at this point but on a female one as well, whose trajectories constantly overlap and differ from the normative, conventional scheme. In summation, their literary work de-territorializes the fixity of prior models, as it does not limit itself to a 'dialectical role-reversal that usually sees the former slaves in the position of new masters or the former mistresses in the position of dominatrix.'[9] It goes much further than this.

My study has approached Italian novels by looking at ways in which we can undo gender crystallization in reading by understanding instead how transpersonal modes can work. Never more than today has Bakhtin's polyphonic concept of the novel as revealing the author's ability to incorporate and absorb outside elements been more relevant. The novel is important in that it can still represent our more immediate real referents, while simultaneously impressing upon readers not only everything that can come close to the real, but also that which, while not real, we would perhaps like reality to be. Whether it be the fantastic, on the threshold between the real and the impossible, like the girls hanging in suspension between a plasticized moon and their bedroom in Isabella Santacroce's novels, or the surreal travelogues written in the desert by Fabrizia Ramondino, the Italian contemporary novel by women can represent multiple (hyper)realities. Telling stories, Adriana Cavarero notes,[10] does not die and actually forms the very glue that bonds women together after our mothers have taught us how to speak. What we see dying, perhaps, is our own obsolete approach to the natural evolution of the novel genre, a highly hybrid form already at the outset. If we keep forcing old conjectures onto what we think a novel should be as a text, we deny its very power to describe us.

I hope that the examples I have chosen clearly indicate the continued interest of Italian women novelists in expressing their views with respect to the society in which they work and to their subjective thinking, be it on religion and its restrictive powers, on sexual desire, on motherhood and procreation, or on father figures and literary parents. I also have suggested positive appropriations of feminist theories – aside from more conventional critical theories on the novel – to understand the value we can add to a novel when providing it with a reading that relies on tradition *and* recent feminist theory.

Far from proposing essentialism in my approach, I believe that we live in a period in which women artists – more than ever – can feel free to experiment with techniques, adopt genres, and analyse themes that can extol a modified view of society within the realm of the novel. Reading the novel is, after all, what makes the text a novel. It is more the attitude by which we look at a written text than the text itself. But it is also who is writing it that makes that very act of reading 'different.' Hélène Cixous's famous words on feminine writing might sound obsolete today, and yet, for some of us, they still resound: 'Woman must write her self: must write about women and bring women to writing, from which they have been driven away as violently as from their bodies – for the same reasons, by the same law, with the same fatal goal. Woman must put herself into the text – as into the world and into history – by her own movement.'[11] Far from making an essentialist statement, Cixous emphasizes how, in spite of the darkness in which women have lived for a long time, there is 'no general woman, no one typical woman.'[12] It is of this multitude than she can speak and discuss only what women might have in common. In the complex picture regarding the work of art, and however hopeful Cixous's beginning might sound, the study of women's art and the propagation of its value in academia and non-academic environments present various issues that require attention in order for us to be actually able to commit ourselves to our self, to 'women's imaginary,' regardless of how 'inexhaustible' this might be.

Raising questions about narrative style, perspective, and character construction in the novel has been another goal of my study. I have analysed contemporary works in which notions of female subjectivity and voice may still reflect the interiorization of male authority. This interiorization could delay the possibility of an authentic voice for liminal characters unless they are written by an adept and sympathetic author. The intimate relationship – thanks to identification – that bridges the gap between such an author and her readers plays an important role in the transformation that has occurred in understanding the contemporary novel by women. The 'erotics of talk' are there and are informing our work as critics. While Italo Calvino's Ludmilla[13] would read a novel and eventually marry the male novelist, we want more Ludmillas reading women authors' novels, looking for different strategies to understand a reality that has never been more complex and fascinating. 'By writing her self, woman will return to the body which has been more than confiscated from her, which has been turned into the uncanny stranger on display,'[14] to that body humiliated, as in *La Dea dei baci*. But at this point in history, the rejection of traditional male examples of literature is no longer necessary or advantageous. Besides, it would obscure some of the uniqueness of this 'multitude of women' in the Italian novel is based.

Many years before Cixous's statement, Virginia Woolf indicated the 'foreignness' of women's themes in writing, their difficulty in 'surmount[ing] the opposition' of male critics who showed bewilderment towards themes outside their system of conventions.[15] In dissimilar ways, both Cixous and Woolf were inviting the re-evaluation of the gender politics informing literary criticism, regardless of the country and of the period in which these writers and thinkers were active. Today, as in the 1970s or the 1920s, women writers employ style as politics to stress their own displacement from loci of authority and to demonstrate that language is a flexible tool for the destabilization of society and the novel. When a multitude of women such as the one I have presented here reconsider the notion of style in a 'materialist mode,' as a vehicle to process and offer 'textual effects so as to engender processes of becoming,'[16] we need to reconsider all the elements that actually make the novel what it is. Value is an 'added' item, one 'that is all the more precious for being new and unexpected ... Literature after feminism, at its best, continues this opening up of new terrain, this enlargement of our horizons. Literature after feminism is an expanded field, not a diminished one.'[17]

Barbara Herrnstein Smith once wrote a sentence of Cartesian simplicity: 'To exist is to evaluate.'[18] It followed me throughout my dissertation writing. With this sentence she indicated the relationship between what we read, see, and ourselves and what this might entail. To tell us that 'to exist is to evaluate' charges us with considerable responsibility. We always put things on a scale of values, unconsciously, whether we work on a text or we read exclusively for pleasure. After many years, I have come to realize that the endurance of a text is neither the 'continuous appreciation of the timeless virtues of a fixed object by succeeding generations of isolated readers' or, merely, 'a series of continuous interactions among a variably constituted object, emergent conditions, and mechanisms of cultural selection and transmission.'[19] It can hardly be solely either. In fact, who are the 'authorities' deciding the 'emergent conditions' or the 'mechanisms of cultural selection' by which a text may enter or stay within the canon? A body of criticism about a work allows for its entrance into and permanence within the canon. And those who have access to it are also the ones decreeing the validity, permanence, and usefulness of works. Eventually, as Herrnstein Smith contends, once works have achieved canonical status, it is hard to disprove their canonicity, or make room for other works that have become more important in different emergent situations. In the language of fiction as utilized by Italian women writers we witness a wrenching historical change. Far from displaying a linear evolution, the novel by women writers takes on the shape of a capillary map in which their writings produce a multitude of variations on the traditional understanding of what a novel should do, or rather, how it should function. At this juncture, we can unproblematically look at some women novelists as 'canonical' ones, and not merely within the 'female' canon of the novel.

But how can we define an alternate canon in Italian literature when the whole concept of canonization in itself is problematic? And how can we talk of a women's canon, when women artists, even today, are discriminated against in Italian literature? My answer is that such a canon is not only definable, but at this point even necessary. Without commenting upon the works of women writers that have constituted and still represent a point of reference for contemporary writers, I would argue that we can hardly understand the changes the Italian novel has undergone in the past twenty years. As Rita Felski contends, the great examples of the novel, heroes like Gatsby or Huck, are 'highly specific.'[20] In my view, the universality expressed by characters like Italo Svevo's Zeno is just as specific as Gatsby. That is to say, it is a 'universality' critics *found* for the author, identifying with the hero's problems without taking into account other possible (women?) readers. There is no such a thing as a universal work. And for this reason, it is indispensable that scholars make room for a critical praxis based on texts by women artists. If not, the list of soon-to-be-forgotten Medusas will continue to grow, while Zeno will remain the undisputed character on which all Italians mirror themselves. The endurance of a text is not a self-made product. Someone makes it.

Notes

Note: Unless otherwise noted, all translations in this text are mine.

Introduction

1 Sharon Wood has designed a very important thread among writers of the past century in her *Italian Women's Writing 1860–1994* (London: Athlone, 1995). In 'Passion and Sexual Difference: The Risorgimento and the Gendering of Writing in Nineteenth-Century Italian Culture,' in *Making and Remaking Italy: The Cultivation of National Identity around the Risorgimento*, ed. Albert Russell Ascoli and Krystina von Henneberg (Oxford: Berg, 2001) Lucia Re highlights the patriarchal exploitation of the 'cult of domesticity and the politics of feeling' after unification. In her reading of Anna Maria Mozzoni's famous writings on the subjection and abjection of Italian women even after unification that followed her translation of John Stuart Mill's *The Subjection of Women,* Re stresses the evidence that not only the Church, but also political powers (moderate and less moderate) had a clear interest in keeping women in a state of illiteracy and backwardness, while eliciting their role as 'angel of the hearth,' which saw its natural follow-up in the bourgeois construction of women's identity in twentieth-century Italian cultural history. 'Thus,' Re states, 'the new bourgeois cult of domesticity of the Italian Risorgimento was promoted not only through a discourse about the nature and the spontaneous inclinations of the genders but also through a regulatory discourse that sought to contain and "domesticate" female passions, especially the passions that may be aroused by excessive learning and reading' (173). See also Ann Caesar's 'Women Readers and the Novel in Nineteenth-Century Italy,' *Italian Studies* 56 (2001): 80–97.

2 Antonio Negri and Michael Hardt, *Multitude: War and Democracy in the Age of Empire* (New York: Penguin Press, 2004).
3 Ibid., xiii.
4 Rosi Braidotti, *Metamorphoses: Towards a Materialist Theory of Becoming* (Cambridge: Polity Press, 2002), 38.
5 Many of the causes and almost institutionalized issues regarding the novel and its relative lack of theory in Italy are the subject of Remo Ceserani and Pierluigi Pellini's 'The Belated Development of a Theory of the Novel' in *The Cambridge Companion to the Italian Novel*, ed. Andrea Ciccarelli and Peter Bondanella (Cambridge: Cambridge University Press, 2003), 1–19.
6 In English literature, the regional novel is intended to be, for instance, the Irish one, indicating by this the peculiarities of Irish people vis-à-vis the British. I contend that in Italian literature regionalism is made more evident by the linguistic richness and different societies they utilize and represent. See Alastair Fowler, *A History of English Literature* (Cambridge, MA: Harvard University Press, 1987), 197. The anachronistic isolation of a specifically 'Italian' narrative context should be debunked, with a reassertion of some of its most relevant characteristics that only too often have been concealed behind the historical novel tradition which began with Alessandro Manzoni's *The Bethrothed* (*I promessi sposi*), ed. Vittorio Spinazzola, 3rd. ed. (Milan: Garzanti, 1972).
7 See *Donne, filosofia e cultura nel Seicento*, ed. Pina Totaro (Rome: Consiglio nazionale delle ricerche, 1999).
8 See Antonia Arslan's *Dame, galline, e regine: La scrittura femminile fra '800 e 900* (Milan: Guerini studio, 1998).
9 See Luisa Ricaldone, *La scrittura nascosta: Donne di lettere e loro immagini tra Arcadia e Restaurazione* (Fiesole: Cadmo, 1996); Anna Santoro and Francesca Veglione, *Catalogo della scrittura femminile a stampa presente nei fondi librari della Biblioteca Nazionale di Napoli* (Naples: Federico e Ardia, 1984); Santoro, *Narratrici italiane dell'Ottocento* (Naples: Federico e Ardia, 1987); and Santoro, *Il Novecento: Antologia di scrittrici italiane del primo ventennio* (Rome: Bulzoni, 1997). I am only citing some of the most relevant works, fully aware that many more are being published or researched at this time.
10 Angela Bianchini, with *Voce donna* (Milan: Frassinelli, 1996), is probably one of the few Italian critics (she is also a writer) who presents us with an organic study and assessment of Western female fiction since its origins. Much on the wave of Hélène Cixous's just published theories on *écriture féminine*, Elisabetta Rasy interrogates the role of female writing in *La lingua della nutrice*, (Rome: Edizioni delle donne, 1978), while in *Le donne e la letteratura: Scrittrici eroine e ispiratrici nel mondo delle lettere* (Rome: Editori Riuniti, 1984) she draws one of the first accounts in Italian of feminist literature and the 'tormented history' of the rela-

tionship women have entertained with literature. Critic and novelist Giuliana Morandini, with *La voce che è in lei: Antologia della narrativa femminile italiana tra '800 e '900* (Milan: Bompiani, 1980), follows Bianchini's more traditional attempt a female writers' taxonomy, with a specific focus on Italian female fiction in the 1800s and early 1900s. Very interesting are the passages Morandini has chosen from the work of several artists who, relatively unknown today, enjoyed a considerable number of readers in their time.

11 See Santoro and Veglione, *Catalogo della scrittura femminile*.
12 The introduction to Santoro's *Il Novecento* is a useful overview of Italian women writers. Also, the volume has an expansive bibliography focused on critical and theoretical works on Italian female writing up to 1997.
13 Robert S. Gordon, 'Other Voices,' in *An Introduction to Twentieth-Century Italian Literature* (London: Duckworth, 2005), 123–39.
14 In *A Literature of Their Own* (Princeton: Princeton University Press, 1977) Showalter names these phases respectively *feminine, feminist, female* (3). She holds the firm belief that these are not rigid categories, but entirely flexible ones to which writers would simultaneously respond in the same periods, and that the three phases at times could overlap each other (13).
15 Gianni Vattimo and Pier Aldo Rovatti, eds, *Il pensiero debole* (Milan: Feltrinelli, 1983).
16 Elisabeth Badinter, *Fausse route* (Paris: Odile Jacob, 2003), 34.
17 Paola Bono, 'Women's Biographies and Autobiographies: A Political Project in the Making,' in *Across Genres, Generations, and Borders: Italian Women Writing Lives*, ed. Susanna Scarparo and Rita Wilson (Newark: University of Delaware Press, 2004), 15.
18 Ibid., 14.
19 Andrea Dworkin and Catharine A. MacKinnon have been active speakers on feminist legal theories. Their work has been fundamental to the understanding of how much still needed to be accomplished before women could rely on actual equality from a legal standpoint. Their radicalism, though, cannot be considered as the only voice of feminist theories, particularly when it comes to analysing works by European, and therefore differently situated, female writers. With respect to the diversification of feminist studies, Rita Felski notes that '[t]he field of feminist criticism is ever more fragmented; many scholars focus on a specific genre, field, or subgroup of women, or alternatively spend their time deconstructing or endlessly qualifying the concept of woman.' See *Literature after Feminism* (Chicago: University of Chicago Press, 2003), 3–5.
20 Ibid., 5.
21 I have dealt elsewhere with the problematic (for me) approach of Dworkin

and MacKinnon to feminist theoretical thought. See Stefania Lucamante, 'Everyday Consumerism and Pornography "above the Pulp Line,"' in *Italian Pulp Fiction: The New Narrative of the Giovani Cannibali Writers*, ed. Lucamante (Madison, NJ: Fairleigh Dickinson University Press, 2001), 98–134.
22 Felski, *Literature after Feminism*, 12.
23 Ibid., 12.
24 Ibid., 20–35.
25 Ibid., 6.
26 Ibid., 8.
27 Ibid., 12.
28 Ibid., 12.
29 Ibid., 10.
30 Lucamante, 'Everyday Consumerism and Pornography,' 99.
31 Giancarlo Lombardi's *Rooms with a View: Feminist Diary Fiction 1952–1999* (Madison, NJ: Fairleigh Dickinson University Press, 2002) explores this particular and much frequented form of writing in a more European context.
32 A relevant study for this topic is Adalgisa Giorgio's recent edition of transnational essays on the mother–daughter relationship, *Writing Mothers and Daughters: Renegotiating the Mother in Western European Narratives by Women* (New York: Berghahn Books, 2002). Also very interesting is the recent autobiographical work in which writer Dacia Maraini and psychologist Silvia Vegetti Finzi describe their war experiences, *Madri e figlie: Ieri e oggi* (Bari: Laterza, 2003). Psychoanalyst Anna Salvo's *Madri e figlie: Legami e conflitti fra due generazioni* (Milan: Mondadori, 2003) deals with the topic, using instead an epistolary form. To this date, Francesca Sanvitale's *Madre e figlia* (Turin: Einaudi, 1980) remains the most important novel in Italian literature depicting the difficult mother–daughter interaction.
33 Mauro Covacich, 'Unabomber,' in *Patrie impure: Italia, Autoritratto a più voci*, ed. Benedetta Centovalli (Milan: Rizzoli, 2003), 130.
34 This was the denomination for Milanese youth in the mid-1980s. Italy (mainly Northern Italy) boasted a 'youth cult' consisting primarily of youngsters dedicated to fashionable clothes like Timberland boots, motor scooters, and large sandwiches known as *panini* (the plural of *panino*). These youngsters were referred to as *paninari* – or, singular, *paninaro*.
35 Adriana Cavarero, *A più voci: Filosofia dell'espressione vocale* (Milan: Feltrinelli, 2003), 210.
36 Rossana Campo, *Mai sentita così bene* (Milan: Feltrinelli, 1995).
37 For the use of chatting, please see my article '"Una laudevole fine": Femminismo e identificazione delle donne nella narrativa di Rossana Campo,' *Italianistica* 31.2–3 (May–Dec. 2002): 295–306.
38 See Monica Cristina Storini's *L'esperienza problematica: Genesi e scrittura nella*

narrativa italiana del Novecento (Rome: Carocci, 2005), 246–66; see also my monograph *Isabella Santacroce* (Fiesole: Cadmo, 2002).
39 Isabella Santacroce, *Fluo: Storie di giovani a Riccione* (Rome: Castelvecchi, 1995).
40 Paola Presciuttini, *Non dire il mio nome* (Padua: Meridiano Zero, 2004), 149.
41 Linda Nicholson, 'The Question of Essentialism,' in *The Second Wave: A Reader in Feminist Theory*, ed. L. Nicholson (London: Routledge, 1997), 319–20.
42 Negri and Hardt, *Multitude*, xiii.
43 The 51st Venice Biennale Exposition – even if this field is open to eternal discussion – was a clear recognition of the role of women in the arts. In the summer of 2005, for the first time, the *Arsenali* space was almost entirely occupied by the work of female artists. The New York–based anonymous collective Guerrilla Girls in the *Arsenali* played quite a strategic role, with posters condemning the highly marginal role academia has always decreed for women artists. Also, the French artist Annette Messager won the prize for the best national pavilion. Far from limiting the notion of art to a gendered one, this Biennale shows instead the importance of giving visibility to women artists in the visual arts' space. See Rosa Martínez and María de Corral's catalogue *La Biennale di Venezia. 51 Esposizione Internazionale d'Arte. L'esperienza dell'arte. Sempre un po' più lontano. Partecipazioni nazionali, eventi nell'ambito*, ed. *Italiana* (Venice: Marsilio, 2005).
44 Massimo Onofri, 'La retorica del sublime basso: Salvatore Niffoi, Erri De Luca, Isabella Santacroce,' in *Sul banco dei cattivi*, ed. G. Ferroni, M. Onofri, F. La Porta, and A. Berardinelli (Rome: Donzelli, 2006), 52.
45 Ibid., 53.
46 Felski again writes: 'A critic who thinks that the most exciting thing about *Medea* or *Middlemarch* is the author's use of metonymy or catachresis is surely missing a great deal' (*Literature after Feminism*, 13).
47 Although the case of the famous feminist writer Dacia Maraini could confute everything I said in this sentence, it is nevertheless true that conventional novels by female writers present fewer sites of ambiguity to a (male) critic and this even when the text presents experimental approaches to the genre. This could be the case with Anna Maria Ortese, like Fleur Jaeggy, or more recently Melania Mazzucco, if it were not for the fact that critics seem to 'miss the point' in many scenes and passages even in their relatively non-transgressive novels.
48 For a detailed close reading and theoretical investigation of Rossana Campo's narrative, please see Silvia Contarini, 'L'eredità della neoavanguardia nei romanzi di Silvia Ballestra, Rossana Campo, Carmen Covito,' *Narrativa* 8 (1995): 75–99; and 'Riflessioni sulla narrativa femminile degli anni '90,' *Narrativa* 10 (1996): 139–63. See also my own 'Per uno sguardo diverso:

Cinema, Santa Cecilia e Mickey Rourke nell'*Attore americano*,' *Narrativa* 20–21 (2001): 19–34.

49 Melissa P. (Panariello), *One Hundred Strokes of the Brush before Going to Bed*, trans. Lawrence Venuti (London: Serpent's Tail, 2005); orig. *Cento colpi di spazzola prima di andare a dormire* (Rome: Fazi, 2003). See also Frank Bruni's review, 'A Teenager Takes Italy by Storm, with Her Tale of Lust,' *New York Times*, 24 December 2003: A3; and Lenora Todaro, 'Oops! I Did It Again,' *The New York Times Review of Books*, 7 November 2004: 17.

50 Michel Foucault, *The History of Sexuality*, vol. 2, *The Use of Pleasure*, trans. Robert Hurley (New York: Pantheon Books, 1985): 31–2.

51 Braidotti, *Metamorphoses*, 15.

52 Harold Bloom declares to 'abhor ... extra-aesthetic considerations' and that 'critics do not make canons, any more than resentful networks can create them.' In this, however, he seems to contradict himself, as canons are based on aesthetic considerations that, in turn, reveal how an artistic text can, also culturally, still resonate decades after its composition. And it is often thanks to the work of critics – living in other times and different societies – that literary works 'talk' after decades. In the Italian part of Bloom's canonical prophecy we only have one female exponent, Natalia Ginzburg, with one title, *Family.* See Bloom, *The Western Canon: The Books and School of the Ages* (New York: Harcourt Brace, 1994), 548–9.

53 bell hooks, *Feminism Is for Everybody: Passionate Politics* (Cambridge, MA: South End Press, 2000), 20.

54 Carla Kaplan, *The Erotics of Talk: Women's Writing and Feminist Paradigms* (Oxford: Oxford University Press, 1996), 19.

55 In 'Everyday Consumerism and Pornography "above the Pulp Line"' I already argued that Italian female writers challenge the canon while there is no actual recognition for their efforts, particularly in academia. Renate Holub, one of the most brilliant readers of Italian feminism in the United States, has written extensively about the Italian female canon and eventual comparisons with American feminist theory. See Renate Holub, 'Between the United States and Italy: Critical Reflections on Diotima's Feminine/Feminist Ethics,' in *Feminine Feminists: Cultural Practices in Italy*, ed. Giovanna Miceli Jeffries (Minneapolis: University of Minnesota Press, 1994), 233–60; and 'Italian Difference Theory: A New Canon?' in *Italian Women Writers from the Renaissance to the Present*, ed. Maria Ornella Marotti (University Park: Pennsylvania State University Press, 1996), 37–52.

56 Ippolita Avalli, *La Dea dei baci* (Milan: Baldini e Castoldi, 1995).

57 Francesca Mazzucato, *Hot Line: Storia di un'ossessione* (Turin: Einaudi, 1996).

58 Pia Pera, *Diario di Lo* (Venice: Marsilio, 1995).

59 Nicholson Baker, *Vox* (New York: Vintage, 1993).

60 Dacia Maraini, 'Lettera sull'aborto,' *Nuovi Argomenti* 1–2 (Jan. 1996); Repr. in *Un clandestino a bordo* (Milan: Rizzoli, 1996), 9–34; 'Letter on Abortion,' in *Stowaway on Board*, trans. Giovanna Bellesia and Victoria Offredi Poletto (West Lafayette, IN: Bordighera Press, 2000), 1–19.
61 Teresa de Lauretis, *The Practice of Love: Lesbian Sexuality and Perverse Desire* (Bloomington: Indiana University Press, 1994).

Chapter 1

1 The intellectual and aesthetic affinities between Elsa Morante and another writer, Fabrizia Ramondino, have been the subject of my '"*Teatro di Guerra*": Of History and Fathers' in *Under Arturo's Star: The Cultural Legacies of Elsa Morante*, ed. Stefania Lucamante and Sharon Wood (West Lafayette, IN: Purdue University Press, 2005), 221–56.
2 Luisa Muraro, *L'ordine simbolico della madre* (Rome: Editori riuniti, 1991).
3 See Renate Holub's use of the term 'matronage' to translate *affidamento*. 'Between the United States and Italy: Critical Reflections on Diotima's Feminine/Feminist Ethics,' in *Feminine/Feminists: Cultural Practices in Italy*, ed. Giovanna Miceli Jeffries (Minneapolis: University of Minnesota Press, 1995), 233–60. See also Rebecca West, 'Su differenza sessuale ed eguaglianza in epoca postmoderna,' in *Nuova Prosa* 44 (2006): 163–79.
4 'L'avvento della legge del padre (del patriarcato) che si sovrappone alla positività dell'opera della madre, scinde la logica dall'essere ed è causa del nostro perdere e riperdere il senso dell'essere' (Muraro, *L'ordine simbolico*, 27).
5 For Teresa de Lauretis the daughter's relationship to the mother is an absolutely central one, and is virtually unquestioned in feminist psychoanalytic studies in spite of the disregard that both Sigmund Freud and Jacques Lacan have shown for the maternal figure in relation to female sexuality and creativity (by default). Lacan assumes, in fact, that only by separating from the mother figure one can access the symbolic. See de Lauretis, *The Practice of Love*, 53.
6 Carla Locatelli stresses the performativity of a text, reminding us that '[t]he Barthesian notion of *texte* involves its significance as a process of signification – at once generator and subverter of meaning).' See her 'Co(n)texts,' in *Co(n)texts: Implicazioni testuali*, ed. Carla Locatelli (Trent: Dipartimento di Scienze Filologiche e Storiche, 2000), 17.
7 While Carl Gustav Jung and Jacques Lacan speak of 'devouring mothers,' Luisa Muraro speaks of 'devouring *the* mother.' In her theory, this expression signifies the act of appropriation that philosophers have invariably always done to the detriment of female thinkers. See Luisa Muraro, in *Duemilaeuna: Donne che cambiano l'Italia*, ed. A. Buttarelli, L. Muraro, and L. Rampello (Milan: Pratiche editrici, 2001), 147; emphasis added.

8 Paola Zaccaria talks about processes of transformation by addressing the necessity of subjectivity in terms of a complex web of the word, the language, affectivity, experience, the feeling of any individual, and sexed subjectivity. See Zaccaria, 'Oltre il materno, il palinsesto,' in *Co(n)texts: Implicazioni testuali*, ed. Carla Locatelli (Trent: Dipartimento di Scienze Filologiche e Storiche, 2000), 267.
9 Adalgisa Giorgio's edited volume *Writing Mothers and Daughters: Renegotiating the Mother in Western European Narratives by Women* (New York: Berghahn Books, 2002) has an extensive bibliography on the contemporary discourse of mothers and daughters, and some specific passages in which the theories of Rich, Irigaray, Kristeva, and Cixous on this subject are discussed (8–9, 39–45, 150–4).
10 Ibid., 1–9.
11 Marianne Hirsch, *The Mother-Daughter Plot: Narrative, Psychoanalysis, Feminism* (Bloomington: Indiana University Press, 1989).
12 The topic of my forthcoming study is the work of two foreign authors, Helena Janeczek and Edith Bruck, who have chosen to write in Italian and live in Italy.
13 Giorgio, *Writing Mothers and Daughters*, 17–18.
14 Nancy Chodorow, *The Reproduction of Mothering: Psychoanalysis and the Sociology of Gender* (Berkeley: University of California Press, 1978).
15 Carla Kaplan, *The Erotics of Talk: Women's Writing and Feminist Paradigms* (Oxford: Oxford University Press, 1996), 29.
16 Ibid., 30. See Susan Gubar's fundamental article on an Isak Dinesen short story, '"The Blank Page" and the Issues of Female Creativity,' *Critical Inquiry* 8.2 (Winter 1981): 243–63, for more on the subject of the blank page and how women artists have overcome since the beginning of the twentieth century the reification of women as characters or even 'blank pages' in the work of male writers and critics (245).
17 Sandra M. Gilbert, 'Life's Empty Pack: Notes toward a Literary Daughteronomy,' *Critical Inquiry* 11 (March 1985): 357.
18 Ibid., 358.
19 Kaplan, *The Erotics of Talk*, 30.
20 Lucamante and Wood, 'Introduction,' in *Under Arturo's Star*, 13.
21 I suggest my *Elsa Morante e l'eredità proustiana* (Fiesole: Cadmo, 1998) for an analysis of a plausible hypothesis concerning Morante's rereading of Proustian themes and strategies.
22 Elsa Morante, *Opere*, ed. Cesare Garboli and Carlo Cecchi (Milan: Mondadori, 1988), 1: lvi.
23 Elsa Morante, 'Sul romanzo,' in '*Pro o contro la bomba atomica*' *ed altri scritti*, intro. Cesare Garboli (Milan: Adelphi, 1987), 50.
24 Adalgisa Giorgio, 'Nature vs. Culture; Repression, Rebellion and Madness in Elsa Morante's *Aracoeli*,' *Modern Language Notes* 109 (1994): 116.

25 Ibid.
26 I refer to Ena Marchi's *postscriptum* in the commemorative insert of *Linea d'ombra* (104 [May 1995]) dedicated to the prematurely deceased writer. Marchi praises Di Lascia's novel, though she insinuates that all the positive comments the novel received were motivated more by the author's premature death than by its actual literary merits. Marchi thinks of *Passaggio in ombra* as a novel that is far (in the negative) from the models to which it has been likened (Morante, Ortese, Tomasi di Lampedusa). According to Marchi, the merit of the novel resides chiefly in having made evident the presence of a great writer *in fieri* ('Ricordo di Mariateresa,' 46).
27 'Canonical works are expected to provide knowledge of the world represented, to exemplify powers for making representations that express possible attitudes or produce artistic models, and to articulate shared values in a past culture that influence the present or to clarify means of reading other works we have reason to care about.' Charles Altieri, 'An Idea and Ideal of a Literary Canon,' in *Canons*, ed. Robert von Hallberg (Chicago: University of Chicago Press, 1984), 58.
28 See Daniela Pasti, 'Di Lascia: un caso che divide,' *La repubblica*, 8 July 1995: 30.
29 Cesare Garboli, 'Elsa come Rousseau' (orig. 'Elsa Morante, pessima matrigna') repr. in *Il gioco segreto: Nove immagini di Elsa Morante* (Milan: Adelphi, 1995). The note in which Morante's text is quoted is in the second version (244n2).
30 Garboli, 'Elsa come Rousseau,' 223; emphasis added.
31 See Muraro, *L'ordine simbolico*, 230.
32 Kaplan, *The Erotics of Talk*, 33.
33 'there exist secure, tested models, to which a woman interested in literature could refer' (Garboli, 'Elsa come Rousseau,' 221).
34 'none of Morante's messages addresses women' (ibid., 223).
35 'Morante does not love women. She loathes them' (ibid., 225).
36 One of the variables of Morante's writing constitutes, in fact, what Filippo La Porta defines as 'Italian ideology,' which is essential for understanding her impact on successive writers. If we adapt La Porta's concept to Morante's works, we conclude that they incorporate all the features that in disparate ways construct the quintessential Italian art, 'the attitude to the theatre (of existence) and mise-en-scène, to melodrama and soft tunes (of conflicts), to the spectacularization of the apocalypse.' See Filippo La Porta, *La Nuova narrativa italiana: Travestimenti e stili di fine secolo*, 2nd ed. (Milan: Bollati Boringhieri, 1999), 15.
37 Garboli, 'Elsa come Rousseau,' 223.
38 Goffredo Fofi, 'I riti della memoria e del futuro,' *Linea d'ombra* 104 (May 1995): 43.

39 Pier Paolo Pasolini, 'L'isola di Arturo,' in *Il portico della morte*, ed. Cesare Segre (Rome: Associazione fondo Pier Paolo Pasolini, 1988), 170; angle quote marks in original.
40 Ibid., 170. In the review of Giovanna Rosa's *Cattedrali di carta: Elsa Morante romanziere* (Milan: Il Saggiatore, 1995) and the already mentioned Cesare Garboli's *Il gioco segreto: Nove immagini di Elsa Morante*, Carlo Madrignani still reiterates, as late as 1996, Garboli's favourite standpoint in assessing Morante's work, well expressed in his Preface (1988) to the Meridiani edition of Morante's *Opere*: 'Al di là della congruità del confronto [tra la Morante e Rousseau], è giusto ricordare la mancanza di ruolo di questa grande artista in un'Italietta di scriventi-vati' ('Elsa, l'inattuale,' *L'Indice dei libri del mese* 1 [Jan. 1996]: 10; 'aside from the congruity of the comparison [between Morante and Rousseau], it is right to recall that this great artist had no role in a provincial Italy made of poet-bards').
41 Madrignani, 'Elsa, l'inattuale,' 10.
42 Pasolini, 'L'isola di Arturo,' 170.
43 When speaking of the Southern setting for the two novels, Garboli comments, '[L]'età rappresentata in *Menzogna e sortilegio* è fortemente, ossessivamente marcata dalle contraddizioni sociali. I conflitti sociali interessano ogni più piccola cellula del romanzo e ne promuovono le grandi storie passionali. Ma da un punto di vista più generale, questo tipo di contraddizione, o di dinamica, ruota intorno all'asse nobiltà–piccola borghesia, nobiltà e contadini, signori e cafoni ... funzionari di Stato. Siamo nel Sud, in Sicilia, e manca il terzo stato. Manca la grande borghesia industriale, e quindi mancano le fabbriche' ('*Menzogna e sortilegio*,' in *Il gioco segreto*, 41; 'The age represented in *Menzogna e sortilegio* is strongly, obsessively marked by social contradictions. Social conflicts permeate the tiniest part of the novel and they ignite great passions. But from a general point of view, this kind of contradiction, or dynamic, rotates around the nobility–small bourgeoisie axis, nobility and contadini, signori and cafoni, ... State employees. We are in the South, in Sicily, and we lack the third State. We miss the great industrial bourgeoisie, and as such, we don't have the factories').
44 Di Lascia's relatives were deeply discomforted by the publication of the novel for its autobiographical traits. In Rocchetta S. Antonio, as in a Southern drama, Di Lascia's relatives refused to make any comment on the novel, offended by how Di Lascia could have exhibited the family's secrets in her book. Such secrets, according to Southern criteria, must be kept most secret: they are everybody's domain, but can never be discussed, and, above all, never accepted. See Francesco Erbani, 'Nel paese di Mariateresa la Strega,' *La repubblica*, 12 August 1995: 25.

45 Although the author Di Lascia claimed to have never read Morante's novel, Di Lascia's editor Ena Marchi referred how Di Lascia's high school teacher had confirmed her doubt, that the writer had read 'almeno due volte' ('at least twice') *Menzogna e sortilegio*, contrary to what Di Lascia had told her over the phone. See Marchi, 'Ricordo di Mariateresa,' *Linea d'ombra* 104 (May 1995): 45.
46 Ibid., 45.
47 Garboli, '*Menzogna e sortilegio*,' 55.
48 The modifier *propre* is meant to apply to those qualifications of institutional or spatial localization in which the relations of force among individuals take place. I take this meaning from Michel de Certeau's *The Practice of Everyday Life*, trans. Steven Rendall (Berkeley: University of California Press, 1984), xix.
49 'In this way, I go back to the past, and meet the girl I once was; I follow her while she keeps in her heart the unfailing lack of an eternal love.' Henceforth, the novel will be referred to as PO.
50 How not to remember that Rosaria also wanted the same bright future in studies for Elisa? See Elsa Morante, *Menzogna e sortilegio*, *Opere*, 1: 21; henceforth MS. Elsa Morante, *House of Liars*, trans. Adrienne Foulke, with editorial assistance by Andrew Chiappe (New York: Harcourt, 1951), 10; henceforth HL.
51 See the interesting analysis of this particular moment in the novel in Lucio Lugnani's '*Logos kai Ananke*,' in *Per Elisa: Studi su menzogna e sortilegio*, ed. L. Lugnani and Emanuella Scarano (Pisa: Nistri-Lischi, 1990), 13 ff.
52 Emanuella Scarano, 'La "fatua veste" del vero,' in Lugnani and Scarano, *Per Elisa*, see 152–3.
53 Marina Jarre notes, 'E altrettanto instabili [aside from the characters], mai fissi, anch'essi non destinati al futuro, sono quei sentimenti che pur sono il tema stesso del libro. Mutano di colpo, la passione diviene odio, l'avversione amore, non si arrendono a nessun ragionamento, seguono alla cieca le loro vie oscure' ('Le ombre impietose di Mariateresa,' *L'indice dei libri del mese* 6 [June 1995]: 16); 'Just as unstable [aside from the characters], never fixed, and also not destined to have a future, are those feelings that yet constitute the theme of the book. They suddenly change, passion becomes hatred, aversion turns into love; they do not surrender to any reasoning, blindly following their dark paths').
54 For the lexicon, it could be sufficient to note the intended usage of archaic and obsolete terms that greatly contribute to creating the atmosphere of a hardly circumscribable, yet limited in its borders, province. That flavour of *romanzo smesso* (a type of reading not in use for a long time, one could say) comes with those words belonging to an early-twentieth-century lexicon, provided with verbal voices like '*vagolo*' (PO 135) or modifiers like '*serotina*'

(PO 168), which the use of elevated synonyms and, aside from the lexicon, the many truncations can offer. What to say of the nickname of the protagonist, '*Tripoli*,' one that resuscitates immediately the nicknames of Morante characters, '*Il butterato*' of *Menzogna e sortilegio* or '*Parodia*' in *L'isola di Arturo?*

55 Already on page 13 the capitalized word 'NECESSITÀ,' almost screamed by the sick narrator, is mindful of Morante's frequent imperatives, her usage of capital letters in *Menzogna e sortilegio* and in *L'isola di Arturo*. Such use reappears on other pages of *Passaggio in ombra* (PO 59, 62, 76, 125, etc.). In Morante's work, the use of capitalized words and self-imperatives derives from Arthur Rimbaud. Rimbaud was an authentic icon for the novelist to the point that Marco Bardini advances the notion of an introjection of 'Elsa' in the Arturo-Arthur of *L'isola di Arturo*. See Bardini, 'Osservazioni preliminari su *l'isola di Arturo*,' in *Riscrittura Intertestualità transcodificazione*, ed. Emanuella Scarano and Donatella Diamanti (Pisa: Tipografia editrice pisana, 1992), 553–88.

56 In Garboli's view, Anna's fake letters were at the very core of the novelistic project of *Menzogna e sortilegio*; '*Menzogna e sortilegio*,' in *Il gioco segreto*, 32. Unfortunately, as Marco Bardini illustrates in his '*House of Liars*: The American Translation of *Menzogna e sortilegio*,' the entire section of fake letters is missing from the American translation of the novel, thus making difficult to make sense of the notion of disease and its transmission in the family. See Bardini, ibid., and Lucamante and Wood, *Under Arturo's Star*, 112–28.

57 Kaplan, *The Erotics of Talk*, 40.

58 Morante, *Aracoeli*, in *Opere* 2: 1174 ('But you, Mamita, help me. As mother cats do with ill-born kittens, eat me again. Receive my deformity in your pitying abyss'; *Aracoeli*, trans. William Weaver [New York: Random House, 1984], 102).

59 Ibid., 1172 ('The mamma's boy fairy tale is stagnant'; *Aracoeli*, 101).

60 Jacques Lacan as quoted in Bruce Fink, *The Lacanian Subject: Between Language and Jouissance* (Princeton, NJ: University Press, 1995), 56.

61 Simona Vinci, *Come prima delle madri* (Turin: Einaudi, 2003); henceforth CPM.

62 With *Dei bambini non si sa niente* (Turin: Einaudi, 1997) Simona Vinci won the Elsa Morante Prize for the first-published narrative work category.

63 Paul Ricoeur, *Time and Narrative*, trans. Kathleen McLaughlin and David Pellauer, vol. 2 (Chicago: University of Chicago Press, 1985), 8.

64 Ricoeur notices the expansion of emplotment, a process in which 'character and emplotment influence each other'; *Time and Narrative*, 2: 23.

65 Tzvetan Todorov, *The Poetics of Prose*, trans. Richard Howard (Oxford: Basil Blackwell, 1977), 47.

66 Simona Vinci, at http://www.studioprogetto.net/incubatoio16/I/simona/htm (Vinci's old website, which no longer exists).

67 Ricoeur, *Time and Narrative*, 2: 10.
68 See Philip Zelazo's levels-of-consciousness mode in his 'Minds in the (re-) Making: Imitation and the Dialectic of Representation,' in *Minds in the Making: Essays in Honour of David R. Olson*, ed. David R. Olson and Janet Wilde Astington (Oxford: Blackwell Publishers, 2000), 143–64.
69 Paul Ricoeur, *The Symbolism of Evil*, trans. Emerson Buchanan (Boston: Beacon Press, 1969), 70.
70 It should be noted that Georges Bataille's *Ma mère* (*My Mother*, trans. Austryn Wainhouse [London: Jonathan Cape, 1972]) could be another subtext, as Vinci needs to go deeper into the incestuous world of Tea and Pietro. Vinci operates an interesting juxtaposition of Bataille's evil on Morante's characters and their intricate relations as a means to corroborate her basic conviction that evil acts in more subtle and perverse ways than the ones proposed by Morante.
71 This initiation is Vinci's reply – and theoretical subplot – to Bataille's novel. Bataille's boy is named Pierre, and his full name should read Pierre Angélique, one of the pseudonyms under which Bataille published. The casual detail that *Pierre* is *Pietro* in Italian allows for my connection. Bataille and Vinci share a striking similarity of views about evil. For Bataille, God's divinity is still seen as part of Pierre Angélique's autobiographic trilogy. By an odd chance the two connect God to the female body that is revealed through the corporeal topology of orifices. As François Bruzzo explains, God's divinity is anchored to the female body, as only in this is there the inscription of a topology of openness to the impossible. Only the female body has, thus, the capacity of going beyond the mystic experience of divinity. This, in Bruzzi's words, is a gift that the female body holds as exclusive to itself. See François Bruzzi, 'Bataille scrittore,' in *Georges Bataille: Tutti i romanzi*, ed. Guido Neri (Turin: Bollati Boringhieri, 1992), vii.
72 Todorov, *The Poetics of Prose*, 47.
73 Ricoeur, *Time and Narrative*, 2: 9.
74 For instance, the tales of the Brothers Grimm abound in gory details. Horror construes scenes with a didactic approach. Surprisingly enough, these narratives are directed to young and innocent children who, frightened by such absurd cruelties, should avoid temptation.
75 My parallel with Morante is not only drawn by my reading of these two authors' texts, but is also recognized by Simona Vinci herself who, in an interview, said that 'dopo Elsa Morante non h[a] letto più niente' ('After Elsa Morante [she] did not read anything anymore'; as quoted in Antonella Fiori, 'I bambini ci guardano: E il loro gioco innocente e crudele diventa tragedia,' *L'Unità*, 17 September 1997: 25.

76 Morante, *Aracoeli*, in *Opere* 2: 1289; emphasis in original.
77 Morante, *Aracoeli*, 189.
78 Garboli, '*Menzogna e sortilegio*,' 36.
79 'Consciousness can exist only through continual recognition of the unconscious, just as everything that lives must pass through many deaths': Carl Gustav Jung, *Aspects of the Feminine*, trans. R.F.C. Hull (Princeton: Princeton University Press, 1982), in *Collected Works*, 6: 125.
80 Todorov, *The Poetics of Prose*, 47.
81 The notion of present time, though, appears varied with respect to the traditional notion of 'present' in Vinci's novel. In speaking of the posmodern novel, Katia Renna notes, 'There is no life in the *present*, which is a convention, a functional knot of dynamic relation between the *past*, which anchors individuals to the roots of an experience constituting their identity, and the *future*, which moves individual destinies towards an unforeseen "opening," projecting them in a horizon of happenings often intuited and prenarrated. The present, when artificially released from its natural contextuality, is thus mere suspension: it gains reality and meaning only within the direction of its movement, in its constant orienting itself, in its trascendental choice of a continuous tension towards a direction, in its intrinsic intentionality. It is a kind of *vectorial* present, natural and dynamic, in opposition to a *punctuative* present, artificial and immoble' ('Daniel Pennac e le reti del romanzo,' in *Il Romanzo: Autori e stili*, ed. Alessandro Catalano and Katia Renna [Rome: La Sapienza, 1997] 181).
82 Civil war is the backdrop for the novel. In this, Vinci follows a trend of the last five years: Carlo Lucarelli's *Guernica* (Turin: Einaudi Tascabili Stile Libero Noir, 2000) and Marcello Fois's *Gap* (Milan: Frassinelli, 1999) are only two examples. Vinci's novel belongs to a trend reminiscent of Giorgio Scerbanenco's strategies, particularly in *Traditori di tutti* (Milan: Garzanti, 1999). Above all, I would say that Vinci's main suggestions are drawn from Italian neo-realism, particularly from Italo Calvino's Pin, the unforgettable protagonist of the 1947 novel *Il sentiero dei nidi di ragno* (Milan: Mondadori, 1993; *The Path to the Spiders' Nest*, trans. Archibald Colquhoun and Martin McLaughlin, New York: HarperCollins, 2000); Roberto Rossellini's trilogy on the Second World War, and *Paisà* especially. It would be problematic, in fact, not to see references to the images of the dead bodies floating in the Po River, to the children as acting partisans and envoys. The descriptions of the partisans' dialogues evoke those of our cinematic legacy of the civil war, one that has built for all of us a visual and collective imaginary from which we draw inevitably. Rossellini's influence is visible also in the image of the hedonistic, nihilistic, and suffocating atmosphere inside Pietro's house, the

incessant smoking and drug ingestion of Tea and Kurt, that remind one of the Gestapo headquarters in *Open City*.
83 Jung, *Aspects of the Feminine*, 6: 107, 110.
84 Ibid., 6: 110.
85 Ibid., 6: 7.
86 See Elsa Morante, *Il mondo salvato dai ragazzini*, in *Opere*, 2: 122.
87 One could, of course, advance the position of Bruzzi about the name Bataille chose for his character: Pietro, the stone, like Saint Peter, upon which the Church has laid its foundations. The Church is the Mother of the faithful ones ('Bataille scrittore,' ix).
88 Morante, *Il mondo salvato dai ragazzini*, in *Opere*, 2: 71.
89 See Adriana Cavarero, *Corpo in figure: Filosofia e politica della corporeità* (Milan: Feltrinelli, 1995), 187 ff.
90 Morante, 'I personaggi,' in '*Pro o contro la bomba atomica*' *e altri scritti*, intro. Cesare Garboli (Milan: Adelphi, 1987), 12.
91 Ibid.
92 'They are among the blackest souls, and different faults weigh them down to the depth.' *Inferno*, VI, 85–7, as in CPM 42. All references to the *Commedia* in Italian are taken from Emilio Pasquini and Antonio Quaglio's edition (Milan: Garzanti, 1987), and those in English from John Sinclair's translation (Oxford: Oxford University Press, 1939).
93 Morante, 'I personaggi,' 12.
94 It is understood that Pietro does not perform his role as detective in the sense that Siegfried Kracauer assigns to such characters, since he will never be believed to have reached a logical conclusion (as in Renna, 'Daniel Pennac e le reti del Romanzo,' 216–17).
95 Claire Johnston, 'Double Indemnity,' in *Women in Film Noir*, ed. Emily Ann Kaplan (London: British Film Institute, 1998), 93.
96 Laura Mulvey, ibid.
97 Jung suggests the dragon as a diabolic and devouring figure (*Aspects of the Feminine*, 6: 109–10).
98 Jung, *Aspects of the Feminine*, 6: 10.
99 In his *Les complexes familiaux dans la formation de l'individu* (Paris: Navarin, 1984) Jacques Lacan notes: 'La saturation du complexe [*de sevrage*] fonde le sentiment maternel; sa sublimation contribue au sentiment familial; sa liquidation laisse des traces où on peut la reconnaître: c'est cette structure de l'imago qui reste à la base des progrès mentaux qui l'ont remaniée. S'il fallait définir la forme la plus abstraite où on la retrouve, nous la caractériserions ainsi: une assimilation parfaite de la totalité à l'être. Sous cette formule d'aspect un peu philosophique, on reconnaîtra ces nostalgies de l'humanité:

mirage métaphisique de l'harmonie universelle, abyme mystique de la fusion affective, utopie sociale d'une tutelle totalitaire, toutes sorties de la hantise du paradis perdu avant la naissance et de la plus obscure aspiration à la mort' (35; 'The saturation of the weaning complex is at the core of the maternal feeling; its sublimation contributes to family affects; its settlement leaves imprints where one can recognize it; it is this structure of the image that remains at the base of the mental progress that has reworked it. If it was difficult to define the most abstract form where one finds it, we characterize it in this way: a perfect assimilation of the totality to being. From this rather philosophical point of view, one will recognize this nostalgia of humanity: metaphysical mirage of universal harmony, mystical void of fusion of sentiments, social utopia of a totalitarian tutelage, all born out of the haunting of the paradise lost before birth and of the most obscure aspiration to death').

100 'Isn't every man's ambition to spoil a woman's life?' Margherita Giacobino, *Casalinghe all'inferno* (Milan: Baldini & Castoldi, 1996), 6.
101 Janette Winterson, *Written on the Body* (New York: Alfred Knopf, 1992), 39.
102 Simone de Beauvoir, *La femme rompue* (Paris: Gallimard, 1967) ; henceforth FR. *The Woman Destroyed*, trans. Patrick O'Brian (New York: Pantheon Books, 1969); henceforth DW.
103 Toril Moi makes a good point in showing how hard de Beauvoir tries to detach and distance herself from that 'darkness.' 'Intentions and Effects: Rhetoric and Identification in Simone de Beauvoir's "The Woman Destroyed" (1988),' in *What is a Woman? And Other Essays* (Oxford, Oxford University Press, 1999), 451–75.
104 See Ellen Nerenberg's *Prison Terms: Representing Confinement during and after Italian Fascism* for a brilliant analysis of confinement, prison, and reclusion during Mussolini years and post–Second World War (Toronto: University of Toronto Press, 2001).
105 Elena Ferrante, *I giorni dell'abbandono* (Rome: Edizioni e/o, 2002), 7; henceforth GA.
106 All translated passages from Ferrante's novel are taken from *The Days of Abandonment*, trans. Ann Goldstein (New York: Europe Editions, 2005), 9; henceforth DA.
107 Elena Ferrante, *L'amore molesto* (Rome: Edizioni e/o, 1992); henceforth AM.
108 René Girard, *The Scapegoat*, trans. Yvonne Freccero (Baltimore: Johns Hopkins University Press, 1986), 104.
109 Pia Pera's *Diario di Lo* is a case in point of this rereading as somewhat detrimental – though done with good intent. See my analysis of her book in chapter 2.

110 Simone de Beauvoir, *All Said and Done*, trans. Patrick O'Brian (Harmondsworth: Penguin, 1987), 140–5.
111 Moi, *What Is a Woman?* 455.
112 Toril Moi, 'Ambiguity and Alienation in *The Second Sex*,' *Boundary 2* 19.2 (1992): 98.
113 Ferrante's most recent novel, *La figlia oscura* (Rome: Edizioni e/o, 2006) is also a story of abandonment, of bad mothers and daughters. My reading of this novel appears in 'L'atroce smacco della madre,' in *Leggendaria* 60 (January 2007): 42–3.
114 Moi, 'Ambiguity and Alienation in *The Second Sex*,' 98.
115 Moira Gatens, *Imaginary Bodies: Ethics, Power and Corporeality* (London and New York: Routledge, 1996), 42.
116 In his unconscious misreading of female anguish, Garboli wondered whether Morante's works were indeed 'misogynist novels,' since they almost exclusively portray women as afflicted, passive, and ultimately unresolved creatures. See Garboli, *Il gioco segreto*, 65.
117 Note by comparison Rossana Campo's disenchanted feminism, Isabella Santacroce's androgynous protagonists, and Simona Vinci's ventures towards borderline perversion.
118 Whatever of the theatrical that remains in Wolf's *Medea* lies precisely in the excess of anger and frustration a woman displays when she has invested all of herself in performing the role of the perfect wife and mother. Love, in Medea's case, is measured by loss, precisely as Jeanette Winterson's epigraph (p. 80) states. Loss measures the intensity of your love. In Greek tragedies loss for a woman reaches the point of killing her own children when her husband deserts the marital bed. It is his doing that the abandoned wife becomes a monster in the murder she commits. Medea, the protagonist of such a tragedy, must mourn. But mourning, and not melancholia, comes only after the rage that sudden loss brings you. Children and your husband are yourself, what you are and what you possess(ed); they represent(ed) you in the world, as you possess(ed) no identity of your own. In this case, they also represent what, until then, society endowed Olga with: power and position. However, she also sees the husband and his name being carried over to some other woman, thus making clear the relationship love–power. What they have in common remains under his name. The wife loses her identity; she is an outcast.
119 Christa Wolf, 'From Cassandra to Medea: Impulses and Motives behind My Work on Two Mythical Figures,' at http://www.randomhouse.com/boldtype/0498/wolf/notebook.html. About the 'banality of every day,' in a 2002 production by the Abbey Theatre, actress Fiona Shaw presented, for

once, a rather believable Medea. Not boasting a dramatic Maria Callas's flair, Shaw's *Medea* was close to Wolf's conceptualization of the myth. Wolf speaks, in fact, of tragic Medea as a character born out of the need of men to overcome their fear of women as sole life-givers. They needed 'the image of the savage, evil woman dominated by uncontrolled urges: the sorceress of black magic, the witch' (Wolf). Fiona Shaw's portrayal deconstructs this image by entwining tragic feelings and irony in her role as wife abandoned for a younger woman. Revenge in the case of Greek tragedies, as I said, takes a slightly more poignant significance than in real life, and yet, Shaw's acting made me think of Ferrante's Olga and the banality of life.

120 Wolf, 'From Cassandra to Medea.'
121 It is the same reaction as Delia's in *L'amore molesto*. Delia rejects Naples and, more generally, the South. Constructing a parallel city-mother, Delia cannot cope with both. Since their language is Amalia's familiar dialect, it has to be rejected. See Giancarlo Lombardi, 'Scambi d'identità: Il recupero del corpo materno ne *L'amore molesto*,' *Romance Languages Annual* 10 (1999): 289. During Amalia's funeral, Delia's menstrual fluids indicate her body's involuntary reaction to being there, in that hated city, following the cadaver of her mother: 'Sentivo la città disciolta nel calore, sotto una luce grigia e polverosa, e ripassavo mentalmente il racconto dell'infanzia e dell'adolescenza che mi spingeva a divagare per la Veterinaria fino all'Orto Botanico, o per le pietre sempre umide, coperte di verdure marce, del mercato di Sant'Antonio Abate. Avevo l'impressione che mia madre si stesse portando via anche i luoghi, anche i nomi delle vie' (AM 12–13; 'I felt the city coming apart in the heat, in the dusty grey light, and I went over in my mind the story of childhood and adolescence that impelled me to wander along the Veterinaria to the Botanic Gardens, or over the cobbles of the market of Santo Antonio Abate, which were always damp and strewn with rotting vegetables. I had the impression that my mother was carrying off the places, too, and the names of the streets'; *Troubling Love*, trans. Ann Goldstein [New York: Europe Editions, 2006], 17); henceforth TL. I would like to point out, however, that similar contradictory feelings can also be found in another Morantian writer, Fabrizia Ramondino, who sees Naples as a *città-balia*, but her conflictual relationship with the city is never made as entirely clear in her works (the most important for this topic being *Dadapolis*), as Ferrante does with respect to the construction of her characters' subjectivity.
122 'Donne che tengono al loro io, lo irrobustiscono, si fanno agguerrite e poi scoprono che basta un taglio di capelli per causare crolli e perdere compattezza, sentirsi un flusso eterogeneo di rottami, utili ancora e inservibili, avvelenati o bonificati' ('Women who care for their ego, they strengthen it,

they train themselves only to realize that a haircut is enough to make them crumble and lose firmness, to feel like an heterogeneous flux of scraps still useful and yet useless, be they poisoned or reclaimed'). See Elena Ferrante, *La frantumaglia* (Rome: Edizioni e/o, 2003), 112; henceforth LF.
123 My emphasis. In his cinematic adaptation of *I giorni dell'abbandono* (Medusa, 2004), Roberto Faenza reifies the ghost of *la poverella* into a homeless woman. She lives in front of Olga's building in Turin, and she embodies Olga's possible failure. The surreal image of Olga's childhood has been turned into a sociological case, which has little to do with the topic of abandoned women and more with current Italian alienation in society.
124 Reference to food and cooking are briefly made in a traditional way to establish a connection between Eros, family, and the senses that resounds as 'familiar' to many. For instance, Olga wants to show all her love with a sauce, 'Volevo che vedesse in quel piatto di pasta tutto ciò che, andandosene, non avrebbe più potuto sfiorare con lo sguardo, o lambire, o accarezzare, ascoltare, annusare: mai più (GA 17; 'I wanted him to see in that plate of pasta everything that, by leaving, he would no longer be able to see, or lick, or caress, listen to, smell: never again,' DA 16).
125 Tommaso Ottonieri defines *intensità* as follows: 'cioè il carattere proprio di ogni lingua che manifesti in qualche minimo o abnorme sintomo la sua crisi ... *Intensità*, per cui ogni stato mentale può fissarsi in un plastico evento linguistico. In liquida plastica narrativa ... Cioè allora: stati della lingua? *Stati-di-scrittura?* – E allora: attraverso che cosa (ci) parla questa *lingua*: su che cosa (ci) scrive questa scrittura?' 'the proper identity of each language, that is, that manifests its crisis in some minimal or abnormal symptom ... *Intensity*, by which each mental state can firmly settle in a linguistic plastic event. In liquid narrative plastic ... Which amounts to saying: States of language? *States-of-Writing?* – And so: through which channel does this language speak to us? On what is this writing writing about?') See Tommaso Ottonieri, *La plastica della lingua* (Milan: Bollati Boringhieri, 2000), 77.
126 Lombardi, 'Scambi d'identità,' 289.
127 Simone de Beauvoir, *The Second Sex*, trans. and ed. H.M. Parshley (New York: Knopf, 1952), 34.
128 Julia Kristeva, *Powers of Horror: An Essay on Abjection*, trans. Leon S. Roudiez (New York: Columbia University Press, 1982), 38. In *A Sister to Scheherazade*, trans. Dorothy S. Blair (Portsmouth, NH: Heinemann, 1993), Assia Djebar writes about the meaning behind the fact that in Arabic the word *Derra* means both 'wound' and 'wife' (91). Olga's woundedness thus comes to us as a condition within her own identity. Olga as a wife is a 'wound,' but also wound(ed).

129 She asks Mario, 'Vuoi dire che t'angosciavo? Vuoi dire che a dormire con me ti sentivi invecchiato? La morte la misuravi sul mio culo, su come era soffice una volta e su come è diventato adesso? Questo vuoi dire?' (GA 43; 'You mean that I brought you anguish? You mean that sleeping with me you felt yourself growing old? You measured death by my ass, by how once it was firm and what is it now? Is that what you mean?' DA 40).

130 See Ferrante's own example of men's speech in *L'amore molesto*. Men are depicted quite differently from the conformist, hypocritical bourgeois Mario. They curse in the middle of the street, they touch women on the bus, and their speech is often 'un fiotto di oscenità in dialetto, un morbido rivolo di suoni che coinvolse in un frullato di seme, saliva, feci, orina dentro orifizi d'ogni genere, me, le mie sorelle, mia madre' (AM 15; 'a stream of obscenities in dialect, a soft river of sound that involved me, my sisters, my mother in a concoction of semen, saliva, feces, urine in every possible orifice,' TL 19).

131 *Il Nuovo Zingarelli: Vocabolario della lingua italiana*, ed. Miro Dogliotti and Luigi Rosiello, 11th ed. (Bologna: Zanichelli, 1986), 353.

132 'Cosa mi si leggeva addosso? Che non dormivo con un uomo da quasi tre mesi? Che non succhiavo cazzi, che nessuno mi leccava la fica? Che non chiavavo? Perciò quei due non facevano altro che parlarmi ridendo di chiavi, di toppe, di serrature? Avrei dovuto blindarmi io, rendermi imperscrutabile ... Seguivo pedissequamente la prassi dell'autodegradazione, mi ero arresa, non cercavo più di trovare una mia nuova misura?' (GA 65, 66) ('What could they read in me? That I hadn't slept with a man for almost three months? That I wasn't sucking cocks, that no one was licking my pussy? That I wasn't screwing? Was that why those two men kept speaking to me, laughing, of keys, of keyholes, of locks? I should have armored myself, made myself inscrutable ... Was I following, literally, the process of self-degradation, had I surrendered, was I no longer trying to find a new measure of myself?' [DA 59–60, 61]).

133 Ferrante's scene recalls Nora's death in Morante's *La Storia*. Nora drowns in her illness and loss of memory after her husband's death, whereas the *poverella* dies in complete madness. But isn't Amalia's death in *L'amore molesto* also reminiscent of Nora's death by the shore?

134 It's interesting to note how the image of the madwoman is used here, as a point of reference almost, feared and yet seen as inevitable. A similar treatment of this motif can be found in Marguerite Duras's *The Lover*, trans. Barbara Bray, intro. Maxine Hong Kingston (New York: Pantheon Books, 1997). A French woman fell for a Chinese man, who hung himself while she was having a party. Left to wander the streets of the village, the French lady

turns into a madwoman, also a reflection of the writer who sees only in her writing the escape from a similar existence. Duras was giving voice to herself, but also to the French madwoman back in Cholon (in Saigon).

135 'I can feel the stillness of this tea hour yet ... Every day, at the same time, the idle gossip would be resumed, interspersed with stifled laughter, with tittle-tattle about the neighbors. Chatter punctuated only by the tireless hum of the seamstress's Singer ... Suspense reflected in the mosaics, under the drooping jasmine.' See Djebar, *A Sister to Scheherazade*, 78.

136 Domenico Starnone recounts in vivid tones stories of post-war Neaples in his *Via Gemito* (Milan: Feltrinelli, 2002), as does Francesco Costa in *La volpe a tre zampe* (Milan: Baldini e Castoldi, 1996). Their writing entails, however, a much more realistic setting, in which the notion of the abused wife is present, but always from the point of view of the little boy, thus respecting the Freudian treatment of the mother–son relationship.

137 Lucien Dällenbach, *Le récit spéculaire: Essais sur la mise en abyme* (Paris: Éditions du Seuil, 1977), 18.

138 Jacques Derrida, *Given Time: I. Counterfeit Money*, trans. Peggy Kamuf (Chicago: University of Chicago Press, 1992), 13; emphasis in original.

139 Ibid., 13.

140 A 'reason why marriage is enjoined is that woman's function is also to satisfy a male's sexual needs and to take care of his household. These duties placed upon woman by society are regarded as a *service* rendered to her spouse: in return he is supposed to give her presents, or a marriage settlement, and to support her. Through him as intermediary, society discharges its debt to the woman it turns over to him.' See Beauvoir, *The Second Sex*, 427.

141 Olga now invokes her own strength: 'Ridarmi io stessa una misura. Cos'ero? Una donna fiaccata da quattro mesi di tensioni e di dolore; non certo una maga che, per disperazione, secerne un veleno capace di dare la febbre al figlio maschio, uccidere un lupo domestico, mettere fuori uso la linea telefonica, corrodere l'ingranaggio di una porta blindata ... Ero un'inetta, prigioniera in casa mia' (GA 132–3) ('Give back to me a sense of proportion. What was I? A woman worn out by four months of tension and grief; not, surely, a witch who, out of desperation, secretes a poison that can give a fever to her male child, kill a domestic animal, put a telephone line out of order, ruin the mechanism of a reinforced door lock ... I was an incompetent, a prisoner in my own house [DA 118–19]).

142 Moi, 'Ambiguity and Alienation in *The Second Sex*,' 108.

143 Moi, 'Intentions as Effects,' 452.

144 Ibid., 453.

145 Ibid.

264 Notes to pages 105–10

146 Ibid., 467.
147 'Generally speaking, I take too peremptory a tone in my essays, some people have told me; a more temperate approach would be more convincing. I don't think so ... My essays reflect my practical choices and my intellectual certitudes; my novels, the astonishment into which I am thrown both by the whole and by the details of our human condition.' See Simone de Beauvoir, *Hard Times: Force of Circumstance*, vol. 2, trans. Peter Green (New York: Paragon House, 1992), 41.
148 Ibid., 469.
149 Ibid., 472.
150 Ibid.
151 Moi, 'Ambiguity and Alienation in *The Second Sex*,' 108.
152 See Anna Patrucco Becchi, '*Stabat Mater*. Le madri di Elsa Morante,' *Belfagor* 31 (July 1993): 436–51.

Chapter 2

1 Lynda Zwinger, *Daughters, Fathers, and the Novel: The Sentimental Romance of Heterosexuality* (Madison: University of Wisconsin Press, 1991), 9. Here, I use the terms romance and novel in the same conflated way that Zwinger does.
2 Jane Gallop, *The Daughter's Seduction* (Ithaca: Cornell University Press, 1982). For a general discussion that introduces several helpful theories on this topic, see Jane M. Ford, *Patriarchy and Incest from Shakespeare to Joyce* (Gainesville: University Press of Florida, 1998); Barbara H. Sheldon, *Daughters and Fathers in Feminist Novels* (New York: Peter Lang, 1997); and *His Hands, His Tools, His Sex, His Dress: Lesbian Writers on Their Fathers*, ed. Catherine Reid and Holly K. Iglesias (New York: Alice Street Editions, 2001). In Italy also we have studies on this topic, based, however, on examples offered by Anglo-American literature, as in Chiara Briganti's *Anche tu, figlia mia!: Figlie e padri nelle letterature anglofone* (Urbino: Quattroventi, 1995).
3 This is a theme that has seen several treatments not only in Italy, but in Europe in general, and also in cinema. *Mon père*, by Eliette Abecassis (Paris: Albin Michel, 2002), is a sort of first-person diary of a woman aiming at finding her own identity via the retrieval of family memories. Agnes Jaoui participated at the 2004 Cannes Film Festival with her *Comme une image*, 'Look at Me,' which deals almost exclusively with a daughter's problems with facing her father's larger-than-life ego.
4 Alberto Moravia's novels epitomize the Oedipal relationship at the very core of Italian family narratives. *Agostino* and *The Conformist* best depict the desire (also physical) of the son for his mother, a desire that prolongs the

son's Oedipal stage into puberty, and eventually even into his adult life. While I am aware that the desire for the mother is not exclusively pertinent to sons, I also think that, in Italian novels, it usually is portrayed in the mother–son relationship.
5 I deal with Dacia Maraini's *Voci*, and her treatment of this topic, in the following chapter on sexual politics.
6 Fleur Jaeggy, *Proleterka* (Milan: Adelphi, 2001); *S.S. Proleterka*, trans. Alastair McEwen (New York: New Directions, 2003).
7 Anna Santoro, *Pausa per rincorsa* (Cava dei Tirreni: Avagliano, 2003), 126 (henceforth PPR); 'Death does not justify anything. Death raises problems of freedom. It clarifies and reveals its ambiguities. Freedom from what?'
8 Rossana Campo, *Sono pazza di te* (Milan: Feltrinelli, 2001).
9 Christa Wolf highlights this concept in her work on female rewrites of myth. Please see my comments on Wolf's work in the previous chapter.
10 Zwinger, *Daughters, Fathers, and the Novel*, 9.
11 Henceforth DB.
12 Henceforth HL.
13 Henceforth DL. Its English translation, *Lo's Diary*, trans. Ann Goldstein (New York: Foxrock, 1999), will be referred to as LD.
14 Isabella Santacroce, *Destroy* (Milan: Feltrinelli, 1996).
15 Isabella Santacroce, *Luminal* (Milan: Feltrinelli, 1998).
16 See Donna Haraway, 'Manifesto for Cyborgs,' a classic of her theories on women and cyborgs, in *The Haraway Reader* (New York: Routledge, 2004), 7–46.
17 Ippolita Avalli, *Nascere non basta* and *Mi manchi* (Milan: Feltrinelli, 2003 and 2008).
18 'The act of will and the action of the body are not two different states objectively known connected by the bond of causality; they do not stand in the relation of cause and effect, but are one and the same thing, though given in two entirely different ways, first quite directly, and then in perception for the understanding. The action of the body is nothing but the act of will objectified, i.e., translated into perception.' See Arthur Schopenhauer, *The World as Will and Representation*, trans. E.F.J. Payne (London: Dover Edition, 1969), 17.
19 Such a setting, the region of Lombardy made immortal by Alessandro Manzoni's nineteenth-century writings, offers an immediate literary reference to his masterpiece *I promessi sposi* (*The Betrothed*). Manzoni's *Promessi sposi* employs the Lodigiano and the Adda River as backdrop for some of Renzo's travails, though with a hopeful and rather optimistic outcome.
20 Giovanni Pascoli's poetry, intended in a non-rhetorical way, feeds Avalli's novel. Pascoli's poetry knows well how to tune words that re-create a by-now lost world of innocence in spite of the traumas experienced.

21 Vladimir Propp, *Morphology of the Folktale*, trans. Laurence Scott (Austin: University of Texas Press, 1968), 22.
22 The new personage, the child's stepmother, Maria Bernini, has the role of disturbing the peace in the family 'to cause some form of misfortune, damage, or harm.' Only later will Giovanna realize who the real 'villain' was. See Propp, *Morphology of the Folktale*, 27.
23 Ibid., 39. I consider Giovanna as a seeker-heroine for several reasons. Hers is a successful, however bitter, departure from the world that wanted to segregate her off in the role of the scapegoat, as we shall see in my study.
24 Frank Kermode, *The Sense of an Ending* (New York: Oxford University Press, 1967), 39.
25 In the recordings of Giovanna, Maria is a well-endowed young woman, whose body brings to mind the sinuosity of baroque statues, as her name, 'Bernini,' re-evokes that of Gianlorenzo, the baroque sculptor.
26 It is a comparison that finds its confirmation only a few pages later during the scene following the episode of the ruined dress on the wedding day of Giovanna's father to Maria: 'Sorriderle, voglio dire. Subito dopo avrei voluto sprofondare nelle sabbie mobili. La Maria mi fissava gelida, con la mano a mezz'aria. Anch'io sono rimasta sospesa, proprio come il pulcino nell'illustrazione sul libro di scienze' (DB 67; 'Smile at her, I want to say. Soon after I would want to sink into the quicksand. Maria was staring at me gelidly, with her hand in mid-air. I remained suspended, too, much like the chick in the science book illustration').
27 Rosi Braidotti, *Metamorphoses: Towards a Materialist Theory of Becoming* (Cambridge: Polity Press, 2002), 21.
28 Ibid., 45; emphasis added.
29 The agrarian, however rather wealthy, setting of this novel suggests the study of patriarchal voices for Giovanna-Vera. Patriarchal voices, though, work to the benefit of the little girl, in that Homer and Giovanni Pascoli – synonymous with education and culture – constitute a pole of diversion from her experiences in the country. Though fraught with doubts and subterranean travails, Pascoli's poetry still appears endowed with a patriarchal voice.
30 If we look at female illnesses, they appear to be a possible representation of the feminine, as in fact Monica Baroni argues, 'both in the meaning of self-narrative and social narrative, that begs to be read as a cultural affirmation, as an affirmation on gender' (*Streghe, madonne e sante postmoderne: Eccedenze femminili tra cronaca e fiction*, ed. Monica Baroni [Rome: Meltemi, 2003], 14.)
31 Jane Wood, *Passion and Pathology in Victorian Fiction* (Oxford: Oxford University Press, 2001), 210.

32 Lilian R. Furst and Peter W. Graham, 'Introduction,' in *Disorderly Eaters: Texts in Self-Empowerment*, ed. Furst and Graham (University Park: Pennsylvania State University Press, 1992), 5–6.
33 Paulo Medeiros, 'Cannibalism and Starvation: The Parameters of Eating Disorders in Literature,' ibid., 11–12.
34 Medeiros ties the concept of nutritional disorders to the first example of sacrifice, that of Adam and Eve who were thrown out of Eden, and in the myth of Tantalus, who was punished by divinity for having dared to steal the ambrosia from the table of the gods. Both examples serve to define the human condition as impossible to be separated from the question of consumption ('Cannibalism and Starvation,' 13). Giuliana Giobbi recalls how anorexia is often linked to religion; Giobbi cites the cases of St Catherine and of the hermits. Here anorexia has a dual function, as it represents the privation of food but also the cure against the danger of sexual pleasure. Anorexia represents the lack of all possible appetites of the flesh and becomes a 'redeeming illness' that leads to purity, to communion with God. In Giobbi's view, 'the sacrifice of corporeal pleasure is a supreme self-punishment that aspires to assure the pre-eminence of the spirit on the flesh' ('"No Bread Will Feed My Hungry Soul": Anorexic Heroines in Female Fiction – from the Example of Emily Brontë as Mirrored by Anita Brookner, Gianna Schelotto and Alessandra Arachi,' *Journal of European Studies* 27 [1997]: 76). Also Grazia Menechella has published a study rich with interesting reflections on anorexia, 'La rappresentazione dell'anoressia nel discorso medico e nei testi di Alessandra Arachi, Nadia Fusini e Sandra Petrignani,' *Italica* 78.3 (2001): 387–409.
35 According to Susan Bordo, an alimentary disorder becomes an instrument of self-expression that must be understood as a form of rebellion generated against a domineering ethos, which in our novel cannot be accepted by Giovanna-Vera, and this for obvious reasons. The result of this operation does not influence the sick person in the sense that there is no specific goal in her/his voluntary fasting. The important element, Bordo argues, is the self-expressive capacity of a choice – be it even expressed in the sense of the refusal of nourishment – in order to protest against a pernicious family dynamics. See Bordo, *Unbearable Weight: Feminism, Western Culture, and the Body* (Berkeley: University of California Press, 1993), 5–6.
36 Luisa Muraro, 'Partire da sé e non farsi trovare,' in Diotima, *La sapienza di partire da sé* (Naples: Liguori, 1996), 20.
37 Ibid., 20; emphasis in original.
38 Ibid.
39 Ibid.
40 Ibid., 21.

41 René Girard, *The Scapegoat*, trans. Yvonne Freccero (Baltimore: Johns Hopkins University Press, 1986), 117.
42 Ibid., 186.
43 'Research has shown that the content of one's memory trace is susceptible to postevent distortion when the individual is unaware of this happening, and that this type of distortion is very prevalent among abused children.' See *Child Abuse, Child Development, and Social Policy*, ed. Dante Cicchetti and Sheree L. Toth (Norwood: Ablex Publishing, 1993), 8: 128.
44 Girard, *The Scapegoat*, 119.
45 Ibid., 119.
46 Luisa Muraro, *Il Dio delle donne* (Milan: Mondadori, 2003), 157.
47 The integral text of the document can be found at http://www.vatican.va/archive/hist_councils/ii_vatican_council/documents/vatii_const_19631204_sacrosanctum-concilium_en.html.
48 I don't agree with Lynda Zwinger about the erotic aspect as being omnipresent in a father–daughter relationship. Unlike *Hot Line*, *La Dea dei baci* is not a romance about feminine desirability, or desire – at least not as related to the father. As such the novel cannot match all the criteria Zwinger discusses in her study. See Zwinger, *Daughters, Fathers, and the Novel*, 70.
49 'Perdition is an equitable exchange because it results from reciprocal evil desires and evil behaviour. The only innocent victims are children on whom scandal is imposed from the outside without any participation on their part. Fortunately, all men were once children.' See Girard, *The Scapegoat*, 134. Girard makes no distinction between those children who eventually become women, and those who become men, a distinction that, in our case, proves to be of fundamental importance owing to the relationship of Giovanna with her father and the other fathers that define her life.
50 Don Bruno, a long-time ally of Giovanna's, invokes sacrifice as a way of overcoming the incidental adversity, thus making his own the voice of the Church and repeating the law of the Commandments.
51 Sigmund Freud, *Totem and Taboo: Resemblances between the Psychic Lives of Savages and Neurotics*, trans. A.A. Brill (Amherst: Prometheus Books, 2000), 87; emphasis in original.
52 Girard, *The Scapegoat*, 101.
53 Ibid.
54 Ibid., 103.
55 Ibid., 104.
56 'The greatest symbol of this possibility – "its most glorious and succinct expression," Arendt states – is the Christian gospels' announcement of "glad tidings": "A child has been born unto us." It is this Christian figuration of the

miraculous through the image of the newborn that gives Arendt the term "natality."' See Fredrick M. Dolan's 'An Ambiguous Citation in Hannah Arendt's *The Human Condition,' Journal of Politics* 66.2 (May 2004): 606.
57 Hannah Arendt, *The Human Condition*, intro. Margaret Canovan (Chicago: University of Chicago Press, 1998), 178.
58 Girard, *The Scapegoat*, 175.
59 Giorgio Agamben, *Homo Sacer: Il potere sovrano e la nuda vita* (Turin: Einaudi, 1995), 94.
60 Arendt, *The Human Condition*, 246.
61 Zwinger, *Daughters, Fathers, and the Novel*, 9.
62 A brilliant exception to this trend in feminist thought is represented by the collection of essays *Refiguring the Father: New Feminist Readings of Patriarchy*, ed. Patricia Yaeger, Beth Kowaleski-Wallace, and Jerry Aline Flieger (Carbondale: Southern Illinois University Press, 1989). In the introduction, Yaeger, Kowaleski-Wallace, and Flieger revise obsolete monolithic notions of patriarchy, while propelling rereadings of the father figure that return to an abstraction of it or, better put, to a 'paternal metaphor' (18).
63 Henceforth HL.
64 It can never be stressed enough that, unlike in Anglo-American critical studies, in which many pages are devoted to the father–daughter relationship as a topic of investigation, in Italian studies this is a relatively unexplored topic.
65 Francesca Mazzucato, *Web Cam* (Venice: Marsilio, 2002).
66 Zwinger, *Daughters, Fathers, and the Novel*, 138.
67 Ibid., 9. See, for a different treatment of the feminist novel subgenre about fathers and daughters, Barbara Sheldon's *Daughters and Fathers in Feminist Novels* (New York: Peter Lang, 1997).
68 Zwinger, ibid., 187.
69 'Covering its object with the funereal trappings of mourning, melancholy confers upon it the phantasmagorical reality of what is lost; but insofar as such mourning is for an unobtainable object, the strategy of melancholy opens a space for the existence of the unreal and marks out a scene in which the ego may enter into relation with it and attempt an appropriation such as no other possession could rival and no loss possibly threaten.' Giorgio Agamben, *Stanzas: Word and Phantasm in Western Culture*, trans. Ronald L. Martinez (Minneapolis: University of Minnesota Press, 1993), 20.
70 'C'è davvero un legame tra la scelta di una professione scomoda e l'affetto morboso per un padre da sempre lontano?' (HL, front flap).
71 In *La bocca più di tutto mi piaceva* (Rome: Donzelli, 1996), Nadia Fusini verbalizes the adoration of a daughter for her father: 'Nessuno era bello come il mio innamorato ... Noi eravamo la vera coppia, ma quello era un segreto tra

noi ... Io lo amavo più della mamma' (9–10; 'No one was as beautiful as my love ... We were the real couple, but that was a secret between us ... I loved him more than my mother').
72 'A daughter is an apprentice; how she treats her father is how she'll treat her man.' Zwinger, *Daughters, Fathers, and the Novel*, 8.
73 Sigmund Freud, 'Mourning and Melancholia,' in *The Standard Edition of the Complete Psychological Works of Sigmund Freud*, ed. James Strachey (London: Hogarth Press, 1953), 14: 239–58.
74 'Freud's early hope that an attachment might be withdrawn and then given anew implied a certain interchangeability of objects as a *sign of hopefulness*, as if the prospect of entering life anew made use of a kind of promiscuity of libidinal aim.' See Judith Butler, *Precarious Life: The Powers of Mourning and Violence* (London: Verso, 2004), 21; emphasis added.
75 Ibid., 21.
76 Freud, 'Mourning and Melancholia,' 251.
77 'Because she is dutiful, she both acquiesces to her father's desire and exists to deny its very possibility; because she is desirable, she both provokes the very desire sentimental pieties exist to deny and embodies the fiction under cover of which the desire and the pieties alike operate.' Zwinger, *Daughters, Fathers, and the Novel*, 119.
78 Sigmund Freud, 'The Dissolution of the Oedipus Complex,' in *Standard Edition of Complete Works*, ed. Strachey, 19: 173–9.
79 Ibid., 173.
80 Ibid.
81 Although fully aware of the homosexual nature of Dora K.'s neurosis, I find *Hot Line* to be a text based on therapeutic needs, a self-written case of neurosis, and that is why I dare liken the two in this part of my study.
82 Freud, 'The Dissolution of the Oedipus Complex,' 178.
83 Ibid.
84 In *Hot Line* the connection with the then current event is explicitly allowed, 'Una volta l'ho vista piangere. So che parlava con Andrea ... un suo cliente fisso, vuole solo lei, telefona tutte le sere, se rispondo io mi chiama Bobbit' (HL 24; 'Once I saw her crying. I know she was talking to Andrea ... one of her regular clients, he only wants her, he calls her every evening, if I pick up he calls me Bobbit'). Later in the novel Lorena explains to a client instead that she chose her name because she liked this region of France.
85 Sigmund Freud, 'Medusa's Head,' in *Standard Edition of Complete Works*, ed. Strachey, 5: 105–6.

86 'Freud's theory of penis envy is deeply embedded in a scopic economy that privileges the visible; woman's sexual organ, which is neither seen nor one, is thus counted as none. It is the negative of the visible – and thus the only morphologically designatable – organ, the penis.' See Claire Kahane, 'The Woman with a Knife and the Chicken without a Head: Fantasms of Rage and Emptiness,' in *Psychoanalyses/Feminisms*, ed. Peter L. Rudnytsky and Andrew M. Gordon (Albany: State University of New York Press, 1999), 184.
87 Ibid.
88 Robert K. Barnhart, ed., *The Barnhart Concise Dictionary of Etymology*, 1st ed. (New York: HarperCollins Publishers, 1995), 516.
89 Slavoj Žižek, 'Melancholy and the Act,' *Critical Inquiry* 26.4 (Summer 2000): 658.
90 Freud, 'Mourning and Melancholia,' 246.
91 In *Hot Line* the notion of the sacrificial lamb of God is presented along with the notion of sacrifice – a scapegoat – for the betterment for society (HL 25), as previously seen in *La Dea dei baci*.
92 Freud, 'Female Sexuality,' in *The Standard Edition of Complete Works*, ed. Strachey, 5: 261.
93 Freud, 'Femininity,' in *Freud on Women: A Reader*, ed. and intro. Elisabeth Young-Bruehl (New York: W.W. Norton, 1990), 353.
94 Jacques Lacan, Jacques-Alain Miller (ed.), and Bruce Fink (trans.), *On Feminine Sexuality, the Limits of Love and Knowledge: The Seminar of Jacques Lacan*, book 20 (New York: Encore W.W. Norton, 1999), 73.
95 Nadia Fusini, 'Woman-Graphy,' in *The Lonely Mirror: Italian Perspectives on Feminist Theory*, ed. Paola Bono and Sandra Kemp (New York: Routledge, 1993), 49. Despite the innovative ways in which women write on pornography, Dacia Maraini comments (negatively) on how their specific interest in 'parts of the body' is somewhat 'grotesque' (*Un clandestino a bordo*, 58; *Stowaway on Board*, 37).
96 Silvia Vegetti Finzi writes: 'The law is engraved in her flesh, written on her nerves, but it is not possible for her to decipher it; she follows its command without ever understanding either its letter or its meaning. For its absence of herself to herself, she is excluded from wielding the *logos*. Her voice is pure *phone*, not speech; because speech demands a subject of discourse ... Whoever is not a subject in discourse, does not know how to say "I," cannot even be a subject of desire and pleasure, as we understand it.' Vegetti Finzi, 'The Female Animal,' in *The Lonely Mirror*, in Bono and Kemp, eds, *The Lonely Mirror*, 141.

97 Lorena's colourful descriptions of her female body, the bra being size E, the netfish hose, everything fits the mould of the female masquerade. The distinction between female masquerade and womanliness is that 'masquerade is present as the context provoking the patient's reaction-formation.' Mary Ann Doane, 'Masquerade Reconsidered: Further Thoughts on the Female Spectator,' *Discourse* 11.1 (Fall–Winter 1988–9): 49.
98 Žižek, 'Melancholy and the Act,' 658.
99 Ibid., 660.
100 I am working with the Freudian notion of the third woman, even if this has little to do with a physical third woman in the father's life. For further reference, please read Elizabeth Berg's 'The Third Woman,' *Diacritics* 12.2 (Summer 1982): 11–20.
101 Žižek, 'Melancholy and the Act,' 660.
102 'Freud was aware, of course, that every person repeats his relationship with his parents in the course of his ostensibly adult relationships. But it was left to [Melanie] Klein to grasp the meaning of this repetition for mourning. Beneath the loss of the adult other, she argues, there always lurks the threatened loss of the (internal) mother: "the poignancy of the actual loss of a loved person is ... greatly increased by the mourner's unconscious phantasies of having lost his *internal* 'good' objects as well." This is why, according to Klein, mourning is typically both so painful and prolonged: "early mourning is revived whenever grief is experienced in later life."' See Isaac D. Balbus, *Mourning and Modernity: Essays in Psychoanalysis of Contemporary Society* (New York: Other Press, 2005), 82.
103 Žižek, 'Melancholy and the Act,' 661.
104 The example Žižek makes about Archer and Olenska's love in *The Age of Innocence* is a case in point ('Melancholy and the Act,' 661).
105 Vladimir Nabokov, 'Good Readers and Good Writers,' in *Lectures on Literature*, ed. Fredson Bowers (New York: Harcourt Brace Jovanovich, 1980), 3.
106 Vladimir Nabokov, *Lolita* (New York: Vintage Books, 1989), 16. Henceforth LO.
107 In 1996 Pia Pera participated to the *Salone del Libro* of Turin dedicated to women writers with her talk entitled 'Migrazioni femminili' ('Female migrations'), later published in *L'Indice dei libri del mese* 8 (1996): 46. On this occasion Pera explained the different parameters in which the female character is situated within a novel: 'While in folk tales it is common practice to move characters from one story to another, it is rare to find this movement in the novel. When it happens there is the authorial awareness that he/she is putting his/her text in relationship with another. Unlike the folk tale variations which

are anonymously and collectively produced – something in which textual critique appears devoid of a specific projectuality – a textual (novelistic) deviation from a text is a particular form of criticism.'
108 According to Vladimir Nabokov, the other two possible 'grenades' for American society might have been, 'a Negro-White marriage which is a complete and glorious success resulting in lots of children and grandchildren; and the total atheist who lives a happy and useful life, and dies in his sleep at the age of 106.' Nabokov, 'On a Book Entitled *Lolita*,' in *Lolita*, 314.
109 Nabokov was not interested in 'didactic fiction,' nor did he ever want Lolita to have a 'moral in tow.' Ibid.
110 Umberto Eco was one of the first authors to see the absurd behind Nabokov's novel and parody it in his pastiche 'Nonita,' in *Diario Minimo* (1963) (Milan: Mondadori, 1988), 11–16. Playing on his evident homonymy with the protagonist, Eco imagines a perverse love for an old woman whose fond memories mark the incipit, 'Fiore della mia adolescenza, angoscia delle mie notti. Potrò mai rivederti. Nonita. Nonita. Nonita. Tre sillabe, come una negazione fatta di dolcezza. Nonita che io possa ricordarti sinché la tua immagine non sarà tenebra e il tuo luogo sepolcro' (11; 'Flower of my youth, anguish of my nights. Will I ever see you again? Nonita. Nonita. Nonita. Three syllables, like a negation made with sweetness. Nonita, that I might remember you until your image will be darkness and your site your grave'). In Eco's case, perversion is love for an old *parchetta* (as from the three female figures cutting the thread of life in mythology), a horrifying term to designate 'quelle creature già segnate dai rigori di un'età implacabile, piegate dal ritmo fatale degli ottant'anni, minate atrocemente dal fantasma desiderabile della senescenza' (12; 'those creatures already implacably marked by their age, bent by the fatal pace of their eighty years, atrociously sapped by the longed-for ghost of senescence'). Of course, there is also the issue of the Lolita short story by Heinz von Eschwege, whose tale appeared in 1916 under the pseudonym Heinz von Lichberg. Michael Maar casts much (believable) doubt on whether Nabokov – living in Berlin at the time – knew of von Lichberg's story. See Michael Maar, *The Two Lolitas*, trans. Perry Anderson (London: Verso, 2005).
111 Ralph Blumenthal, 'Disputed "Lolita" Spinoff Is Dropped by Publisher,' *New York Times*, 7 November 1998: B7.
112 See the distinction that Linda Hutcheon makes in her *A Theory of Parody: The Teachings of Twentieth-Century Art Forms* (New York: Methuen, 1985), 40.

113 Clearly the issue of copyright was much more at stake than any artistic or ideological principle, a mere excuse when talking copyright money. Likewise, Dmitri Nabokov's lawyer, Peter Skolnic, showed a similar display of theoretical 'misunderstanding' when, upon hearing the decision of Farrar, Straus & Giroux to cancel publication of *Lo's Diary*, he said: 'If Pera's "version" of Lolita would have been allowed to stand the next author is free to say, "Ah, there's a good idea: I'll tell it from the perspective of another character."' See Blumenthal, 'Disputed "Lolita,"' A15, A22.

114 Dmitri Nabokov, 'On a Book Entitled *Lo's Diary*,' in Pera, *Lo's Diary*, vii–viii.

115 Ibid., ix.

116 Examples of rewriting without legal suits and filings abound, as in Jean Rhys's case with *Wide Sargasso Sea* (New York: Norton, 1992), a rewriting of *Jane Eyre*. In Rhys's novel, Jane Eyre's mad woman retells the story from her point of view, that is, the experiences of the mistreated first wife. Rhys therefore utilizes, just as Nabokov's lawyer so vehemently complained about with Pia Pera's story, a different perspective from the one Charlotte Brontë chose for her rendition of the story. Perhaps it succeeded because Rhys's was more a case of Gérard Genette's 'transposition' rather than parody. Whereas parody is a limited modification, 'transposition can give rise to works of vast dimensions, such as *Faust* or *Ulysses*, whose textual amplitude and aesthetic and/or ideological ambition may mask or even completely obfuscate their hypertextual character.' See Genette, *Palimpsests: Literature in the Second Degree*, trans. Channa Newman and Claude Doubinsky (Lincoln: University of Nebraska Press, 1997), 213. Or perhaps, I would argue, because it was the rewriting of a deceased woman's novel – with no immediate heirs – and came from the same tradition apparently, nobody accused Jean Rhys of sheer plagiarism.

117 'In a case closely followed by publishers because of its implications for copyright law, a retelling of Vladimir Nabokov's "Lolita" from the nymphet's point of view, whose publication was abruptly canceled last fall, will go forward as a result of an unusual agreement worked out over the last six months.' See Peter Applebome, 'Pact Reached on U.S. Edition of *Lolita* Retelling,' *New York Times*, 17 June 1999: E1, E10.

118 When it was first published, however, *Lolita* was certainly considered to be, at the very least, a controversial book, as evidenced by the story of its tormented publication. Controversies are instrumental for the development of the novel genre. It should not be forgotten that Nabokov's *Lolita* gained a reputation as a canonical text, as part of class reading lists – even becoming a key reading in Teheran for women who seek advancement in their society

– only in rather recent times, and certainly not when it was published. See Azar Nafisi's recent *Reading* Lolita *in Teheran: A Memoir in Books* (New York: Random House, 2003).

119 In *Dopo la fine: Sulla condizione postuma della letteratura* (Turin: Einaudi, 1996) Giulio Ferroni states, 'La permanenza fisica dei segni grafici e dei testi con essi composti ... hanno diffuso fin dai tempi più remoti la nozione del carattere 'postumo' delle scritture stesse, facendole sentire come tracce e lasciti di vite (individuali e collettive) concluse, paradossali conservatrice e prosecutrici di vita oltre morte. Nei modi più diversi l'atto dello scrivere ha rinviato a una vita futura, a un agire e persistere "dopo," quando sarebbero per sempre venuti meno il corpo, la mano, e la mente dello scriba; e all'inverso nell'atto del leggere si è riconosciuto un guardare da "dopo," un modo di riappropriarsi di tracce fisiche di realtà consumate, di sentire vivo un passato morto' (3; 'The physical permanence of graphic signs and the texts they have composed ... has propagated the notion of the 'posthumous' of written texts since remote times. It establishes them like traces and legacies of concluded lives [individual and collective], paradoxically keepers and pursuers of life beyond death. In various ways, the act of writing has been deferred to a future life, to acting and persisting "after," when the body, the hand, and the mind of the scribe would have expired forever; inversely, in the act of reading it has been recognized as an act of looking from "after," from aftertime, as a way of re-appropriation of physical traces of consumed realities, of feeling a dead past as alive.').

120 The most convincing analysis of the positive/negative dichotomy of postmodernism is the one proposed by Margaret Rose in *Parody: Ancient, Modern, and Post-modern* (Cambridge: Cambridge University Press, 1993), 197. 'The historically neutral dichotomy of Negative/Positive ... has been used largely in order to describe the way in which some theories of the post-modern have moved from the negative function of describing the end or failings of modernism, or of other theories of the post-modern, to describing something more creative or innovative. Further to this, the dichotomy of Negative/Positive is intended to show the way in which the negative and positive conceptions, and uses, of post-modernism have sometimes interacted with each other in ways similar to the negative and positive poles of an electric charge, to produce a variety of different views as well as certain continuous negative versus positive streams of thought.'

121 This is how Linda Hutcheon puts the question central to the novel in contemporary times: 'The novel today often still claims to be a genre rooted in the realities of historical time and geographical space, yet narrative is

276 Notes to pages 166–7

presented as only narrative, as its own reality – that is, as artifice. Often overt narratorial comment or an internal self-reflecting mirror (a *mise-en-abyme*) will signal this dual ontological status to the reader. Or ... the pointing to the literariness of the text may be achieved by using parody: in the background will stand another text against which the new creation is implicitly to be both measured and understood ... What is interesting is that, unlike what is more traditionally regarded as parody, the modern form does not always permit one of the texts to fare any better or worse than the other. It is the fact that they *differ* that this parody emphasizes and, indeed, dramatizes.' See Hutcheon, *A Theory of Parody*, 31; emphasis in original.

122 'The hypertext invites us to engage in a relational reading, the flavor of which, however perverse, may well be condensed in an adjective recently coined by Philippe Lejeune: a palimpsestuous reading.' See Genette, *Palimpsests*, 399.

123 The intertextual thread linking the two novels even reinvents the generic limits dictated by the concept of national literature, following, it would seem, a path already taken by Nabokov himself and by his contribution to the concept of transnationality as intended in modern times.

124 Hutcheon, *A Theory of Parody*, 35.

125 Ibid., 34.

126 Genette, *Palimpsests*, 25.

127 Ferroni, *Dopo la fine*, 3.

128 In speaking of the transformation of codes in her seminal *Alice Doesn't: Feminism, Semiotics, Cinema* (Bloomington: Indiana University Press, 1984), Teresa de Lauretis notes that 'different contents are culturally assigned to the same sign-vehicle or whenever new sign-vehicles are produced. In this manner a new text, a different interpretation of a text – any new practice of discourse – sets up a different configuration of content, introduces other cultural meanings that in turn transform the codes and rearrange the semantic universe of the society that produces it' (34).

129 By these two adjectives, Hutcheon means that parodic use of another text is limited to the discourse between the stylistic features of the two texts, while satire puts into play the social and moral components of the period and history in which such texts are written. See Hutcheon, *A Theory of Parody*, 43. Margaret Rose criticizes the elimination of the comic from Hutcheon's theory on parody, perhaps in fear that the comic can be reductive with respect to parody. See Rose, *Parody*, 238–42. For Hutcheon, parody must be considered as difference (see note 121 above), which brings her to define parody as the postmodern genre. Seymour Chatman, in 'Parody and Style,' *Poetics*

Today 22.1 (Spring 2001), has much to say about the 'making of parody the prototypical postmodern genre' (28). Drawing distinctions between parody, pastiche, satire, and intertexuality *tout court*, Chatman seems to agree with Hutcheon on many things, though with different words. They share the necessity for segregating parody from the conventionally comic; the notion of the duplicitous homage and ridicule the new text makes on the previous; the understanding that parody can be achieved only when readers are familiar with the previous text; and, last, that parody can only work on what 'has been *already* textually modeled' (30).

130 Linda Hutcheon argues that 'if a new parodic form does not develop when an old one becomes insufficiently motivated, the old form tends to degenerate into pure convention.' Hutcheon, *Narcissistic Narrative: The Metafictional Paradox* (Waterloo, ON: Wilfrid Laurier University Press, 1980), 24.

131 In speaking of the transformation of codes, Teresa de Lauretis notes that 'different contents are culturally assigned to the same sign-vehicle or whenever new sign-vehicles are produced. In this manner a new text, a different interpretation of a text – any new practice of discourse – sets up a different configuration of content, introduces other cultural meanings that in turn transform the codes and rearrange the semantic universe of the society that produces it.' De Lauretis, *Alice Doesn't*, 34.

132 Ellen White, 'Editorial Review,' at http://www.amazon.com/gp/product/0964374021/104-2391390-5442331?v=glance&n=283155.

133 It's interesting to see how the use of names is another parameter by which Dolly vindicates the exact knowledge of her story and does not want to hide anything from readers. For instance, Nabokov's Mrs "Richard F. Schiller" becomes Mrs Schlegel, and her maiden name Haze becomes Maze.

134 'His blindness is wholly in keeping with his transgressions against her – his violation, as he ultimately admits, of the sacred rights of childhood.' See Ellen Pifer, *Demon or Doll: Images of the Child in Contemporary Writing and Culture* (Charlottesville: University of Virginia Press, 2000), 79.

135 Produced by the mutations in the treatment of the nymphet motif as by the profound revision in its form, linguistic and structural translation, the most innovative aspect of the discourse is achieved through the recovery of Lolita's voice as a narrative element, integrally revisited, and obeying thus a female desire of justice for Lolita already expressed by poetess Kim Morrissey: 'Lolita is a book where the fictional character of Dolores – Lolita – has no voice. And you never hear her side of the story. And so there's a great desire, I think, for women to have those voices that are traditionally left out of literature heard.' See her interview with Camille Paglia, in *Vamps and Tramps: New Essays* (New

York: Vintage Books, 1994), 157. With her collection titled *Poems for Men Who Dream of Lolita* (Regina, SK: Coteau Books 1992), Morrissey manifests an interest for the character in American society, and in feminist writing in particular. She explains to Paglia: 'When I wrote these poems, I wanted people to *never* be able to say the word "Lolita" again and use it in the clichéd way that we have' (*Vamps and Tramps*, 157).

136 'How can techniques in narrative point of view control a reader's sympathy for other characters? ... (1) We are more likely to sympathise with people when we have a lot of information about their lives, motivations, fears etc. (2) We sympathise with people when we see other people who do not share our access to their inner lives judging them harshly or incorrectly. In life, we get this kind of information through intimacy, friendship or Oprah Winfrey. In fiction we get it through the narrator, either reliably reported by the narrator or through direct access to the minds of characters.' Mark Currie, *Postmodern Narrative Theory* (New York: St Martin's Press, 1998), 19.

137 Pifer, *Demon or Doll*, 76.

138 Fascination with this particular aspect of Lolita goes a long way. In Jim Jarmusch's *Broken Flowers* (Focus Features, 2005) Sharon Stone and her fictional daughter play a scene in which not only the classic heart-shaped glasses but the same suffocating small-town atmosphere is conveyed. *Broken Flowers*, like *Lolita*, is a road picture. The element of stillness seems to be emphasized by the apparent paradox of movement vs. stillness of the topic.

139 In talking about the migration of characters, Pera notes: 'When a character is a citizen of a work that denies him/her an all-round portrayal, he/she prefers to migrate to other books where he/she hopes to find justice, to see her/his most elementary "human rights" recognized' ('Migrazioni femminili,' 46).

140 Linda Hutcheon, 'Modern Parody and Bakhtin,' *Rethinking Bakhtin: Extensions and Challenges*, ed. Gary Saul Morson and Caryl Emerson (Evanston: Nortwestern University Press, 1989), 102–3.

141 Leona Toker does not spare any contempt for those critics who have perpetuated Lolita's image without possibility for her redemption. Toker states: 'Repeated reading reveals that Dolly's troubled inner life, although not conventionally pure, is by no means vulgar or callous. It is amazing, though, how often the effect of the first reading persists and how many critics never change their attitude that they share with Charlotte Haze and with Humbert at his worst moments.' Toker, *Nabokov: The Mystery of Literary Structures* (Ithaca: Cornell University Press, 1989), 205–6. In agreement with this line of thought, I would cite a passage from one of the most read manuals on the Russian author, Douglas Fowler's *Reading Nabokov*, which corrobo-

rates Toker's point about the critics misogyny: 'Thus many different factors work to keep Humbert out of the center of our conception of moral crime and our condemnation of it, to maintain his status as a Nabokovian favorite: he does not kill Charlotte; he does not seduce Lolita; his sexual enjoyment of her is imperfect because of her indifference; her thralldom to him depends in part on her own indifference, rootlessness, and meretriciousness, for Lolita wants to be entertained. Humbert goes to enormous lengths to try to make her happy, and she encourages this. He is in the grip of a real passion, is constantly aware of his own guilt, and does not fool himself about the cruelty for which he is responsible.' Fowler, *Reading Nabokov* (Ithaca: Cornell University Press, 1974), 152. Fowler speaks of a twelve-year-old girl as if she were a full-grown woman with her mind already set as to how to entertain an erotic and sentimental relationship with her stepfather! Not to mention Leslie Fiedler who, as Pifer reports, assumes that 'it is the naïve child, the female, the American who corrupts the sophisticated adult, the male, the European.' Pifer, *Demon or Doll*, 69.

142 Maurice Couturier notes in speaking of Humbert's trial: 'He tries to persuade himself that his crime is not that grave; after all, it is Lolita who has taken the initiative and, further, she was no longer a virgin. In reading these contradictory comments, the reader wonders if Humbert actually believes himself to have committed a crime by abusing this twelve-year-old girl; taking into account Lolita's boldness and bawdiness, one tends to say to oneself sometimes that Humbert is as much a victim as a criminal, as in these lurid stories in which the woman, after provoking the man, accuses him of having raped her. After all these ethical and juridical derivations, we don't quite know what to think anymore and we would tend to justify the accused' (*Nabokov, ou la tyrannie de l'auteur* [(Paris: Éditions du Seuil, 1993)], 178; '[I]l tente de se persuader que son crime n'est pas d'une telle gravité; après tout, c'est Lolita qui a pris l'initiative et, d'ailleurs, elle n'était plus vierge. En lisant ces commentaires contradictoires, le lecteur se demande si Humbert croit vraiment avoir commis un crime en abusant de cette fille de douze ans; compte tenu de la hardiesse et de la paillardise de Lolita, il a tendance à se dire parfois que Humbert est autant victime que criminel, comme dans ces histoires louches où la femme, après avoir provoqué l'homme, accuse celui-ci de l'avoir violée. Après toutes ces dérives éthiques et finalement juridiques, nous ne savons plus très bien quoi penser et serions disposés à gracier tout bonnement l'accusé').

143 Couturier notes, in slightly different terms, that Nabokov often would make fun of and mock illustrious writers. He argues: 'In any case, he incites us to show our critical sense and to not succumb to the authority of more famous

writers, himself included' ('Nabokov convoquait les écrivains les plus illustres pour les contrer, se moquer d'eux parfois. Dans tous les cas, il nous incite à faire preuve de sens critique et à ne jamais succomber passivement à l'autorité des écrivains les plus célèbres, lui compris'; *Nabokov*, 77).

144 See Marita Nadal's 'The Death of a Beautiful Woman Is, Unquestionably, the Most Poetical Topic in the World: Poetic and Parodic Treatment of Women in Poe's Tales,' in *Gender, I-deology: Essays on Theory, Fiction and Film*, ed. Chantal Cornut-Gentille D'Arcy and José Ángel García Landa (Amsterdam: Rodopi, 1996), 151–63.

145 Speaking in the third person about himself, Humbert Humbert tries to assimilate his love for nymphets to illustrious cases of young muses loved by artists, namely, Dante's Beatrice and Petrarch's Laura (LO 19).

146 According to Nomi Tamir-Ghez, Nabokov makes four key strategic decisions about *Lolita*'s rhetorical structure, all geared to ensure a 'desired delicate balance between the reader's feelings of identification with and rejection of Humbert' ('The Art of Persuasion in Nabokov's *Lolita*,' in *Vladimir Nabokov's Lolita: A Casebook*, ed. Ellen Pifer (Oxford: Oxford University Press, 2002), 23; emphasis in original. Humbert's emotional world – narrated in the first person – shapes the context for the story, for 'the author wishes the reader to sympathize (at least partially or temporally) with the hero' (23). The *choice of character* appears to be among the novel's best strategies: 'In order further to secure our empathy for the criminal-speaker, Nabokov presents us with an intelligent, well-educated, middle-class man with good manners and a sharp tongue, a man with whom the average reader can easily identify,' but a man who is also 'a sophisticated rhetorician' (23). Last but not least, we have Nabokov's most important decision: '*to give Humbert full control over the discourse*' (23).

147 Maria Nadotti was the most brilliant reviewer of the novel, bringing to the fore many of the most relevant points of Pera's parody. See Nadotti, 'Lolita II, la vendetta,' *L'Unità*, 13 November 1995: 16.

148 As I was finishing the writing of this book, echoes of the famous suit still resonated in American newspapers and journals. Peter Skolnic, Dmitri Nabokov's lawyer, wrote a letter in response to a piece by D.T. Max about literary licence, 'The Injustice Collector' (*The New Yorker*, 19 June 2006), which appeared ibid., 10–17 July 2006, 8. Skolnic claims that the battle against the publication of *Lo's Diary* was anything but unsuccessful – as Max's article appeared to claim. In Skolnic's letter, there is no reference to the name of the author, Pia Pera, nor to the fact that she did not write any postface to the American translation of her own novel.

149 See Hutcheon, *A Theory of Parody*, 34.

Chapter 3

1 Braidotti, *Metamorphoses: Towards a Materialist Theory of Becoming* (Cambridge: Polity Press, 2002), 30.
2 This is the already mentioned case of Dworkin and MacKinnon in which too strong a radical position can pay service to ultra-conservative groups. For a better understanding of MacKinnon's position about sexual politics, please read her fundamental discussion 'Not a Moral Issue,' in *Feminism Unmodified: Discourses on Life and Law* (Cambridge, MA: Harvard University Press, 1987), 146–62.
3 Braidotti, *Metamorphoses*, 32.
4 Ibid., 11–12.
5 Judith Butler, *Bodies That Matter: On the Discursive Limits of Sex* (New York: Routledge, 1993), 30.
6 Braidotti, *Metamorphoses*, 33.
7 Judith Butler, *Undoing Gender* (New York: Routledge, 2004), 5; emphasis added.
8 Ibid., 8.
9 Maria Rosa Cutrufelli's edition of *Nella città proibita* (Milan: Marco Tropea, 1997), a collection of short stories by Italian women writers (*In the Forbidden City: An Anthology of Erotic Fiction by Women*, trans. Vincent Bertolini [Chicago: University of Chicago Press, 2000]) contributed to a more general awareness of this mode of Italian women writers' attempts to break with tradition in all senses. In 2004 Einaudi published another anthology, *Ragazze che dovresti conoscere: The Sex Anthology* (Turin: Einaudi, 2004), which lists known writers of a younger generation such as Simona Vinci, Teresa Ciabatti, and Elena Stancanelli. The most recent collection is *Tua, con tutto il corpo: Antologia di racconti erotici al femminile*, ed. Francesca Mazzucato (Faloppio: Lietocolle, 2005), an anthology of erotic short stories by emerging female writers (Daniela Gambino, Monica Maggi, and Laura Guglielmi among others) that looks at the meanderings of eroticism much in the same garb as Anaïs Nin.
10 To my knowledge, only Guido Morselli's *Un dramma borghese* (Milan: Adelphi, 1978) deals with this theme.
11 Melania Mazzucco, *Il bacio della Medusa* (Milan: Baldini e Castoldi, 1996); henceforth BM.
12 In *Il doppio itinerario della scrittura: La donna nella tradizione letteraria italiana* (Turin: Einaudi, 1998), yet another critical project to explain the void created by the absence of women in Italian literary tradition and histories, Marina Zancan indicates heterosexuality as indispensable for a correct understanding of influences, of the son's need for domination of the

mother, his source of life, and demonstrates how, in that union mother–son, one finds the origin of the 'immaginario poetico' that unites both sexes, (vi–viii).
13 Anne Sexton, 'The Abortion,' in *Collected Poems* (Boston: Houghton Mifflin, 1999), 62.
14 Luce Irigaray, *Thinking the Difference: For a Peaceful Revolution*, trans. Karin Montin (New York: Routledge, 1994), xiv. Within the context of Italian political engagement for women's rights should be mentioned Irigaray's seminal lecture 'Come diventare delle donne civili?' given in Rome on 8 April 1988, to the Italian Communist Women, later published in *Reti* 3–4 (May–August 1988): 6–16.
15 Social protest appears to Maraini as the tool for a concrete change of woman's conditions. The *parola* is the medium through which Maraini chooses to reconsider the role of woman in Italian society. As Maria Grazia Sumeli Weinberg writes in *Invito alla lettura di Dacia Maraini* (Pretoria: University of South Africa Press, 1993), 'In women's case, victims for centuries of seclusion, the word serves to relate the unsaid and to reveal in a more open and flexible speech all that society has always forbidden them: the existence of their own speaking body, in other words, of a legitimate feminine representation' (21).
16 For the development of Italian women's struggles for the abortion law, see 'History of Two Laws' in *Italian Feminist Thought: A Reader*, ed. Paola Bono and Sandra Kemp (New York: Routledge, 1991), 211–33. Bono and Kemp translated relevant documents on the abortion issue such as 'Manifesto, 1978,' offering their point of view on the 'questionable links' of abortion with sexuality and explaining how solidarity among women was strongly fuelled by the 'repressive nature of the legislation which considered abortion a crime' (211).
17 'Lettera sull'aborto,' in *Un clandestino a bordo. Le donne: La maternità negata il corpo segnato* (Milan, Rizzoli, 1996), 7–34; henceforth LA. 'Letter on Abortion,' in *Stowaway on Board*, trans. Victoria Poletti Offredi and Giovanna Bellesia (Lafayette: Bordighera Press, 2000), 3–19; henceforth LA 2.
18 The double condition of Dacia Maraini as a writer and as an activist in the women's movement is rooted in her conviction that only a woman can speak about another woman, as Maryse Jeuland-Meynaud pertinently points out in her article 'Dacia Maraini: Polémique ou littérature?' in *Les femmes écrivains en Italie aux XIXe et XXe siècles*, Actes du colloque international, Aix-en Provence, 14–16 November 1991, ed. Marie-Anne Rubat de Mérac (Aix-en-Provence: Publications de l'Université de Provence, 1993) : 'Dacia's feminism is engagement plus writing. The writer delivers us a pressing message whose constituents will immediately be seen to later evaluate their *literariness*' (206).

19 The expression 'political aesthetic' is Sharon Wood's. See her essay on Maraini, 'The Silencing of Women: The Political Aesthetic of Dacia Maraini (born 1936),' in her *Italian Women's Writing 1860–1994* (London: Athlone, 1995), 216–31.
20 Ibid., xiv.
21 Rita Felski, *Beyond Feminist Aesthetics: Feminist Literature and Social Change* (Cambridge, MA: Harvard University Press, 1989), 83.
22 Substantial documentation about the years preceding the abortion law is offered in the chapter 'Aborto: La decisione alle donne. E il conflitto si fa manifesto,' in *UDI. Laboratorio di politica delle donne*, ed. Maria Michetti, Margherita Repetto, and Luciana Viviani (Rome: Cooperativa Libera Stampa, 1984), 405–38. This chapter also documents Maraini's involvement in women's rights as a member of groups of prominent women who denounced clandestine abortions in 1974 (416).
23 See Bono and Kemp, eds, *Italian Feminist Thought*, 37. Women's autonomy is being challenged again in Italy. See Ritanna Armeni, *La colpa delle donne: Dal referendum sull'aborto alla fecondazione assistita. Storie, battaglie e riflessioni* (Milan: Ponte alle Grazie, 2006) for an interesting analysis of what – from being a woman's right to choose – has now become an opposition between 'the culture of death' and 'the culture of life,' particularly after the approval of the law on assisted procreation. Though this is a topic of great import, there are few contemporary literary narratives on this new aspect of choosing or not to give life.
24 Oriana Fallaci, *Lettera a un bambino mai nato* (Milan: Rizzoli, 1975).
25 Tommasina Gabriele, 'The Pregnant Nun: Suor Attanasia and the Metaphor of Arrested Maternity in Dacia Maraini,' *Italica* 81.1 (Spring 2004): 70.
26 Dacia Maraini, *L'età del malessere* (Turin: Einaudi, 1963); *The Age of Malaise*, trans. Frances Frenaye (New York: Grove Press, 1963).
27 Dacia Maraini, *La vacanza* (Rome: Lerici, 1962).
28 Stuart Flexner, ed., *Random House Dictionary*, 2nd ed. (New York: Random House, 1987), 6, 1128.
29 *Il Nuovo Zingarelli*, ed. Miro Dogliotti and Luigi Rosiello, 11th ed. (Bologna: Zanichelli, 1986), 9.
30 *Isolina: La donna tagliata a pezzi* (Milan: Mondadori, 1985) is the account of a homicide in Verona. This story of a young woman who was literally cut in pieces and thrown in the Adige to save an officer's honour because of her death from an unwanted and thus forced abortion is representative of Maraini's moral standpoint in her accusations against a society in which women are 'used' for men's benefit, and is thus closer to her activism of the 1970s.
31 Dacia Maraini, *Donna in guerra* (Turin: Einaudi, 1975); *Woman at War*, trans. Mara Benetti and Elspeth Spottiswood (New York: Italica Press, 1988).

32 In this vision of abortion, Vannina's character embodies an Italian feminist understanding of abortion as an unpleasant, but at times necessary, option for a woman. Adriana Cavarero words the issue of maternity in the same terminology, '[T]he mother is the *container* of the unborn child.' Cavarero, *In Spite of Plato*, trans. Serena Anderlini-D'Onofrio and Aine O'Healy (New York: Routledge, 1995), 67; emphasis added.
33 Maraini, *Donna in guerra*, 262. In 'Dacia Maraini's *Donna in guerra*: Victory or Defeat?' in *Contemporary Women Writers in Italy: A Modern Renaissance*, ed. Santo Aricò (Amherst: University of Massachusetts Press, 1990), Anthony J. Tamburri underscores the transcendent sexual imagery, rich in its mimetical, yet metaphorical meanings, utilized by Maraini as a linguistic and rhetorical technique for showing repression, as well as Giacinto's role in exemplifying 'male objectification of a female and society's expectations' for submissive creatures able to reproduce, since 'motherhood is the essence of a female's nature' (146). While this novel is widely considered by women scholars of Maraini's work as her most programmatically narrative work, a response and a follow-up to Sibilla Aleramo's *Una donna*, Tamburri wonders whether *Donna in guerra*, 'actually contains an anti-male stance merely because she does not advocate "separatism"' (148).
34 Tamburri, 'Dacia Maraini's *Donna in Guerra*,' 148.
35 Maraini, *Donna in guerra*, 246.
36 Dacia Maraini, *La donna perfetta* (Turin: Einaudi, 1975).
37 Dacia Maraini, *Lettere a Marina* (Milan: Bompiani, 1981); *Letters to Marina*, trans. Dick Kitto and Elspeth Spottiswood (Freedom, CA: The Crossing Press, 1987).
38 Dacia Maraini, *Il treno per Helsinki* (Turin: Einaudi, 1984); *The Train*, trans. Dick Kitto and Elspeth Spottiswood (London: Camden Press, 1988).
39 Dacia Maraini and Piera degli Esposti, *Storia di Piera* (Milan: Bompiani, 1980), 64. See Aine O'Healy's article on Marco Ferreri's cinematic adaptation of the book, 'Filming Female "Autobiography": Maraini, Ferreri, and Piera's Own Story,' in *Feminine Feminists: Cultural Practices in Italy*, ed. Giovanna Miceli Jeffries (Minneapolis: University of Minnesota Press, 1995), 190–298.
40 Felski, *Beyond Feminist Aesthetics*, 138.
41 Maraini, *Lettere a Marina*, 43.
42 Dacia Maraini, *La lunga vita di Marianna Ucrìa* (Milan: Rizzoli, 1990).
43 Maraini, *Lettere a Marina*, 15–16; emphasis added. Unlike in the English language, in Italian the foetus is not an 'it' but a 'he.' Mention of the foetus is always made in the masculine, the Italian linguistic convention for the neuter form. Maraini's own foetus was a boy, and it is natural for her to discuss the foetus in terms of the sex of her own baby.
44 *Letters to Marina*, 17; emphasis added.

45 *Lettere a Marina*, 16–18; emphasis added.
46 *Letters to Marina*, 18–20; emphasis added.
47 Use of this locution is made in both *Il treno* (65) and in *Lettere a Marina* (15).
48 Maraini, *Il treno per Helsinki*, 74; emphasis added.
49 Maraini, *The Train*, 65, 66; emphasis added.
50 At the Turin Book Fair, in 1996, while reiterating her position on the gendered aspect of writing, Maraini also expressed renewed concerns for women's condition. Further, she poignantly demonstrated that women are forced to make choices in order to pursue a career (*professione*) because jobs are still modelled after male ideals and needs, and are unfit to meet women's needs. These statements were taped and graciously provided to me by Silvia Verdiani of Turin.
51 See note 17 above.
52 Dacia Maraini, *Voci*. (Milan: Rizzoli, 1994); *Voices*, trans. Dick Kitto and Elspeth Spottiswood (London: Serpent's Tail, 1997).
53 Maraini, *Voci*, 262, 265, 268.
54 Maraini, *Voices* 215, 217, 220.
55 In her analysis of contemporary novels that employ the abortion motif, Wilt remarks: 'Abortion, a malleable topos, seems to work most often under this law of plot: if abortion represents the unholy domain of control, the plot will dissent from, perhaps thwart it. To support abortion, which lends itself so easily to the unholy domain of control, the novelist will have to place the act in the domain of surprise, resistance to control. If a man attempts to control a woman through pregnancy the plot will resist with abortion ...; if a man attempts to control a woman through abortion, or a woman attempts to control 'nature' with choice, the plot will resist with pregnancy.' See her *Abortion, Choice, and Contemporary Fiction: The Armageddon of Maternal Instinct* (Chicago: University of Chicago Press, 1990), 4. Maraini seems to resist this notion of surprise, and prefers to engage her characters in more traditional narratives of power and subjection.
56 An interesting study could be undertaken in regard to Maraini's account of Conrad's story in *Voci* (272–3). The narrating voice – Michela – employs this plot to justify and explain to herself the sense of identification with Angela and her tragedy. The similitude between a woman and a boat is, of course, nothing new, but what probably makes Conrad's story so striking for Maraini – who also translated *The Secret Sharer* (*Il compagno segreto* [Milan: Rizzoli, 2001]) – is the possessive form, which in English makes clear the possessor of the object.
57 Vessel is an oft-used metaphor. In 'Abortion Rights Alchemy and the United States Supreme Court: What's Wrong and How to Fix It,' in *Perspectives on the Politics of Abortion*, ed. Ted G. Jelen (Westport: Praeger, 1995) Eileen McDonagh

discusses the *Roe v. Wade* decision of the U.S. Supreme Court. In making its decision, the Court did not carefully analyse the condition of pregnancy. Through her in-class discussions with her students, McDonagh was able to identify five different perceptions (and definitions) of pregnancy, namely, those of (1) women as vessels carrying children in their bodies, (2) the one regarding the fetal development, (3) pregnancy as result of sex, (4) as a burdensome condition, and (5) its value to society (23–30). In 2006 we are all too aware of the reversibility of such a decision, which might affect – once again – women's possibility of controlling of their sexuality and reproductive functions. In a recent article, 'Reversing Roe' (*The New Yorker*, 26 June 2006), Cynthia Gorney highlights the dangerous situation in South Dakota, where law HB1215 banning abortion was just passed in plain violation of the Roe v. Wade 1973 Supreme Court decision. This South Dakota law shows the 'on-going dispute over the tactics of managing Americans' ambivalence about abortion – whether to work at it bit by bit, in an effort to convince voters, politicians, and judges of the merits of laws that close off access to abortion without banning it outright; or whether that saves only some babies' lives, to use the movement's vernacular, while doing violence both to other babies and to the whole philosophical construct of "right to life"' (52). Also Lea Melandri complains about the relative lack of power that women have today in Italian politics and social reform, a case in point being the fight over stem-cell research. Trying to address many issues in the name of feminism today has not meant possessing a stronger ability to modify ourselves and the existing environment; 'Il femminismo è ancora in silenzio' (*Liberazione*, 12 January 2005).

58 Maraini, 'Lettera sull'aborto,' 16; 'Letter on Abortion,' 7.
59 Marina Warner, *Six Myths in Our Time: Little Angels, Little Monsters, Beautiful Beasts, and More* (New York: Random House, 1995), 3–23.
60 Cavarero, *In Spite of Plato*, 64.
61 Rosi Braidotti, *Nomadic Subjects: Embodiment and Sexual Difference in Contemporary Feminist Theory* (New York: Columbia University Press, 1994), 79.
62 Cavarero would object to Maraini's current reconsiderations on abortion and the power of women. The philosopher writes in her analysis of Demeter's myth: 'Regardless of how the law addresses the problem, it is clear that by now birth has been removed not only from sovereignty of maternal power but also from the basic feminine experience of maternity. Here indeed not only maternity, understood as reproductive function, and the fetus, understood as a legal subject, are concerns of the state, but so is the ovum, in its aseptic separateness and unpredictable wanderings through more or less compliant wombs ... Risking their lives and breaking the law, or, more precisely, risking their lives because they are breaking the law, women

demonstrate that they know that maternity is indeed their own concern, not an issue of public law. It is a question of the irreducible individuality of every woman as a living whole made of body and mind ... When she decides to have an abortion she decides for *herself* and for *no one else* (she does not decide for the embryo that as such is still within her body, not yet born). In any case, she is alone and entirely responsible for her decision.' *In Spite of Plato*, 78.

63 Simone de Beauvoir, *The Second Sex*, trans. and ed. H.M. Parshley (New York: Knopf, 1952), 484.

64 De Beauvoir states in the chapter titled 'The Mother' that reproduction has never been a mere 'biological chance.' Rather 'it has always come under the voluntary control of human beings ... There are few subjects on which bourgeois society displays greater hypocrisy; abortion is considered a revolting crime to which it is indecent even to refer' (*The Second Sex*, 484–85).

65 Ibid., 490.

66 Diane Elam, *Deconstruction and Feminism: Ms. En Abyme* (New York: Routledge, 1994), 78–9.

67 Ibid., 79.

68 Mary O'Brien, *Reproducing the World: Essays on Feminist Theory* (Boulder, CO: Westview Press, 1989), 303.

69 In talking about the reticence of Italian women in using contraceptives because of religious reasons Maraini wonders how can it be 'possible that the teachings of the Church, that carry so little weight as far as sexuality in general is concerned, could be so influential in this matter of contraception?' (LA2 8, 18).

70 Maria Antonietta Cruciata, *Dacia Maraini* (Fiesole: Cadmo, 2003), 136–7.

71 Maria Zingarelli, 'Dacia Maraini: Il paese è contro questa legge,' *L'Unità*, 26 September 2004: 10.

72 In *The Reproduction of Mothering: Psychoanalysis and the Sociology of Gender*, Nancy Chodorow draws a correct representation of what gender differentiation has meant for centuries: 'The social organization of gender, in its relation to an economic context, has depended on the continuation of the social relations of parenting. The reproduction of these social relations of parenting is not reducible to individual intention but depends on all the arrangements which go into the organization of gender and the organization of the economy' ([Berkeley: University of California Press, 1978] 34). She adds: 'In the case of mothering, the economic system has depended for its reproduction on women's reproduction of particular forms of labor power in the family. At the same time, income inequality between men and women makes it more rational and even necessary, in any individual conjugal family for fathers,

rather than mothers, to be primary wage-earners. Therefore, mothers, rather than fathers, are the primary caretakers of children and the home' (35). Chodorow's conclusions, that 'women's capacities for mothering and abilities to get gratification from it are strongly internalized and psychologically enforced, and are built developmentally into the feminine psychic structure' (39), are accurate in that they are indeed some of the reasons why women still accept their traditional role in society. I argue, however, that these reasons do not entirely explain women's desire for having children.

73 Butler, *Undoing Gender*, 11.
74 As Maraini states in her interview with Maria Zingarelli, lack of female representation in the two chambers of government has long been a problem for the cause of defending women's rights in politics, a lack that in turn produced a large majority of (male) supporters of the new laxity for procreation. 'Women need to defend their right to be mothers.' Zingarelli, 'Dacia,' 10.
75 Butler, *Undoing Gender*, 12.
76 Ibid.
77 Elsa Morante, *Menzogna e sortilegio*, in *Opere* 1:9 ('When I recognize myself, I stand motionless, staring as though I glimpsed the head of Medusa'; *House of Liars*, 3).
78 'And who looks at the Gorgon? Everybody moves, slips away, they don't see, they hope to get away. To make you gaze at her, the Gorgon must grab you but she has no arms. She won't be the one to petrify me, not me.' See Rossana Rossanda, *La ragazza del secolo scorso* (Turin: Einaudi, 2005), 61.
79 Butler, *Undoing Gender*, 36.
80 Cathy Caruth, *Unclaimed Experience: Trauma, Narrative, and History* (Baltimore: Johns Hopkins University Press, 1996), 3.
81 Ibid., 7.
82 Butler, *Undoing Gender*, 14.
83 The title of this part of the novel makes evident the allusion to the musical terms *tempo* and *controtempo*. It confirms Mazzucco's thesis that her entire novelistic construction is based on the concept of melodrama, not for its tones, but for the essential fusion between music and words, apparently attested to also by the name 'Norma,' the protagonist of a famous opera Vincenzo Bellini composed in 1832.
84 As already seen in chapter 2 in the case of Ippolita Avalli's Giovanna-Vera, it is Medusa's own marginality, her not being owned by patriarchy, that makes her an ideal target for collective sacrifice. See René Girard, *Violence and the Sacred*, trans. Patrick Gregory (Baltimore: Johns Hopkins University Press, 1977), 4–13. I would even say that the entire novel is more about readingthe dreams and traumas of the protagonists than about actual

facts, a contention I find corroborated by the multiple endings of this metafictional novel.
85 Sandra Gilbert and Susan Gubar, *The Madwoman in the Attic: The Woman Writer and the Nineteenth-Century Literary Imagination* (New Haven: Yale University Press, 1979), 77–8.
86 Ibid., 78–9. Annis Pratt expresses similar views in her *Dancing with Goddesses: Archetypes, Poetry, and Empowerment* (Bloomington: Indiana University Press, 1994), xii–xiii.
87 Pratt, *Dancing with Goddesses*, 4–5. In discussing the ambiguity inherent in the Victorian binary representations of Medusa as angel and demon, Pratt adds that, aside from recognizing the strength of the archetype as source of energy of a feminist kind, such binary representation attests also to the process of empowerment drawn from previous history(ies) up to the nineteenth century (13).
88 See Dante's *terzina* '"Volgiti 'n dietro e tien lo viso chiuso; / ché se 'l Gorgon si mostra e tu 'l vedessi, / nulla sarebbe di tornare mai suso"' (*Inferno* VI, 55–7; 'Turn back and keep thine eyes shut, for should the Gorgon show herself and thou see her, there would be no returning above'). This *terzina* is also the epigraph to the first part of the novel (BM 7). All references to the *Commedia* in Italian are taken from Emilio Pasquini and Antonio Quaglio's edition (Milan: Garzanti, 1987); and those in English are from John Sinclair's translation (Oxford: Oxford University Press, 1939).
89 See Girard, *Violence and Sacred*, 13–37.
90 Susan Bowers, in 'Medusa and the Female Gaze,' *NWSA Journal* 2.2 (1990): 217–35, and Annis Pratt, in *Dancing with Goddesses*, have brilliantly studied the non-patriarchal retrieval by several female novelists and poets of pre-Olympian Medusian mythology, one that seems strictly pertinent to this interpretative reversal. See also Sigrid Weigel's *Die Stimme der Medusa: Schreibweisen in der Gegenwartsliteratture von Frauen* (Dülmen-Hiddingsel: Tende, 1987); and *The Medusa Reader*, ed. Marjorie Garber and Nancy J. Vickers (New York: Routledge, 2003), for their extensive treatment of the myth in women's literature and across the centuries.
91 Bowers, 'Medusa,' 229.
92 Teresa de Lauretis, *The Practice of Love: Lesbian Sexuality and Perverse Desire* (Bloomington: Indiana University Press, 1994), xiii. I also draw from de Lauretis's discussion of desire in narrative in *Alice Doesn't: Feminism, Semiotics, Cinema* (Bloomington: Indiana University Press, 1984), 136. In the same pages (136–64) de Lauretis offers also a brilliant reading of Medusa in film and society while showing how Hélène Cixous's 'The Laugh of the Medusa' (trans. Keith Cohen and Paula Cohen, *Signs* 1 [1976]) partly parodies

Sigmund Freud's 1922 essay 'Medusa's Head.' See Freud, 'Medusa's Head,' in *The Standard Edition of the Complete Psychological Works of Sigmund Freud*, ed. James Strachey (London: The Hogarth Press, 1953), 5: 105–6.
93 Vladimir Propp, *Morphology of the Folktale*, trans. Laurence Scott (Austin: University of Texas Press, 1968), 22–7.
94 *Écriture féminine* is surely 'utopian,' at least until an effective liberation from the Law of the Father exists, notes Cixous; 'The Laugh of the Medusa,' 887. (But in the meantime it is wonderful to fantasize.) Further, Bowers notes how the paradox of the Olympian Medusa lies in the juxtaposition of her beauty with her horror, this latter represented by the writhing serpents on her head and her power to petrify. In Bowers's opinion, this paradox partly reflects the coexistence of the pre-Olympian myth, given to us by Hesiod in his *Theogony*, with the Olympian one ('Medusa,' 222).
95 Bowers, 'Medusa,' 218.
96 In *The Practice of Love* (21–30) de Lauretis attenuates some of the feminist strong attacks against Freud as she re-evaluates the fascination and interest that drew feminist thinkers to his works in the first place. It was Freud's ambiguity, after all, that constructed the space into which feminist thinkers could insinuate doubt and scepticism of the patriarchal discourse, just as he did for the role of Jewish intellectuals in a Gentile world. Also, in her *Speaking the Unspeakable: Religion, Misogyny, and the Uncanny Mother in Freud's Cultural Texts* (Berkeley: University of California Press, 2001) Diane Jonte-Pace discusses the 'hesitant non-Oedipal speculations,' or what she calls the 'counterthesis,' in Freud's writings. Jonte-Pace demonstrates the possibility of a 'feminist analysis of deeply rooted forms of cultural misogyny and xenophobia' in Freud's cultural texts (3).
97 De Lauretis elucidates many points of ambiguity in Freud's theories on perversion. She convincingly points to the site for discussion left in a passage in which Freud speaks of the separation between sexual instinct and sexual desire (*The Practice of Love*, 35), particularly when he writes, 'It seems probable that the sexual instinct is in the first instance independent of its object; nor is its origin likely to be due to its object's attractions.' See Freud's passage in 'Three Essays on the Theory of Sexuality,' in *Standard Edition of Complete Works of Freud*, ed. Strachey, 7: 147–8.
98 As Jonathan Dollimore notes, the dynamics of perverse desire have widely been a constant theme since the construction of the most ancient mythologies. Dollimore, *Sexual Dissidence: Augustine to Wilde, Freud to Foucault* (Oxford: Clarendon Press, 1991), 204. He also argues that 'to recover the lost histories of perversion' as Freud does means 'also to recognize the inadequacies of the sexological and psychoanalytical accounts of desire generally and of perversion specifically' (170).

99 Bowers, 'Medusa,' 234.
100 The honeymoon was a recurring theme in fin-de-siècle literature that Mazzucco reworks it in her postmodern novel. For a good example see Guy de Maupassant's short story 'Enragée,' translated as 'Hydrophobia' in his *Complete Works: A Life. Unedited Stories Not Found in Other Editions*, trans. Alfred de Sumichrast (Boston: C.T. Brainard Publishing Co., 1910), 252–60. In the garb of a letter to her friend Geneviève, the protagonist retells her honeymoon to Normandy, particularly of her own ignorance towards sex and her relationship with the man she married.
101 'The nuptial pact is frequently ... a legal prostitution. In the upper classes it is a deal in dowries and heraldic quarterings; in the lower class, a vast manufactory of proletarians. Marriage today is one of the most fertile sources of woes, a slow poison that saps domestic felicity, the morale of a people, the economic development of the forces of a country. Matrimony is often the patent of irresponsibility for woman and an easy way to polygamy for man; it is a hypocritically virtuous disguise which conceals vice in modern society.' Paolo Mantegazza, *Physiology of Love*, trans. Herbert Alexander (New York: Eugenics, 1936), 209.
102 This was in fact the sole way in which Norma knew of sex – through her erudite studies in Florence. Until her marriage, Latin poetry, Catullus's Carmen 62 in this case, constituted the space to which Norma's knowledge of human behaviour was confined: 'Quel "signore" si accingeva a profanare il suo santuario di flos cresciuto in saeptis secretus hortis, nullo convolus aratro. E il verso cum tenui carptus defloruit ungui l'aveva colpita fonosimbolicamente fin dai tempi del liceo, inducendola a solidarizzare col fiorellino incalzato dalla lama dell'aratore. E invece, cum castum amisit polluto corpore florem, era ancora viva' (BM 27); (That gentleman was about to desecrate the sanctuary of her *flos* [flower], grown *in saeptis secretus hortis* [secretly in a fenced garden], *nullo convolus aratro* [torn up by no plow]. Since high-school times, the verse about the flower uprooted by the plow phono-symbolically had struck her. And instead, *cum castum amisit polluto corpore florem* [when she has lost her chaste flower with sullied body], she was still alive.)
103 De Lauretis, *The Practice of Love*, 44–55; Dollimore, *Sexual Dissidence*, 196.
104 Dollimore, *Sexual Dissidence*, 181.
105 De Lauretis, *The Practice of Love*, 25; Dollimore, *Sexual Dissidence*, 172.
106 De Lauretis, *The Practice of Love*, 22.
107 As in Dollimore, *Sexual Dissidence*, 175.
108 Victor Robinson, 'Introduction,' in Paolo Mantegazza, *Sexual Relations of Mankind*, trans. Samuel Putnam (New York: Eugenics Publishing Co., 1935), xii–xiii.

109 See de Lauretis, *The Practice of Love*, 18–20.
110 This is also the example chosen by Sigmund Freud as the explanatory cause for the 'fear of the lack' that Medusa's apotropaic gaze ignites in men.
111 Mantegazza, *Sexual Relations of Mankind*, 84.
112 'It is impossible to erect the boundaries between love's physiology and its pathology. The highest rungs of eroticism might be the first steps on the ladder of perversion' (ibid., 78).
113 Mantegazza, *Fisiologia del piacere* (Milan: Bietti, 1947),10.
114 Ibid., 10
115 Ibid.
116 Ibid., 46.
117 De Lauretis, *The Practice of Love*, xix.
118 Mantegazza, *Fisiologia del piacere*, 46.
119 Cesare Lombroso and Guglielmo Ferrero, *Criminal Woman, the Prostitute, and the Normal Woman*, trans. and intro. Nicole Hahn Rafter and Mary Gibson (Durham: Duke University Press, 2004), 41.
120 Ibid., 36. Ibid., 52–7.
121 Ibid., 52–7.
122 Ibid., 37.
123 Ibid., 176.
124 Butler, *Undoing Gender*, 42.
125 Ibid., 51.
126 De Lauretis, *The Practice of Love*, 41. 'The designated subject (lesbian),' claims Monique Wittig, 'is *not* a woman, either economically, or politically, or ideologically. For what makes a woman is a specific social relation to a man, a relation that we have previously called servitude, a relation which implies personal and physical obligation as well as economic obligation ("forced residence," domestic corvée, conjugal duties, unlimited production of children, etc.), a relation which lesbians escape by refusing to become or to stay heterosexual.' See Wittig, *The Straight Mind and Other Essays*, trans. Marlene Wildeman (Boston: Beacon Press, 1992), 20.
127 I believe that her story could hardly have been written before the Freudian discoveries about the Oedipal complex being applicable – as de Lauretis theorizes – also to the little girl, and not only to Hans, the little boy.
128 Sergi in Lombroso and Ferrero, *Criminal Woman*, 59; emphasis added.
129 As ibid., 64.
130 Ibid., 64.
131 Ibid., 69.
132 Marcel Proust, *Swann's Way*, trans. Lydia Davis (New York: Viking, 2003), 18. See also Michael Riffaterre's 'On Narrative Subtexts: Proust's Magic Lantern,' *Style* 22.3 (1988): 450–6.

133 De Lauretis, *The Practice of Love*, 262.
134 Ibid., 156.
135 Ibid., 51.
136 'The mirror of Medusa is more profound than the topos of decadent beauty conceived as the appeal of corruption would have us believe: it is the same profundity as a hallucinating conciousness of ones's own mysteries to fall into the *terror antiquus* of its subterranean world; the unconscious strips the Self of its presumed stability in the very same moment it believes to possess it.' See Ferruccio Masini, *Lo sguardo della Medusa: Prospettive critiche sul Novecento tedesco* (Bologna: Cappelli, 1977), 80.
137 Freud, 'Medusa's Head,' 105.
138 Pratt contends that this is just another gynophobic assertion of the period in which Freud and Ferenczi were active (*Dancing with Goddesses*, 34). Bowers expands on such a concept and claims that 'patriarchal males have had to make Medusa – and by extension all women – the object of the male gaze as a protection against being objectified themselves by Medusa's gaze ('Medusa,' 220).
139 Further, Freud states that 'since the Greeks were in the main strongly homosexual, it was inevitable that we should find among them a representation of woman as a being who frightens and repels because she is castrated' ('Medusa's Head,' 106). In Freud's essay, there is a basic confirmation that 'the feminine, to use a catachresis, is domesticated and rendered unintelligible within a phallogocentrism that claims to be self-constituting. Disavowed, the remnant of the feminine survives as the *inscriptional space* of the phallogocentrism, the spectacular surface that receives the marks of a masculine signifying act only to give back a (false) reflection and guarantee of phallogocentric self-sufficiency, without making any contribution of its own.' See Butler, 'Bodies That Matter,' in *Engaging with Irigaray: Feminist Philosophy and Modern European Thought*, ed. Carolyn Burke, Naomi Schor, and Margaret Whitford (New York: Columbia University Press, 1994), 152.
140 In speaking about film and gaze, de Lauretis wonders, 'how did Medusa feel looking at herself being slain and pinned up on screens, walls, billboards, and other shields of masculine identity, is really a political question ... the relation of female subjectivity to ideology in the representation of sexual difference and desire, the positions available to women in film, the conditions of vision and production, for women' (de Lauretis, *Alice Doesn't*, 136).
141 Bowers, 'Medusa,' 217.
142 In the novel there is a description of an 1897 painting by Giulio Aristide Sartorio, *La Gorgone e gli Eroi* (*The Gorgon and the Heroes*), that only reconfirms the stereotypical fright of men before Medusa (BM 313–14) vis-à-vis Mazzucco's argument of Medusa's gaze that empowers women.

143 Jane Gallop, 'The Other Woman,' in *Thinking through the Body* (New York: Columbia University Press, 1988), 167.
144 This is in spite of class inferiority, a class notion that impedes the fullness of the subversive intent. In the clear intimacy between the two characters, there is also the notion of work with an artistic meaning as facilitated by Medusa's gaze, one that questions her stereotypical reading.
145 Starting with the notion of the talismanic fetish-object, Emily Apter demonstrates how such objects were endowed with the ability to destabilize the threshold between the proprietor and the property. See her *Feminizing the Fetish: Psychoanalysis and Narrative Obsession in Turn-of-the-Century France* (Ithaca: Cornell University Press, 1991), 43. As a corollary, such objects would also destabilize the same concept that would juxtapose the woman to the fetish (245).
146 Arthur Schnitzler, *Fräulein Else: A Novel*, trans. Robert A. Simon (New York: Simon and Schuster, 1971).
147 Arthur Schnitzler, *Traumnovelle*, trans. Otto P. Schinnerer (New York: AMS Press, 1971).
148 Medusa's powers have been so unanimously recognized that a verb was coined to make evident the fearful feelings that her presence produces. In French, *méduser* is, in fact, a synonym for petrify. See Paul Robert, *Dictionnaire alphabétique et analogique de la langue française* (Paris: Société du nouveau littré, 1973), 1064.
149 As in Braidotti, *Metamorphoses*, 46.
150 Masini, *Lo sguardo della Medusa*, 76.
151 See Renate Holub, 'Between the United States and Italy: Critical Reflections on Diotima's Feminine/Feminist Ethics,' in *Feminine/Feminists: Cultural Practices in Italy*, ed. Giovanna Miceli Jeffries (Minneapolis: University of Minnesota Press, 1995), 250.
152 For an extensive and convincing analysis of de Beauvoir's theories, see Toril Moi's 'Is Anatomy Destiny? Freud and Biological Determinism,' in *'What Is a Woman?' And Other Essays* (Oxford: Oxford University Press, 1999), 369–93.
153 'Ambiguous beauty, bearer of the final fruit of the unfathomable ocean.' See Maria Zambrano, *Claros del bosque* (Barcelona: Editorial Sexi Barral, 1977), 145.
154 'On the hidden and jealously guarded logos' (ibid., 146).
155 Elizabeth Viti, 'Marcel and the Medusa: The Narrator's Obfuscated Homosexuality in *À la recherche du temps perdu*,' *Dalhousie French Studies* 26 (1994): 64.
156 On the notion of contract, see Wittig, *The Straight Mind*, 6.
157 Cixous, 'The Laugh of Medusa,' 888.

158 Butler, *Undoing Gender*, 15, 40–1.
159 Not incidentally, in *Undoing Gender* Butler explains two elements derived from Foucault's theory on power to mistrust: '(1) regulatory power not only acts upon a preexisting subject but also shapes and forms that subject; moreover, every juridical form of power has its productive effect; and (2) to become subject to a regulation is also to become subjectivated by it, that is, to be brought into being as a subject precisely through being regulated' (41).

Conclusions

1 Sigmund Freud, 'New Introductory Lectures on Psycho-Analysis,' in *The Standard Edition of the Complete Psychological Works*, ed. and trans. James Strachey (London: Hogarth, 1953), 22: 112–35.
2 Sandra M. Gilbert, '"Life's Empty Pack": Notes toward a Literary Daughteronomy,' *Critical Inquiry* 12.2 (March 1985): 358.
3 For a discussion on *buonismo* and *cattivismo*, the two trends into which Italian critics in the mid-1990s had divided emerging writers, please see Gian Paolo Renello's 'The Mediatic Body of the Cannibale Literature,' in Stefania Lucamante, ed., *Italian Pulp Fiction* (Madison, N.J.: Fairleigh Dickinson University Press, 2001), 98–134.
4 Simona Vinci, www.studioprogetto.net/incubatoio16/I/simona.htm (Vinci's old website which no longer exists).
5 Virginia Woolf, *A Room of One's Own* (New York: Harvest, 1981), 109.
6 Gilbert, '"Life's Empty Pack,"' 357.
7 Ibid., 358.
8 The five mothers are Lalla Romano, Anna Banti, Elsa Morante, Natalia Ginzburg, and Anna Maria Ortese. Maraini's grandmother is Grazia Deledda. She also claims to have had fathers to look up to, namely, Svevo, Moravia, Bassani, Cassola, Pasolini, Calvino, and Landolfi, not to mention Conrad, Melville, Dostoevsky, and Proust. This is what Maraini stated in her interview with Maria Luisa Cruciata, *Dacia Maraini* (Fiesole: Cadmo, 2003), 135.
9 Rosi Braidotti, *Metamorphoses* (Cambridge: Polity Press, 2002), 85.
10 While Adriana Cavarero convincingly reiterates such concept in several studies, in *Tu che mi guardi, tu che mi racconti* narrative is the focus of her analysis (Milan: Feltrinelli, 1997).
11 Hélène Cixous, 'The Laugh of the Medusa,' *Signs* 1 (1976): 875.
12 Ibid., 876.
13 Italo Calvino, *If on a Winter's Night a Traveler*, trans. William Weaver (New York: Harvest, 1979).

14 Cixous, 'The Laugh of the Medusa,' 880.
15 'It is probable, however, that both in life and in art the values of a woman are not the values of a man. Thus, when a woman comes to write a novel, she will find that she is perpetually wishing to alter the established values – to make serious what appears insignificant to a man, and trivial what is to him important. And for that, of course, she will be criticized; for the critic of the opposite sex will be genuinely puzzled and surprised by an attempt to alter the current scale of values, and will see in it not merely a difference of view, but a view that is weak, or trivial, or sentimental, because it differs from his own.' See Virginia Woolf, *Women and Writing* (New York: Harvest, 2003), 49.
16 Braidotti, *Metamorphoses*, 96.
17 Rita Felski, *Literature after Feminism* (Chicago: University of Toronto Press, 2003), 169.
18 Barbara Herrnstein Smith, 'Contingencies of Value,' in *Canons*, ed. Robert von Hallberg (Chicago: University of Chicago Press, 1983), 30.
19 Ibid., 30.
20 Felski, *Literature after Feminism*, 15.

Works Cited

Abecassis, Eliette. *Mon père*. Paris: Albin Michel, 2002.
Agamben, Giorgio. *Homo Sacer: Il potere sovrano e la nuda vita*. Turin: Einaudi, 1995.
– *Stanzas: Word and Phantasm in Western Culture*. Trans. Ronald L. Martinez. Minneapolis: University of Minnesota, 1993.
Aleramo, Sibilla. *Una donna* (1906). Milan: Feltrinelli, 2001.
Alighieri, Dante. *Commedia*. Ed. Emilio Pasquini and Antonio Quaglio. Milan: Garzanti, 1987.
– *The Divine Comedy: Inferno*. Ed. John Sinclair. Oxford: Oxford University Press, 1939.
Altieri, Charles. 'An Idea and Ideal of a Literary Canon.' In *Canons*, ed. Robert von Hallberg, 41–64. Chicago: University of Chicago Press, 1984.
American Beauty. Dir. Sam Mendes. DreamWorks, 1999.
Applebome, Peter. 'Pact Reached on U.S. Edition of *Lolita* Retelling.' *New York Times*, 17 June 1999: E1, E10.
Apter, Emily. *Feminizing the Fetish: Psychoanalysis and Narrative Obsession in Turn-of-the-Century France*. Ithaca: Cornell University Press, 1991.
Arendt, Hannah. *The Human Condition*. Intro. Margaret Canovan. Chicago: University of Chicago Press, 1998.
Armeni, Ritanna. *La colpa delle donne: Dal referendum sull'aborto alla fecondazione assistita. Storie, battaglie e riflessioni*. Milan: Ponte alle Grazie, 2006.
Arslan, Antonia. *Dame, galline e regine: La scrittura femminile italiana fra '800 e '900*. Milan: Guerini studio, 1998.
Attridge, Derek. *The Singularity of Literature*. New York: Routledge, 2004.
Avalli, Ippolita. *Nascere non basta*. Milan: Feltrinelli, 2003.
– *La Dea dei baci*. Milan: Baldini e Castoldi, 1995.
– *Mi manchi*. Milan: Feltrinelli, 2008.
Badinter, Elisabeth. *Fausse route*. Paris: Odile Jacob, 2003.

Baker, Nicholson. *Vox*. New York: Vintage, 1993.
Balbus, Isaac D. *Mourning and Modernity: Essays in Psychoanalysis of Contemporary Society*. New York: Other Press, 2005.
Bardini, Marco. '*House of Liars*: The American Translation of *Menzogna e sortilegio*.' In *Under Arturo's Star: The Cultural Legacies of Elsa Morante*, ed. Stefania Lucamante and Sharon Wood, 112–28. West Lafayette: Purdue University Press, 2005.
– 'Osservazioni preliminari su *l'isola di Arturo*.' In *Riscrittura Intertestualità transcodificazione*, ed. Emanuella Scarano and Donatella Diamanti, 553–88. Pisa: Tipografia editrice pisana, 1992.
Barnhart, Robert K., ed. *The Barnhart Concise Dictionary of Etymology*. 1st ed. New York: HarperCollins Publishers, 1995.
Baroni, Monica, ed. *Streghe, madonne e sante postmoderne: Eccedenze femminili tra cronaca e fiction*. Rome: Meltemi, 2003.
Bataille, Georges. *My Mother*. Trans. Austryn Wainhouse. London: Jonathan Cape, 1972.
Beauvoir, Simone de. *All Said and Done*. Trans. Patrick O'Brian. Harmondsworth: Penguin, 1987.
– *La femme rompue*. Paris: Gallimard, 1967.
– *Hard Times: Force of Circumstance*. 2 vols. Trans. Peter Green. New York: Paragon House, 1992.
– *Mémoires d'une jeune fille rangée*. Paris: Gallimard, 1958.
– *The Second Sex*. Trans. and ed. H.M. Parshley. New York: Knopf, 1952.
– *The Woman Destroyed*. Trans. Patrick O'Brian. New York: Pantheon Books, 1969.
Bellini, Vincenzo. *Norma*. 1832.
Berg, Elizabeth. 'The Third Woman.' *Diacritics* 12.2 (1982): 11–20.
Bianchini, Angela. *Voce donna*. Milan: Frassinelli, 1996.
Bloom, Harold. *The Western Canon: The Books and School of the Ages*. New York: Harcourt Brace, 1994.
Blumenthal, Ralph. 'Disputed "Lolita" Spinoff Is Dropped by Publisher.' *New York Times*, 7 November 1998: B7, B14.
– 'Nabokov Son Files Suit to Block a Retold "Lolita". *New York Times*, 10 October 1998: B9.
Boecklin, Arnold. *Die Toteninsel*. (1883) Bâle: Öffentliche Kunstsammlung Kunstmuseum.
Bono, Paola. 'Women's Biographies and Autobiographies: A Political Project in the Making.' In *Across Genres, Generations, and Borders: Italian Women Writing Lives*, ed. Susanna Scarparo and Rita Wilson, 10–21. Newark: University of Delaware Press, 2004.

Bono, Paola, and Sandra Kemp, eds. *Italian Feminist Thought: A Reader.* Cambridge: Blackwell, 1991.
- *The Lonely Mirror: Italian Perspectives on Feminist Theory.* New York: Routledge, 1993.
Bordo, Susan. *Unbearable Weight: Feminism, Western Culture, and the Body.* Berkeley: University of California Press, 1993.
Bowers, Susan. 'Medusa and the Female Gaze.' *NWSA Journal* 2 (Spring 1990): 217–35.
Braidotti, Rosi. *Metamorphoses: Towards a Materialist Theory of Becoming.* Cambridge: Polity Press, 2002.
- *Nuovi soggetti nomadi.* Rome: Luca Sossella, 2002.
- *Nomadic Subjects: Embodiment and Sexual Difference in Contemporary Feminist Theory.* New York: Columbia University Press, 1994.
- 'Oltre il genere.' *Leggendaria* 23 (2000): 5–7.
Briganti, Chiara. *Anche tu, figlia mia!: Figlie e padri nelle letterature anglofone.* Urbino: Quattroventi, 1995.
Brontë, Charlotte. *Jane Eyre.* Ed. Heather Glen. New York: St Martin's Press, 1997.
Bruni, Frank. 'A Teenager Takes Italy by Storm, with Her Tale of Lust.' *New York Times,* 24 December 2003: A3.
Bruzzi, François. 'Bataille scrittore.' In *Georges Bataille: Tutti i romanzi,* ed. Guido Neri. v–xxvi. Turin: Bollati Boringhieri, 1992.
Butler, Judith 'Bodies That Matter.' In *Engaging with Irigaray: Feminist Philosophy and Modern European Thought,* ed. Carolyn Burke, Naomi Schor, and Margaret Whitford, 141–73. New York: Columbia University Press, 1994.
- *Precarious Life: The Powers of Mourning and Violence.* London: Verso, 2004.
- *Undoing Gender.* New York: Routledge, 2004.
Caesar, Ann. 'Women Readers and the Novel in Nineteenth-Century Italy.' *Italian Studies* 56 (2001): 80–97.
Calvino, Italo. *If on a Winter's Night a Traveler.* Trans. William Weaver. New York: Harvest, 1979.
- *The Path to the Spiders' Nest.* Trans. Archibald Colquhoun and Martin McLaughlin. New York: HarperCollins, 2000.
- *Il sentiero dei nidi di ragno* (1947). Milan: Mondadori, 1993.
Campo, Rossana. *Mai sentita così bene.* Milan: Feltrinelli, 1995.
- *Sono pazza di te.* Milan: Feltrinelli, 2001.
Caruth, Cathy. *Unclaimed Experience: Trauma, Narrative, and History.* Baltimore: Johns Hopkins University Press, 1996.
Catullus, Gaius Valerius. *Catullus: The Complete Poems for Modern Readers.* Trans. Reney Myers and Robert J. Ormsby. London: Allen and Unwin, 1972.

Cavarero, Adriana. *Corpo in figure: Filosofia e politica della corporeità*. Milan: Feltrinelli, 1995.
– *A più voci: Filosofia dell'espressione vocale*. Milan: Feltrinelli, 2003.
– *In Spite of Plato*. Trans. Serena Anderlini-D'Onofrio and Aine O'Healy. New York: Routledge, 1995.
– *Tu che mi guardi, tu che mi racconti: Filosofia della narrazione*. Milan: Feltrinelli, 1997.
Centovalli, Benedetta, ed. *Patrie impure: Italia, autoritratto a più voci*. Milan: Rizzoli, 2003.
Certeau, Michel de. *The Practice of Everyday Life*. Trans. Steven Rendall. Berkeley: University of California Press, 1984.
Ceserani, Remo, and Pierluigi Pellini. 'The Belated Development of a Theory of the Novel.' In *The Cambridge Companion to the Italian Novel*, ed. Andrea Ciccarelli and Peter Bondanella, 1–19. Cambridge: Cambridge University Press, 2003.
Chatman, Seymour. 'Parody and Style.' *Poetics Today* 22.1 (Spring 2001): 25–39.
Chodorow, Nancy. *The Reproduction of Mothering: Psychoanalysis and the Sociology of Gender*. Berkeley: University of California Press, 1978.
Cicchetti, Dante, and Sheree L. Toth, eds. *Child Abuse, Child Development, and Social Policy*. Vol. 8. Norwood: Ablex Publishing, 1993.
Cixous, Hélène. 'The Laugh of the Medusa.' Trans. Keith Cohen and Paula Cohen. *Signs* 1 (1976): 875–93; orig. 'Le rire de la Méduse,' *L'Arc* (1975): 39–45.
Conrad, Joseph. *The Secret Sharer*. New York: Dove, 1993. *Il compagno segreto*. Trans. Dacia Maraini. Milan: Rizzoli, 2001.
Contarini, Silvia. 'L'eredità della neoavanguardia nei romanzi di Silvia Ballestra, Rossana Campo, Carmen Covito.' *Narrativa* 8 (1995): 75–99.
– 'Riflessioni sulla narrativa femminile degli anni '90.' *Narrativa* 10 (1996): 139–63.
Costa, Francesco. *La volpe a tre zampe*. Milan: Baldini e Castoldi, 1996.
Couturier, Maurice. *Nabokov, ou la tyrannie de l'auteur*. Paris: Éditions du Seuil, 1993.
Covacich, Mauro. 'Unabomber.' In *Patrie impure: Italia, autoritratto a più voci*, ed. Benedetta Centovalli, 121–37. Milan: Rizzoli, 2003.
Cruciata, Maria Antonietta. *Dacia Maraini*. Fiesole: Cadmo, 2003.
Currie, Mark. *Postmodern Narrative Theory*. New York: St Martin's Press, 1998.
Cutrufelli, Maria Rosa, ed. *In the Forbidden City: An Anthology of Erotic Fiction by Women*. Trans. Vincent Bertolini. Chicago: University of Chicago Press, 2000.
Cutrufelli, Maria Rosa, ed. *Nella città proibita*. Milan: Marco Tropea, 1997.
Dällenbach. Lucien. *Le récit spéculaire: Essais sur la mise en abyme*. Paris: Éditions du Seuil, 1977.

De Lauretis, Teresa. *Alice Doesn't: Feminism, Semiotics, Cinema.* Bloomington: Indiana University Press, 1984.
– *The Practice of Love: Lesbian Sexuality and Perverse Desire.* Bloomington: Indiana University Press, 1994.
Derrida, Jacques. *Given Time: I. Counterfeit Money.* Trans. Peggy Kamuf. Chicago: University of Chicago Press, 1992.
Devoto, Giacomo, and Gian Carlo Oli. *Dizionario della lingua italiana.* Florence: Le Monnier, 1971.
Diaconescu-Blumenfeld, Rodica, and Ada Testaferri, eds. *The Pleasure of Writing: Critical Essays on Dacia Maraini.* West Lafayette: Purdue University Press, 2000.
Di Lascia, Mariateresa. *Passaggio in ombra.* Milan: Feltrinelli, 1995.
Diotima. *Il cielo stellato sopra di noi: L'ordine simbolico della madre.* Milan: La Tartaruga, 1992.
– *La sapienza di partire da sé.* Naples: Liguori, 1996.
Djebar, Assia. *A Sister to Scheherazade.* Trans. Dorothy S. Blair. Portsmouth, NH: Heinemann, 1993.
Doane, Mary Ann. 'Film and Masquerade: Theorizing the Female Spectator.' In *Writing on the Body: Female Embodiment*, ed. Kate Conboy, Nadia Medina, and Sarah Stanbury, 176–94. New York: Columbia University Press, 1997.
– 'Masquerade Reconsidered: Further Thoughts on the Female Spectator.' *Discourse* 11.1 (Fall–Winter 1988–9): 42–53.
Dolan, Frederick M. 'An Ambiguous Citation in Hannah Arendt's *The Human Condition.*' *Journal of Politics* 66.2 (May 2004): 606–10.
Dollimore, Jonathan. *Sexual Dissidence: Augustine to Wilde, Freud to Foucault.* Oxford: Clarendon Press, 1991.
Duras, Marguerite. *The Lover.* Trans. Barbara Bray, intro. Maxine Hong Kingston. New York: Pantheon Books, 1997.
Eco, Umberto. 'Nonita.' In *Diario minimo* (1963), 11–16. Milan: Mondadori, 1988.
Elam, Diane. *Feminism and Deconstruction: Ms. En Abyme.* New York: Routledge, 1994.
Eliot, Thomas Stearns. *The Waste Land and Other Writings.* Intro. Mary Karr. New York: Modern Library, 2001.
Erbani, Francesco. 'Nel paese di Mariateresa la Strega.' *La repubblica*, 12 August 1995: 25.
Euripides. *Medea.* Trans. Kenneth McLeish and Frederic Raphael. Dir. Deborah Warner. Perf. Fiona Shaw. Brooks Atkinson Theatre, New York, 4 December 2002–14 February 2003.
Faenza, Roberto. *I giorni dell'abbandono.* Medusa, 2004.
Fallaci, Oriana. *Lettera a un bambino mai nato.* Milan: Rizzoli, 1975.

Felski, Rita. *Beyond Feminist Aesthetics: Feminist Literature and Social Change.* Cambridge, MA: Harvard University Press, 1989.
– *Literature after Feminism.* Chicago: University of Chicago Press, 2003.
Ferrante, Elena. *L'amore molesto.* Rome: Edizioni e/o, 1992.
– *The Days of Abandonment.* Trans. Ann Goldstein. New York: Europe Editions, 2005.
– *La figlia oscura.* Rome: Edizioni e/o, 2006.
– *La frantumaglia.* Rome: Edizioni e/o, 2003.
– *I giorni dell'abbandono.* Rome: Edizioni e/o, 2002.
– *Troubling Love.* Trans. Ann Goldstein. New York: Europe Editions, 2006.
Ferroni, Giulio. *Dopo la fine: Sulla condizione postuma della letteratura.* Turin: Einaudi, 1996.
Fiori, Antonella. 'I bambini ci guardano. E il loro gioco innocente e crudele diventa Tragedia.' *L'Unità,* 17 September 1997: 25.
Flexner, Stuart, ed. *Random House Dictionary.* 2nd ed. New York: Random House, 1987.
Fofi, Goffredo. 'I riti della memoria e del futuro: Il romanzo di Mariateresa Di Lascia.' *Linea d'ombra* 104 (May 1995): 43–4.
Fois, Marcello. *Gap.* Milan: Frassinelli, 1999.
Ford, Jane M. *Patriarchy and Incest from Shakespeare to Joyce.* Gainesville: University Press of Florida, 1998.
Foucault, Michel. *The History of Sexuality.* Vol. 2, *The Use of Pleasure.* Trans. Robert Hurley. New York: Pantheon Books, 1985.
Fowler, Alastair. *A History of English Literature.* Cambridge, MA: Harvard University Press, 1987.
Fowler, Douglas. *Reading Nabokov.* Ithaca: Cornell University Press, 1974.
Freud, Sigmund. *The Standard Edition of the Complete Works of Sigmund Freud.* 24 vols. Ed. James Strachey. London: Hogarth Press, 1953.
– *Totem and Taboo: Resemblances between the Psychic Lives of Savages and Neurotics.* Trans. A.A. Brill. Amherst: Prometheus Books, 2000.
Furst, Lillian R., and Peter W. Graham, ed. *Disorderly Eaters: Texts in Self-Empowerment.* University Park: Pennsylvania State University Press, 1992.
Fusini, Nadia. *La bocca più di tutto mi piaceva.* Rome: Donzelli, 1996.
– 'Woman-graphy.' In *The Lonely Mirror: Italian Perspectives on Feminist Theory,* ed. Paola Bono and Sandra Kemp, 39–54. New York: Routledge, 1993.
Gabriele, Tommasina. 'The Pregnant Nun: Suor Attanasia and the Metaphor of Arrested Maternity in Dacia Maraini.' *Italica* 81.1 (Spring 2004): 65–80.
Gallop, Jane. *The Daughter's Seduction.* Ithaca: Cornell University Press, 1982.
– 'The Other Woman.' In Gallop, *Thinking through the Body,* 160–78. New York: Columbia University Press, 1988.

Ganeri, Margherita. 'Narratrici coi nervi tesi.' In *Tirature '98. Una modernità da raccontare: La narrativa degli anni novanta*, ed. Vittorio Spinazzola, 46–50. Milan: Il Saggiatore, 1997.
Garber, Marjorie, and Nancy Vickers, ed. *The Medusa Reader.* New York: Routledge, 2003.
Garboli, Cesare. *Il gioco segreto: Nove immagini di Elsa Morante.* Milan: Adelphi, 1995.
Gatens, Moira. *Imaginary Bodies: Ethics, Power and Corporeality.* London and New York: Routledge, 1996.
Genette, Gerard. *Palimpsests: Literature in the Second Degree.* Trans. Channa Newman and Claude Doubinsky. Lincoln: University of Nebraska Press, 1998.
Giacobino, Margherita. *Casalinghe all'inferno.* Milan: Baldini & Castoldi, 1996.
Gilbert, Sandra M. '"Life's Empty Pack": Notes toward a Literary Daughteronomy.' *Critical Inquiry* 11 (March 1985): 355–84.
Gilbert, Sandra M., and Susan Gubar. *The Madwoman in the Attic: The Woman Writer and the Nineteenth-Century Literary Imagination.* New Haven: Yale University Press, 1979.
Ginzburg, Natalia. *Famiglia.* Turin: Einaudi, 1977.
– *Family: Two Novellas.* Trans. Beryl Stockman. New York: Seaver Books / H. Holt, 1988.
Giobbi, Giuliana. '"No Bread Will Feed My Hungry Soul": Anorexic Heroines in Female Fiction – from the Example of Emily Brontë as Mirrored by Anita Brookner, Gianna Schelotto and Alessandra Arachi.' *Journal of European Studies* 27 (1997): 73–92.
Giorgio, Adalgisa, 'Nature vs. Culture: Repression, Rebellion and Madness in Elsa Morante's *Aracoeli*.' *Modern Language Notes* 109 (1994): 93–116.
Giorgio, Adalgisa, ed. *Writing Mothers and Daughters: Renegotiating the Mother in Western European Narratives by Women.* New York: Berghahn Books, 2002.
Girard, René. *The Scapegoat.* Trans. Yvonne Freccero. Baltimore: Johns Hopkins University Press, 1986.
– *Violence and the Sacred.* Trans. Patrick Gregory. Baltimore: Johns Hopkins University Press, 1977.
Gordon, Robert S.C. *An Introduction to Twentieth-Century Italian Literature.* London: Duckworth, 2005.
Gorney, Cynthia. 'Reversing Roe: Is Mainstream Right-to-Life Ready for an Abortion Ban.' *New Yorker,* 26 June 2006: 46–53.
Gubar, Susan. '"The Blank Page" and the Issues of Female Creativity.' *Critical Inquiry* 8.2 (Winter 1981): 243–63.
Haraway, Donna. *The Haraway Reader.* New York: Routledge, 2004.
Herrnstein Smith, Barbara. 'Contingencies of Value.' In *Canons,* ed. Robert von Hallberg, 5–40. Chicago: University of Chicago Press, 1983.

Hirsch, Marianne. *The Mother-Daughter Plot: Narrative, Psychoanalysis, Feminism.* Bloomington: Indiana University Press, 1987.
Holub, Renate. 'Between the United States and Italy: Critical Reflections on Diotima's Feminine/Feminist Ethics.' In *Feminine/Feminists: Cultural Practices in Italy,* ed. Giovanna Miceli Jeffries, 233–60. Minneapolis: University of Minnesota Press, 1995.
– 'Italian Difference Theory: A New Canon?' *Italian Women Writers from the Renaissance to the Present,* ed. Maria Ornella Marotti, 37–52. University Park: Pennsylvania State University Press, 1996.
hooks, bell. *Feminism Is for Everybody: Passionate Politics.* Cambridge, MA: South End Press, 2000.
Hutcheon, Linda. 'Modern Parody and Bakhtin.' In *Rethinking Bakhtin: Extensions and Challenges,* ed. Gary Saul Morson and Caryl Emerson, 87–103. Evanston: Northwestern University Press, 1989.
– *Narcissistic Narrative: The Metafictional Paradox.* Waterloo: Wilfrid Laurier University Press, 1980.
– *A Theory of Parody: The Teachings of Twentieth-Century Art Forms.* New York: Methuen, 1985.
Irigaray, Luce. 'Come diventare delle donne civili?' *Reti* 3–4 (May–August 1988): 6–16.
– *Thinking the Difference: For a Peaceful Revolution.* Trans. Karin Montin. New York: Routledge, 1994.
Jaeggy, Fleur. *Proleterka.* Milan: Adelphi, 2001.
– *S.S. Proleterka.* Trans. Alastair McEwen. New York: New Directions, 2003.
Jaoui, Agnes. *Comme une image* (Look at me). Paris: Les films A4 41, 2003.
Jarmusch, Jim. *Broken Flowers.* Focus Features, 2005.
Jarre, Marina. 'Le ombre impietose di Mariateresa.' *L'indice dei libri del mese* 6 (June 1995): 16.
Jeuland-Meynaud, Maryse. 'Dacia Maraini: Polémique ou littérature?' In *Les femmes écrivains en Italie aux XIXe et XXe siècles,* Actes du colloque international, Aix-en-Provence, 14–16 November 1991, ed. Marie-Anne Rubat de Mérac, 205–38. Aix-en-Provence: Publications de l'Université de Provence, 1993.
Johnston, Claire. 'Double Indemnity.' In *Women in Film Noir,* ed. Emily Ann Kaplan, 89–98. London: British Film Institute, 1998.
Jonte-Pace, Diane. *Speaking the Unspeakable: Religion, Misogyny, and the Uncanny Mother in Freud's Cultural Texts.* Berkeley: University of California Press, 2001.
Jung, Carl Gustav. *Aspects of the Feminine.* Vol. 6 of Collected Works. Trans. R.F.C. Hull. Princeton: Princeton University Press, 1982.

Kahane, Claire. 'The Woman with a Knife and the Chicken without a Head: Phantasms of Rage and Emptiness.' In *Psychoanalyses/Feminisms*, ed. Peter L. Rudnytsky and Andrew M. Gordon, 179–92. Albany: State University of New York Press, 1999.
Kaplan, Carla. *The Erotics of Talk: Women's Writing and Feminist Paradigms*. Oxford: Oxford University Press, 1996.
Kaplan, Louise. *Female Perversions: The Temptations of Emma Bovary.* New York: Doubleday, 1991.
Kermode, Frank. *The Sense of an Ending.* New York: Oxford University Press, 1967.
Kristeva, Julia. *Powers of Horror: An Essay on Abjection.* Trans. Leon S. Roudiez. New York: Columbia University Press, 1982.
Lacan, Jacques. *Les complexes familiaux dans la formation de l'individu.* Paris: Navarin, 1984.
– *On Feminine Sexuality, the Limits of Love and Knowledge: The Seminar of Jacques Lacan.* Book 20. Ed. Jacques-Alain Miller. Trans. Bruce Fink. New York: Encore W.W. Norton, 1999.
La Porta, Filippo. *La nuova narrativa italiana: Travestimenti e stili di fine secolo.* 2nd ed. Turin: Bollati Boringhieri, 1999.
Locatelli, Carla, ed. *Co(n)texts: Implicazioni testuali.* Trent: Dipartimento di Scienze Filologiche e Storiche, 2000.
– 'Co(n)texts.' In *Co(n)texts: Implicazioni testuali,* 11–36.
Lombardi, Giancarlo. *Rooms with a View: Feminist Diary Fiction 1952–1999.* Madison, N.J.: Fairleigh Dickinson University Press, 2002.
– 'Scambi d'identità: Il recupero del corpo materno ne *L'amore molesto*.' *Romance Languages Annual* 10 (1999): 288–91.
Lombroso, Cesare. *L'uomo delinquente.* Milan: Hoepli, 1876.
Lombroso, Cesare, and Guglielmo Ferrero. *Criminal Woman, the Prostitute, and the Normal Woman.* Trans. and intro. Nicole Hahn Rafter and Mary Gibson. Durham: Duke University Press, 2004.
Lucamante, Stefania. 'L'atroce smacco della madre.' *Leggendaria* 60 (January 2007): 42–43.
Lucamante, Stefania, ed. *Italian Pulp Fiction: The New Narrative of the Giovani Cannibali Writers.* Madison, N.J.: Fairleigh Dickinson University Press, 2001.
Lucamante Stefania, and Sharon Wood. *Under Arturo's Star: The Cultural Legacies of Elsa Morante.* West Lafayette, IN: Purdue University Press, 2005.
– *Elsa Morante e l'eredità proustiana* (Fiesole: Cadmo, 1998).
– 'Everyday Consumerism and Pornography "above the Pulp Line."' In S. Lucamante, ed., *Italian Pulp Fiction*, 98–134.
– *Isabella Santacroce.* Fiesole: Cadmo, 2002.

- '"Una laudevole fine": Femminismo e identificazione delle donne nella narrativa di Rossana Campo.' *Italianistica* 31.2–3 (May–Dec. 2002): 295–306.
- 'Per uno sguardo diverso: Cinema, Santa Cecilia e Mickey Rourke nell'*Attore americano.*' *Narrativa* 20–1 (2001): 19–34.
- 'Teatro di Guerra: Of History and Fathers.' In S. Lucamante and S. Wood, eds, *Under Arturo's Star,* 221–56.

Lucarelli, Carlo. *Guernica.* Turin: Einaudi Tascabili Stile Libero Noir, 2000.

Lugnani, Lucio. '*Logos kai Ananke.*' In *Per Elisa: Studi su* Menzogna e sortilegio, ed. Lucio Lugnani and Emanuella Scarano, 9–94. Pisa: Nistri-Lischi, 1990.

Maar, Michael. *The Two Lolitas.* Trans. Perry Anderson. London: Verso, 2005.

MacKinnon, Catharine A. *Feminism Unmodified: Discourses on Life and Law.* Cambridge, MA: Harvard University Press, 1987.

Madrignani, Carlo. 'Elsa, l'inattuale.' *L'Indice dei libri del mese* 1 (January 1996): 10.

Mantegazza, Paolo. *Fisiologia del piacere.* Milan: Bietti, 1947.
- *Physiology of Love.* Trans. Herbert Alexander. New York: Eugenics Publishing Co., 1936.
- *Sexual Relations of Mankind.* Ed. and intro. Victor Robinson. Trans. Samuel Putnam. New York: Eugenics Publishing Co., 1935.

Manzoni, Alessandro. *I promessi sposi.* Ed. Vittorio Spinazzola. 3rd ed. Milan: Garzanti, 1972.

Maraini, Dacia. *The Age of Malaise.* Trans. Frances Frenaye. New York: Grove Press, 1963.
- *Un clandestino a bordo. Le donne: La maternità negata il corpo segnato.* Milan: Rizzoli, 1996.
- *Donna in guerra.* Turin: Einaudi, 1975.
- *La donna perfetta.* Turin: Einaudi, 1975.
- *L'età del malessere.* Turin: Einaudi, 1963, 1976.
- *The Holiday.* Trans. Stuart Hood. London: Weidenfeld and Nicolson, 1966.
- *Isolina: La donna tagliata a pezzi.* Milan: Mondadori, 1985.
- 'Letter on Abortion.' In Maraini *Stowaway on Board,* 1–19.
- 'Lettera sull'aborto.' *Nuovi Argomenti* 1–2 (January 1996). Repr. In Maraina, *Un clandestino a bordo,* 9–34.
- *Lettere a Marina.* Milan: Bompiani, 1981.
- *Letters to Marina.* Trans. Dick Kitto and Elspeth Spottiswood. Freedom, CA: Crossing Press, 1987.
- *La lunga vita di Marianna Ucrìa.* Milan: Rizzoli, 1990.
- *Stowaway on Board.* Trans. Giovanna Bellesia and Victoria Offredi Poletto. West Lafayette, IN: Bordighera Press, 2000.
- *The Train.* Trans. Dick Kitto and Elspeth Spottiswood. London: Camden Press, 1988.

- *Il treno per Helsinki.* Turin: Einaudi, 1984.
- *Voci.* Milan: Rizzoli, 1994.
- *Voices.* Trans. Dick Kitto and Elspeth Spottiswood. London: Serpent's Tail, 1997.
- *La vacanza.* Rome: Lerici, 1962.
- *Woman at War.* Trans. Mara Benetti and Elspeth Spottiswood. New York: Italica Press, 1988.

Maraini, Dacia, trans. *Il compagno segreto.* (Joseph Conrad, *The Secret Sharer.*) Milan: Rizzoli, 2001.

Maraini, Dacia, and Piera degli Esposti. *Storia di Piera.* Milan: Bompiani, 1980.

Marchi, Ena. 'Ricordo di Mariateresa.' *Linea d'ombra* 104 (May 1995): 44–6.

Martinéz, Rosa, and María de Corral. *La Biennale di Venezia, 51 Esposizione Internazionale d'Arte. L'esperienza dell'arte: Sempre un po' più lontano. Partecipazioni nazionali, eventi nell'ambito,* ed. *Italiana.* 3 vols. Venice: Marsilio, 2005.

Masini, Ferruccio. *Lo sguardo della Medusa: Prospettive critiche sul Novecento tedesco.* Bologna: Cappelli, 1977.

Maupassant, Guy de. 'Hydrophobia.' In *Complete Works. A Life. Unedited Stories Not Found in Other Editions,* 252–60. Trans. Alfred de Sumichrast, Boston: C.T. Brainard Publishing Co., 1910.

Max, D.T. 'The Injustice Collector.' *The New Yorker,* 19 June 2006: 22–45.

Mazzucato, Francesca. *Hot Line: Storia di un'ossessione.* Turin: Einaudi, 1996.
- *Web Cam.* Venice: Marsilio, 2002.

Mazzucato, Francesca, ed. *Tua, con tutto il corpo: Antologia di racconti erotici al femminile.* Faloppio: Lietocolle, 2005.

Mazzucco, Melania. *Il bacio della Medusa.* Milan: Baldini e Castoldi, 1996.

McDonagh, Eileen. 'Abortion Rights Alchemy and the United States Supreme Court: What's Wrong and How to Fix It.' In *Perspectives on the Politics of Abortion,* ed. Ted G. Jelen, 21–53. Westport: Praeger, 1995.

Medeiros, Paulo. 'Cannibalism and Starvation: The Parameters of Eating Disorders in Literature.' In *Disorderly Eaters: Texts in Self-Empowerment,* ed. Lilian R. Furst and Peter W. Graham, 11–27. University Park: Pennsylvania State University Press, 1992.

Melandri, Lea. 'Il femminismo è ancora in silenzio.' *Liberazione,* 12 January 2005.

Melissa P. (Panariello). *Cento colpi di spazzola prima di andare a dormire.* Rome: Fazi, 2003.
- *One Hundred Strokes of the Brush before Going to Bed.* Trans. Lawrence Venuti. London: Serpent's Tail, 2004.

Menechella, Grazia. 'La rappresentazione dell'anoressia nel discorso medico e nei testi di Alessandra Arachi, Nadia Fusini e Sandra Petrignani.' *Italica* 78.3 (2001): 387–409.

Miceli Jeffries, Giovanna, ed. *Feminine Feminists: Cultural Practices in Italy.* Minneapolis: University of Minnesota Press, 1995.
Michetti, Maria, Margherita Repetto, and Luciana Viviani, eds. *UDI. Laboratorio di politica delle donne.* Rome: Cooperativa Libera Stampa, 1984.
Moi, Toril. 'Ambiguity and Alienation in *The Second Sex.*' *Boundary 2* 19.2 (1992): 96–112.
– 'Intentions and Effects: Rhetoric and Identification in Simone de Beauvoir's "The Woman Destroyed" (1988),' in *What Is a Woman?* 451–75.
– *What Is a Woman? And Other Essays.* Oxford: Oxford University Press, 1999.
Morandini, Giuliana. *La voce che è in lei: Antologia della narrativa femminile italiana tra '800 e '900.* Milan: Bompiani, 1980.
Morante, Elsa. *Aracoeli.* Trans. William Weaver. New York: Random House, 1984.
– *House of Liars.* Trans. Adrienne Foulke with ed. assistance of Andrew Chiappe. New York: Harcourt Brace and Co., 1951.
– 'I personaggi.' In *Pro o contro la bomba atomica,* 11–14.
– *Opere.* 2 vols. Ed. Cesare Garboli and Carlo Cecchi. Milan: Meridiani Mondadori, 1988 and 1990.
– *'Pro o contro la bomba atomica' e altri scritti.* Intro. Cesare Garboli. Milan: Adelphi, 1987.
– 'Sul romanzo.' In *Pro o contro la bomba atomica,* 41–73.
Morrissey, Kim. *Poems for Men Who Dream of Lolita.* Regina, SK: Coteau Books, 1992.
Morselli, Guido. *Un dramma borghese.* Milan: Adelphi, 1978.
Muraro, Luisa. *Il Dio delle donne.* Milan: Mondadori, 2003.
– *L'ordine simbolico della madre.* Rome: Editori Riuniti, 1991.
– 'Partire da sé e non farsi trovare.' In Diotima, *La sapienza di partire da sé,* 5–22. Naples: Liguori, 1996.
Muraro, Luisa, Annarosa Buttarelli, and Liliana Rampello, eds. *Duemilaeuna: Donne che cambiano l'Italia.* Milan: Pratiche editrici, 2001.
Nabokov, Dmitri. 'On a Book Entitled *Lo's Diary.*' In Pia Pera, *Lo's Diary,* trans. Ann Goldstein, vii–x. New York: Foxrock, 1999.
Nabokov, Vladimir. 'Great Readers and Great Writers.' In *Lectures on Literature,* ed. Fredson Bowers, 1–6. New York: Harcourt Brace Jovanovich, 1980.
– *Lolita.* New York: Vintage Books, 1989.
– 'On a Book Entitled *Lolita.*' In *Lolita.* 311–17.
Nadal, Marita. 'The Death of a Beautiful Woman Is, Unquestionably, the Most Poetical Topic in the World: Poetic and Parodic Treatment of Women in Poe's Tales.' In *Gender, I-deology: Essays on Theory, Fiction and Film,* ed. Chantal Cornut-Gentille D'Arcy and José Ángel García Landa, 151–63. Amsterdam: Rodopi, 1996.

Nadotti, Maria. 'Lolita II, la vendetta.' *L'Unità*, 13 November 1995: 16.
Nafisi, Azar. *Reading Lolita in Teheran: A Memoir in Books*. New York: Random House, 2003.
Negri, Toni, and Michael Hardt. *Multitude: War and Democracy in the Age of Empire*. New York: Penguin Press, 2004.
Nerenberg, Ellen. *Prison Terms: Representing Confinement during and after Italian Fascism*. Toronto: University of Toronto Press, 2001.
Nicholson, Linda. 'The Question of Essentialism.' In L. Nicholson, ed. *The Second Wave: A Reader in Feminist Theory*, 319–20. London: Routledge, 1997.
Il Nuovo Zingarelli: Vocabolario della lingua italiana. 11th ed. Ed. Miro Dogliotti and Luigi Rosiello. Bologna: Zanichelli, 1986.
O'Brien, Mary. *Reproducing the World: Essays on Feminist Theory*. Boulder, CO: Westview Press, 1989.
O'Healy, Aine. 'Filming Female "Autobiography": Maraini, Ferreri, and Piera's Own Story.' In *Feminine Feminists: Cultural Practices in Italy*, ed. Giovanna Miceli Jeffries (Minneapolis: University of Minnesota Press, 1995), 190–298.
Onofri, Massimo. 'La retorica del sublime basso: Salvatore Niffoi, Erri De Luca, Isabella Santacroce.' In *Sul banco dei cattivi*, ed. Giulio Ferroni, Massimo Onofri, Filippo La Porta, and Alfonso Berardinelli, 33–54. Rome: Donzelli, 2006.
Ottonieri, Tommaso. *La plastica della lingua*. Milan: Bollati Boringhieri, 2000.
Ovid. *Metamorphoses*. Trans. and ed. Charles Martin, intro. Bernard Knox. New York: W.W. Norton & Co., 2004.
Paglia, Camille. *Vamps and Tramps: New Essays*. New York: Vintage Books, 1994.
Palieri, Maria Serena. 'Intervista a Simona Vinci.' *L'Unità*, 12 February 2004: 25.
Pasolini, Pier Paolo. 'L'isola di Arturo.' In *Il portico della morte*, ed. Cesare Segre. Rome: Associazione fondo Pier Paolo Pasolini, 1988.
Pasti, Daniela. 'Di Lascia: Un caso che divide.' *La repubblica*, 8 July 1995: 30.
Patrucco Becchi, Anna. '*Stabat Mater*: Le madri di Elsa Morante.' *Belfagor* 31 (July 1993): 436–51.
Pera, Pia. *Diario di Lo*. Venice: Marsilio, 1995.
– *Lo's Diary*. Trans. Ann Goldstein. New York: Foxrock, 1999.
– 'Migrazioni femminili.' *L'Indice dei libri del mese* 8, (1996): 46.
Picchietti, Virginia. *Relational Spaces: Daughterhood, Motherhood, and Sisterhood in Dacia Maraini's Writings and Films*. Madison, NJ: Fairleigh Dickinson University Press, 2002.
Pifer, Ellen. *Demon or Doll: Images of the Child in Contemporary Writing and Culture*. Charlottesville: University of Virginia Press, 2000.
Pifer, Ellen, ed. *Vladimir Nabokov's Lolita: A Casebook*. Oxford: Oxford University Press, 2002.

Pratt, Annis. *Dancing with Goddesses: Archetypes, Poetry, and Empowerment.* Bloomington: Indiana University Press, 1994.
Presciuttini, Paola. *Non dire il mio nome.* Padua: Meridiano Zero, 2004.
Propp, Vladimir. *Morphology of the Folktale.* Trans. Laurence Scott. Austin: University of Texas Press, 1968.
Proust, Marcel. *Swann's Way.* Trans. Lydia Davis. New York: Viking, 2003.
Ragazze che dovresti conoscere: The Sex Anthology. Turin: Einaudi, 2004.
Ramondino, Fabrizia. *Althénopis.* Turin: Einaudi, 1995.
– *Guerra di infanzia e di Spagna.* Turin: Einaudi, 2001.
Ramondino, Fabrizia, and Andreas Friedrich Müller, eds. *Dadapolis: Caleidoscopio napoletano.* Turin: Einaudi, 1992.
Rasy, Elisabetta. *Le donne e la letteratura: Scrittrici eroine e ispiratrici nel mondo delle lettere.* Rome: Editori Riuniti, 1984.
– *La lingua della nutrice.* Rome: Edizioni delle donne, 1978.
Re, Lucia. 'Passion and Sexual Difference: The Risorgimento and the Gendering of Writing in Nineteenth-Century Italian Culture.' In *Making and Remaking Italy: The Cultivation of National Identity around the Risorgimento*, ed. Albert Russell Ascoli and Krystina von Henneberg, 155–200. Oxford: Berg, 2001.
Reid, Catherine, and Holly K. Iglesias, eds. *His Hands, His Tools, His Sex, His Dress: Lesbian Writers on Their Fathers.* New York: Alice Street Editions, 2001.
Renello, Gian Paolo. 'The Mediatic Body of the *Cannibali* Literature.' In Lucamante, *Italian Pulp Fiction*, 135–60.
Renna, Katia. 'Daniel Pennac e le reti del Romanzo.' In *Il Romanzo: Autori e stili*, ed. Alessandro Catalano and Katia Renna, 157–234. Rome: La Sapienza, 1997.
Rhys, Jean. *Wide Sargasso Sea.* New York: Norton, 1992.
Ricaldone, Luisa. *La scrittura nascosta: Donne di lettere e loro immagini tra Arcadia e Restaurazione.* Fiesole: Cadmo, 1996.
Ricoeur, Paul. *The Symbolism of Evil.* Trans. Emerson Buchanan. Boston: Beacon Press, 1969.
– *Time and Narrative.* Vol. 2. Trans. Kathleen McLaughlin and David Pellauer. Chicago: University of Chicago Press, 1985.
Riffaterre, Michael, 'On Narrative Subtexts: Proust's Magic Lantern.' *Style* 22.3 (1988): 450–6.
Robert, Paul. *Dictionnaire alphabétique et analogique de la langue française.* Paris: Société du nouveau littré, 1973.
Robinson, Victor. 'Introduction.' In Mantegazza, *Sexual Relations of Mankind*, ix–xiv.
Rosa, Giovanna. *Cattedrali di carta: Elsa Morante romanziere.* Milan: Il Saggiatore, 1995.
Rose, Margaret. *Parody: Ancient, Modern, and Post-Modern.* Cambridge: Cambridge University Press, 1993.

Rossanda, Rossana. *La ragazza del secolo scorso*. Turin: Einaudi, 2005.
Rowe-Finkbeiner, Kristin. *The F Word: Feminism in Jeopardy. Women, Politics, and the Future*. Emeryville, CA: Seal Press, 2004.
'Sacrosanctum Concilium.' 9 August 2005, Vatican website, http://www.vatican
   . va/archive/hist_councils/ii_vatican_council/documents/vatii_const_
   19631204_sacrosanctum-concilium_en.html.
Salvo, Anna. *Madri e figlie: Legami e conflitti fra due generazioni*. Milan: Mondadori, 2003.
Santacroce, Isabella. *Destroy*. Milan: Feltrinelli, 1996.
– *Fluo: Storie di giovani a Riccione*. Rome: Castelvecchi, 1995.
– *Luminal*. Milan: Feltrinelli, 1998.
Santoro, Anna. *Pausa per rincorsa*. Cava dei Tirreni: Avagliano, 2003.
– *Il Novecento: Antologia di scrittrici italiane del primo ventennio*. Rome: Bulzoni, 1997.
– *Narratrici italiane dell'Ottocento*. Naples: Federico e Ardia, 1987.
Santoro, Anna, and Francesca Veglione. *Catalogo della scrittura femminile a stampa presente nei fondi librari della Biblioteca Nazionale di Napoli*. Naples: Federico e Ardia, 1984.
Sanvitale, Francesca. *Madre e figlia*. Turin: Einaudi, 1980.
Sanvitale, Francesca, ed. *Le Scrittrici dell'Ottocento (da Eleonora de Fonseca Pimentel a Matilde Serao)*. 1st ed. Rome: Istituto poligrafico e Zecca dello Stato, 1995.
Sartorio, Giulio Aristide. *The Gorgon and the Heroes*. Rome: Galleria Nazionale d'Arte Moderna.
Scarano, Emanuella. 'La "fatua veste del vero."' In *Per Elisa: Studi su* Menzogna e
– Sortilegio, ed. Lucio Lugnani and Emanuella Scarano, 95–17. Pisa: Nistri-Lischi, 1990.
Scarparo, Susanna, and Rita Wilson, ed. *Across Genres, Generation, and Borders: Italian Women Writing Lives*. Newark: University of Delaware Press, 2004.
Scerbanenco, Giorgio. *Traditori di tutti*. Milan: Garzanti, 1999.
Schnitzler, Arthur. *Fräulein Else: A Novel*. Trans. Robert A. Simon. New York: Simon and Schuster, 1971.
– *Traumnovelle*. Trans. Otto P. Schinnerer. New York: AMS Press, 1971.
Schopenhauer, Arthur. *The World as Will and Representation*. Trans. E.F.J. Payne. London: Dover Edition, 1969.
Sexton, Anne. *The Collected Poems*. Boston: Houghton Mifflin, 1999.
Sheldon, Barbara H. *Daughters and Fathers in Feminist Novels*. New York: Peter Lang, 1997.
Showalter, Elaine. *A Literature of Their Own*. Princeton: Princeton University Press, 1977.
Skolnic, Peter. Letter in 'The Mail.' *The New Yorker*, 10 July 2006: 8.

Starnone, Domenico. *Via Gemito*. Milan: Feltrinelli, 2002.
Storini, Monica Cristina. *L'esperienza problematica: Genesi e scrittura nella narrativa italiana del Novecento*. Rome: Carocci, 2005.
Tambling, Jeremy. *Confession: Sexuality, Sin, the Subject*. Manchester: Manchester University Press, 1990.
Tamburri, Anthony J. 'Dacia Maraini's *Donna in guerra*: Victory or Defeat?' In *Contemporary Women Writers in Italy: A Modern Renaissance*, ed. Santo Aricò, 138–51. Amherst: University of Massachusetts Press, 1990.
Tamir-Ghez, Nomi. 'The Art of Persuasion in Nabokov's *Lolita*.' In Pifer, ed., *Vladimir Nabokov's Lolita: A Casebook*, 17–38.
Todaro, Lenora. 'Oops! I Did It Again.' *New York Times Review of Books*, 7 November 2004: 17.
Todorov, Tzvetan. *The Poetics of Prose*. Trans. Richard Howard. Oxford: Basil Blackwell, 1977.
Toker, Leona. *Nabokov: The Mystery of Literary Structures*. Ithaca: Cornell University Press, 1989.
Totaro, Pina, ed. *Donne, filosofia e cultura nel Seicento*. Rome: Ed. Consiglio Nazionale delle Ricerche, 1999.
Vattimo, Gianni, and Pier Aldo Rovatti, ed. *Il pensiero debole*. Milan: Feltrinelli, 1983.
Vegetti Finzi, Silvia. 'The Female Animal.' In *The Lonely Mirror: Italian Perspectives on Feminist Theory*, ed. Paola Bono and Sandra Kemp, 128–51. New York: Routledge, 1993.
Vegetti Finzi, Silvia, ed. *Madri e figlie: Ieri e oggi*. Bari: Laterza, 2003.
Vermeer, Johannes. *The Love Letter* (1667–8). Amsterdam: Rijksmuseum.
Vinci, Simona. *Come prima delle madri*. Turin: Einaudi, 2003.
– *Dei bambini non si sa niente*. Turin: Einaudi, 1996.
– www.studioprogetto.net/incubatoio16/I/simona.htm (page no longer available).
Virgil. *The Aeneid*. Trans. Robert Fitzgerald. New York: Vintage Books, 1990.
Viti, Elizabeth. 'Marcel and the Medusa: The Narrator's Obfuscated Homosexuality in *À la recherche du temps perdu*.' *Dalhousie French Studies* 26 (1994): 61–8.
Warner, Marina. *Six Myths in Our Time: Little Angels, Little Monsters, Beautiful Beasts, and More*. New York: Random House, 1995.
Weigel, Sigrid. *Die Stimme der Medusa: Schreibweisen in der Gegenwartsliteratture von Frauen*. Dülmen-Hiddingsel: Tende, 1987.
Weinberg Sumeli, Maria Grazia. *Invito alla lettura di Dacia Maraini*. Pretoria: University of South Africa Press, 1993.
West, Rebecca. 'Su differenza sessuale ed eguaglianza in epoca postmoderna.' *Nuova Prosa* 44 (2006): 163–79.
White, Ellen. 'Editorial Review.' At http://www.amazon.com/gp/product/0964374021/104–2391390–5442331?v=glance&n=283155.

Wilt, Judith. *Abortion, Choice, and Contemporary Fiction: The Armageddon of Maternal Instinct.* Chicago: University of Chicago Press, 1990.
Winterson, Jeanette. *Written on the Body.* New York: Alfred Knopf, 1992.
Wittig, Monique. *The Straight Mind and Other Essays.* Trans. Marlene Wildeman. Boston: Beacon Press, 1992.
Wood, Jane. *Passion and Pathology in Victorian Fiction.* Oxford: Oxford University Press, 2001.
Wood, Sharon. 'The Silencing of Women: The Political Aesthetic of Dacia Maraini (born 1936).' In *Italian Women's Writing 1860–1994.* London: Athlone, 1995. 216–31.
Wolf, Christa. 'From Cassandra to Medea: Impulses and Motives behind My Work on Two Mythical Figures.' 30 July 2005. At http://www.randomhouse.com/boldtype/0498/wolf/notebook.html.
Woolf, Virginia. *A Room of One's Own.* New York: Harvest, 1981.
– *Women and Writing.* New York: Harvest, 2003.
Yaeger, Patricia. 'Afterword.' In *Feminism, Bakhtin, and the Dialogic,* ed. D.M. Bauer and Susan Kinstry, 239–46. Albany: State University of New York Press, 1991.
Yaeger, Patricia, Beth Kowaleski-Wallace, and Jerry Aline Flieger, eds. *Refiguring the Father: New Feminist Readings of Patriarchy.* Carbondale: Southern Illinois University Press, 1989.
Young-Bruehl, Elisabeth, ed. *Freud on Women: A Reader.* 1st ed. New York: W.W. Norton, 1990.
Zaccaria, Paola. 'Oltre il materno, il palinsesto. La mitopoiesi generativa di Frida Kahlo e H.(ilda) D.(oolittle).' In *Co(n)texts: Implicazioni testuali,* ed. Carla Locatelli, Trent: Dipartimento di Scienze Filologiche e Storiche, 2000. 267–88.
Zambrano, Maria. *Claros del bosque.* Barcelona: Editorial Seix Barral, 1977.
Zancan, Marina. *Il doppio itinerario della scrittura: La donna nella tradizione letteraria italiana.* Turin: Einaudi, 1998.
Zingarelli, Maria. 'Dacia Maraini: Il paese è contro questa legge.' *L'Unità,* 26 September 2004: 10.
Žižek, Slavoj. 'Melancholy and the Act.' *Critical Inquiry* 26.4 (Summer 2000): 657–81.
Zwinger, Lynda. *Daughters, Fathers, and the Novel: The Sentimental Romance of Heterosexuality.* Madison: University of Wisconsin Press, 1991.

Index

Abecassis, Eliette, 264 n. 3
Abortion, 14, 26, 185–205, 285–6 n. 57 (*Roe v. Wade*)
Achmatova, Anna, 179
Acker, Kathy, 144
Adam (and Eve), 267 n. 34
Aeneid (Virgil), 122
Agamben, Giorgio, 141, 269 n. 69
Alighieri, Dante, 179; *Inferno*, 22, 73, 79, 257 n. 92, 289 n. 88
Aleramo, Sibilla (Rina Faccio), 6–7; *Una donna*, 110–11, 284 n. 33
Altieri, Charles, 38, 251 n. 27
Amazons, 209
American Beauty (Mendes), 87
Andersen, Hans Christian, 122
'Annabel Lee' (Poe), 176–7
Anna Karenina (Tolstoy), 103–4, 177
Anorexia nervosa, 126–7
Aphrodite, 212
Applebome, Peter, 274 n. 117
Arendt, Hannah, 9, 142, 161, 236; *The Human Condition*, 235, 268–9 n. 56
Aristotle, 220; Aristotelian tragedy, 79
Armeni, Ritanna, 283 n. 23
Athena (Medusa's head), 227
Australian Aborigines, 215

Avalli, Ippolita, 25, 116–18, 120, 133, 139, 265 n. 20, 288 n. 84; *La Dea dei baci*, 116–43, 145

Bacio della Medusa, Il (Mazzucco), 206–34
Badinter, Elisabeth, 9–10, 245 n. 16
Baker, Nicholson, 26
Balbus, Isaac D., 272 n. 102
Ballestra, Silvia, 14, 247 n. 48
Banti, Anna (Lucia Lopresti) 7
Barca, Calderón de la: *La vida es sueño*, 37
Bardini, Marco, 254 nn. 55, 56
Barnhart, Robert K., 271 n. 88
Baroni, Monica, 266 n. 30
Bataille, Georges: *Ma mère*, 74, 75, 236, 255 nn. 70, 71, 257 n. 87
Beatrice (Dante), 179, 280 n. 145
Beauvoir, Simone de, 25, 28, 37, 80–8, 90, 92, 93, 96, 101–2, 104–7, 143, 203, 234, 258 n. 103, 259 n. 110, 263 n. 140, 264 n. 147, 287 n. 64, 294 n. 152; *La femme rompue*, 80–106; *Mémoirs d'une jeune fille rangée*, 143; *The Second Sex*, 202–3. *See also* Ferrante

316 Index

Belfagor, 264 n. 152
Belle de jour (Buñuel), 157
Bellini, Vincenzo: *Norma*, 288 n. 83
Berardinelli, Alfonso, 247 n. 44
Berg, Elizabeth, 272 n. 100
Berlusconi, Silvio, 5
Bianchini, Angela, 244 n.10
Bloom, Harold, 21, 34, 248 n. 52
Bobbitt, Lorena, 148–9
Bocca più di tutto mi piaceva, La (Fusini), 145, 269 n. 71
Boecklin, Arnold: *Die Toteninsel*, 78
Bono, Paola, 9, 282 n. 16
Bordo, Susan, 267 n. 35
Bowers, Susan, 210, 227, 289 n. 90, 290 n. 94, 291 n. 99, 293 nn. 138, 141
Braidotti, Rosi, 4, 10, 17, 21, 125; and metamorphosis (*potestas* and *potentia*), 184; reproductive powers, 200; and sexuality, 181–4
Briganti, Chiara, 264 n. 2
Broken Flowers (Jarmusch), 278 n. 138
Brontë, Charlotte: *Jane Eyre*, 274 n. 116
Brothers Grimm, 69, 76, 255 n. 74
Bruck, Edith, 250 n. 12
Bruzzi, François, 255 n. 71, 257 n. 87
Buñuel, Luis: *Belle de jour*, 157
Butler, Judith, 146–7; and matter, 229; and reorganization, 184, 204–6; sexuality and social norms, 207; and speaking subject, 233, 270 n. 74, 295 n. 159

Callas, Maria, 259–60 n. 119
Calvino, Italo, 23–6, 239; *Il sentiero dei nidi di ragno*, 256 n. 82
Campo, Rossana, 15–20, 113–14, 246 n. 37, 247 n. 48, 259 n. 117

Cannibali writers, 14
Canon, literary, 23; canonicity and canon expansion, 28–38; canon and Morante, 59–60
Carmen (Merimée), 176
Catholic Church, 119, 150–1, 215
Cattivismo, 236, 295 n. 3
Catullus (Gaius Valerius), 213, 222, 291 n. 102
Cavarero, Adriana, 15, 200 (Demether myth), 238, 257 n. 89, 284 n. 32, 286–7 n. 62
Cerati, Carla, 33
Certeau, Michel de, 253 n. 48
Ceserani, Remo, 244 n. 5
Céspedes, Alba de, 8
Chatman, Seymour, 276–7 n. 129
Chodorow, Nancy: *The Reproduction of Mothering*, 33, 287 n. 72
Ciabatti, Teresa, 281 n. 9
Cicchetti, Dante, 268 n. 43
Cyclops, 140
Cinderella, 123
Circe, 124. See also *La Dea dei baci*, 124
Cixous, Hélène, 31, 239–40, 244 n. 10, 250 n. 9; *écriture feminine*, 290 n. 94; '*Le rire de la Méduse*,' 211
Clifton, Gladys M., 278 n. 141
Clytemnestra, 132
Combray (Proust), 222
Come prima dei bambini (Vinci), 60–80
Confession (Tambling), 156
Conrad, Joseph (Józef Teodor Nałęcz Konrad Korzeniowski), 198; *The Secret Sharer*, 199–200, 205
Contarini, Silvia, 247 n. 48
Corneille, Pierre: *Médée*, 86
Corral, María de, 247 n. 43
Costa, Francesco: *La volpe a tre zampe*, 263 n. 136

Côte d'Azur, 230
Couturier, Maurice, 279 nn. 142, 143
Covacich, Mauro, 15
Covito, Carmen, 247 n. 48
Currie, Mark, 278 n. 136
Cutrufelli, Maria Rosa, 15, 113, 281 n. 9

D'Annunzio, Gabriele, 18
Darwin, Charles, 215
Dea dei baci, La (Avalli), 116–43, 145
d'Este, Isabella, 55
degli Esposti, Piera, 191
Deledda, Grazia, 6–7
Deleuze, Gilles, 4, 238
De Luca, Erri, 247 n. 44
Deneuve, Catherine; *Belle de jour*, 157
Derrida, Jacques, 165
Diamanti, Donatella, 254 n. 55
Diario di Lo (*Lo's Diary*) (Pera), 162–80, 274 n. 113
Di Lascia, Mariateresa, 24, 28–9, 37–41, 44–60, 106, 108, 235, 251 nn. 26, 28, 252 n. 44, 253 n. 45; *Passaggio in ombra*, 44–60, 92
Dinesen, Isak (Karen Blixen), 250 n. 16
Diotima, 9, 181, 248 n. 55
Diritto alla sessualità, 204
Djebar, Assia: *A Sister to Scheherazade*, 95, 261 n. 128, 263 n. 135
Doane, Mary Ann, 272 n.97
Dollimore, Jonathan, 214, 290 n. 98
Don Quixote, 72
Duras, Marguerite, 234, 262–3 n. 134
Dworkin, Andrea, 10–11, 245 nn. 19, 21, 281 n. 2

Eco, Umberto, 83, 273 n. 110
écriture feminine, 211, 290 n. 94

Eden, 267 n. 34
Elam, Diane, 203–4
Eliot, George, 35, 237; *Middlemarch* and Dorothea Brooke, 213, 247 n. 46
Ellis, John, 11
Emma Bovary (Flaubert), 177
Emplotment (Ricoeur), 61–3
Erbani, Francesco, 252 n. 44
Erotic writing, 184
Eros, 228, 261 n. 124
Eugene Onegin (Pushkin), 26
Euripides: *Medea*, 86

Faenza, Roberto: *I giorni dell'abbandono*, 261 n. 123
Fallaci Oriana: *Lettera a un bambino mai nato*, 188, 198
Farrar, Straus, & Giroux, 164, 274 n. 113
Felski, Rita, 10–12, 15, 19, 187, 241, 245 n. 19, 247 n. 46
Feminist movement (*doppia militanza*), 8
Femme fatale, 76–8, 176
Femme rompue, La (de Beauvoir), 80–107
Ferrante, Elena, 24, 28–9, 80–92, 96, 106–7, 120, 182, 235, 259 n. 113 (*La figlia oscura*), 259–60 n. 119, 260 n. 121, 260–1 n. 122, 262 nn. 130, 133; *L'amore molesto* (Troubling Love), 83, 91; and *frantumaglia*, 89, 96; *I giorni dell'abbandono* (The Days of Abandonment) as reading of *La femme rompue*, 80–106; and *napoli-tanità* 87; and *sorveglianza*, 89, 91
Ferroni, Giulio, 165–7, 247 n. 44, 275 n. 119
Feste dell'Unità, 150–1

318 Index

Fiedler, Leslie, 279 n. 141
Fini restaurant, 153–4
Fink, Bruce, 254 n. 60, 271 n. 94
Fiori, Antonella, 255 n. 75
Flieger, Jerry Aline, 269 n. 62
Florence, 212, 215, 221
Fofi, Goffredo, 41
Fois, Marcello, 256 n. 82
Ford, Jane M., 264 n. 2
Foucault, Michel, 7, 20
Fowler, Alastair, 244 n. 6
Fowler, Douglas, 278 n. 141
Freud, Sigmund, 108, 126, 138, 146–9, 152, 158, 207–8, 214, 215, 232, 249 n. 5, 271 n. 86; 'The Dissolution of the Oedipus Complex,' 147, 270 nn. 78, 82; Dora K., 147, 219, 270 n. 81, 271 n. 92; 'Medusa's Head,' 148, 227, 293 n. 139; 'Mourning and Melancholia,' 146; and perverse desire, 212–13; *Sexualartrieb*, 214; Stiffening, 228; 'Three Essays on the Theory of Sexuality,' 213; *Totem and Taboo*, 138
Fusini, Nadia: *La bocca più di tutto mi piaceva*, 145, 269 n. 71, 271 n. 95

Gallop, Jane, 109–10, 228, 264 n. 2, 294 n. 143
Gambino, Daniela, 281 n. 9
Garboli, Cesare, 8, 38–41, 43, 45, 60, 65–6, 106, 251 nn. 29, 33, 252 nn. 40, 43, 254 n. 56, 256 n. 78, 257 n. 90, 259 n. 116, 295 n. 8
Gatens, Moira, 85
Genette, Gérard, 83, 166, 192, 274 n. 116, 276 nn. 122, 126
Gertrude (Manzoni), 182
Gilbert, Sandra M., 34–6, 39, 81, 237

Ginzburg, Natalia, 7–8, 182, 248 n. 52
Giobbi, Giuliana, 267 n. 34
Giorgio, Adalgisa, 32–3, 37, 246 n. 32
Girard, René, 130, 134, 138–9, 268 n. 49; and Gospel of Luke, 139; and mimetic triangle, 177; scapegoat theory 130–43
Gorgon (Medusa), 206, 209, 224, 227–8, 230, 233, 293 n. 142 (painting of by Sartorio)
Gordon, Andrew M., 271 n. 86
Gordon, Robert S., 7, 245 n. 13
Gorney, Cynthia, 286 n. 57
Gubar, Susan, 34–5, 39, 250 n. 16
Guerrilla Girls, 247 n. 43
Guglielmi, Laura, 281 n. 9
Gull, William W., 127

Hallberg, Robert von, 251 n. 27
Hamlet, 72, 75
Haraway, Donna, 116, 265 n. 16
Hardt, Michael, 4
Heidegger, Martin, 9
Hemingway, Ernest, 56
Hernnstein Smith, Barbara, 240–1
Hesiod, 211
Hirsch, Marianne: *The Mother-Daughter Plot: Narrative, Psychoanalysis, Feminism*, 32
'Hydrophobia' (de Maupassant), 291 n. 100
Hoffmann, E.T.A., 101
Holub, Renate, 248 n. 55, 249 n. 3
Homer, 126, 130, 266 n. 29
hooks, bell, 22
Hot Line: Storia di un'ossessione (Mazzucato), 142–61
Howard, Richard, 254 n. 65
Human Condition, The (Arendt), 235, 268–9 n. 56, 269 nn. 57, 60

Hutcheon, Linda, 83, 166–7, 180, 273 n. 112, 275–6 n. 121, 276 n. 124, 276–7 n. 129, 277 n. 130, 278 n. 140
Hybrid phase of women's artistic production, 4, 8–10, 13–14, 17, 21, 181, 234

I giorni dell'abbandono (Faenza), 261 n. 123
I giorni dell'abbandono (The Days of Abandonment) (Ferrante), 24–5, 80–107, 120, 182, 235, 259 n. 105, 261 n. 123
Iglesias, Holly K., 264 n. 2
Iphigenia, 132
Iliad, 122
Irigaray, Luce, 10, 125, 152, 157, 250 n. 9, 282 n. 14
Isolina: La donna tagliata a pezzi (Maraini), 283 n. 30

Jaeggy, Fleur, 113, 247 n. 47, 265 n. 6
Janeczek, Helena, 250 n. 12
Jane Eyre (Brontë), 274 n. 116
Janeczek, Helena, 250 n. 12
Jaoui, Agnes, 264 n. 3
Jarre, Marina, 253 n. 53
Jesus Christ, 131, 134, 136–7. *See also under* Girard
Jeuland–Meynaud, Maryse, 282 n. 18
Jonte–Pace, Diane, 290 n. 96
Jouissance, 216
Jung, Carl Gustav, 70–1, 79, 249 n. 7, 256 n. 79, 257 n. 97
Justine (Sade), 175

Kahane, Claire, 148, 271 n. 86
Kaplan, Carla, 22, 31, 34–5, 40, 60
Kaplan, Emily Ann, 257 n. 95

Kemp, Sandra, 282 n. 16
Kermode, Frank, 121
Klein, Melanie, 147, 149, 158, 272 n. 102
Kowaleski-Wallace, Beth, 269 n. 62
Kracauer, Siegfried, 257 n. 94
Kristeva, Julia, 31, 108, 250 n. 9; and the *abject* 94, 103
Kubrick, Stanley: *Lolita*, 117, 176

Lacan, Jacques, 108, 147, 232, 249 nn. 5, 7, 254 n. 60, 257 n. 99, 271 n. 94
La Porta, Filippo, 247 n. 44, 251 n. 36
Laura (Petrarch), 179, 280 n. 145
Lauretis, Teresa de, 26, 167, 211–16, 219, 232, 249 n. 5, 276 n. 128, 277 n. 131, 289 n. 92, 290 nn. 96, 97, 291 n. 99, 292 n. 103, 293 n. 140
Legge 40/2004 (law 40/2004), 204
Legge 194 (law 194), 187
Lejeune, Philippe, 276 n. 122
Levi, Primo, 21
Lichberg, Heinz von (Heinz von Eschwege), 273 n. 110
Locatelli, Carla, 249 n. 6
Lolita (Kubrick), 117, 176
Lolita (Nabokov), 25–6, 116–17, 160–80
Lombardi, Giancarlo, 92, 246 n. 31, 260 n. 121
Lombroso, Cesare, 217–20; *Criminal Man* (*L'uomo delinquente*), 217; *Criminal Woman* (*La donna delinquente*), 217
Lo's Diary. See *Diario di Lo*
Love Letter, The (Vermeer), 228
Loy, Rosetta, 33, 38
Lucamante, Stefania, 245 n. 21, 249 n. 1, 254 n. 56

Lucarelli, Carlo, 256 n. 82
Lugnani, Lucio, 253 nn. 51, 52

Maar, Micheal, 273 n. 110
MacKinnon, Catharine A., 10–11, 245 nn. 19, 21, 281 n. 2
Madrignani, Carlo, 252 n. 40
Maggi, Monica, 281 n. 9
Male homosexual hysteria, 207–15
Manifesto di rivolta femminile, 188
Mantegazza, Paolo, 213, 215–17, 219, 221, 225, 291 n. 101, 108, 292 n.112; *Fisiologia del piacere*, 216; *Sexual Relations of Mankind*, 215; *tribadismo*, 217
Manzoni, Alessandro, 22, 40, 119, 182, 244 n. 6, 265 n. 19
Maraini, Dacia, 15, 26, 37, 113, 185, 232–3, 238, 246 n. 32, 247 n. 47, 265 n. 5, 271 n. 95, 282 nn. 15, 18, 283 nn. 19, 22, 25, 26, 27, 30, 31, 285 nn. 50, 56, 286 nn. 58, 62, 287 n. 69, 288 n. 74, 295 n. 8; *Un clandestino a bordo* (Stowaway on Board), 195–6, 198; *Donna in guerra*, 190; *La donna perfetta*, 186, 191; *L'età del malessere*, 189–91, 198; *Isolina: La donna tagliata a pezzi*, 283 n. 30; 'Lettera sull'aborto,' 186–9, 198–204; *Lettere a Marina* (*Letters to Marina*), 186, 191–3, 194, 199, 211, 284 n. 43; *La lunga notte di Marianna Ucrìa* (The Silent Duchess), 193, 198; and the politics of choice, 186–7; sexual politics and abortion 187–206; *Storia di Piera*, 186, 191; *Il treno per Helsinki*, 186, 191–2, 194, 199; *Voci* (Voices), 195–8
Marchi, Ena, 251 n. 26, 253 n. 45
Marianna Ucrìa (Maraini), 193

Marotti, Maria Ornella, 248 n. 55
Martínez, Rosa, 247 n. 43
Maupassant, Guy de: 'Hydrophobia,' 291 n. 100
Masini, Ferruccio, 293 n. 136
Mazzantini, Margaret, 113
Mazzucato, Francesca, 25, 116–17, 155–6, 179, 182, 281 n. 9; *Hot Line: Storia di un'ossessione* 142–61; *Web Cam*, 143, 160–1, 270 nn. 81, 84
Mazzucco, Melania, 14, 26, 185, 206–12, 215, 218–19, 223, 226, 228, 231–4, 247 n. 47, 281 n. 11, 288 n. 83, 291, nn. 100, 293, n. 142; *Il bacio della Medusa*, 206–34; Medusa's myth, 206–10
McDonagh, Eileen, 285–6 n. 57. See also *Roe v. Wade*
Medea, 25, 81, 86–7 (Christa Wolf), 200, 247 n. 46, 259 nn. 118, 119
Medeiros, Paulo, 267 n. 34
Medusa (myth and gaze), 206–10, 288 nn. 78, 84, 289 nn. 87, 88, 90, 92, 290 n. 94, 292 n. 110, 293 nn. 136, 138, 139, 140, 142, 294 nn. 144, 148
Melancholy, 146–61
Melandri, Lea, 286 n. 57
Melissa P. (Panariello), 20
Mendes, Sam: *American Beauty*, 87
Menechella, Grazia, 267 n. 34
Mérimée, Prosper: *Carmen*, 176
Messager, Annette, 247 n. 43
Miceli Jeffries, Giovanna, 248 n. 55
Mill, John Stuart, 243 n. 1
Middlemarch (Eliot), 247 n. 46
Miller, Jacques-Alain, 271 n. 94
Modena (Italy), 147, 153–5, 160
Moi, Toril, 84, 101, 104, 229, 258 n. 103, 294 n. 152

Morandini, Giuliana, 244 n. 10
Morante, Elsa, 8, 23–5, 28–9, 36–46, 52, 54–61, 63–70, 72, 74–5, 79, 82–3, 85, 98, 106–8, 182, 234–6, 249 n. 1, 251 nn. 26, 29, 34, 35, 36, 252 n. 40, 253 nn. 45, 50, 254 nn. 54, 55, 58, 62, 255 nn. 70, 75, 259 n. 116, 262 n. 133, 264 n. 152, 288 n. 77, 295 n. 8; *Alibi*, 65; *Aracoeli*, 75–80; and canonicity, 59; *L'isola di Arturo*, 24, 65–8, 72; and literary entrustment, 36–46; *Menzogna e sortilegio*, 49–57, 98; *Il mondo salvato dai ragazzini*, 60–1, 79; and Vinci, 60–80
Moravia, Alberto, 264 n. 4: *Agostino* and *The Conformist*
Morphology of the Folktale. *See* Propp
Morrissey, Kim: *Poems for Men Who Dream of Lolita*, 277–8 n. 135
Morselli, Guido, 281 n. 10
Mozzoni, Anna Maria, 243 n. 1
Muraro, Luisa, 30, 128–30, 136, 142, 249 nn. 2, 3, 7, 268 n. 46; *ordine simbolico della madre*, 33; *partire da sé*, 129; *Pratica di affidamento* (entrustment), 28, 33–4, 229

Nabokov, Dmitri, 163–4, 170, 274 n. 116, 280 n. 148
Nabokov, Vladimir, 25–6, 116, 172, 234; and *Lolita* 162–80, 273 nn. 108, 109, 110, 274 nn. 113, 117, 118, 276 nn. 123, 277 n. 133, 280 n. 146
Nadal, Marita, 280 n. 144
Nafisi, Azar, 275 n. 118
Napolitanità: and Ferrante, 87; and language, 91, 99
Neera (Anna Radius Zuccari), 6
Negri, Ada, 6

Negri, Toni, 4
Nerenberg, Ellen, 258 n. 104
Nicholson, Lynda, 247 n. 41
Nin, Anaïs, and erotic writing, 184
New York Times, 20, 163, 176, 248 n. 49, 273 n. 111, 274 n. 117
Nora (Ibsen), 177
Norma (Bellini), 288 n. 83
Nuovi Argomenti, 188

Odyssey, 122, 130
Odysseus, 140
O'Neill, Eugene: *Medea*, 86
Onofri, Massimo, 18–21
Ortese, Annamaria, 7–8, 23, 45, 247 n. 47, 251 n. 26
Ottonieri, Tommaso, 261 n. 125
Ovid: *Medea*, 86; *Metamorphoses*, 211

Paglia, Camille, 277–8 n. 135
Parody: and the novel, 162, 164–7, 171–3, 178, 180, 273 nn. 110, 112, 274 n. 116, 275, n. 120, 276 nn. 121, 124, 276–7 n.129, 278 n. 140, 281 nn. 147, 149
Pascoli, Giovanni, 126, 265 n. 20, 266 n. 29
Pasolini, Pier Paolo, 42–4, 295 n. 8
Passaggio in ombra (Di Lascia), 37–60, 92, 251 n.26
Passerini, Luisa, 15
Pavese, Cesare, 23
Pasti, Daniela, 38
Pellini, Pierluigi, 244 n. 5
Pellizza da Volpedo, Giuseppe, 118
Pera, Pia, 25–6, 116–17, 182, 258 n. 109, 272 n. 107, 278 n. 139; and *Diario di Lo* (*Lo's Diary*) 162–80
Perseus, 211

Perverse desire, 212–30. *See also* Freud, de Lauretis, Dollimore
Petrarch, Francesco, 22, 179
Pharmakon, 157, 210
Phoné, 157
Pifer, Ellen, 277 n. 134
Plato, 9
Poe, Edgar Allan: 'Annabel Lee,' 176–7
Poems for Men Who Dream of Lolita (Morrissey), 277–8 n. 135
Pratica di affidamento (entrustment) (Muraro), 28, 33–4
Pratt, Annis, 289 nn. 87, 90, 293 n. 138
Presciuttini, Paola, 16
Pride and Prejudice (Austen), 132
Propp, Vladimir; *Morphology of the Folktale*, 121, 211, 266 n. 22, 290 n. 93
Proust, Marcel, 58, 79, 223, 230–1; *Swann's Way*, 292 n. 132, 295 n. 8
Pushkin, Aleksandr: *Eugene Onegin*, 26

Ramondino, Fabrizia, 15, 33, 238, 249 n. 1, 260 n. 121
Rasy, Elisabetta, 244 n. 10
Re, Lucia, 243 n. 1
Reagan, Ronald, 14
Rendall, Steven, 253 n. 48
Renna, Katia, 256 n. 81, 257 n. 94
Rhys, Jean: *Wide Sargasso Sea*, 180, 274 n. 116
Ricaldone, Luisa, 244 n. 9
Rich, Adrienne, 31, 250 n. 9
Ricoeur, Paul, 61–3, 254 n. 64, 255 n. 73. *See also* emplotment
Rimbaud, Arthur, 254 n. 55
'*Le rire de la Méduse*' (The Laugh of the Medusa) (Cixous), 211

Riviere, Joan, 147, 158
Robinson, Victor, 215
Rocchetta S. Antonio, 252 n. 44. *See also* Di Lascia and *Passaggio in ombra*
Roe v. Wade, 285–6 n. 57
Roman noir, 61–5. *See also* Todorov
Romano, Lalla, 8
Rome, 194
Rosa, Giovanna, 252 n. 40
Rose, Margaret, 275 n. 120, 276 n. 129
Rossellini, Roberto, 256 n. 82
Rovatti, Pier Aldo, 8

Sade (Marquis de): *Justine*, 175
Sacra Rota, 232
Salvo, Anna, 246 n. 32
Santacroce, Isabella, 16–20, 116, 238, 259 n. 117
Sartorio, Giulio Aristide: *La Gorgone e gli Eroi*, 193 n. 142
Santoro, Anna, 6–7, 113–14, 244 n. 9, 245 n. 12, 265 n. 7
Sanvitale, Francesca, 33, 246 n. 32
Scapegoat theory, and *La Dea dei baci*, 117–42
Scarano, Emanuella, 53, 253 n. 51, 254 n. 55, 261 n. 51
Scerbanenco, Giorgio, 256 n. 82
Schelotto, Gianna, 267 n. 34
Schnitzler, Arthur: *Fräulein Else* and *Traumnovelle*, 228; *Mittelbewusstein*, 229
Schopenhauer, Arthur (*The World as Will and Representation*), 118, 265 n. 18
Second World War, 25, 117, 234, 256 n. 82, 258 n. 104
Sentiero dei nidi di ragno, Il (Calvino), 256 n. 82

Serao, Matilde, 6
Sergi, Giuseppe, 219
Sexuality, sexual politics, 181–200; and abortion 14, 26, 185–205, 285–6 n. 57 (*Roe v. Wade*); and lesbianism 206–33
Shaw, Fiona, 259–60 n. 119
Sheldon, Barbara H., 264 n. 2, 269 n. 67
Showalter, Elaine: *A Literature of Their Own*, 8, 13, 245 n. 14
Siciliano, Enzo, 26, 188, 198, 201
Sister to Scheherazade, A (Djebar), 95, 261 n. 128, 263 n. 135
Skolnic, Peter, 274 n. 113, 280 n. 148
Sittlichkeit, 229
Smagamento (disillusionment), 24, 45, 55, 60–1, 66, 70, 74, 82, 236; Morante and Di Lascia, 45–60; Morante and Vinci, 60–82, 236
Snow White, 123
Spielberg, Steven, 103
Stancanelli, Elena, 281 n. 9
Starnone, Domenico: *Via Gemito*, 263 n. 136
Stiffening. *See* Freud
Svevo Italo (Ettore Schmitz), 241

Tambling, Jeremy, 156
Tamburri, Anthony J., 284 n. 33
Tamir-Ghez, Nomi, 280 n. 146
Tantalus, 267 n. 34
Thanatos, 228
Todorov, Tzvetan, 64; and *roman noir*, 64–5, 255 n. 72, 256 n. 80
Toker, Leona, 174, 278 n. 141
Tomasi di Lampedusa, Giuseppe, 251 n. 26
Tommaseo, Niccolò, 222
Toth, Sheree L., 268 n. 43

Turin, 81–2, 86, 88, 95, 99, 212–13, 261 n. 123, 272 n. 107 (*Salone del Libro*), 285 n. 50; Regio Manicomio of, 232

Umberto I, King of Savoy, 210
Unheimliche (*Das*), 227

Vatican II, 135, 137; and 'Sacrosanctum Concilium,' 136
Vattimo, Gianni, 8
Vegetti Finzi, Silvia, 246 n. 32, 271 n. 96
Venice Biennale Exposition, 247 n. 43
Vermeer, Johannes: *The Love Letter*, 228
Vinci, Simona, 14, 24–5, 28–9, 60–80, 106, 108, 234–6, 234 nn. 5, 6, 254 nn. 62, 66, 255 nn. 70, 71, 75, 256 nn. 81, 82, 259 n. 117, 281 n. 9, 294 n. 152, 295 n. 4. See also *cattivismo*
Vintage (publisher), 178
Viti, Elizabeth, 230
Vittorini, Elio, 56
Voci (Voices) Maraini, 195

Wainhouse, Austryn, 255 n. 70
Warner, Marina, 200–1
Web Cam (Mazzucato), 143, 160–1, 269 n. 65
Weinberg, Maria Grazia Sumeli, 282 n. 15
West, Rebecca, 249 n. 3
Wharton, Edith, 35
Wide Sargasso Sea (Rhys), 180, 274 n. 116
Wilde Astington, Janet, 255 n. 68
Wildeman, Marlene, 292 n.126
Wilt, Judith, 197; abortion, 285 n. 55
Winterson, Jeanette, 185, 259 n. 118

Wittig, Monique, 292 n. 126
Wolf, Christa: *Medea*, 86, 259 n. 118, 259–60 n. 119, 265 n. 9; and *Vergangenheitbewältigung*, 86
Wood, Jane, 127
Wood, Sharon, 36, 187, 243 n. 1, 249 n. 1, 254 n. 56, 283 n. 19
Woolf, Virginia, 240, 296 n. 15

Yager, Patricia, 269 n. 62
Young-Bruehl, Elisabeth, 271 n. 93

Zaccaria, Paola, 249 n. 8
Zambrano, Maria, 230, 294 n. 153
Zancan, Marina, 281 n. 12
Zelazo, Philip, 255 n. 68
Zeno (Svevo), 241
Zingarelli (dictionary), 190
Žižek, Slavoj, 158, 160, 272 n. 104
Zwinger, Lynda, 109, 144, 149, 264 n. 1, 268 n. 48, 270 nn. 72, 77

www.ingramcontent.com/pod-product-compliance
Lightning Source LLC
Chambersburg PA
CBHW030303080526
44584CB00012B/423